THE
DRÜG
SOLUTION

THE DRUG SOLUTION

By CHESTER NELSON MITCHELL

CARLETON UNIVERSITY PRESS

Ottawa, Canada

1990

© Carleton University Press Inc. 1990

ISBN 0-88629-116-X paperback
ISBN 0-88629-117-8 casebound

Carleton Public Policy Series #5

Printed and bound in Canada

Canadian Cataloguing in Publication Data
Mitchell, Chester Nelson, 1949 -
  The drug solution

(Carleton public policy series ; 5)
ISBN 0-88629-117-8 (bound)
ISBN 0-88629-116-X (pbk.)

    1. Narcotics, Control of. 2. Drug abuse--Treatment.
3. Narcotic addicts--Legal status, laws, etc.
I. Title. II. Series.

HV5801.M58 1990   362.29   C90-090019-9

Distributed by: Oxford University Press Canada
                 70 Wynford Drive
                 Don Mills, Ontario
                 Canada M3C 1J9
                 (416) 441-2941

Cover design: Y Graphic Design

Acknowledgements:

Carleton University Press gratefully acknowledges the support extended to its publishing programme by the Canada Council and the Ontario Arts Council.

This book has been published with the help of a grant from the Social Science Federation of Canada, using funds provided by the Social Sciences and Humanities Research Council of Canada.

To Shona and Mason

TABLE OF CONTENTS

FOREWORD

Introducing various substances into our bodies by eating, drinking, or other means are basic human acts. At various times and in different places some of these acts are viewed as acceptable, others as unacceptable, some as the "proper use" of a particular substance, others as its "improper abuse." Clearly, use and abuse are judgments, not facts. Unfortunately, after a thirty-year war on drugs, most Americans have come to believe that the dangerousness of particular drugs is a fact, and that this alleged fact is the reason why they are prohibited.

In this important and timely book, Professor Chet Mitchell presents a carefully thought-out legal critique of contemporary drug control legislation. Wisely bypassing the seemingly fruitless debate between criminalizing and legalizing particular drugs, he invites us to reconsider the wisdom of the maxim that what's sauce for the goose is sauce for the gander; and proposes that we base our drug control policies on fundamental principles of equity, reciprocity, and justice, rather than on ad hoc decisions justified by appeals to the real or fantasied properties of particular substances.

Although it is obvious that there can be no purely scientific basis for drug prohibition, we have built an elaborate system of social practices on the premise that the substances our drug laws now proscribe are, in fact, especially dangerous to us, individually and collectively, and hence ought to be made illegal. Of course, as all history teaches us, no matter how absurd or brutal a social practice may be, its very existence and survival over a period of time legitimizes it as good and valid. Once that has occurred — the traditional religious subjection of women and chattel slavery come to mind — the opponents of the practice become viewed as immoral and antisocial. This is our present situation with respect to illicit drugs such as marijuana, heroin, and cocaine, all of which were just as legal as aspirin until 1914. One of the important consequences of the hysteria about drug use and drug prohibition is that nearly everyone forgets that no person has to take any drug he doesn't want to take (except involuntarily hospitalized mental patients); and that the bottom line in the so-called drug problem, therefore, is the decision of the individual to seek or avoid, use or abstain from using, one or another particular drug.

Sadly, the pushers of drug prohibition have been even more successful than the pushers of drugs: as a result, few of us believe that it is our right to use drugs the government decrees to be illegal, but many of us believe that it is right for the government to protect us, by means of the criminal law, from allegedly dangerous drugs. Fortunately, hardly any of us yet believes that it is also the job of the government to protect us from reading "dangerous books," such as this one. And as long as that is true, no effort to confuse and tyrannize the people in the Name of Drugs can succeed.

Dr. Thomas Szasz
Professor of Psychiatry
State University of New York
Syracuse

ACKNOWLEDGEMENTS

I should like to thank the Law Foundation of Ontario and the Social Science and Humanities Research Council for their financial support for my research. Research assistance was ably provided by Christopher Tennant and Shona McDiarmid.

Valuable comments on early drafts of the book were provided by some of the anonymous referees, by Robert Solomon, Patricia Erickson, Clifford Shearing, Shona McDiarmid, and Michael MacNeil. My appreciation as well to Carleton University Press and particularly to David Knight and Michael MacNeil for their enthusiastic and effective support. Ideas, comments and criticisms were also provided by many of the Carleton University students who, over the last four years, participated in my seminar on medical regulation.

I am grateful to Ruth Kelvey for the excellent work she did on the typescript and for her helpful comments. Thanks also to Joan Sargent and Debra Faulkner.

The views expressed herein are my own as are any errors.

Ottawa, January 1990
C. Mitchell

INTRODUCTION

Since at least 1914, the war against users and sellers of illicit drugs has been a staple of the American political diet and, spearheaded by the U.S. government, drug battles now touch every continent. This war on drugs is a dangerous, costly endeavour that should be of concern to everyone. Drug battlefields in the Colombian highlands, Burma's Golden Triangle or the inner city slum may seem remote but consider who the war on drugs is actually against. The primary targets are the producers, smugglers and traders of the forbidden products yet these professional traffickers only begin to represent the drug "enemy". By sharing and distributing illicit drugs amongst themselves, most users can be legally classified as traffickers. Current laws also criminalize mere possession of many drugs, making at least 25 million Americans liable to serious penalties according to a 1985 survey conducted by the National Institute on Drug Abuse. Nor does the list of American drug offenders stop there. One must also add over 10 million adolescents guilty of "underage" tobacco or alcohol use and unknown numbers of prescription drug users who commit crimes by carrying their drugs in unmarked containers or by sharing them with family or friends. The Canadian situation is similar though on a smaller scale.

Despite the drug war's broad coverage, most voters probably feel secure in the belief that the drug enemy is a limited, easily distinguished group - a group that does not and will not include themselves. Actually, almost everyone is at risk of finding themselves on the wrong side of the drug laws. The potential for inflating the drug war can be traced to one fundamental fact - no pharmacological differences separate licit from illicit drugs. Taken under identical conditions, illicit drugs are no more dangerous, attractive or habit forming than licit drugs such as alcohol, caffeine, diazepam or nicotine. All mood-altering or psychoactive drugs are dangerous. Use of any drug can impair health, cause birth defects or lead to chronic consumption.

Since no pharmacological barrier divides legal from illegal drugs, legislators could justifiably outlaw any substance. Admittedly, caffeine or alcohol are not about to be made "narcotics" but no constitutional limits in Canada or the U.S. preclude such reclassification. Should the popularity of smoking tobacco continue to decline, smokers could find themselves behind enemy lines. Alcohol's Prohibition serves warning that even a drug used by most voters can become a drug war target, and according to Chris Reed, temperance sentiment is growing again in the United States (*Globe & Mail*, November 28, 1989). Yet heedless of these possibilities, many nicotine and alcohol users stand by or even applaud while users of equivalent drugs are fined, imprisoned or involuntarily "treated".

Why are governments waging a too-literal "war" on millions of their citizens? Political leaders claim the war fights crime, reduces drug use, promotes health and protects children. In fact, far from reducing crime, the drug war incites it. Formerly legitimate businesses are turned over to crime syndicates and law enforcement agencies are corrupted. The law detracts from safety because illegal products are of poor quality or because government deliberately poisons the prohibited drugs. During the 1920s, pyridine, benzine, nicotine and mercury served to poison American commercial alcohol. Thousands of Americans were blinded, killed or paralyzed. Similar injuries continue. As for protecting children, the law plainly fails to do that. Yale Brozen, I think, correctly recognized that in actual practice the transportation industry is more thoroughly regulated than the narcotics industry. [1]

As to the genuine motives behind the drug wars, George Orwell provides a clue. In *1984* Big Brother waged a contrived, perpetual war to deceive and dominate the public. During war, governments find it easier to raise taxes, run deficits, confiscate private property, curtail civil liberties, expand police forces, practice secrecy and conceal failure. Wars are so useful that unethical governments seek them out or even invent them. Inventing a war has its advantages. By comparison with civil wars or foreign adventures, a drug war is rather ideal. The enemy are mostly ordinary citizens, not armed guerrillas. The Soviets do not complain, indeed, they pursue similar campaigns. Best of all, there is no serious threat to combat so utter failure to win the war does not force capitulation. As a bonus, the drugs prohibited are usually foreign-sourced. This protects domestic drug producers while excusing aggressive intervention in less developed countries. Napalming or "Spiking" Colombian coca fields wins extensive press coverage and doubles as a non-tariff trade barrier. In terms of health protection, Latin Americans might be tempted in response to attack and burn Carolina tobacco fields but this fair turnabout would be identified by American governments as foul terrorism.

Finally, what does the drug war cost? Hamowy reports that drug enforcement amounts to the "most expensive intrusion into the private lives of Americans ever undertaken in the nation's history." [2] In the U.S. it costs more than 600,000 criminal law arrests every year. It costs over $10 billion in administrative expenses for police, courts, lawyers and prisons. It costs more billions in foregone tax revenues. It costs widespread disrespect for the law, police corruption and foreign policy failure. It costs loss of personal autonomy and the pitting of citizens, even family members, against one another. It costs medical fraud and a seriously compromised medical profession.

Fortunately, there appears to be a new understanding that the drug laws are fatally flawed. Notable and influential drug war opponents include Nobel economist Milton Friedman, Simon Fraser psychologist Bruce Alexander, Princeton's Ethan Nadelmann, Alan Dershowitz and Lester Grinspoon at Harvard, psychiatrist Thomas Szasz, Dr. Luigi Del Gatto, David Boaz of the Cato Institute and conservative pundit William F. Buckley, Jr. Arnold Trebach, of Washington's American University, recently established the Drug Policy Foundation, a rapidly growing organization dedicated to seeking practical methods of peaceful drug law reform. Equally noteworthy are early signs of dissent among politicians and police. In his speech to the U.S. Conference of Mayors in April 1988, Baltimore Mayor Kurt Schmoke, a former prosecutor, called for a national debate on whether to legalize currently prohibited drugs. Washington's Mayor Marion Barry, Mayor Donald Fraser of Minneapolis and at least two Democratic congressmen, Steny Hoyer of Maryland and Fortney Stark of California support Schmoke's initiative. Joseph McNamara, a California police chief, also favours debating legalization because his department allocates more than half of its resources to what McNamara considers a futile effort to enforce existing drug laws. A number of other public officials are "bitterly disillusioned" about the war on drugs according to a recent *Time* (May 30, 1988) cover story on legalizing drugs. While noting that "drug legalization has become the idea of the moment", *Time*'s report was instructively entitled "Thinking the Unthinkable". The *Washington Post*, the *Boston Globe* and the *New York Times* have featured front-page coverage on the legalization debate.

The general case for legalization has been examined at length by E.M. Brecher, Andrew Weil, Jock Young, John Rublowsky, John Kaplan, Peter Hedblom, R. Schroeder, Neil Boyd, Rufus King, David Richards, Eric Goode and Steven Wisotsky, to name a few. Most proponents of legalization argue that narcotics prohibitions cause far more damage than does use of the drugs themselves. A similar argument persuaded U.S. legislators in 1932 to repeal the prohibition against alcohol. Although circumstances have changed, the antiprohibitionist arguments are still compelling. [3] But that persuasion only takes us over the first hurdle, the conviction that our drug laws should be altered.

This book briefly reviews the evidence for and against legalizing drugs but its main objective is to consider the alternative methods of legalization. The book therefore concentrates on the question not of whether to legalize illicit drugs but rather of how to deal with drug use were it to be legalized. As the aforementioned *Time* article explains, "Advocates of legalization are still ... disunited when it comes to spelling out a practical program, which hardly anyone has ventured to do." The *Economist* (May 21, 1988) likewise observed that the legalization debate "lacks focus". Providing a focus and spelling out a drug regulatory program are what this book ventures to do. As Stinson observes, this means establishing drug control policy objectives, analyzing alternative control methods and relating such methods to education, treatment, criminal defenses, advertising, product liability and a host of other legal matters. [4]

Earlier, in "A Comparative Analysis of Cannabis Regulation" (1983), I investigated the extent to which the regulation of alcohol and tobacco constituted models of effective drug control that could be extended to marijuana. I concluded that alcohol-tobacco regulations were not ideal but that the general scheme of a basic right to use drugs tempered by certain legal restrictions, such as taxes and

serving licenses, was a better program for cannabis users than prohibition. Subsequently, I broadened coverage beyond marijuana to
include all illicit drugs as well as medical psychoactives. While
marijuana remains the illicit drug of choice and while law reform
limited to cannabis products, as advocated by the National Organization for Reform of Marijuana Laws (NORML) and as considered by
various government commissions would be a positive step, a drug-
by-drug reform of the narcotics laws is inefficient. Moreover, a
reading of the scientific literature suggests to me that psychoactive
drugs are more alike than different. Just as the multiple differences
between people are no longer used to justify drastic legal discrimination, eventually drug laws will evolve from differentiation toward
equivalency. In practical terms this prediction leads me to consider
a system designed to regulate all psychoactives including such
drugs as nicotine, caffeine, diazepam, cocaine, alcohol, amphetamine and morphine.

This book also seeks to provide a comprehensive set of legal,
ethical and scientific criteria by which to make choices between
competing methods of regulation. In another earlier work, "A Justice-Based Argument for the Uniform Regulation of Psychoactive
Drugs" (1986), I went back to basics by asking what principles justify any government intervention in the case of drug use. I found
both cost-benefit and rights-based analyses capable of providing
useful guidance. I describe both analytical methods at greater
length here but I also rely on democratic processes to provide some
fundamental answers as to how drug users should be governed.
Democratically, the drug control question is fairly framed when
every citizen is asked: what restraints on your own drug use will
you accept in order to defend yourself against the social costs imposed by the drug use of others? Besides offering a lengthy speculation on how voters will answer this question, I examine public
choice mechanisms and contemporary democratic systems and review the type of measures required to increase democratic control of
law making. Arguably, lack of democracy and constitutional protection permitted politicians to create the war on drugs in the first
place. This does not imply that significant drug reform cannot be
accomplished within the current institutional framework. Repeal of
alcohol Prohibition in 1932 is a possible precedent. Without serious
democratic reform, however, drug law revisions will likely occur

piecemeal without assurance that government will not launch equally ill-considered wars in the future against other targets such as cosmetics or pop music, both currently prohibited by Iranian political authorities. Drug use merely exemplifies a large class of mildly antisocial behaviours that affluent societies must eventually learn to efficiently regulate.

In order to consider every point of view, the book analyses all the existing models of drug regulation. In broad terms, five major legal systems of drug regulation can be identified. These are criminal law prohibition, medical prescription, rationing, taxation and private law. Principles of justice require that if drug use is legally regulated then all psychoactive drug users and producers should be assigned to one system. Fairness demands would be satisfied if all drugs were prohibited, if all were prescription-only or if all were free of public law restrictions. To assist citizens in making this hypothetical choice I examine each regulatory scheme on a best-case basis. That is, I try to make the best possible case for a uniform criminal law prohibition of all drugs and then speculate on whether most people would willingly inflict such a system on themselves. The evidence suggests that prohibition and medical prescription would be the least favoured choices for a uniform drug regulation program. Between rationing, taxation and private law the choice is less obvious.

This idealized framework may seem unrealistic and remote from current political realities but it need not be adopted to serve a useful function. Evaluating the competing drug control paradigms in uniform, idealized isolation provides a clear and convenient basis for judging their strengths and weaknesses.

A simple, idealized framework may also provide a focus for debate and political action more effectively than can a detailed "realistic" plan that must necessarily be complex and compromising. It may be instructive here to recall Friedrich Hayek's observation that those "who have concerned themselves exclusively with what seemed practicable in the existing state of opinion have constantly found that even this has rapidly become politically impossible as the result of changes in a public opinion which they have done nothing to guide". [5] Furthermore, an idealized analysis does nothing to impede less comprehensive engagements with drug policy. Practical politicians already have the knowledge and skill needed to shift illicit drugs to alcohol style regulations. At some point, the advantages gained by such a strategy will outweigh whatever benefits politicians now derive from scapegoating illicit drug users. A clear cataloguing of drug prohibition costs versus potential drug tax revenues can only hasten that eventuality. Still, while that limited reform would solve the most pressing drug control problems, it would leave unaddressed most of the issues discussed in this volume. In particular, it would do little to help us avoid similar disasters in the future.

Notes

[1]   Y. Brozen, "Is Government the Source of Monopoly?" (Cato Institute, 1980).

[2]   R. Hamowy, "Introduction: Illicit Drugs and Government Control" in R. Hamowy (ed), *Dealing with Drugs — Consequences of Government Control* (Mass: Lexington Books, 1987) at 1-2.

[3]   M. Woodiwiss, *Crime, Crusaders and Corruption: Prohibitions in the United States, 1900-1987* (Totowa: N.J.: Barnes & Noble, 1988).

[4]   G. Stinson, "The war on heroin: British policy and the international trade in illicit drugs" in *Tackling Drug Misuse: A Summary of the Government's Strategy* (British Home Office, 1986) at 57.

[5]   F. Hayek, "The Intellectuals and Socialism" cited in the Introduction to Brozen, *supra* note 1.

I   A Policy Primer on Drug Control

1. The Failure of Current Drug Policy

On most counts, drug prohibition can be judged a failure. The extent of that failure and the reasons for it are thoroughly documented and analyzed by the numerous researchers and scientists cited in this chapter. Yet despite prohibition's costly problems, most governments remain firmly opposed to any retreat from severe criminal controls. This political intransigence in the face of critical evidence helped inspire at least two opposition groups: The Drug Policy Foundation, created in 1987, and the International League Against Prohibition, founded in 1989.[1] Membership in these international bodies is not limited to civil libertarians or academics but also includes police chiefs, physicians, social workers, and some politicians. The potential significance of these groups lies partly in the fact that for the first time since 1908, when most governments started enacting narcotic controls, the prohibitionists face an organized, influential opposition.

The international complexion of the anti-prohibitionist groups is also worth noting. Drug laws are an international concern because most regimes enacted similar legislation, because formal treaty obligations exist and because the illicit drug trade involves north-south foreign affairs. There are also considerable advantages to using comparative scientific studies. For these reasons, this book's coverage is not restricted to Canadian or even to North American drug affairs.

The case against current drug policies rests on the following observations:
1. prohibition publicizes obscure drugs and, with enthusiastic media support, generates new fashions in drug use;[2]
2. prohibition fails to eradicate the importation or domestic prozduction of illicit drugs but perversely succeeds in shifting users to more potent forms of a drug or to more dangerous methods of ingestion;[3]
3. efforts to eliminate illicit drugs "at the source" in Third World countries are futile, expensive and destructive;[4]

4. mass demand for prohibited drugs creates an extensive black market that feeds organized crime, increases violence, destroys respect for the law, corrupts enforcement, aids tax evasion, glamorizes crime and wastes police resources;[5]
5. drug law enforcement relies on informants, entrapment and undercover agents and creates a warlike atmosphere conducive to the abuse of human rights;[6]
6. current drug laws ignore constitutional guarantees of legal equality;[7]
7. current drug laws are elitist and undemocratic because they minimize voter input and reject citizen autonomy while granting unjustified drug control monopolies to police and physicians;[8]
8. ending prohibition would destroy black markets, unclog prisons and courts, decriminalize millions of citizens, better protect youngsters and restore a good deal of tolerance and civility to society.[9]

These eight points merely summarize the thorough documentation of many researchers. Readers unfamiliar with the evidence are encouraged to consult the sources cited.

For those who carefully examine the consequences of present drug laws, both in North America and abroad, the case for some type of reform is compelling. But research has also disclosed the existence of major obstacles to drug reform. To begin with, some groups are satisfied with current policies and will block radical departures. According to Marie-Andrée Bertrand, the reform-resistant factions include police groups, organized medicine, pharmacists, pharmaceutical producers, distillers and brewers, the tobacco industry, and finally a broad category of "moral entrepreneurs".[10] These are powerful interests.

A second reform obstacle is the natural hesitancy engendered by any major legal change. Uncertainty may lead many people to reason that although prohibition is a costly, ineffective mess, might not some new scheme be even worse? Anti-drug crusaders amplify these uncertainties by recklessly claiming that without the "thin blue line" of narcotics police to protect us, countries will plunge into anarchy, families will disintegrate and most of us will become drugged zombies. Sufficient evidence already exists to refute such claims, but that evidence is not widely known. Uncertainty and propaganda can be overcome by changing political incentives, by

2

broadcasting existing knowledge about drugs more effectively and by producing even more convincing evidence. Perhaps the best avenue for pursuing superior evidence is to encourage governments at every level and in every jurisdiction to experiment with drug control. Once people learn that governments in Alaska, the Netherlands or New Zealand can revoke criminal controls without significant problems, the drug crusaders' myths will be undermined. The movement against drug prohibition is, in a sense, a replay of the historical battle between science and the church. Now it is social scientists rather than astronomers who fight against a censoring establishment for the freedom to test, criticize and experiment.

A third reform obstacle is the plain fact that disparate dissatisfactions do not necessarily add up to a cohesive reform agenda. Complaints motivate a search for solutions, and that search is now definitely underway, but what is also required is a systematic way of thinking about the "drug problem." The analytical method should be accessible, to encourage the widest participation, and it should also facilitate the formation of common goals, to focus reform resources. I believe such an analytical method is available, and it is the purpose of this book to describe and apply that analysis.

In a nutshell, systematic thinking about drug control should rest on three foundations: science, justice and cost-benefit social accounting. Why these three elements? Science is the starting point because our long-term success depends on beginning with the best evidence. This is as true for law as for chemistry. As to what policy makers should do with the evidence, two broad routes can be taken. One route searches for the policy that will deliver the greatest social benefits at least cost. The other route searches for the policy that is fairest, that can be administered justly and that is the fruit of a genuine democratic selection. If carefully and thoroughly explored, both routes will guide us to similar policy destinations. Criminal prohibition of certain drugs, for example, is criticized by both methods: First, because prohibition is a high cost/low benefit system, and second because prohibition is unjust. But since cost-benefit and rights-based analyses do not cover the same issues, it is necessary to employ both methods.

A general survey of drug benefits and costs is made in Chapter Two. The human rights side of the drug control debate is the focus of Chapter Three. Subsequent chapters employ both methods to evaluate alternative drug control strategies. Chapter One's task is to set the scene by reviewing the basic components of drug policy. These components include political assumptions about drugs, the scientific evidence, a political theory of current drug legislation and arguments both for and against serious liberalizing reform.

2. Political Assumptions About Drugs

All laws are premised on assumptions, and drug laws are no exception. But are the assumptions true?

Perhaps the most important assumption underlying every nation's drug laws is that drugs possess inherent qualities such that some drugs are unalterably dangerous and others are quite safe. Along the same lines, drug laws assume that only some drugs possess therapeutic properties and only some drugs are habit-forming. That psychoactive drugs are thought to differ tremendously from one another is apparent in the assignment of drugs to different legal categories. According to the usual legislative pattern, the production, sale and use of morphine, tobacco, diazepam (Valium) and alcohol are regulated under entirely different statutes. Even when a number of drugs are assigned to a general statute, such as Britain's *Misuse of Drugs Act 1971*, Canada's *Narcotic Control Act* or the U.S. *Comprehensive Drug Abuse Prevention and Control Act* of 1970,the law invents separate categories or "schedules.[11] In the U.S. scheme, Schedule I drugs like heroin allegedly pose a serious threat and have no medical value so they cannot be prescribed or even possessed. Four other Schedules differentiate between drugs like cocaine, amphetamines, barbiturates, and codeine. All but Schedule I can be medically prescribed. Criminal penalties for trafficking apply to all five Schedules. Numerous other rules about storage, manufacturing quotas, import licenses, record keeping and registration also apply to the different Schedules.[12] Canadian law differentiates between "narcotics" (heroin, marijuana, cocaine), "controlled drugs" (methaqualone) and "designated drugs" (amphetamine). Additional rules control special category drugs such as LSD, methadone and thalidomide.[13]

The penalty scale legislated for drug offences highlights a second assumption, namely that the use and sale of some drugs (narcotics) causes severe social harm equivalent to sabotage, treason or murder, whereas the sale of other drugs is mildly damaging or not damaging at all. From this premise flows a matching variation in penalties ranging from coffee sellers (no penalties), alcohol users (small punitive taxes) to narcotic sellers (life imprisonment, execution).[14] The day M.D.M.A., a methamphetamine analogue, was moved to Schedule I by the U.S. Drug Enforcement Administration (DEA), its sellers became subject to fines of up to $125,000 and to 15-year prison terms.

A third assumption, derived from the first two premises, is that since drugs have specialized features they should be assigned to specialized professions. Drugs that are inherently "medical" (listed in the *Physician's Desk Reference*) therefore properly belong to the medical profession just as "criminal" substances (including most drugs listed in the *High Times Encyclopedia of Recreational Drugs*) are naturally the exclusive property of police. The appropriateness of such drug control assignment is founded on the expectation that without medical supervision the number of adverse drug events will increase (see Chapter Five); that without police, drug abuse and related crime will explode (see Chapter Four) or that without liquor licence agents the damage from alcoholic excess will mushroom (see Chapters Seven and Eight). Are these assumptions well-founded?

3. A Summary of the Scientific Evidence

a. Drugs and Social Context

Alcohol and diazepam are both depressants yet diazepam is not legally available at taverns and alcohol is not prescribed for anxiety. Orthodox *opinion* explains the different legal status of these two central nervous system depressants by reference to their different pharmacological attributes. In contrast, the *evidence* available suggests that drugs are medicinal or recreational because of historical circumstances and that every drug can be used as a symptom reliever, ceremonial substance or for social recreation.[15] Rather than focus on the drug, many researchers focus on the drug takers and drug controllers. Erich Goode, Norman Zinberg, John Marks, Andrew Weil, Jock Young, Jerome Jaffe and others demonstrate that social context influences and even determines drug definitions, drug effects, drug-related behaviour and the drug experience.[16] Whether a drug is considered "hard" or "soft," "medicinal" or "abusive," addicting or benign is primarily determined by politics, not

5

pharmacology, just as the difference between water and holy water, as Szasz points out, is a matter of religion, priests and faith, not chemistry.

Cross-cultural and historical comparisons confirm that our drug discriminations are artificial. Alcohol today is not usually classified as medicine, but for millennia alcohol was lauded as excellent treatment for practically all diseases.[17] In the 19th century, alcohol was the most prescribed drug within psychiatric institutions and the fifth most prescribed drug overall following opiates, ether, quinine and sodium bicarbonate.[18] Physicians may assume that alcohol's medical eclipse was due to their acquisition of superior substitutes, such as the barbiturates and more recent tranquillizers, but there is little evidence to show that new sedatives are more medicinal than alcohol. Instead, Julien reports that the sedative/depressants are "all virtually identical pharmacologically."[19] All depressants can "tranquillize." Opiates were the tranquillizer of choice prior to 1914 for middle and upper class American women, the same group that became benzodiazepine users in the 1970s.[20] Rosenberg expects that if heroin were again legally available it would compete with the modern tranquillizers.[21] Opiates boast a long medical history as sedatives, pain killers and cough suppressors.[22] An 1880 textbook listed 54 diseases treatable by morphine injection. Heroin, which is a form of morphine, is largely interchangeable with synthetic opiates like methadone, meperidine (Demerol), hydrocodone and fentanyl. Marijuana also tranquillizes.[23] Under U.S. federal law marijuana is a Schedule I drug, but actually the drug's abuse potential is low and it can alleviate symptoms of insomnia, anxiety, asthma, glaucoma and epilepsy.[24]

Stimulants are also flexibly employed. Tobacco served ceremonial purposes for native Americans and was launched in Europe as a medicine possessing marvelous curative powers.[25] Coca leaf was chewed in the Andes to suppress hunger and fatigue, treat stomach ailments, measure distance, facilitate religious visions and mark special occasions.[26] Over the last century in North America, cocaine served as a general health tonic, a specialized anesthetic, a symptom alleviator and, most recently, as a recreational "party drug" and social differentiator establishing users as progressive, adventurous, open-minded and youth-oriented.[27] Though their legal status is at great variance, nicotine and cocaine can trigger similar effects as can pemoline, lidocaine, amphetamine (Benzedrine), phenmetrazine (Preludin) and methylphenidate: experienced cocaine users usually cannot distinguish intranasal cocaine from amphetamines or other synthetics.[28] New stimulants are classified as medicines though they are not more medicinal than cocaine, a fact that is now apparent with amphetamine after medical reports in the 1950s praising the efficacy and safety of amphetamine were discredited in the 1970s.[29] It also appears that "hallucinogens" like LSD and mescaline are a sub-branch of the stimulants.[30] Fort finds that given the right dosage and a conducive setting, any psychoactive drug "can sometimes produce hallucinations."[31] Along the same lines, many psychoactives - including alcohol, tea, cocaine, tobacco and opium - have been regarded as divine instruments capable of connecting users with a higher reality. Wine cults flourished in ancient Greece, and in some African cultures beer still has a sacred character. William James, the noted American psychologist, affirmed in 1900 that alcohol had the power "to stimulate the mystical faculties."[32]

Just as supposedly non-medical drugs like nicotine and alcohol have well-established medical pedigrees, some accepted medicines were once "fun drugs." When Humphrey Davy isolated nitrous oxide in 1772 he saw its potential as a surgical anesthetic, but until about 1850 the drug was taken at parties as "laughing gas."[33] Ether was also used for amusement. Ether drinking enjoyed a brief popularity in 19th century Ulster during a government-induced whisky shortage.[34] Aspirin, the most familiar over-the-counter (OTC) drug, is taken primarily as an analgesic but some people use it as a sedative.[35] Although aspirin abuse, or "salicylism," can lead to delirium, hallucinations and the mental confusion condemned when associated with illicit drugs, no politician attacks aspirin abusers.[36]

The variable employment of drugs is masked by customs, habits and legal restrictions. Today we lack the legal opportunity to attend nitrous oxide parties, drink ether or chew coca leaf, but perhaps more restricting are the conditioned limitations that stop most of us from even considering an aspirin binge, an injection of caffeine or a diazepam wedding toast. Many North American parents give their young children aspirin, caffeine and similar drugs but would probably be shocked at the idea of youngsters chewing coca or taking diluted wine, though these practices are common in Peru and Portugal. Part of our cultural limitation is the fixed association of certain drugs with certain methods of ingestion. To North Ameri-

7

cans, caffeine means weak beverages usually taken with food. Caffeine does not mean intravenous injection, gangsters and self-destructive movie stars, all of which are associated with cocaine. Some readers will feel that by its very nature caffeine cannot be associated with high dosage abuse, high rollers and organized crime — but why not? These abusive elements are as remote from the Peruvian peasants' coca leaf as they are from our breakfast coffee bean.

What we naturally tend to overlook is the influence of pervasive cultural conditioning. Just as Europens do not consider dogs "food," although other people do, we do not consider caffeine to be a "drug," let alone an abusable party drug. We, therefore, never try to ascertain whether caffeine could be put to this or other uses, just as we never eat dogs though they are readily available. Few people see through the biases. During a debate in Britain's Parliament on alcohol abuse, one Member, who was also a physician, complained about tea swilling hypocrites who denounced alcohol while intoxicating themselves on caffeine, a drug Stanley Einstein describes as "a very potent central nervous stimulant."[37] Such insight is rare. Generally our lack of experimentation and our habitual use of certain drugs for certain purposes continually reaffirms the "rightness" of our arbitrary drug divisions. Since all cultures, including our own, are permeated with taboos about food, cosmetics, apparel, drugs and the like, it is difficult to think objectively about such matters. Clothing is an example. Like drug choices, clothing fashions exhibit strongly ritualistic and class elements, especially within the sexual division of fashion.[38] Although most contemporary "feminine" elements have been part of the male costume in other cultures, most men would strenuously oppose adoption of feminine accoutrements; indeed, some men would wage civil war to avoid a legally enforced program of "cross-dressing." Arbitrary fashions become significant because a given fashion element comes to stand for status, power and high office. There is little inherently dangerous in lipstick, eyeshadow, hose or earrings, yet most men religiously avoid such fashions. Moreover, men have used legislative power to criminalize fashion deviance by imprisoning men for wearing lipstick or women for sporting pants.[39] Drug-related choices are similarly dominated by taboo and fashion. If this point is not grasped, our laws and attitudes about drugs cannot be understood.

8

Social customs and long experience with a drug bring about startling changes in perceptions, a point illustrated by sugar. Around 1000 A.D., refined white sugar was rare, expensive and employed as a medicine, a status made official in the 12th century, when Thomas Aquinas judged that taking sugar did not break a fast since "sugared spices" were not eaten for nourishment but as medicinal aids to digestion. Sidney Mintz, an anthropologist and student of sugar, observes that of all the tropical "drug foods" adopted in Europe, including tea, coffee, chocolate, tobacco, rum and sugar, it was only sugar that completely escaped religious proscription. Mintz's explanation of this development is worth quoting at length:

> That sugars, particularly highly refined sucrose, produce peculiar physiological effects is well known. But these effects are not so visible as those of such substances as alcohol; or caffeine - rich beverages... And all of these substances, sucrose included, seem to have a declining and less visible effect after prolonged or intensified use... In all likelihood, sugar was not subject to religion-based criticisms like those pronounced on tea, coffee, rum and tobacco, exactly because its consumption did not result in flushing, staggering, dizziness, euphoria, changes in the pitch of voice, slurring of speech, visibly intensified physical activity, or any of the other cases associated with the ingestion of caffeine, alcohol, and nicotine.[40]

b. Drug Specificity and Drug Generality

Drugs do possess inherent differences. Various drugs take effect at different rates, have different potencies and trigger some unique consequences. The relevant policy question is: Do these differences suffice to justify current legal discrimination?

Certain legal incentives encourage the individuality of drugs to be emphasized. Alcohol sellers enjoy a legal monopoly in the market for recreational sedatives. All other competitors are either restricted (diazepam, ether) or prohibited (marijuana, opium). Since alcohol sellers do not want their drug to be prohibited (again) or restricted to medical use, they wisely ignore or deny the close similarities between their drug and other sedatives. Moreover, for commercial

9

reasons alcohol advertisements attempt to create differentiation where almost none exists, as between different brands of lager. Medical incentives likewise compel pharmaceutical producers to downplay similarities and highlight differences. If the inventors of Valium had reported that their new drug was very similar to alcohol they might have been denied both patent protection and regulatory approval.[41]

Marketing medical psychoactives also depends on product differentiation, so among the benzodiazepines, for instance, flurazepam (Dalmane) is marketed as a sleeping pill whereas diazepam (Valium) is sold as a daytime tranquillizer although they could, in fact, be reversed. Drug specificity is therefore stressed even when a drug has many other effects than the ones advertised. Drugs like phenothiazine, lithium, amphetamine, iproniazid and others were relabelled when their "side effects" proved more valuable than their "main effect." Chlorpromazine, the first "wonder drug" for schizophrenia, was first marketed as an antihistamine. What about other antihistamines? Gordon Claridge admits that "hayfever remedies" produce drowziness and lethargy, which are typical signs of sedation, but he claims such drugs "would not be considered psychotropic in the accepted sense."[41] By "accepted sense" Claridge means customary medical practice. A drug's full range of possibilities is ignored although its specified action, say for anxiety, may not even be its major action.[43] Lennard, *et al.*, report that although drugs have specific physiological impact, their effects upon behaviour and experience are "largely nonspecific." They stress how a drug experience derives primarily from the drug taker's social and psychological background so that even high doses of LSD or chlorpromazine are open to a range of interpretation. In various blind studies they found users unable to judge the potency of the drugs being taken and observers unable to judge what sort of drug a subject took or even whether they took a drug. They conclude that drug effects are "always nonspecific and general" but that in the case of illicit and medical drugs the illusion of specific effects holds sway. The specific effects desired, they write, are labelled the "main effects" and all other effects "are labelled side effects, regardless of whether they are positive, negative, uncomfortable, dangerous, or massive...[thus the specificity of drugs is] "to quite a considerable extent, a fiction."[44]

10

Drug specificity is also stressed in medicine to distinguish licit from illicit chemicals. Borrowing a sexual metaphor, medical psychoactives are represented as prim, god-fearing women who decorously serve as angels of mercy without inciting lust or debauchery. On the other hand, bad drugs like marijuana are uncouth, wicked temptresses who lead men astray. To redeem marijuana it must be transformed by industry into THC, the "active ingredient" in *cannabis sativa*, and then it must be taken as pills available only through physicians, as copulation was once legally available only with the approval of priests. Then, THC medicine must be officially available only for recognized afflictions like glaucoma.[45] Dozens of apparently precise pharmacological categories falsely imply that medical psychoactives possess only specific actions. This specificity allows the drugs to masquerade as specialized weapons ("magic bullets") in the physician's arsenal. These commercial and professional biases make medical categorization unsuitable for legal purposes because law must take into account not only what a drug now happens to be used for, but also what it could be used for.

Drug generality begins with basic questions such as: How do drugs work? Why do people take drugs? All psychoactives are alike insofar as no one knows fully how any drug interacts biochemically with its consumers. Despite technical advances in studying drugs, there is not a single drug for which the complete mode of operation is known.[46] Canada's *Commission of Inquiry into the Non-Medical use of Drugs* (the LeDain Commission) concluded that the "details of cellular physiology are largely unknown and with rare exceptions there is little information as to the mechanism by which any particular drug changes the activity of the nervous system."[47] This is as true for caffeine as for heroin.

Recognizing that observations of cellular physiology alone cannot explain how drugs work, some theorists take a more psychological approach. These researchers observe that drugs do not provide nutrients or necessary trace elements. Moreover, they observe that at a given dosage drugs are generally fatal. All our familiar drugs like alcohol, diazepam, caffeine and nicotine can serve as poisons; indeed, "pharmakos," the Greek root of pharmaceutical, means poison. Infants can be killed by eating one cigaret, drinking a martini or chewing a half dozen aspirins.[48] Nicotine itself is a pesticide produced by the tobacco plant as part of its chemical warfare against insect pests. Why should people take potential poisons?

11

Drugs disrupt normal brain function.[49] If extreme (10 grams of caffeine), such disruption can be fatal, but minor (0.5 grams of caffeine) disruptions can trigger effects humans and other animals find desirable. D.G. Garan explains that the central nervous system operates as a governor controlling energy outlays and organic demand priorities.[50] When the need arises, a brain will produce sedation or energization naturally. Hibernation is a dramatic example of what inner chemical signals are capable of achieving. By disrupting chemical signals, drugs can artificially achieve similar effects. Some drugs shortcircuit organic mechanisms that normally inhibit energy release. Ingestion of such drugs will result in a satisfying release felt as vigour, relief from fatigue, better attention level, higher energy. Writing about cocaine, Andrew Weil makes an important observation true of all psychoactives: "Cocaine does not miraculously bestow energy on the body; it merely releases energy already stored chemically in certain parts of the nervous system."[51] Other drugs suppress cellular responses designed to alert the brain to organic demands such as hunger, fear or pain. Use of this type of drug results in pain relief, tranquillization or sedation.

This view of drug effects does not distinguish between alcohol and heroin. Both disrupt normal functioning of the central nervous system. Both are potentially fatal and in both cases the satisfying response pursued by means of the drug is temporary. Garan explains that the disrupted organism inevitably attempts to restore equilibrium by counteracting the drug's disruption. As a result, the psychic gain in relief or energy achieved through drug use does not last. Even worse, Garan suggests that the gain is eventually met by an equal loss felt as hangover, depression, fatigue, headache or whatever, depending on the results achieved by using a given drug. Other researchers agree that drug use creates organic "debts" which, being self-induced, are inescapable.[52] From the process of "opposite causation" flows the typical consequences of chronic drug use, namely habituation, tolerance, withdrawal discomforts and reversals. These countereffects or reversals appear to be universal features of drug use. Alcohol intoxication is reversed by fatigue and headache, caffeine arousal leads to drowsiness and cocaine highs are followed rapidly by equal lows. Regular use of soporifics leads to insomnia, purgatives eventually cause constipation, nose sprays appear to worsen nasal congestion in the long run and frequent antacid use causes acid "rebound."[53] Finally, the modern trend in drug studies is to recognize that mood alteration can be achieved not only through hundreds of different drugs but also through music, sex, food, frantic activity, fantasy or any other strategy that directly manipulates natural biochemical stimulants or sedatives. Representative of this literature are J. Orford's *Excessive Appetites: A Psychological View of Addictions* (1985), *Commonalities in Substance Abuse and Habitual Behaviour* (1983), edited by Levinson, Gerstein and Molff, and the previously mentioned work of Rice, Garan, Marvel and Hartmann, Goode, Weil, Bonnie and Zinberg.

If mood-altering, psychoactive or psychotropic drugs are self-defeating and harmful, why do people willingly consume them? Except for attempted suicides, humans ingest drugs to trigger satisfying disruptions in their biochemical economy. Considerable evidence supports the familiar hedonistic thesis that humans consistently strive to attain satisfaction and avoid dissatisfaction.[54] Our choice of drugs reinforces this theory because among the thousands of plants and chemicals with psychoactive impact, we assiduously avoid those that directly trigger headaches, anxiety, pain, fatigue or other discomforts and choose instead those with the opposite impact. Pain causing drugs probably exist in equal number to pain relieving drugs, but they remain undiscovered or unused. To be precise, drugs are not *purely* pleasant or unpleasant. What matters is whether the drug's *net* impact is satisfying. A drug may cause vomiting, cramps, dizziness or sore throat but be taken anyway because its dominant effects are satisfying for at least some people.

So we take drugs to achieve some desirable state, be it symptom relief, peace of mind, inspiration or euphoria. But why, if drug effects are temporary and eventually reversed, do we keep taking them? One answer can be found in our innate optimism and positive biases that cause us to discount future risks.[55] Simply put, the immediate advantages gained by drug use often count more than the disadvantages that come later. Young adults, who are biologically most optimistic and who discount future consequences most, are also the heaviest users of drugs. The second reason for drug use is pragmatic. Even though financial loans must be repaid, people are often justified in assuming a debt. Likewise with drugs, a point I will return to in Chapter Two. What I want to emphasize here is that unlike medical and political approaches, which focus on and even create drug differences, scientific research tends to report on the basic features shared by all psychoactives and to treat drugs as a single class.

c. Variation in Drug-Related Harm

The second assumption guiding lawmakers is that the degree of harm engendered by drug use varies tremendously because some drugs are inherently "soft" while others are hard, harder or hardest. The scientific evidence is very much at odds with governments here since research indicates that there is nothing especially harmful about illicit drugs and that drug harm results from many factors apart from a drug's inherent properties. Under certain conditions caffeine use is more harmful than heroin use.

The harms attributed to drug use include accidental death, chronic disease, birth defects, cognitive impairment, misuse of resources, violence and acquisitive crime.[56] Chapter Two examines in detail measurements of drug-related harm. To summarize that material, we know far less about drug harm than politicians claim, and what we do know refutes orthodox political positions. Despite the heady confidence with which politicians around the world have erected criminal penalty scales for different drug offences, no one has yet formulated a well-documented ranking of inherent drug dangers. Some experts rate alcohol and nicotine use as more harmful than use of cannabis or heroin.[57] One medical authority ranks glue and amphetamine as most dangerous, followed by alcohol, tobacco, barbiturates, heroin, LSD and, finally, marijuana as least dangerous.[58] Both of these rankings reverse the judgment about drug dangerousness implicit in current drug laws.

In assessing the harm caused by different drugs, the first point to clarify is that an unbiased assessment cannot be made simply by comparing drugs as they now happen to be used. A drug's impact depends upon dosage, duration of use, purity, legal status, method of ingestion and a host of social factors.[59] Tobacco and alcohol use now account for the bulk of all drug harm, with nicotine-related deaths alone 100 times greater than all deaths related to illicit drugs, but this is to be expected given that tobacco and alcohol are, with caffeine, the most heavily consumed drugs. For every American regularly using cocaine, there are 100 using alcohol, and for every cocaine-related death in 1986 there were 500 deaths related to tobacco.[60] Smith concludes that the U.S. government is "waging

14

an irrational and unconscionably costly war against [illicit] substances that cause fewer than 5 percent of all drug-related deaths."[61] But a fair comparison between nicotine and cocaine must hold dosage constant. Conversely, evidence that marijuana smoking damages the lungs more than tobacco cigarets or that injecting heroin is more dangerous than drinking beer is unjust. Tobacco cigarets are filtered, refined, machine-made and use mild leaf developed over centuries of devoted horticulture, whereas marijuana "joints" are hand made, unfiltered and composed of crudely processed leaf. Moreover, marijuana is illegal and expensive so people naturally tend to maximize the value of a given amount by inhaling deeply, by holding in the smoke and by not letting the joint "idle." If tobacco cigarets cost $100 a pack smokers would behave similarly.

Comparing heroin and beer is equally unfair because heroin's illicit status puts it at a disadvantage. A fair comparison would pit beer against a pure, mild and legal opiate beverage used by a similar group under comparable circumstances. When such a comparison was possible prior to 1910, a number of commentators claimed that alcohol was more damaging than morphine or heroin.[62] In those days, alcohol was "hard" and cocaine-based beverages, like Coca-Cola, were "soft" drinks. Anti-alcohol opinion from that period, however, is often unreliable because some prohibitionists slandered alcohol to further their political cause. Poverty, crime, labour unrest, illiteracy and the like were then blamed on alcohol in the same way that every social ill is now attributed to "drugs."[63]

Unbiased drug rankings are possible. One method is to feed comparable doses of the major drugs to laboratory animals.[64] A much better method, though less practical, would compare human groups each using only one psychoactive over a long period — perhaps two generations. Each drug-using group would also be evaluated against a drug-abstaining control group. This ideal experiment remains undone; after all, how much would we have to pay people to limit themselves to one drug (or no drugs), and how would adherence to the experimental rules be monitored? Nonetheless, certain results can be anticipated from such a test. First, natural control groups exist, like the Seventh-day Adventists, who mostly avoid alcohol, nicotine and even caffeine. Among Adventists who adhere strictly to their no-drug regime, average life expectancy is 12 years

15

longer than the American average, and lower than average death rates are achieved for all ten of the leading causes of death.[65] The non-drug control group will therefore likely prove to be healthier than any of the drug using groups. I also predict that the abstinent group will be as happy overall as the drug-using groups.[66]

The other important result I anticipate is that drug damage will generally vary more among individuals than among groups using different drugs. Alcohol and opiates can be used as an example. Both drugs will exhibit the same sort of use distribution: most people will be sporadic or light users, a smaller portion will be regular users and an even smaller fraction will be heavy "abusers." Differences in harm between light and heavy alcohol users will be far greater than the average differences between the alcohol and opiate-using groups. Indeed, there probably will not be significant average differences between these two groups. In other words, the damage a given drug causes depends more on the user than on the drug.

In our culture a one-drug restriction is highly artificial since multi-drug use is the norm, especially among high-rate users. Most heavy drinkers smoke tobacco and most heavy smokers drink more coffee than 90% of non-smokers.[67] Still, if we could restrict various groups to one drug it would demonstrate an additional point; ingenious people can do many different things with a single drug. There exist a hundred recipes and methods for caffeine preparation alone, as Italian coffee aficionados demonstrate. As a beverage, caffeine is taken as tea, coffee or colas, but it can also be eaten, processed as pills, injected, sniffed as powder or smoked like hashish. When cocaine was legal it was available in a similar range of products. If restricted to caffeine, most people would consume the drug moderately or "socially" as a mild beverage, but some persons (the young and the restless) would take more potent concentrations and use more dangerous ingestion methods. This risk-taking group would binge on caffeine at parties, combine sex and caffeine, mainline caffeine for the greatest "rush," and discover psychedelic dosage levels. Their elders would still protest about drug use, but would focus on all the variables *except* choice of drug. Far from being an odd hypothesis, this situation matches the modern case of music in which, generically, music is accepted but parents sometimes prohibit their children's musical activities for being too raucous, too "black," too lascivious or too anti-intellectual. Bach (music as tea-ceremony) is

16

commendable but Twisted Sister, Judas Priest or Megadeth (music mainlined) is deplorable. However, all drugs may not lend themselves to such broad, flexible usage. Zinberg distinguishes between "bread and butter" drugs like alcohol, cannabis and opiates, which have consistent, flexible effect and are socially adaptable, and "exotic" drugs like amphetamine and LSD, which he claims have little potential for long-term recreational use.[68]

Political assessments about drugs' relative impairment potential are now thoroughly warped by bias. Commercially important and widely accepted drugs like alcohol, tobacco and caffeine have their dangers downplayed. During World War II, tobacco was declared an "essential crop" by the U.S. government and many governments today market tobacco through a state monopoly.[69] Extensive tobacco-related damage is now acknowledged, but it still receives less emphasis than the minor harm caused by illicit drugs. This occurs largely because illicit drug dangers are exaggerated by government officials who fabricate horror stories that are spread by compliant media. As a result, most people now believe that heroin and cocaine are incredibly harmful. In contrast, Grinspoon and Hedblom conclude that heroin's dangers are "vastly overestimated"; Rosenberg finds that heroin is not particularly harmful and Helmer marvels at the propaganda process that turned an analgesic and cough suppressant like heroin into the number one public enemy.[70] Bellis reports that heroin is no more dangerous than tobacco or alcohol; Lauderdale and Inverarity speculate that without prohibition the opiates today would be no more feared than nicotine, and Michaels argues that "stereotypes of addiction bear scant resemblance to actual use patterns."[71] Marijuana's reputation was similarly slandered by alcohol-using law enforcement agents after 1930.[72] And presently, politicians and editorial writers are engaged in an orgy of defamation against cocaine.[73] In every case the anti-narcotics propaganda is founded on the same causal errors: the effects of the black market, which exist because of the law, are falsely blamed on the drug; the dangerous ways in which high-risk takers use cocaine are falsely attributed to the drug; and the drug-crime connection, which is primarily a legal artifact, is wrongly tied to the drug itself. Under different laws and social conditions, everything now said about cocaine could be said about nicotine.

The dangers of government-approved medical psychoactives are distorted in the opposite direction of illicit drugs. Prescription and OTC drug dangers are underestimated in order to confirm their status as official medicines.[74] Like alcohol, medical drugs are establishment products. As Mathew Dumont explains:

> By every physical, psychological and social parameter, barbiturate and amphetamine abuse should be of greater public concern than heroin addiction. The fact that these chemicals are produced by the most profitable and respectable industry in the nation and in large part distributed by the most prestigious group of people has blunted the edge of political indignation.[75]

Box explains how "political indignation" was blunted. Hoffman-La-Roche and other firms in the U.S. spent large sums lobbying Congress to prevent their drugs from being slotted into an overly restrictive schedule.[76] New psychoactives are launched on waves of commercial enthusiasm from drug companies, affiliated researchers, anecdotal medical surveys and uncritical trade reports.[77] New drugs are normally advertised as delivering symptom relief without acute toxicity or dependence potential, but with experience these claims are eventually refuted.[78] Many physicians promoted amphetamine in the 1950s as safe and useful but now experts report that amphetamine is neither safe nor useful, that it has "an insignificantly small part to play in the legitimate practice of medicine."[79] The story is or will be the same with sedatives like thalidomide or tranquillizers like diazepam.[80] According to some medical cynics, new drugs should be prescribed as soon as possible "before they stop working."[81] But as medicines like barbiturates and amphetamine are discredited, newer ones replace them, and the pretence is maintained that licit and illicit drugs are worlds apart. Schroeder reports that aspirin may retard sperm cell formation, damage chromosomes and cause "numerous undesirable effects" but he then cautions that the "point to be made is not that aspirin is a 'dangerous' drug that should be placed in the same category as cocaine or heroin."[82] But that is the point. Taken in five grain tablets, heroin and aspirin (both developed by Bayer) are comparable.

d. Addiction Variations

Illicit drugs, especially cocaine and heroin, are supposedly so addicting that their users become powerless to reduce or stop drug intake even when their health and well being are threatened.[83] Addiction to illicit drugs is frequently compared to enslavement. Richard Nixon, then U.S. President, said in 1972 that the people conducting the "global heroin trade are literally the slave traders of our time. They are traffickers in living death. They must be hunted to the end of the earth."[84] It is also alleged that drug habituation creates financial crises that force users into acquisitive crimes. In fact, the evidence indicates that illicit drugs are not especially addicting, that the portrait of compulsive alcoholics and enslaved heroin addicts is overblown and inaccurate, and that habituation is a common experience not restricted to drug use.

Taking the most general point first, Scitovsky reports that people acquire consumptive habits much more readily than they abandon them.[85] Humans are habit prone. Scitovsky argues that most consumptive behaviour, including brand-name fixation, is psychologically equivalent to drug habituation. Every product or activity capable of satisfying a human need is capable of inducing psychological dependence.[86] Thus people become habituated to their regular dose of spectator sports, cosmetics, television, religion or gambling. John Marks draws a parallel to drugs by labelling these other recreations "social psychoactives".[87] Reports of parents neglecting their children by spending time and money on alcohol or cocaine can be matched by tales of neglect tied to gambling, sports or soap-operas.[88] Zincone argues that millions of people worship soccer (football) and that some extreme fans starve themselves to help pay for the star athlete crucial to their team's prominence.[89]

How compulsive are drug addictions? Orthodox opinion since the rise of a deterministic modern psychiatry contends that alcoholism is a permanent disease or that once "hooked" on heroin one is, at best, a heroin addict in remission. But this now standard refrain that alcoholics, for example, are helpless compulsives who cannot drink moderately finds little support in the scientific literature despite wide popular and medical acceptance of E. Jellinick's *The Disease Concept of Alcoholism* (1960).[90] Beauchamp's thesis that alcoholism is a myth is substantiated by research revealing that chronic heavy drinkers can limit their drinking and return to moderate alcohol intake.[91] A new survey of the alcoholism literature by H. Fingarette lends support to Beauchamp's position.[92] Two other notewor-

19

thy explorations of addiction are Stanton Peele's *Diseasing of America: Addiction Treatment Out of Control* (1989) and Bruce Alexander's *Peaceful Measures: Canada's Alternatives to the War on Drugs* (1990).

Habituation does not inevitably follow the use of certain drugs, nor are any drug habits unbreakable once acquired. Most users of heroin, cannabis, alcohol or tobacco are not strongly habituated. In one study, 24 smokers were supplied unmarked cartons of both regular and very low nicotine cigarets. During the experiment, six smokers did not notice being shifted from regular to low nicotine, nine noticed or complained about the change and nine cheated on the test by returning to their regular brand when they were given the low nicotine batch.[93] I expect similar variations in allegiance will be observed amongst other drug users. The instant, perpetual heroin addict is a myth. Even committed opiate users regulate quantity and frequency of use, often abstain voluntarily and usually "mature out" of use after about 10 years.[94]

Finally, while the habituation potential of drugs varies, the drugs classified as illicit are not necessarily the most addicting. In the Health Consequences of Smoking : *Nicotine Addiction* (1988), the U.S. Surgeon General, C. Everett Koop, concluded that tobacco should be treated as cautiously as heroin. Not surprisingly, a Senator from North Carolina attacked Koop's report for comparing tobacco to "insidious narcotics."[95] Actually, people taking both heroin and nicotine often report that the greater challenge is to quit tobacco. Most smokers are regular, dependent users who rarely go an hour or more without a "fix"; a few extremists even wake during the night to smoke. Perhaps no other unnecessary substance means so much to so many people in the world as tobacco.[96] Still, 30 million Americans quit using tobacco in the last two decades and 95% of these quit without professional help.[97]

Drugs need not be intoxicating or exhilarating to be habit-forming, nor must they be entirely satisfying. A survey of 71 heroin users found that only 8 found the effect "thrilling"; most merely reported that the drug "relaxed" them.[98] Drug addictiveness, however, is confused by the usual legal and social biases and is strongly effected by expectations. While Murphree notes that all drug addictions are "the same phenomenon," leading theories of addiction reflect the position of specific drug users in the social-legal hierarchy.[99] After the opiate prohibition deterred middle and upper class users and left opiates in the hands of the "criminal" class and the poor ("junkie" derives from scrap collector or junkman), theories of opiate addiction mirrored the theorists' disdain for the subject group of "wretched" addicts. Now the pathology of cocaine use is stressed. Once or twice a year since 1982, *Time* articles have claimed that cocaine cannot be used moderately; one article stated: "By definition, people addicted to cocaine are out of control... [and] on or over the edge of ruin."[100] Official pronouncements provide a basis for such "definitional" opinions. A recent National Institute on Drug Abuse publication, *Cocaine Use in America* (1985), opines that "If we were to design deliberately a chemical that would lock people into perpetual use, it would probably resemble the neuro-psychological properties of cocaine... anyone with access to cocaine in quantity is at risk" (p. 151). In fact, most cocaine users are social users, few match the journalistic or police stereotype, and chewing coca leaf, even for decades, is apparently not addicting.[101]

Tobacco use produces physical tolerance and addiction, but this was a fact of no compelling interest prior to the 1970s because the drug was socially acceptable and readily available at low prices. Tobacco use was not viewed as pathological, few experts studied nicotine addiction and users were not pushed into a corner by artificial limitations on supply. Evidence of extreme or "crazed" behaviour by smokers caught in a suppliers' strike or war-time rationing was discounted.[102] The addictiveness of a medical psychoactive like amphetamine was similarly overlooked.[103] One pharmacology textbook claimed that "psychotherapeutic agents do not make healthy people feel 'happy,' nor improve their disposition," hence no danger of addiction existed.[104] Some drugs, like lithium, do not trigger positive mood elevation, but in the case of psychoactive medicines the introduction of every new drug is followed eventually by reports of chronic, habitual use.[105] Finally, the drug user's addiction and withdrawal experience are influenced by social norms that lead heroin users, for example, to expect their withdrawal to be exceedingly frightful.[106]

The conclusion I draw from the evidence is that recreational, medical and illicit drugs are all habituating to various degrees unrelated to their legal status. Marijuana, for example, appears to be less habit-forming than tobacco or coffee. Furthermore, drug dependence is now the normal state for the majority of adults so the impact of such addiction should not be exaggerated. Most caffeine, nicotine or alcohol habitues lead responsible, productive lives. What would wreak havoc on these ordinary drug users would be to prohibit their drugs.

4. The Politics of Drugs

The evidence surveyed so far suggests that current drug control policies are both counter-productive and factually unfounded. Byck and van Dyke conclude in their *Scientific American* (1982) article on cocaine that the present law is "based neither on science nor sense" primarily because the law "most appropriately should relate to human behaviour, not chemical entities." If these criticisms are true, the question that naturally arises is why such policies were ever enacted. The answer, I think, cannot be found by referring to issues of public safety, quality control, informed choice or social welfare. Instead, an explanation of current drug laws should be based on competition in the drug field and on the success of some competitors in exploiting the political process to gain unfair advantage. This analysis builds on familiar work in critical criminology and on classic texts of criminal law sociology.[107]

War is a form of competition and the war against drugs is no exception, being the result of drug-based competition in three spheres: commercial, occupational and cultural. Commercial battles over the drug trade are an historical constant with tea, rum, tobacco, coffee, opium, coca and other drugs playing central roles in the founding of various commercial and colonial empires.[108] Governments involve themselves in this drug trade by granting monopolies to certain companies, by promoting the export of domestic drugs and by limiting the import of "foreign" drugs. Canadian and U.S. governments conform to standard mercantalist, beggar-thy-neighbour policies by exporting alcohol, tobacco and pharmaceuticals to Third World countries while banning the import of opium, marijuana and coca from those same countries. Coffee exports from South America seem an exception, but coffee use spread from Africa and Arabia into Europe centuries before coffee production was transplanted to Colombia by Western investors.

Within every society a struggle occurs between groups fighting for the power to produce and distribute drugs. Drugs are an attractive, popular commodity and their control confers significant benefits. As one might expect, in a political contest the powerful tend to dominate; thus drugs have historically begun their social careers in the hands of priests, royalty or organized medicine.[109] With the eclipse of organized religion and the rise of the medical profession in the 20th century, it is understandable that modern drug control debates focus on a medical versus non-medical dichotomy. Chapter Five offers a detailed analysis of medical politics and the competition between police and physicians, and between physicians and the other professionals desiring to distribute drugs without benefit of a medical licence.

The final and broadest form of drug competition is cultural. Cultures naturally propagate their own languages, fashions, symbols and practices as God-given, natural and wholesome while rejecting "alien" customs. After 1900, Canadian and American lawmakers passed discriminatory laws against drugs such as opium, marijuana and cocaine that were associated with foreign cultures or opposed minorities.[110] Stringent laws against alcohol and tobacco use were also enacted, but these were generally beaten back except as they applied to people below the voting age. The continued vigour of the narcotics laws through the 1960s, 1970s and 1980s is also explicable in terms of cultural competition between a white, male, alcohol-using establishment and various factions of black activists, native groups, anti-war rebels and most importantly, a youth "counterculture."[111] The British Royal College of Psychiatrists reports that often drugs regarded by some governments as a dire threat are considered harmless pleasures by other authorities, and that it is usual to view drugs from other cultures with deep suspicion. The different treatment of opium and alcohol traders this century is attributed by the College to "the ability of Western Europeans to impose their assumptions, customs and prejudices on other people through financial power, war and domination of international bodies."[112]

Drug classifications and methods of drug control are all explicable in terms of political incentives and social conditions. Legal controls over drug matters, almost absent prior to 1900, have proliferated in this century, but then the legal regulation of most everything has undergone unprecedented growth. Our drug laws are complex and discriminatory, but this reflects a sophisticated social structure where numerous professional, ethnic, sexual and class divisions exist. In stable, archaic societies a drug's status and control is so firmly governed by custom that few overt laws need apply. Industrial cultures partly depend on customary control over older drugs, but this is not true for the many new drugs added to the social crucible by invention and exploration. The modern era also rapidly intermixes different cultures, a process that brings together drug habits familiar to one group but feared by another. In this cultural conflict, the drug customs officially sanctioned follow the lines of political hegemony which has meant, over the last century or more, that occidental drugs have superceded oriental drugs. A final factor in shaping drug legislation is the powerful hand of fashion. People's choice of drug, method of use, form and brand usually reflects their gender, race, age and socio-economic status, so laws discriminating between cigars and cigarets or between opium smoking and laudanum drinking can be enacted as proxies for social discrimination.

The claim that a drug's legal status depends on the status and political clout of the drug's sellers and users, and not on the drug's pharmacology, can be readily tested. Caffeine is the most popular, widely used drug. Predictably, it is also the least restricted drug. Caffeine is a habit forming stimulant but its nearly universal acceptance obscures its drug status.[113] Statistics Canada includes tea and coffee in "Food Industries." Objectors might argue that caffeine retailers need no licence, pay no special tax, advertise freely and sell to minors because caffeine is entirely benign and the law merely recognizes this fact. Sheehan, a fitness and health columnist, claims that coffee is safe and in all likelihood "is actually good for you. It probably has physiological benefits."[114] An admitted coffee addict, Sheehan cites only short-term studies in support of his claim. If Sheehan were to read the *Fitness Institute Bulletin* he would find an article by M. Baldwin, "The Pros and Cons of Coffee" (December 1980), in which Baldwin concludes that if your goal is fitness and health, caffeine "should have no part in your life." Baldwin explains that using caffeine is like "buying on credit" because after caffeine triggers an initial energy release "by blocking normal shutoff mechanisms" there follows within one to three hours a hangover effect of under stimulation, motor impairment and mental inefficiency. Caffeine use, she reports, is also linked to hypoglycemia, greater risk of coronary heart attack and stomach ulcer. Certain other facts undercut the benign caffeine argument. In other places and times, authorities classified caffeine beverages as dangerous substances.[115] Health concerns also exist. About one third of adult caffeine users in North America are estimated to be at risk.[116] Finally, drugs classified as dangerous in North America are judged elsewhere as benign. South American Indians consider coca a food and Jamaican women and children drink ganja tea (cannabis), but both practices are prohibited in North America and are considered extremely dangerous.

Alcohol and tobacco, the next two most popular drugs, occupy a broad middle ground between caffeine and "real drugs" like the narcotics. Where these drugs are taken almost universally (wine in Southern Europe, tobacco in many countries), they are legally classified as agricultural commodities or quasi-foods like coffee. Where per capita intake declines, as it did with alcohol in North America from 1850 to 1930 and as it is doing now with tobacco, there is usually an increase in legislated restrictions. Since 1960 the proportion of tobacco smokers has fallen from 50% to about 30% of American adults. Further declines in tobacco's popularity will be met by higher tobacco taxes and more anti-smoking initiatives.[117] Early anti-cigaret efforts between 1895 and 1914 probably arose in large part because urban immigrants in the U.S. were the first users of cigarets. In contrast to tobacco, most alcohol regulations have been liberalized since 1950 as alcohol consumption regained popularity.

Few legal restraints affect the purchase and use of OTC psychoactives such as aspirin. These drugs tend to be viewed as a single class of medicines, and as such come close to universal acceptance. Different, more restrictive laws apply to medical psychoactives that, since 1938, fall under the monopoly control of physicians. In almost every case, prescription-only drugs are new drugs that had no committed band of loyal users to protest physician control. Politically, physicians could not turn alcohol into a prescription-only drug except under the bizarre conditions created by Prohibition in the U.S. from 1918 to 1932. Finally, legally proscribed drugs are the least used and the least integrated into Western culture. Complications develop, however, when drugs like marijuana move from the remote fringes of society to mainstream youth,

25

as happened in the late 1960s. Earlier laws developed to subjugate Chinese immigrants and Mexican labourers were suddenly turned on the sons and daughters of the middle class. Legalizing marijuana became a respectable position and a lobbying group was created — the National Organization for the Reform of Marijuana Laws (NORML). Drugs like heroin and cocaine that were not adopted by the youth movement remained entirely despicable. Recently, however, cocaine's renaissance is altering opinion on that drug.

Political biases are allowed nearly free reign in the regulation of drugs because lawmakers in democracies and dictatorships alike enjoy legislative licence to classify drugs any way they please. Numerous legal categories can be created and any drug can be assigned to any category. Legislators need not demonstrate that drug use is dangerous, they need merely assert that it is harmful. Drug classifications are not based on drug effects, harmfulness, addictiveness or any objective measure.[118] Instead, drugs are grouped according to the legal restrictions imposed on their users, producers or sellers.[119] Obviously such a scheme is entirely circular — a drug is declared a "narcotic" not because its chemical structure resembles morphine, not because it induces drowziness, and not because it is especially dangerous, but because legislators assign it to the "narcotic" classification. Without factual tests, burdens of proof or constitutional laws to impede them, politicians can make any substance a "narcotic." Cocaine, a sleep-preventing stimulant, is legally classified a "narcotic," that is a sleep-inducer.[120] Cannabis is also frequently made a "narcotic," a decision the LeDain Commission admitted was arbitrary since cannabis is similar in effect to a wide variety of drugs including "alcohol, LSD and mescaline, nitrous oxide, amphetamines, atropine, opiate narcotics, barbiturates and the minor and major tranquillizers."[121] If cannabis can be a "narcotic," then so can any psychoactive including aspirin, alcohol or atropine.[122]

Given that current drug classifications at law are not based on pharmacological properties, addictiveness or abuse potential, it is clear that the law is aimed at people, not drugs. Since the drug laws served, and still serve, as an indirect means of inflicting unethical and unconstitutional discrimination against minorities, the only complete ethical remedy is to abolish discrimination and treat all drug users alike. The scientific evidence surveyed, which stresses

26

the generality of drug effects and the major role played by the user and by social taboos, fashions and expectations, tends to the same conclusion — that psychoactive drug use is a general phenomenon. Finally, I draw support from drug policy experts like Ed Brecher, who also condemned current drug categories and recommended a more unified approach : "a sound policy for any of these drugs ... will almost certainly be a consistent policy for all of them."

5. Arguments Against Legalization

If drug laws are actually the result of covert competitive struggles between professions, cultures and businesses, what do anti-drug crusaders offer by way of justification for continuing the war?

William von Rabb, commissioner of the U.S. Customs Service in 1988, offers invective, propaganda and diversion. Rabb feels that talking about legalizing cocaine is "madness" and that such talk is the result of people being "so desperate and afraid" that they would surrender to "drug thugs."[124] Rabb claims, without any reference or evidence, that drugs are extremely dangerous. His position is consistent with the U.S. *Anti-Drug Abuse Act* of 1988, P.L.100-690, which declares that legalizing drugs would be "an unconscionable surrender in a war [where] there can be no substitute for total victory." (Sec. 5011) Section 5251 of the same Act promises a "Drug-Free America by 1995." To achieve that goal, William Bennett, U.S. National Drug Control Director, considers beheading drug dealers to be a morally plausible strategy.[125]

In 1988, Ostrowski wrote to the leading Washington figures and organizations behind the war on drugs, asking them to cite any study demonstrating the beneficial effects of drug prohibition when weighed against its costs. Of those who bothered to reply, none could cite any study that would justify the official policy.[126] Their omission is not surprising given that present drug policies ignore the findings of every impartial, scholarly commission that has researched drug issues. These commissions include the Indian Hemp Drugs Commission, *Marijuana*, 1893-94; The Panama Canal Zone Military Investigations, 1916-1929; Advisory Commission on Drug Dependence, *Cannabis*, 1968 (The Wooton Report); the Canadian Goevernment's Commision of Inquiry, 1970-72; and the National

Research Council of the National Academy of Sciences, *An Analysis of Marijuana Policy*, 1982.

Canadian columnist Diane Francis cites with approval Ontario provincial court judge Robert Dnieper who, when sentencing on marijuana possession charges, said that the casual user of such drugs 'is a murderer. He is the evil one.'[127] In favouring harsher measures against illicit drug sellers and users, Francis makes the usual mistake of blaming enforcement costs and drug-related violence on illicit drugs rather than on politicians.

Time's cover story of May 30, 1988, entitled "Thinking the Unthinkable," mentions a number of anti-reform arguments. The authorities cited — mostly police, politicians and drug abuse rehabilitators — are against any form of legalization because they believe that:

1. illicit drugs destroy lives, transforming users so that they are "no longer normal human beings";
2. legalization would result in "an enormous increase in drug abuse", a "vast army of people who would be out of control";
3. legalization would "send a message of unrestricted hedonism" and thus amount to a "moral surrender";
4. legalization is disguised racism since it would "write the death warrants for people in the lower socio-economic classes";
5. legalization will not reduce crime because few "addicts" can hold regular jobs, so they would continue "to steal or prostitute themselves for drug money"; and because the drugs themselves are criminogenic;
6. legalization would tacitly approve of drug use — "You can't say drugs are bad at the same time that you are making them legal";
7. since licit drugs like alcohol and tobacco already cause tremendous damage, it would be a mistake to allow cannabis, cocaine and the opiates to be as widely used.

Anti-reformers in the drug policy literature make more detailed but essentially similar claims. Oregon law professor H. Titus argues that marijuana use is rooted in Eastern religious thought which "threatens the very values upon which our system is based."[128] J.B. MacDonald, then head of Ontario's Addiction Research Foundation, dismissed attempts to regulate illicit drugs along the alcohol model because that would only compound our drug problems.[129] The *Time* article, while itself staunchly anti-reform, at least discusses some

28

pro-legalization arguments. What the article fails to do is mention a single scientific study about drug effects, addictiveness or comparative drug dangers. Without any scientific input, a number of unfounded claims about "addicts" and about the inherent dangers of "narcotics" (1, 2, 4 & 5 on the previous page) are allowed to pass unchallenged. Other arguments (2, 3, 6 & 7) stand or fall on claims that can only be confirmed or refuted by experiment, but the necessary experiments are conveniently ruled out by *Time* as "too risky." Furthermore, whether legalization will really send a message of "unrestricted hedonism" or increase total drug-related damage depends in large part on which alternative to prohibition is chosen. Converting all illicit drugs to prescription-only medicines would hardly be interpreted as hedonistic. Likewise, subjecting all drugs, including alcohol, caffeine and tobacco, to rationing controls could reduce total drug use even while allowing the possibility of greater use of cannabis and opium. It seems not to occur to anti-narcotics crusaders that pro-legalizers could be more effectively anti-drug-use than they are, a lapse largely due to their cultural bias in refusing to count alcohol, coffee, tobacco and diazepam as "drugs."[130]

The anti-legalizers deal with the argument that drug laws actually result from professional and cultural competition by ignoring it. The entire focus is on the allegedly unique dangers inherent in illicit drug use. John Lawn, head of the DEA, simply asserts that, "Drugs are bad not because they're illegal. They're illegal because they're bad."

Also missing from the *Time* article are discussions about fairness, democratic choice, and whether government should have to actually demonstrate an activity's serious harmfulness before subjecting people to lengthy prison terms. Anti-legalizers also tend to cloak their case in moral indignation and contrast their commitment to "values" with the legalizers' supposedly pragmatic sell-out to drug pushers. Given the long history of consistent immorality behind the anti-narcotics crusade, their self-righteousness is a text book example of historical revisionism.

The most thorough and recent case against legalization I found is by Inciardi and McBride.[131] These authors lodge eight criticisms against legalization. First, they argue that legalizers have so far failed to provide detailed, concrete proposals. Even if this was true, the problem ended with the publication of this book. Second, they suggest that illicit drugs ought to remain illegal because they are highly dangerous. Their claims are exaggerated. The third criticism is odd because it is based on their denial of the enslavement theory of addiction. Most legalizers, including myself, agree with them. Criminals who use illicit drugs will not quit being criminals just because drugs are legalized. Their fourth concern is that once drugs are legal, the vast persuasive powers of modern marketers will create great demand for these substances. Fear of advertising, as I show in Chapter Seven, is as unwarranted as fear of narcotics. Five, they assume incorrectly that alcohol and other drugs are seriously criminogenic. Six, they assert without evidence that legalization will devastate black, inner city ghettos. Seven, they point to surveys of declining illicit drug use to prove that the drug war is succeeding. Only by ignoring all the rights-based arguments for legalization can they cite such surveys as measures of "success." Even if only one person wanted to use cocaine, the law would still be as unjust as it is today. Finally, they play their democratic card: opinion surveys indicate that about 90% of Americans oppose drug legalization and support harsh punishment for drug felons. While true, this argument is quite weak as I will explain in more detail later.

Political opposition to reform will be discussed again in Chapter Nine after we have made a close inspection of the various ways in which drug-related activities can be regulated.

Notes

1   A. Trebach, *The Great Drug War* (NY: Macmillan, 1987). Trebach is the founder and President of the Washington-based Drug Policy Foundation. Marie Andrée Bertrand, a Montreal criminologist, is President of the International League Against Prohibition.

2   See E.M Brecher and the Editors of *Consumer Reports, Licit and Illicit Drugs* (Boston: Little, Brown, 1972); A. Lamberti: "Criminal organizations as incentives to spreading drug consumption" in *The Cost of Prohibition on Drugs* (Brussels: CORA, 1989) 13-21.

3   S. Wisotsky, *Breaking the Impasse in the War on Drugs* (Westport: Greenwood Press, 1986); G. Jonas, "The Myths of Drug Abuse" *Canadian Lawyer* October 1988.

4   C. Mitchell, "Le Crime Organisé et La Guerre aux Stupéfiants: Crise et Réforme" (1989) 12 *Criminologie* 41-65; T. Carpenter, "The U.S. Campaign Against International Trafficking: A Cure Worse Than The Disease" *Policy Analysis - Cato Institute* #63 December 1985.

5   *The Cost of Prohibition of Drugs,* Papers of The International Anti-Prohibitionist Forum, (CORA, Brussels, 1989); J. Ostrowski, "Thinking About Drug Legalization" *Cato Policy Analysis* 121: 1-64, 1989; J. Inciardi, *The War on Drugs - Heroin, Cocaine, Crime and Public Policy* (Palo Alto: Mayfield, 1986); J. Moore & C. Hager, "Drugs and Crime: A Bad Connection" (1973) 3 *Yale Review of Law & Social Action* 228-45; "Where the War is Being Lost" *Time* March 14, 1988 19-20; "The Miami Connection" *The Nation* February 18, 1984 186-198.

6   E.J. Epstein, *Agency of Fear: Opiates and Political Power in America* (New York: G.P. Putnam's, 1977); J. Kaplan, "Drugs and Crime: Legal Aspects" 643-52 *Encyclopedia of Crime & Justice* Vol. 2 S. Kadish (ed) (New York: Free Press, 1983); P. Smith, "The Soldiers' Story" *Reason* August/September 1988 31-33.

[7] C. Mitchell, "A Justice-Based Argument for the Uniform Regulation of Psychoactive Drugs" (1986) 31 *McGill Law Journal* 212-263; J. Fort, *The Pleasure Seekers: The Drug Crisis, Youth and Society* (New York: Grove Press, 1969); C. Lidz & A. Walker, *Heroin, Deviance and Morality* (London: Sage Pub., 1980); D. Musto, *The American Disease: Origins of Narcotic Control* (New Haven: Yale University Press, 1973).

[8] C. Mitchell, "Deregulating Mandatory Medical Prescription" (1986) 12 *American Journal of Law and Medicine* 207-239; O. Ray, *Drugs, Society and Human Behaviour* (St. Louis: C.V. Mosby, 1978); K. Satinder, *Drug Use: Criminal, Sick or Cultural* (New York: Libra Pub., 1980).

[9] E. Nadelmann, "The Case for Legalization" (1988) 92 *The Public Interest* 3-31; E. Nadelmann, "Drug Prohibtion in the United States: Costs, Consequences, and Alternatives" (1989) 245 *SCIENCE* 939-947: T. Stachnick, "The Case Against Penalties for Illicit Drug Use" (1972) 27 *American Psychologist* 637; M. Kurzman and M. Magell, "Decriminalizing possession of all controlled substances: an alternative whose time has come" (1977) *Contemporary Drug Problems* 245; "Fighting a losing battle" *Maclean's* June 20, 1988 48; P. Hadaway, B. Beyerstein & J. Youdale, "Canadian drug policies: Irrational, futile and unjust" (1990) 20 (4) *Journal of Drug Issues*.

[10] M. Bertrand, "The immorality of prohibition" in *The Cost of Prohibition on Drugs* (1989) 175-77.

[11] B. MacFarlane, *Drug Offences in Canada* (Toronto: Canada Law Book, 1986). According to Manning, the U.S. drug classification scheme is accepted without question by drug enforcement officers as an "invisible credo, isolated and unsupported by unequivocal research findings." P. Manning, *The Narc's Game: Organizational and Informational Limits on Drug Law Enforcement* (MIT Press, 1980) 10.

[12] W. Vodra, "The Controlled Substances Act" (1978) 2 *Drug Enforcement* 2-7; P. Bucknell & P. Ghodse, "Notes on Some Controlled Drugs" (1985) *Criminal Law Review* 260, and (1988) *Criminal Law Review* 275.

[13] See the *Food and Drugs Act*, R.S.C. 1970, C. F-27; the *Nar-*

cotic Control Act R.S.C. 1970, C. N-1 and various schedules set out in *Food and Drug Regulations*, C.R.C. 1978, c. 870, c. 01.041 and the *Narcotic Control Regulations*, C.R.C. 1978, c. 1041. For a general discussion of the relevant legislation concerning "medical" drugs, see W.M. Wardell (ed), *Controlling the Use of Therapeutic Drugs: An International Comparison* (Washington: American Enterprise Institute for Public Policy Research, 1978).

[14] See H.R. Levin, *Legal Dimensions of Drug Abuse in the United States* (Springfield, Ill.: Charles C. Thomas, 1974) 7-8; R. Smart, *Forbidden Highs* (Toronto: Addiction Research Foundation, 1983) 224; R. Ferguson, *Drug Abuse Control* (Boston: Holbrook Press, 1975).

[15] T. Szasz, *Ceremonial Chemistry: The Ritual Persecution of Drugs, Addicts and Pushers* (New York: Anchor Press/Doubleday, 1974) at 150; A. Weil, *The Natural Mind* (Boston: Houghton Mifflin, 1972) Chapter 2.

[16] E. Goode, *Drugs in American Society*, 2nd ed (New York: Alfred A. Knopf, 1984) 5; J. Young, *The Drugtakers* (London: MacGibbon & Kee, 1971) 9-10; J. Marks, *The Benzodiazepines: Use, Overuse, Misuse, Abuse* (Baltimore: U. Park Press, 1978) at 69, 73; J. Jaffe, "What Counts As A 'Drug Problem'" in C. Edwards, A. Arif, J. Jaffe,(eds.) *Drug Use and Misuse - Cultural Perspectives* (London: Croom Helm, 1983); J. Krivanek, *Addictions* (Sydney: Allen & Unwin, 1988).

[17] S. Lucia, *A History of Wine as Therapy* (Philadelphia: J.B. Lippincott, 1963); C.D. Leake and M. Silverman, *Alcoholic Beverages in Clinical Medicine* (Chicago: Year Book Medical, 1966).

[18] S. Williams, "The Use of Beverage Alcohol as Medicine, 1790-1860" (1980) 41 *J. Stud. Alcohol* 543; N. Longmate, *The Water Drinkers: A History of Temperance* (London, Ontario: Hamish, 1968) 178; M. Smith and D. Knopp, *Pharmacy, Drugs, and Medical Care* (Baltimore: Williams and Wilkins, 1972) 158-161.

[19] R. M. Julien, *A Primer of Drug Action* (San Francisco: Freeman, 1981) 209.

[20] D.T. Cartwright, *Dark Paradise: Opiate Addiction in America Before 1940* (Cambridge, Mass.: Harvard University Press, 1982) 113.

[21] P. Rosenberg, "The Abusers of Stimulants and Depressants" in J. Cull and R. Hardy (eds), *Types of Drug Abusers and Their Abuses* (Springfield: Charles C. Thomas, 1974) 123-129.

[22] J. Rublowsky, *The Stoned Age - A History of Drugs in America* (New York: Putnam, 1974) 118-21.

[23] L. Grinspoon & J. Bakalar, "Medical Uses of Illicit Drugs" in *Dealing with Drugs* (1987) 183-219; J. Kaplan, "Classification for Legal Control" in R. H. Blum (ed), *Controlling Drugs* (San Francisco: Jossey, Bass, 1974) 293.

[24] S. Snyder, "What We Have Forgotten about Pot - a Pharmacologist's History" *New York Times Magazine* December 13, 1970, 124; J. Ungerleider and T. Andrysiak, "Therapeutic Issues of Marijuana and THC" (1985) 20 *Int. J. Add.* 691.

[25] H.S. Diehl, *Tobacco and Your Health, The Smoking Controversy* (1969) at 2-7; L. Jeger, "The Social Implications" in H. Cole and C. Fletcher, eds. *Common Sense About Smoking* (London: Penguin 1963) at 79-80.

[26] R. Martin, "The Role of Coca in History, Religion and Medicine" in *The Coca Leaf and Cocaine Papers* (G. Andrews & D. Solomon, (eds), New York: Harcourt Brace Jovanovich, 1975); J. Kennedy, *Coca Exotica: The Illustrated Story of Cocaine* (New York: Cornwall Books, 1987).

[27] N. Stone, M. Fromme, D. Kagan, *Cocaine: Seduction and Solution* (New York: Clarkson Potter, 1984) 15; L. Grinspoon & J. Bakalar, *Cocaine* (New York: Basic Books, 1976). See also J. Orcutt, "Normative Definitions of Intoxicated States: A Test of Several Sociological Theories", (1977-78) 25 *Social Problems* 385-396.

[28] Julien, *supra* note 19, at 87; C. van Dyke & R. Byck, "Cocaine" 246(3) *Scientific American* (1982) 128-141.

[29] Rosenberg, *supra* note 21 at 166.

[30]   J. Rice, *Ups and Downs: Drugging and Doping* (New York: Macmillan, 1972) 3-6.

[31]   J. Fort, "The Marijuana Abuser and the Abuser of Psyche-delic-Hallucinogens" in J.G. Cull & R. E. Hardy (eds), *Types of Drug Abusers and Their Abuses* (Springfield: Charles C. Thomas, 1974)   135; P. Furst, *Hallucinogens and Culture* (Novato, CA: Chandler & Sharp, 1982).

[32]   William James, *The Varieties of Religious Experience* (Fontana Library, London, 1960)   373.

[33]   See M. Crichton, *Five Patients: The Hospital Explained* (New York: Alfred A. Knopf, 1970)   87-88.

[34]   N. Longmate, *supra* note 18, 12.

[35]   *Consumer Reports* (eds), *The Medicine Show* (New York: Pantheon Books, 1974)   13. Analgesics are not supposed to se-date, which is why one textbook writer classifies "light-head-edness, dizziness, sleepiness and nausea" as "side-effects" of Robaxin (methocarbamol). See   R. Poitevin, *Understanding Medications* (Montreal: Habitex, 1973) 41.

[36]   S. Einstein, *Beyond Drugs* (Pergamon Press, 1975) 82-85.

[37]   *ibid.*, 86.

[38]   See P. Fussell, *Class* (New York: Ballantine, 1984).

[39]   T. Conry, *Consumer's Guide to Cosmetics* (New York: Anchor Books, 1980) 17-19; L. Plommer, "Iran: no place to be a woman" *The Globe and Mail* August 29, 1987 D3. Czechoslovakian officials cancelled a Bruce Cockburn concert in 1985 because his wearing an earring was "subversive."

[40]   Sidney W. Mintz, *Sweetness and Power - The Place of Sugar in Modern History* (New York: Elisabeth Sifton Books, Viking, 1985) 99, 100.

[41]   W. N. Hubbard Jr., "Preclinical Problems of New Drug Development" in R. L. Landau, ed. *Regulating New Drugs* (Chicago: University of Chicago Center for Policy Study, 1973) 36, 50

and E.W. Kitch, "The Patent System and the New Drug Application: An Evaluation of the Incentives for Private Investment in New Drug Research and Marketing" in Landau 82, 85.

[42] G. Claridge, *Drugs and Human Behaviour* (New York: Praeger, 1970) 19.

[43] R. H. Blum, "Interest Groups" in *Controlling Drugs, supra* note 22, 64-65.

[44] H. Lennard, L. Epstein, A. Bernstein, D. Ranson, *Mystification and Drug Misuse* (San Francisco: Jossey-Bass, 1971) 57-67, 78-83. See also Maloff, *et al.* whose anthropological evidence about how different tribes use the same drug as an energizer and tranquillizer highlights the "cultural plasticity" of drug taking. D. Maloff, *et al.*, "Informal Social Controls and Their Influence on Substance Use" (1979) 9 *Journal of Drug Issues* 161.

[45] S. Rosenblatt and R. Dodson, *Beyond Valium: The Brave New World of Psychochemistry* (New York: Putnam, 1981) 234-235. See also A. N. Angier, "Marijuana: Bad News and Good" (1981) *Discover*, August, 15; S. Cohen, "Marijuana as Medicine" (1978), *Psychology Today* April 60-64, 73.

[46] E. R. Gritz and M. E. Jarvick, "Psychoactive Drugs and Social Behaviour" in K. R. Hammond and C.R.B. Joyce (eds), *Psychoactive Drugs and Social Judgment: Theory and Research* (New York: Wiley, 1975) 7, 8.

[47] Government of Canada, *Report of the Commission of Inquiry into the Non-Medical Use of Drugs: Marijuana* (Ottawa: Information Canada, 1972), 20, (Chair: G. LeDain).

[48] P. Leach, *The Parents' A to Z* (London: Allen Lane, 1983) 42-43.

[49] Rice, *supra* note 30, 6.

[50] D. G. Garan, *Against Ourselves: Disorders from Improvements under the Organic Limitedness of Man* (New York: Philosophical Library, 1979) 58.

51 A. Weil, "The Green and the White" in *The Coca Leaf and Co-caine Papers, supra* note 26, at 331.

52 G. Marvel and B. Hartman, "An 'Economic' Theory of Addic-tion, Hypomania, and Sensation Seeking", (1986) 21 *Interna-tional Journal of Addiction* 495, 496-500. See also University of Pennsylvania psychologist R. Soloman quoted in "A Painful Theory on Pleasures" *Time*, November 10, 1980, 10.

53 A. Malleson, *Need Your Doctor Be So Useless?* (London: George Allen & Unwin, 1973).

54 C. Mitchell, "The Mispursuit of Happiness: Divorcing Norma-tive Legal Theory from Utilitarianism" 1986 16 *Manitoba Law Journal* 123-147.

55 ibid., 129-130.

56 On birth defects and other health problems see R. Hughes and R. Brewin, *The Tranquilizing of America* (New York: Har-court Brace Jovanovich, 1979) ch. 2 and ch. 4; J. Elkington, *The Poisoned Womb - Human Reproduction in a Polluted World* (New York: Viking, 1985); *The Globe & Mail*, March 4, 1985, 4.

57 See H. Teff, *Drugs, Society and the Law* (Westmead, England: Saxon House, 1975) 146-8. In the U.K. during 1974 there were 61 deaths connected with heroin, 1,829 with alcohol and 1,930 with barbiturates.

58 R. Schroeder, *The Politics of Drugs - An American Dilemma* (Washington: Congressional Quarterly Press, 1980) 99.

59 M. Green, "Towards Rational Drug Scheduling" in J. Black-well & P. Erickson, *Illicit Drugs in Canada* (Toronto: Nelson, 1988) 186-208.

60 H. Levine and C. Reinarman, "What's Behind 'Jar Wars'" *The Nation* March 28, 1987, 388; for unbiased definitions of "drug abuse" see R. E. Carney, "The Abuser of Tobacco" in J. G. Cull and R.E. Hardy (eds), *Types of Drug Abusers and Their Abuses* (Springfield, Ill.: Charles C. Thomas, 1974) 160, 162; Julien, *supra* note 19, 214.

[61] M. Smith, "The Drug Problem - Is There an Answer?" (1988) *Federal Probation* 3-6 (March).

[62] J. L. Phillips and R. Wynne, *Cocaine: The Mystique and Reality* (New York: Avon Books, 1980).

[63] C. Mitchell, "The Intoxicated Offender - Refuting the Legal and Medical Myths" (1988) 11 *International Journal of Law & Psychiatry* 77-103, 81.

[64] As an example of the method, see M. Bozarth & R. Wise, "Toxicity Associated with Long-Term Intravenous Heroin and Cocaine Self-Administration in the Rat" (1985) 254 *Journal of the American Medical Association* 81-83. But on the dangers of learning from laboratory rats, see B. Alexander, P. Hadaway, R. Coambs, "Rat Park Chronicle" (1988) *Illicit Drugs in Canada* 63-68.

[65] J. Brody, "Adventists Are Gold Mine for Research on Disease" *New York Times*, November 11, 1986, C1.

[66] Mitchell, *supra* note 54.

[67] J. Istvan and J. Matarazzo, "Tobacco, Alcohol and Caffeine Use: A Review of Their Interrelationships", (1984) 95 *Psychol. Bulletin* 301-326. Drugs like alcohol and tobacco in combination may have synergistic impact. See, J. O'Connor and M. Daly, *The Smoking Habit* (Ireland: Gill and Macmillan, 1985) 128.

[68] N. Zinberg, "The Use and Misuse of Intoxicants" in *Dealing with Drugs* (1987) 253.

[69] R. Sobel, *They Satisfy: The Cigarette in American Life* (New York: Anchor Books/Doubleday, 1978) 131.

[70] L. Grinspoon and R. Hedblom, *The Speed Culture: Amphetamine Use and Abuse in America* (Cambridge, Mass.: Harvard University Press, 1975) 67; Rosenberg, *supra* note 21, 128; J. Helmer, *Drugs and Minority Oppression* (New York: Seabury Press, 1975) 4-6.

[71] P. Lauderdale & J. Inverarity, "Regulation of Opiates" (1984)

3 *Journal of Drug Issues* 567; D. Bellis, *Heroin and Politicians - The Failure of Public Policy to Control Addiction in America* (Westport: Greenwood Press, 1981) 11, 208; R. Michaels, "The Market for Heroin Before and After Legalization" in *Dealing with Drugs* (1987) 291, 305. Also see T. Bennett & R. Wright, "The Drug-Taking Careers of Opioid Users" (1986) 25 *Howard Journal* 1.

72 See M. Schofield, *The Strange Case of Pot* (Harmondsworth, England: Penguin Books, 1971); P. Cavalluzo, "Marijuana, The Law and the Courts" (1970) 8 *Osgoode Hall Law Journal* 215-248; L. Sloman, *Reefer Madness - The History of Marijuana in America* (NY: Bobbs - Merrill, 1979).

73 See A. Weisman, "Confessions of a Drug-Type Junkie" *The New Republic* 28 July, 1986.

74 See "Too many painkillers can hurt" *The Economist*, March 19, 1983, 106; P. Temin, *Taking Your Medicine - Drug Regulation in the United States* (Harvard University Press, 1980) 3-4.

75 M. Dumont, "Civil Commitment of the Addict: A Critical Analysis" in L. Simmons & M. God (eds), *Discrimination and the Addict* (London: Sage Publishers, 1973) 256.

76 S. Box, *Power, Crime and Mystification* (London: Tavistock, 1983).

77 Mintz notes the "grotesque exaggerations" of therapeutic potency and the "sensationally favorable" press new drugs received in the 1950s. M. Mintz, *The Therapeutic Nightmare* (Boston: Houghton Mifflin, 1965) 57-62, 185.

78 See Rice, *supra* note 30, 68.

79 See W. B. Mendelson, *The Use and Misuse of Sleeping Pills: A Clinical Guide* (New York: Plenum, 1980) 39.

80 E. Bargmann *et al.*, *Stopping Valium, Ativan, Centrax, Dalmane, Librium, Paxipan, Restoril, Serax, Tranxene and Xanax* (Washington: Public Citizen, 1982) 27-39.

81 See S. Fredmann and R. E. Burger, *Forbidden Cures: How the*

FDA Suppresses Drugs That Could Save Your Life (New York: Stein and Sage, 1976) 174.

[82] Schroeder, *supra* note 58, 10.

[83] For Crick, "hard" drugs preclude moderate use. He suggests that it is "doubtful whether Sherlock Holmes could have *occasionally* taken Cocaine..." B. Crick, *Crime, Rape and Gin* (London: Elek/Pemberton, 1974) 73-75.

[84] Ray, *supra* note 8, 48.

[85] T. Scitovsky, *The Joyless Economy* (Oxford University Press, 1976); T. Scitovsky, "Asymmetries in economies", (1978) 25 *Scottish Journal of Political Economy* 227. See also C. Herman & L. Kozlowski, "Indulgence, Excess and Restraint: Perspectives on Consummatory Behaviour in Everyday Life" 85 (1979) *Journal of Drug Issues* 185.

[86] Garan, *supra* note 50.

[87] Marks, *supra* note 16.

[88] See, for example, C. Welles, "America's Gambling Fever" *Business Week* April 24, 1989 112-120.

[89] G. Zincone, "Brussels just battle in soccers' religious wars" *The Globe & Mail* 8 June, 1985, 7.

[90] See, K. Poikolainen, "Alcoholism: A Social Construct" (1982) 12 *Journal of Drug Issues* 361; R. Tournier, "The Medicalization of Alcoholism: Discontinuities in Ideologies of Deviance" (1985) 15 *J. Drug Issues* 39; J. Schneider, "Deviant Drinking as Disease: Alcoholism As a Social Accomplishment" (1977-78) 25 *Social Problems* 361-372.

[91] D. Beauchamp, *Beyond Alcoholism - Alcohol and Public Health Policy* (Philadelphia: Temple University Press, 1980) 78-83; see also, N. Zinberg, *Drug, Set and Setting: The Basis For Controlled Intoxicant Use* (Yale University Press, 1984).

[92] H. Fingarette, *Heavy Drinking - The Myth of Alcoholism As a Disease* (University of California Press, 1987).

93   J. O'Connor & M. Daly, *The Smoking Habit* (Ireland: Gill and MacMillan, 1985) at 50-52. On cocaine, see P. Erickson & B. Alexander, "Cocaine and Addictive Liability" (forthcoming, 1989).

94   Beauchamp, *supra* note 91; D. Waldorf & P. Biernacki, "Natural Recovery from Heroin Addiction, A Review of the Incidence Literature" (1979) *Journal of Drug Issues* 281.

95   *Time*, May 30, 1988, 59.

96   M. A. H. Russell, "Tobacco Smoking and Nicotine Dependence" in Addiction Research Foundation, *Research Advances in Alcohol and Drug Problems*, Vol. 3 (New York: Wiley, 1976) 1.

97   S. Peele, "What Does Addiction Have to do With Level of Consumption? A Response to R. Room", (1987) 48 *Journal of Studies on Alcohol* 84-89; S. Peele, "A Moral Vision of Addiction: How People's Values Determine Whether They Become and Remain Addicts" (1987) 17 *Journal of Drug Issues* 209.

98   See S. Peele, "The Pleasure Principle in Addiction", (1985) 15 *Journal of Drug Issues* 193.

99   H. Murphree, "Addiction and the Pleasure Principle: Pharmacodynamics versus Psychodynamics" in *The Role of Pleasure in Behaviour* R. Heath (ed),(New York: Harper & Row, 1964) 155, 159, 163; A. Lindesmith, "The drug addict as a psychopath" (1940) 5 *American Sociological Review* 914-920; J. Blackwell, "Sin, Sickness, or Social Problem? The Concept of Drug Dependence" (1988) *Illicit Drugs in Canada* 158.

100 "Crashing on Cocaine" *Time* (11 April, 1983) 18-27; "Crack - A Cheap and deadly cocaine is a spreading menace" *Time* (2 June, 1986) 14-16; "The Enemy Within" and "America's Crusade" *Time* (15 September, 1986) 56-74; "Fighting Back" *Time* (11 September, 1989) 16-22.

101 P. Erickson *et al.*, *The Steel Drug: Cocaine in Perspective* (Boston: Lexington Books, 1987) 129; B. Cocks, "Coca: Its Use Among the Aymara Indians of the Bolivian Altiplano", (1978) 2 *Legal Medical Quarterly* 33-35.

41

[102] "Smokers in Israel Left Fuming" The Toronto *Globe & Mail* (5 July, 1985) 9.

[103] Hughes and Brewin, *supra* note 56, 32-36; Goode, *supra* note 16, 228-31; Grinspoon and Hedblom, *supra* note 70, 156.

[104] F. M. Berger, "Introduction" in W.W. Clark and J. del Giudice (eds), *Principles of Psychopharmacology* (New York: Academic Press, 1970) 1, 4.

[105] See, for example, H. Petursson and M.H. Lader, "Benzodiazephine Dependence" (1981) 76 *British Journal of Addiction* 133; Mendelson, *supra* note 79, 128-36. Some hold out the probably futile hope of finding harmless, non-addictive substitutes for alcohol and other drugs. See R.K. Siegel, *Intoxication: Life in Pursuit of Artificial Paradise* (New York: Dutton, 1989).

[106] Peele, *supra* note 97.

[107] T. Sellin, *Culture, Conflict and Crime* (1948); A. Lindesmith, *Opiate Addiction* (1947); E. Sutherland, *White Collar Crime* (1949); J. Gusfield, *Symbolic Crusade* (1963); H. Becker, *Outsiders: Studies in the Sociology of Deviance* (1963); I. Taylor, P. Walton, J. Young, *The New Criminology* (1973) and C. Reasons, "The politics of drugs: An inquiry in the sociology of social problems" (1974) 15 *Sociological Quarterly*; A. Turk, *Political Criminality: The Defiance and Defense of Authority* (Beverly Hills: Sage, 1982).

[108] Goode, *supra* note 16; Rublowsky, *supra* note 22.

[109] Szasz, *supra* note 15.

[110] N. Boyd, "The origins of Canadian narcotics legislation" (1984) 8 *Dalhousie Law Journal* 102-36; R. Solomon & M. Green, "The First Century: The History of Non-Medical Opiate Use and Control Policies in Canada, 1870-1970" (1982) 20 *University of Western Ontario Law Review* 307-36; R. Bonnie and C. Whitebread, "The forbidden fruit and the tree of knowledge: An inquiry into the legal history of American marijuana prohibition" (1970) 56 *Virginia Law Review* 971-1203.

111 J. Cloyd, *Drugs and Information Control* (Westport: Greenwood Press, 1982); A. McNicoll, *Drug Trafficking: A North-South Perspective* (Ottawa: North-South Institute, 1983); W. Walker, *Drug Control in the Americas* (University of New Mexico Press, 1981); J. Ranking, "The Politics of Alcohol and Drug Use" (1974) 7th L. Ball Oration, Victorian Foundation on Alcoholism and Drug Dependence.

112 Royal College of Psychiatrists, *Alcohol: Our Favourite Drug* (London: Tavistock, 1986) 17-20.

113 See A. M. Vener, L. R. Krupka and J. J. Climo, "Drugs (Prescription, Over-the-Counter, Social) and Young Adult: Use and Attitudes" (1982) 17 *International Journal of Addictions* 399; R. Solomon, T. Hammond, S. Langdon, *Drug and Alcohol Law for Canadians* 2nd ed. (Toronto: Addiction Research Foundation, 1986) 3.

114 G. Sheehan, "Coffee's virtues are defended" Toronto *Globe & Mail* November 25, 1988, A23.

115 Satinder, *supra* note 8.

116 J. Gredan, "Coffee, Tea and You", *The Sciences* January 1979, 6-11; S. Einstein, *supra* note 36, at 87.

117 E. Nuehring & G. Markle, "Nicotine and Norms: The Re-Emergence of a Deviant Behaviour" (1973-74) 21 *Social Problems* 512-526.

118 See, R. H. Blum, "Interest Groups" in R. H. Blum *et al.*, *Controlling Drugs* (San Francisco: Jossey-Bass, 1974) 64-65; H. Kalant and O. Kalant, *Drugs, Society and Personal Choice* (Toronto, University of Toronto Press, 1971) 116; J. Krivanek, *Drug problems, people problems* (Boston: George Allen & Unwin, 1982) 15-18; R. Stephens, *Mind-Altering Drugs - Use, Abuse and Treatment* (New York: Sage Publishing, 1987) 21.

119 Solomon *et al.*, *supra* note 113, 4.

120 C. B. Schultz, "Statutory Classification of Cocaine as a Narcotic: An Illogical Anachronism" (1983) 9 *American Journal of Medicine* 225.

121 Le Dain Commission, *supra* note 47, 16.

122 In thirteen states marijuana is a narcotic, but in thirty-seven states it is a hallucinogen. In three states LSD is a narcotic. With equal justification lawmakers could declare alcohol, caffeine or tobacco to be narcotics. Indeed, since no scientific rationale need be given by legislators, they could designate grapefruit or pomegranates as narcotics.

123 Brecher, *supra* note 2, 266, 522-25.

124 W. von Rabb, "Legalizing drug use won't eliminate problems" *Toronto Star* July 29, 1988, A17.

125 A. Trebach, "'Behead the damn drug dealers': When Will We Learn the Lesson of Ayatollah Khalkhali?" (1989) 1(3) *The Drug Policy Letter* 1-3.

126 J. Ostrowski, "Thinking About Drug Legalization", (1989) *Cato Policy Analysis*, 2.

127 D. Francis, "Harsh measures against drugs" *Maclean's* September 12, 1988, 9.

128 H. W. Titus, "Oregon Marijuana Decriminalization: The Moral Question" (1977) 7 *Journal of Drug Issues* 32.

129 J. B. MacDonald, *Cannabis, Health and the Law* (Toronto: Addiction Research Foundation, 1981).

130 J. Kaplan, "Drug-dealing and the Law" in R. Blum (ed.), *Drug Dealers - Taking Action* (San Francisco: Jossey-Bass, 1973) 209.

131 J. Inciardi and D. McBride, "Legalization: A High Risk Alternative in the War on Drugs" (1989) 32(3) *American Behavioral Scientist* 259-289.

II Drug Control and Principles of Justice

The evidence presented in this chapter indicates that drug users impose measurable costs and burdens on other people. The objective is to reduce such costs and, where possible, compensate injured parties. Three basic avenues of cost reduction are available: self-control, social control and government control. Conscience, enlightened self-interest, instinct, peer pressure, religious injunction and employer self-interest all affect drug use choices. Private sanctions alone, however, may not be effective enough to provide the degree of protection and deterrence required. If private regulation is not altogether sufficient, some type of government intervention may be justified. The perennial difficulty is deciding what form state regulation of drug use should take. Should drug users be executed, taxed, forced into medical treatment, issued drug ration cards, or admonished by state-sponsored advertisements praising the benefits of self-restraint? Choosing between these possibilities is facilitated by careful adherence to certain widely recognized principles of justice. According to the first principle, government-imposed restraints should be proportional and appropriate to the harm defended against. The second principle to be honored dictates that legal restrictions should be applied fairly.

1. Justifying State Intervention

Robert Nozick's discussion about the ethical limits to state action concludes, as did John Stuart Mill, that state coercion is only justified when it serves common self-defence.[1] Naturally, different defensive needs justify different types of state action. Armed attack justifies raising a military force. Serious internal threats to citizen security justify criminal/tort prohibitions, and the need to protect general health, welfare and environment justifies regulatory action. The first challenge in governing the government is to allow the state to intervene only when the need is genuine and only to the extent required to meet the need. By creating threats or by responding excessively to genuine needs, governments justify expropriating an unwarranted share of GNP. Conversely, government may fail to act against a genuine threat when those responsible for the damage, like polluting oil refiners, possess the clout to warp the political process in their favour. As a result of these opposing incentives, governments may over and under regulate at the same time in the same field. Drug regulation exemplifies this phenomenon.

Leaving aside the practical for the ideal, principled analyses of state drug controls work through three contingent questions. First, does the production, sale and use of drugs constitute a genuine threat? Second, if a drug threat exists, can it be solved by personal and social controls? Our thinking now tends to be dominated by legal solutions but suasion, education and self-help measures should not be ignored or under-rated. Archaic societies regulate drug use without recourse to formal state controls.[2] Why do we need the government to intervene? If private controls do not suffice, thus making state intervention necessary, the third question is: What type of government action is justified? Is compulsory education through warning labels and school instruction enough? Given the right incentives, will citizens police drug advertising and quality control themselves or are public police a necessity? Should drug sellers be taxed, licensed, sent to medical school or shot, like traitors, by firing squads? In short, what scale and form of state intervention best fits the threat posed by drug use?

a. Net Social Benefits of Drug Use

A responsible social accounting must consider both costs and benefits. Drug use benefits fall into three categories: commercial profits, symptom relief and recreation. None of these are easy to quantify or measure.

Indeed, Garfield reports that no nation has ever done a nationwide cost-benefit analysis on alcohol, one of the major drugs, nor is there consensus on what count as costs and benefits.[3] Drugs' commercial importance cannot be denied. Trade in recreational drugs employs millions of Americans.[4] Corn and grape growers, tobacco farmers, coffee importers, packagers, transporters, brewers, distillers, advertisers and retailers are some of the obvious beneficiaries of this trade. About 414,000 Americans in 1983 were employed directly in tobacco and another two million indirectly; while in Europe, about 1.6 million were employed, including tobacco retailers.[6] In France, one tenth of all employees earn alcohol-related incomes.

The British spend 7.7% of their incomes on alcohol, and the alcohol industry employs 700,000 or 4% of the U.K. labour force. Another 40,000 work in the British tobacco trade. Global tobacco sales run well over $150 billion annually. Excluding China, commercial beer production globally in 1987 stood at 95.5 billion litres. For some countries, exports of tobacco, coffee, tea or cocaine represent the largest source of foreign exchange earnings. Coffee is the second most important legal commodity in international trade, bested only by petroleum. Some 20 million people world wide earn a livelihood through coffee production and distribution. For 24 developing countries, coffee and cocoa exports bring in 20% of total export earnings.[6] The value of the American trade in coffee was $4.6 billion in 1976, a figure comparable to sales in logging, ready-mix concrete, flour and toys.[7] Bolivia's cultivation of coca and marijuana provides livelihood for an estimated 500,000 people, out of a population of 27 million. American states in their colonial period were often similarly dependent on single-product trade in tobacco, rum or slaves.[8]

The gross dollar value of psychoactive drug sales worldwide, though immense, does not constitute absolute economic gain. Almost all resources of soil, machinery and human capital allocated to drugs have alternate uses. Grain, potatoes, corn and grapes yield food as well as alcohol. Furthermore, alcohol has many industrial uses. Land supporting tobacco can support wheat, turkeys, sweet potatoes, peanuts, roses, amaranth, flax or soybeans, albeit at less profit.[9] Net profit for tobacco in North Carolina in 1979 was $1,198 per acre, compared to $233 for peanuts and $72 for soya beans, but tobacco profits then were artificially boosted by government price supports and crop reduction programs. The portion of the industrial infrastructure now devoted to drugs also has alternate uses. The commercial benefit of drugs is therefore only the difference between present yields on capital and yields from the next most profitable usage. Some cost-benefit analyses miss this point and count gross employment receipts or gross sales as drug benefits.[10] A similar logic would count police employment as a benefit of crime or munitions sales as a benefit of war. Drug-related employment and sales represent commercial significance, not necessarily economic benefit. In calculating benefit we must factor in the opportunity cost of alternate employment of capital. Patricia Buchholz, in canvassing some of tobacco's opportunity costs, explains that:

47

Approximately 10 million acres of valuable agricultural and forestland and one billion man-days are devoted to the tobacco crop annually — the fruit of which is consumed daily by smokers around the world at considerable risk to their health... The people and the land are taken from the production of food; the forests are cut to cure the tobacco which results in the spread of deserts.[11]

An additional and potentially important factor in calculating the commercial benefit of drugs is the cost of re-allocating resources now devoted to the drug business. Any severe, sudden change, such as prohibiting alcohol sales, would cause tremendous commercial loss. Resources of land, machinery and human skill may be quite flexible over the long term, but in the short term every business carries fixed investments. A lifetime of expertise in tobacco cultivation and marketing cannot be costlessly transposed to other horticultural pursuits. Distillers cannot switch immediately to the production of fuel alcohol, nor could all taverns survive transformation into coffee houses or water bars. The plight of the 250,000 Americans earning alcohol-related livelihoods in 1918 was ignored by the Prohibitionists. Some breweries converted to ice cream, cheese or cereal beverage production, but most folded.

Drugs (alcohol and tobacco) are also fiscally important as traditional tax department milk cows, but whether tax revenue from drug sales amounts to a social benefit is far from clear. Suffice to say here that drug tax issues, which are numerous and complex, are addressed in Chapter Eight.

The second drug benefit is symptom relief. Symptomatic relief is potentially of societal benefit if it permits employees using caffeine to be more productive, neighbours on diazepam or alcohol to be more cheerful, and children on ritalin or dexedrine to be more attentive or studious. For a number of reasons, benefits from symptom relief are consistently exaggerated. The primary difficulty is causal. Observers tend not to connect the eventual costs of symptom relief with initial benefits. This disconnection, which creates an illusion of something-for-nothing, can be illustrated with three familiar complaints: colds, headaches and anxiety. Numerous drugs temporarily alleviate coughs, fevers, sore throats or nasal congestion. None of these drugs fight viral infections or improve the organism's capacity to resist infection. On the contrary, symptomatic drugs appear to reduce resistance and lead to longer or more frequent colds. These results should not surprise us given that cold "remedies" only mask symptoms by interfering with the organism's own disease defenses.[12] Advertisers do not mention the negative aftereffects of cold relievers, nor are drug users often appreciative of the long-term consequences. People seeking headache relief via psychoactive drug use may believe that aspirin and its analgesic competitors deliver costless, permanent escape from pain. Unhappily, analgesic users probably experience more headaches because of their drug use. Users cannot readily notice this effect because they cannot measure their lifetime supply of headaches had they not taken pain relievers. On each headache occasion the analgesic "works" and the painful symptoms are relieved. Oddly, few if any moralists remark upon the parallel between the way aspirin solves headaches and the way sedatives like alcohol solve more existential complaints.

Symptom relievers, if used repeatedly, create the vicious circle characteristic of all psychoactive drug use. The more drugs are used, the more symptoms arise that call for drug use. Initial relief is easily achieved but counteractions subsequently negate the gain by causing opposite effects. With relatively euphoric drugs like alcohol or cocaine, the counteraction is usually rather obvious and strikes within hours of the initial benefit. Long experience with alcohol has taught us that the drug causes more problems than it cures. The same process is probably operative with aspirin but is manifested in more subtle form. That aspirin use might cause an increase in headache pain is not generally considered, partly because aspirin's countereffects are diffuse and long-term.[13] Anxiety relief, on the other hand, favours alcohol-like drugs such as diazepam. As a result, researchers quickly established a connection between tranquillizer use and increased anxiety.

Reversals limit but do not negate the benefits of symptom relief. In some circumstances one might reasonably turn to drugs knowing that no net gain would be achieved. One may want the same symptom later rather than now. It may be wise to alleviate a headache before a critical sales meeting or relieve a bad cough before a speech. Drug use can also spread a large pain over a longer term, allowing small installment payments. This is the process that follows surgery under anesthetic, demonstrating that in medicine as in business, loans can be productive even though one has to pay them back with interest. Drugs as deficit pain managers can serve a positive role. However, the obvious danger is that accumulating a large deficit can jeopardize one's fiscal or physical condition. Since the psychology of borrowing is comparable, be it drugged relief or monetary debt, it may not be coincidental that in modern Western cultures both personal indebtedness and drug consumption have climbed to unprecedented levels.

Other therapeutic claims for specific drugs, for example that daily aspirin use reduces risk of heart disease or that light alcohol consumption increases longevity, remain controversial, but if established would be counted as drug benefits.

Since the seam of Calvinist restraint in our heritage condemns both commercial and personal indulgence, supporters of symptom relief try to counter traditional reticence about drug taking.[14] People are exhorted to feel no shame about seeking drug relief. Pain killing is misrepresented as a new invention. Johnson explains that we are all afraid of pain and so is puzzled as to why "civilized man took nearly 5,000 years to discover drugs which could readily prevent it."[15] Opium was used in ancient Sumeria and breweries flourished in Egypt more that 5,000 years ago. Recently reserpine was used in "pioneering" therapies for the mentally ill. Yet rauwolfia, the natural source of reserpine, was used millennia ago in India for treatment of "lunacy." Henbane, hemlock, cannabis and mandrake have served as analgesics. Colchicum eased the pain of gout in Hellenic times and Aristotle praised the pain-relieving powers of dittany. In 1248 Theodoric de Lucca, using mandrake oil and opium as an anesthetic, observed that surgical patients could be cut and feel nothing under the drugs' influence. Heedless of this familiar history, Calder in his classic *Medicine and Man* remarked that Sam Colt "nearly discovered anesthetics."[16] Later in the same book, Calder explained that Vedic surgeons used belladonna and Indian hemp (cannabis) as "operational anesthetics." Examples of historical symptom relievers form a lengthy list: rivea corymbosa was an Aztec narcotic, nutmeg and mace were applied by Hindu physicians as sedatives and analgesics, Incans employed jimson weed in surgery, and in Nigeria reserpine was given to relieve epilepsy.

Other historical revisionists admit the prior existence of pain relievers but then suggest that earlier peoples did not appreciate their full potential. In *Arrows of Mercy*, Smith cites a type of plastic surgery common to India 2,500 years ago and remarks that "incredibly, all these operations were carried out without anesthetics as *we know them*...."[17] (emphasis added). Smith draws this odd distinction because his goal is to portray 19th-century medics as the conquerors of pain. By re-inventing pain killing as something new, like radio or television, the attempt is made to circumvent traditional rules that weighed against excessive reliance on psychoactive drugs.[18] Rejecting customary wisdom, modern apologists for unlimited pain relief describe pain as "needless." Pain in mourning, pain in living, pain in childbirth — all allegedly can be and should be chemically eliminated.

The counterargument is that drugs cannot permanently remove pain, they can only re-arrange distress and they do that only at some risk. Compare the management of pain in midwifery and obstetrics. Midwives deal with pain in delivery by teaching clients what to expect, by optimizing birth conditions and by counselling patience and strength. Drug use is minimal. With obstetricians the opposite tends to be true. Major drug use is routine. In extreme cases, anesthetics are needed to permit surgical intervention, but obstetricians intervene far more frequently than is scientifically justified. The traditional non-drug methods of midwives are clearly superior in results achieved.[19]

As to the third benefit, drugs are said to be useful social facilitators and satisfying recreations. One research group explained that their concern with alcohol's harmful effects did not cause them to forget "the pleasure that [alcohol] gives to the great majority of consumers."[20] This statement implies that for most moderate, socially upstanding drinkers, alcohol-induced satisfactions are net gains. Somehow alcohol users are imagined to have more total fun than non-drinkers. Michael Kinsley feels that "alcohol is a small but genuine contribution toward [the] pursuit of happiness..."[21] Pro-tobacco analysts worry that a smoking ban will deprive users of "satisfaction." Moralist Joel Feinberg describes alcohol use as a "wholly innocent and harmless pleasure" for millions of people who "drink moderately to promote pleasant relaxation in company or to cope with stress, and do not thereby make themselves the slightest bit dangerous to others."[22] Feinberg exaggerates. Moderate drinkers can harm others to some slight degree, partly by setting a drug using example whereby chemical coping becomes widely accepted: "moderate" alcohol use is a relative standard established by social practice. Also important here is the untested premise that alcohol-induced satisfactions are a bonus, an extra filip of joy, a "genuine" and lasting contribution to happiness. The capacity of drugs to trigger short-term satisfaction gains is undeniable and important. But if drug effects are reversed, so that drug users achieve no permanent net satisfaction gain, drugged satisfactions are irrelevant to cost-benefit accounting.

As with symptomatic relief, the social and hedonistic benefits of psychoactives appear to be miscalculated because of our short-sighted tendency to measure only initial effects. Alcohol, diazepam, cannabis, cocaine and hundreds of other drugs can foster social intercourse and amplify conviviality, but they do so, some theorists argue, at the cost of longer-term irritability, lethargy or anxiety. Drugs allow us to fly now and pay later. Like deficit financing, this opportunity can be useful but it should probably be regarded as response management, not as a free ride. Similarly, psychoactives can trigger feelings of harmony, purposefulness, creativity and insight. These "religious" experiences are genuine and educative, and they may assist artistic production, but drug insight also seems to be reversed by opposite feelings of stupidity and dullness.

When drug benefits are closely scrutinized, the superficial first impression of extensive gains turns out to be misleading. Drug benefits are modest, and as drug use increases in frequency, duration and dosage, benefits generally decline. The strong case for psychoactive drug use is limited to emergency, short-term or constrained periodic employment.

b. Net Social Costs of Drug Use

On the debit side, drug users inflict costs on other people through litter, smoke damage, fires, productivity losses, higher taxes and insurance rates, and a general escalation of accidents, errors and social risk. The bulk of drug-related costs are borne by users themselves in the form of ill health, incapacity, economic loss and shorter life. One third of all premature fatalities in the U.S. flow from the use of tobacco and alcohol, and the eight-year life expectancy advantage enjoyed by women is due almost entirely to the higher rate of drug consumption by men.[23] The longevity of Seventh Day Adventists cited in Chapter One supports this claim. While lung cancer death rates for men are falling in the U.S., lung cancer death rates for women are rising at 5% a year. From 1900 to 1970, women's longevity gained about 7 years on men. That trend has ended. Biostatisticians report that as women start to behave like men, their death rates begin to match those of men.[24] This self-harm element of drug costs is not a direct component of harm to others: suicide is not comparable to murder. Nonetheless, self-harm is rarely pure or totally isolated. Self-harm does hurt others. The degree of harm inflicted depends on cost-spreading techniques (taxes, insurance) and social interdependence. Knowles, who has explored this point at length, concludes that the "idea of a right to health should be replaced by the idea of an individual moral obligation to preserve one's health."[25] Since use of drugs like tobacco leads to what the Canadian Medical Association calls an "unrivalled tale of illness, disability and death," limiting one's drug use is the type of obligation Knowles has in mind.[26]

Estimates have been made of drug-related costs, with the focus usually on tobacco and alcohol. In current dollars, Bonnie pegged annual costs in the U.S. for alcohol at $86 billion and tobacco $45 billion.[27] U.S. Surgeon General C.E. Koop divides tobacco-related costs into two parts — $20 billion in health care and $30 billion in lost production. The U.S. Office of Technology Assessment estimated that tobacco-related wage losses and government-borne health costs for 1985 were $65 billion or $2.17 per pack.[28] Tobacco costs in Canada for 1982 totalled about $7.1 billion, made up of $1.5 billion in health costs, $4.6 billion in productivity loss, $850 million in disability payments and $12 million in fire damage.[29] On the narrower issue of drug costs borne by American businesses, industries and their customers, Scanlon cites estimates of $20 billion annually from alcohol and another $26 billion from other "drug abuse."[30] These alcohol and tobacco cost estimates should be taken as guides, not firm measures. Problems of causal attribution plague drug cost calculations. For almost every harm associated with drug use, drug use is normally one of many causal factors. Typical of this imprecision are estimates that alcohol use is related to 41-95% of all deaths from cirrhosis of the liver. Some cirrhosis occurs without alcohol use and users may or may not aggravate the condition by developing nutritional deficiencies and other health problems. The causal links between alcohol and crime, traffic damage, ill-health or lower productivity are still very uncertain. McDonnell and Maynard warn readers that:

> Definitional problems in the alcohol field are enormous...The nature of causal links is complex and thus estimates given below relate to alcohol associated consequences. The exact contribution of alcohol has not been identified...The figures below do not purport to be accurate statistical estimates.[31]

Some overestimation of drug costs takes place. For example, drug use may increase health costs, but premature death may also reduce pension and life insurance payouts. These effects will cancel one another to some extent. Estimates of U.S. medical care costs caused by smoking range up to $8 billion (1978); Luce and Schweitzer produced a total social cost estimate for tobacco use of 2.5% of GNP in 1975, but Leu and Schaub cast considerable doubt on the methods employed to produce such figures.[32] Indeed, they argue that health expenditures are higher for *non-smokers* because smokers' higher annual health expenditure rate is more than counterbalanced by lower life expectancy. In other words, non-smokers cost less per year but live longer and thus generate more health costs overall. This effect is due primarily to the fact that health care expenditures increase dramatically with age and non-smokers spend more of their life past 65 than smokers.

Leu and Schaub also criticize current cost estimates on two other important grounds. Existing studies fail to distinguish satisfactorily between correlation and causality. As a result, costs attributed to alcohol use may be actually caused by lack of exercise, poor nutrition or other drugs, particularly tobacco. In researching peptic ulcer and drug use, for example, it was found that with the effects of cigaret smoking removed, heavier drinkers were no more likely to develop peptic ulcer than non-drinkers. Since almost all heavy drinkers are also smokers, alcohol and tobacco cost estimators may count the same damage twice. Studies may also fail to hold other causal factors constant. British smokers are absent from work more than non-smokers, but high absenteeism is characteristic of the hourly wage earners who smoke the most. When occupation is factored in, Leu and Schaub report that no connection between tobacco and absenteeism remains.[33] Researchers must also account for the "smoker type" who causes self-harm and social damage with or without smoking. The increased death rate from accidents, suicide and violence among smokers is not likely caused by tobacco. Similarly, U.S. smokers are 46% more likely to get traffic tickets for speeding, running red lights and other moving violations, not because they smoke but because smoking is a frequent part of a higher-risk age group, gender and lifestyle.

Oster, Colditz and Kelly's economic analysis of health-related costs associated with tobacco smoking took a different approach by estimating costs borne by smokers.[34] The merit of this approach is that most expenses are borne by tobacco users themselves, not society. Furthermore, publicity about such expenses is needed to fill the educational gap left by the almost total emphasis on health consequences. Cigaret packages warn that smoking is unhealthy but there is doubt that such warnings are effective. Perhaps a warning to the effect that smoking, aside from the purchase price of tobacco, will cost the average 30 year old pack-a-day smoker about $61,000 over their lifetime will be more discouraging.

Having briefly described some of the ways in which certain drug-related costs are exaggerated, it is necessary to note the opposite problem of underestimation which occurs because many drug costs are too subtle or private to readily calculate. What is the total cost of air fouled by tobacco smoke? What is the social cost of the bad example heavy drug users set for their children? How can all drug-related birth defects be monitored or quantified? Is premature, drug-related death at 65 years of age a benefit (lower pension burden) or a cost (the loss of an elder's experience and influence)?

Experts may exaggerate or ignore drug-related costs for partisan reasons. During the late 1800s when temperance forces were gathering momentum, many American experts declared alcohol to be a primary cause of labor agitation, crime, poverty and premature death. Conversely, respected authorities in the 1940s denied that alcohol use played a major role in liver disease or highway accidents.[35] Similar exaggerations and oversights are currently made in estimating the cost of illicit drugs such as cannabis. Marijuana is neither the grave menace to health and public safety claimed by supporters of severe anti-cannabis laws, nor the benign stepping stone to an enlightened culture portrayed by others.[36] Research indicates cannabis smoking mirrors the damaging effects of tobacco smoking. But, unlike alcohol, cannabis poses no danger of accidental overdose fatalities. Legal, good quality, marijuana in equivalent doses may result in lower costs than those generated by alcohol or tobacco. The same analysis and conclusions can be drawn about other psychoactives, whether medical or illicit.

In 1977, Ralph Berry and others measured total societal costs associated with American alcohol use and produced a figure of $72 billion, in 1979 funds. Charging Berry with being too conservative, the Institute of Medicine of the National Academy of Sciences revised the estimate to more than $90 billion. Most recently, Leonard Schrifrin reviewed the same data and produced a new estimate for 1979 costs of $113 billion, or about 3.2% of GNP. In comparison, the most detailed study of the Nordic countries, by Veikko Kasurinen in Finland, estimated total alcohol costs at 1.5% of the Finnish GNP.[37] Variations and revisions of this magnitude do not inspire confidence. Perhaps a brief look at the reasoning behind the estimates would be helpful.

Berry's team calculated that $15.5 billion or 36% of total alcohol costs to others flowed from diminished productivity. No direct productivity measures were available, so Berry's figure was produced by measuring income differentials between households with and without male alcohol "abusers" aged 21 to 59 and by attributing 76% of the difference to alcohol abuse. The $15.5 billion estimate arrived at is far too low. Berry's odd definition of alcohol "abuser" omitted some male "abusers" and all female "abusers." Berry also ignored all non-market production losses. When these factors are counted in by Schrifrin, total civilian productivity loss climbs from $15.5 billion to $45 billion. On the other hand, both estimates may be wild exaggerations if the income difference related to alcohol use is mostly a correlation rather than a causal result. According to many researchers, alcohol abuse is consistent with a personality type that is risk-prone, sensation-seeking, and unduly self-indulgent in hundreds of ways.

Using the relevant cluster of behaviours and attributes, psychologists can identify "drinker-types" or "smoker-types," some of whom do not drink or smoke tobacco. To isolate alcohol's contribution, it is necessary to control for the "alcohol-type" by comparing drinkers with non-drinkers in the same group. Cost estimators do adjust for certain variables, mostly age, occupation and gender, but these adjustments are insufficient.

Other problems can be noted. The line between self-harm and societal harm is not clearly drawn. An alcohol abuser's income loss or higher unemployment rate is largely a matter of self-harm. Similarly, the $3.7 billion in income loss from premature death is borne mostly by the deceased alcohol user's estate, not by strangers. Dynamics are also overlooked. Alcohol users may in fact demand an extra 12% of all health costs, but health savings from alcohol users whose premature deaths remove them from public pension rolls must be counted in as well. There is also the issue of arbitrary assumptions and definitions. McDonnell and Maynard purport to measure the costs of "alcohol misuse" but they define "misuse" to include only 750,000 "problem" drinkers out of an English drinking population of 35 million, whereas other surveys characterize at least 10% of all alcohol users as "problem drinkers" with another 26% in the "potential" problem class. To estimate the costs of alcohol-related absenteeism, McDonnell and Maynard guess that between 40% to 100% of excess sick days taken by heavy drinkers are alcohol related. No direct evidence supports this assumption. Though the call for more research is a cliché, the drug cost estimation field certainly needs additional work.

A final problem concerns the nature of causation in social behaviour. Of the $28.7 billion in total motor vehicle crash costs, Berry attributes 18% to alcohol use. But alcohol's well-publicized correlation with bad driving should not tempt us into simple-minded causal analyses. Alcohol use causes unconscious self-injury such as cirrhosis, but the logic of physiological causation does not apply very well to conscious behaviour. Alcohol use *causes* motor vehicle damage only if we assume that drunk drivers are compelled to drive. In the strictest causal sense, driver error is the chief cause of motor vehicle damage; car use, not alcohol use, is the key factor. Alcohol use can amplify error only for people who choose to drive after drinking. Since alcohol use does not compel car use, it is the driver's choice that matters. Moreover, that choice occurs in a technological setting that did not happen by accident. Automobile producers, road builders, suburban developers and their political supporters struggled vigorously and sometimes illegally to create a car-dependent, low-density land-use system that would replace bicycles, pedestrians and public transit with personal automobiles.[38] Whenever city officials decide to build another expressway instead of public transit, their engineers can calculate the additional driving and the extra deaths that will result. The same concerns and complex causal chains apply as well to alcohol-related crimes, a point I will return to.

Keeping in mind the caveats about cost/benefit estimations, I believe it is reasonable to conclude that both licit and illicit drugs deliver modest benefits, and that considerable drug-related costs are passed on to others. There appears to exist, therefore, a genuine need for defense against drug users.

2. Private Intervention

Defensive measures against drug-related damage need not entail state initiatives; fashion, religious injunctions and commercial disincentives already limit drug use as much or more than legal orders. Since these methods are the least expensive and least coercive, they should be considered first.

Fashion is a ubiquitous and powerful influence on human behaviour. The scope for truly independent decisions about clothing, food or drugs is always culturally limited. An entire volume could be dedicated to tobacco fashions alone. English society after Charles II carefully divided tobacco use by class: aristocrats took snuff, commoners smoked pipes. Tobacco fashions still divide the sexes. One cultural survey found that women do not smoke tobacco at all in 55 of 183 societies.[39] Latin American women smoke cigars but almost no North American women do. In Wald et al, *United Kingdom Smoking Statistics* (1988), the survey questionnaire did not even bother asking women: "Do you smoke a pipe?" Very few British men under 25 smoke pipes either.[40] There are also important ethnic differences in American smoking styles. Perhaps the latest trend in smoking is the simple separation of "smokers" and "nonsmokers." Smoking cigarets came in and is now going out of style.[41] U.S. adult per-capita consumption fell from a high of 217 packs in 1963 to 187 packs a year in 1983. When a cigaret smoker strode onto the pages of a turn-of-the-century novel, readers immediately recognized the villain, but by the 1930s cigarets were accepted, even glamorous. Films of that period were shot through gauze filters and a tobacco-smoke haze. Now fashion judges that smoking is no longer smart, attractive or intelligent. If the trend continues, in twenty years smoking in public may be regarded with horror.[42] Fighting back, a Smokers Freedom Society has recently been formed (under the sponsorship of certain tobacco firms) to re-establish the social respectability of smoking. So far, the group appears outclassed and outgunned by non-smoker's rights associations.

Drug fashions, however, are not reliable or comprehensive as the following examples demonstrate. While cigarets fall out of fashion, alcohol continues to gain back some of its pre-1900 popularity. Per capita consumption of alcohol between 1790 and 1830 was at least twice present-day levels. Whiskey was taken at work break rather than coffee and both "eye-openers" and "nightcaps" were common.[43] Meanwhile, coffee drinkers in the U.S. are an aging and perhaps endangered species. The number of adult coffee drinkers dropped 18% from 1963 to 1980; among young adults only one in four is a regular coffee drinker. Youth still take caffeine, but in cola drinks rather than tea or coffee.

Amphetamine consumption declined sharply in the 1970s partly because "speed" lost favour among trend setters. Cocaine's resurgence, however, may have resulted in total stimulant consumption increasing. Fashion change may simply mean people using one stimulant or depressant instead of another, or different forms of ingestion may catch on. Tobacco smoking could disappear without causing a decline in nicotine consumption if spittoons, now relegated to popular duty as plant holders, staged a comeback along with tobacco chewing.

Fashions may lack sufficient adaptability to handle new drugs. Alcohol's introduction devastated many societies unprepared for the drug and the Western culture that came with it. Similarly, Western culture lacks customs, attitudes and traditions for dealing with the hundreds of new psychoactives discovered this past century. Fashions in alcohol and coffee were not extended rapidly enough to enfold the new substances: our fashions were too drug specific. Possibly, a comprehensive anti-drug fashion may arise. But for drugs in general to become unfashionable, people must first recognize drugs as a unified class.

Volunteer organizations also limit drug use. Foremost are churches which ask members, as a condition of membership, to forgo certain drugs. All the successful prohibitions of alcohol appear to be based on religious injunction rather than secular law. Examples include abstaining Buddhists, Hindu Brahmins, Muslims and some fundamental Protestants.[44] History may repeat itself if Peter Berger is correct that the anti-tobacco smoking movement is part of a neo-Protestant health-cult where "any threat to health must take on a devilish quality."[45] Berger also reports that anti-smoking may become an important cause among the Muslim masses.

Some religious organizations ask members to refrain from the use of coffee, tobacco and alcohol. Such churches are necessarily marginal in North America because most adults are regular users of at least one of these three drugs. But churches do not just prohibit, they also regulate drugs. Collective drug use, and even intoxication, is demanded on some occasions and frowned upon at others.

Drug use can also stand as a badge of group membership. In such cases members refrain from using a certain drug not because of health concerns but because that drug is used by an opposing group of heathens, infidels, heretics or dissidents. Many food taboos evolved in this manner and became fixed into a rigid formula. To flaunt group customs about food or drug use is to attack the essential integrity of the group and the authority of the elders. Naturally, such transgressions are not taken lightly. Szasz explains that by "glorifying what one may or may not eat as a matter of the gravest concern to an all-caring deity, true believers elevate ordinary events... say, eating a shrimp cocktail... to acts that are, spiritually speaking, matters of life and death."[46]

Food or drug taboos are of no legal interest when imposed by volunteer organizations. If your club, gang or church only permits coffee on Fridays, tobacco as snuff and alcohol with at least a dozen other members present, that is your affair. But should your group use state power to impose these arbitrary limits on everyone, a very different situation arises. Present drug laws cross that line. Dominant groups have used the state to establish their tastes, preferences and opinions about drugs as mandatory laws. Drugs used predominantly by Mexicans, urban blacks, radical academics, aborigines, Colombians and anti-government protestors have all been subject to legal sanction.[47] Each group lives by historically-rooted patterns of drug use. New drugs or practices falling outside those patterns can threaten group solidarity. But exploiting government to pursue internecine warfare is undemocratic. It is also unjustified since the protection sought is limited, not collective. Sectarian attacks on specific drugs do not necessarily diminish total drug use or rationally deal with real dangers.

A third source of private drug control is the self-interest of employers. Employers are discovering that drug users are costly employees. Tobacco and alcohol users spend more time on sick leave, are less productive when on the job, have lower morale, and have higher disability costs. According to the Industrial Alcoholism Institute, each heavy drinking employee (15% of the total) costs employers about $2,500 annually.[48] William Weis, director of Seattle University's Smoking Policy Institute, advises businesses that banning tobacco can save more that $5,000 per smoker over a five year period. Smokers increase cleaning costs, damage sensitive electronics, and disturb customers. As a result, smokers now have some difficulty finding employment. A survey of personnel managers (some of them smokers) found that 15 out of 16 would hire a non-smoker over a smoker, other things being equal. Northern Life Insurance in Seattle and Turner Broadcasting in Atlanta refuse to hire smokers. Oklahoma fire fighters must not smoke on or off the job.

Flexibility and variety are possible advantages of business-led drug restrictions. If employers want non-smoking employees or if some of their employees complain about smokers, employers can buy off either side, install ventilation, segregate smokers, ban smoking, or hire only smokers or non-smokers. In the absence of legal limits, business will adopt smoking and drug use policies that suit their circumstances.[49] A disadvantage of business initiatives against drug use is that drug users may be unfairly discriminated against.

Many U.S. employers have launched massive urine-testing programs designed to detect employee use of illicit drugs. Among the Fortune 500 corporations, about 29% currently take urine samples from job applicants and 26% sample existing employees. Under the prodding of groups like Partnership for a Drug-Free America, employers arrange for almost 5 million American employees or applicants to submit to tests every year.[50] Some evidence suggests that sampling programs lower accident rates, but serious cause for concern exists. To begin with, some employees learn how to cheat the tests, so that only honest or unprepared users are unmasked. The tests are also not very accurate, especially when conducted incompetently. The Center for Disease Control in Atlanta found some labs had error rates as high as 65%.[51] Immunoassay is the cheapest method, costing as little as $5 per sample, but it is the least accurate. Tests for cocaine may respond to OTC diet "aids," decongestants or asthma drugs. Ibuprofen drugs like Advil and Motrin cross-react for cannabis. Gas chromatography combined with mass spectrometry is very accurate but costs $50-150 per sample.

Despite the frequency of false positives, employers take punitive action on the basis of dubious test results. In the Pettigrew case, an office manager tested positive for cocaine in the first test but not in a second, yet Southern Pacific Transportation Company insisted that Pettigrew submit to four weeks of hospital treatment, abstain from alcohol, attend AA sessions twice weekly and produce more urine samples upon request.[52] Even if the tests are perfectly reliable they do not establish that the employee was drug-impaired on the job, nor do they measure the rate or duration of use. Just as Henry Ford once threatened to fire employees on the Model T assembly line for drinking alcohol at home, some employers today feel it their duty to help enforce narcotics laws. Labour unions have been ambivalent about drug testing, apparently because some members applaud management's campaign against deviant "drug abusers."[53] American labour arbitrators have determined that employers have no general right to control an employee's private behaviour. Rules must directly and demonstrably relate to job-related responsibilities, which holds for the rule limiting pre-flight alcohol use by airline pilots. But most testing programs designed to detect illicit drug use are based on the premise that any use equals "abuse." This assumption is obviously false for people who use illicit drugs sporadically and in moderate amounts and it may be false even for regular users. A recent experiment compared the performance of marijuana-using volunteers with an abstaining control group and found no difference between them in terms of hours worked or total output.[54]

Drug-testing programs, however, are motivated by more than concerns for job-related safety or performance. Mandatory drug testing asserts an employer's authority by threatening employees' jobs and dignity. Positive results can be kept on hand until the employee causes trouble, blows the whistle or becomes redundant. There is also a political angle. President Reagan in 1987 ordered federal agencies to test employees in sensitive positions, and the President's Commission on Organized Crime recommended that every company contracting with the federal government test its employees for illicit drugs.[55] The U.S. military is already conducting millions of immunoassay tests each year, following Defense Department surveys in 1980 that found 36% of 15,000 randomly selected military personnel admitted using illegal drugs.[56] Companies that want to curry favour in Washington would be wise to emulate the Marine Corps. Reportedly, even high-level Justice Department officials opposed to the tests as unconstitutional, expensive and inaccurate refuse to object for fear of being labelled "soft on drugs." As carried out now, drug testing is distinctly unfair because nicotine, alcohol and caffeine are excluded.[57] A fair program would test every member of the organization including top management and board members; it would test for every psychoactive drug; it would carefully set out beforehand the consequences of testing positive, and these consequences would relate only to work-related effects. Given the force of law, these fairness requirements would deter tobacco-, caffeine-, alcohol- and tranquillizer-using managers and owners from penalizing cocaine-or marijuana-using employees. Civil liberties lawyers argue that supervised, compulsory urine tests violate constitutional rights to privacy, to the presumption of innocence, and to protection against self-incrimination and unreasonable searches, but these issues are all secondary to the fundamental unfairness of testing only certain employees for certain drugs and not restricting repercussions to cases where drug use is proven to affect employment duties.[58]

Business will restrict drug use in customer service areas if that policy garners competitive advantage. Airlines, bars, hotels, restaurants and shops are under client pressure to control or eliminate smoking. Drug smoking, however, is a special and limited issue not tied to drug use per se. Objections to public tobacco use would cease if users quietly chewed gum or swallowed nicotine pills. Businesses will also promote drug use if that policy is profitable.

Thus business, fashion, and volunteer organizations are alike in being unreliable. Furthermore, issues of drug safety, product testing, advertising, marketing and liability are mostly untouched by these private control methods. Another drawback is that those forced to bear drug-related costs cannot easily seek compensation through non-legal control systems. For these reasons, purely private disincentives do not provide adequate protection against drug damage.

3. Limits to State Intervention

a. Retribution and Proportionality

State intervention is justified for collective defense, but the degree of intervention called for must fit the harm defended against. This proposition is easily demonstrated. With food distribution, the harms defended against include adulterated products, harmful additives, mislabelling and fraud. These dangers justify consumer protection laws to supervise and regulate the food industry. With murder, extreme harm calls for severe responses.

The demand that government intervene only to the extent necessary is familiar. Current drug laws ignore this demand because they exist not to provide collective defense but to allow certain groups to eliminate their competitors and exploit their customers. Once the state intervenes to benefit special interest groups, no ethical limits restrict the scale or severity of the intervention.

Three methods exist for measuring the degree of coercive state action a given harm deserves. Two of these methods achieve acceptable results; one does not. The first and standard method is to directly measure the wrongfulness of the behaviour in question. An act's wrongfulness consists of the damage caused (or attempted) and the actor's abdication from norms of self-restraint. This second component needs some explaining. Implicitly, we all promise to abide by the terms of a social contract, which may or may not correspond exactly with official law. In breaking this social contract, thieves not only cause economic loss, they also breach the contract others have kept. This breach takes unfair advantage of everyone else's self-restraint. Thus the law draws a major distinction between intentional theft of an automobile and accidental or negligent property damage. The property loss may be identical in both cases,

but the person who accidentally causes a car accident is not punished or viewed with alarm and is only required to compensate the
injured party. Thieves are punished, on the other hand, because
theft breaches a central tenet of the social contract. For the same
reason, murder is much more wrongful than a negligent or accidental homicide.

This second component of wrongfulness should be judged according to actual social practice. Where petty thievery is quite common, a petty thief does not take that much advantage of others. If
everyone stole, theft would be closer to negligence than crime. Tax
evasion exemplifies this relative standard. In some countries tax
evasion is popularly viewed as legitimate sport. Laws may threaten
harsh penalties, but in practice tax evaders expect chronic under-
enforcement and lenient penalties. It then follows that the criminal
law should not prohibit activities, like premarital sex, that many
people engage in. Crimes cannot be serious breaches of the social
contract if most people do not uphold the given standard of restraint.

On both counts of wrongfulness, the harm caused by drug use
is minor. Since most everyone uses drugs, drug use cannot breach
any social agreement. This contrasts markedly with traditional
crimes: almost all citizens do refrain from murder and robbery. As
for direct damages, an individual act of drug taking normally causes
only minuscule harm to others. Based on the estimates of alcohol-
and tobacco-related social costs cited above, one can calculate that
on the average taking one drink causes up to 50 cents in damages
while one cigaret causes about 5 cents in damages. That level of
harm is hardly a major blow against the social order. Of course,
billions of small wrongful acts, like drinking or polluting, when
added up can exceed the total damage caused by murderers. Measuring aggregate damage is vital for an intelligent allocation of legal
resources, but aggregates should not be confused with individual
liability. Collectively, alcohol users and tobacco smokers probably
inflict major damage. Individually, like one locust or one termite,
the harm they cause on any given occasion is small. More on this in
Chapter Six.

Many commentators unfortunately miscalculate drug damages
by attributing harm caused by drug users to the drug use itself.
Alcohol use, for example, is frequently cited as a cause of violent

crime.[59] Obviously alcohol does not cause crime in any absolute sense, since drinking and intoxication are very common whereas murder and robbery are rare. Instead, alcohol use may increase by a small amount the likelihood of violence. On an aggregate basis across the U.S., alcohol use may "cause" 100 murders a year, but this does not mean that alcohol compelled these offenders to kill. It is more likely that alcohol merely influenced people already disposed to murder who, if sober, would have committed only an aggravated assault. Alcohol use also correlates with violence because of the places and social circumstances in which people drink. According to the professional literature, the relationship between alcohol and aggression is subtle, complex and not yet fully understood.[60] If alcohol induces recklessness — and the evidence is mixed — then it does so to a minor degree. Alcohol use does not transform otherwise peaceful people into murderous menaces or cause uncontrolled rampages. Medical testimony at criminal trials to the effect that very intoxicated defendants did not know what they were doing or did not intend their actions cannot withstand close inspection.[61] What alcoholic excess *can* do is impair short-term memory storage so that inebriated offenders may genuinely not remember what transpired the night before.[62] Alcoholic amnesia, however, has no bearing on behavioral control.

Drug-related damage estimates are also inflated by attributing acquisitive crimes to the financial needs of illicit drug users. Inordinate estimates of such crimes are then tallied up by the police in the drug-costs column. This reasoning is biased and inaccurate. Illicit drug users, even of the opiates, are not uniformly compelled to steal by irresistible drug cravings. Most users display considerable flexibility in varying their drug intake.[63] Furthermore, drug-related theft by heroin users (excluding direct theft of specific drugs) is more likely to be committed after alcohol use to earn money to purchase alcohol.[64]

Finally, it is a grave ethical error to solely blame the temptation for the acts of the tempted. Blaming theft on money, rape on women's attractiveness, or murder on jealousy misrepresents humans as irresponsible automatons condemned to act on every whim, impulse or desire. Worse, those who blame only the temptation naturally embark on increasingly brutal attempts to banish all sources of temptation — women are hidden from men's sight and social intercourse is suspended; drugs, music cosmetics and erotica are prohibited; and personal autonomy is ceded to theocratic, therapeutic or militaristic authorities.

A direct measure of the damages necessarily flowing from drug use indicates that drug taking constitutes a level of wrongfulness far below the level justifying criminal law penalties. Different conclusions follow from the second method of assessment, which measures apprehended fears rather than actual damage. This can produce invalid results because fears about drugs, spiders, snakes or Soviets are not always fair or even remotely realistic. The successful maligning of heroin as a "devil drug" illustrates this problem.[65] Without hearing or reading a shred of scientific evidence, and usually without any personal experience with the drug, most people are convinced that heroin causes social damage comparable to plague or war. Misconceptions, propaganda and ignorance are hardly reliable foundations on which to build effective laws.

Exaggerated fears are often sustained because self-esteem is heightened by the presence of hated scapegoats. The more wicked, nasty and degenerate the scapegoat, the kinder, more benevolent and upstanding the persecutors feel. Politicians compete in outslandering heroin users because they know it makes most voters feel good about themselves. The role of heroin or cocaine in this process is historically accidental. Any minority-use psychoactive could be similarly framed and its users/sellers subjected to *any* level of state intervention.

Basing state intervention on subjective attitudes is unfair because dominant groups exempt their behaviour from legal restrictions. Examples abound of legal burdens imposed by male, white, Christian voters on female, black and Jewish citizens. And the reverse occurs when and where the power relations are turned about as in Israel and black African nations.[66] Marijuana was not prohibited by poor Mexican immigrants who found the drug a cheap substitute for the tobacco and alcohol they could not afford. Labor leaders who supported a ban on opium smoking did not represent Chinese workers who could be extradited under the new law.[67] Federal regulations stopping heroin distribution were not introduced by women patent medicine users denied access to alcohol, tobacco and public taverns. The Prohibition movement against alcohol and tobacco was not led by men addicted to those drugs and to men-only clubs and bars.[68]

The democratic challenge is to measure public opinion in a way that is both accurate and fair. Forced-choice analysis, the third method of measuring wrongfulness, is a potentially useful tool in meeting that challenge. A forced-choice survey establishes a relative scale of wrongfulness by having respondents choose the least obnoxious of two harms. Would you, for example, prefer being offered heroin or being compelled at gunpoint to have your leg crushed?[69]

If you and almost everyone else prefer the first crime we can safely conclude that it should be punished less severely than the second crime. By running through a number of such choices, an entire hierarchy of wrongs can be constructed ranging from littering to murder. The superiority of this method lies in importing a market-like costing mechanism into ethical choices. People's spending choices reflect their real scale of values because everyone has limited resources. What is spent on X cannot also be spent on Y. A market-like forced choice departs from the usual survey of public attitudes about drug control. These surveys employ a costless, non-comparative approach and thus elicit superficial, unrealistic and biased responses. People might be asked: "Do you favour longer prison terms for heroin traffickers?" The question provides no incentives for the respondents to acquaint themselves with the facts. Worse, a "yes" answer costs respondents nothing. It may even spark a warm glow of civic pride as they strike a small blow against a group identified by government as terrible enemies of society. Since little personal is at stake in answering the question, respondents can indulge their fantasies. In contrast, a forced-choice survey puts a great deal at stake. A vote for severe penalties against heroin sales, in the example above, would hypothetically cost a crushed leg.

Informal tests of the above choice found that no one preferred violent assault to being offered heroin. Indeed, heroin touting was preferred to every victimizing crime mentioned. Nonetheless, some politicians and commentators call for the death penalty against heroin retailers and wholesalers. One quickly learns, however, that they make this demand not for their own sake but for the sake of others. One recent editorial page letter writer suggested that heroin marketers should be executed because "they are condemning thousands to death by the very nature of their trade." I confidently predict that this man would, himself, much prefer an offer to purchase heroin over a crushed leg because he would reject the offer of heroin and no harm would be done. But many unfortunate sods, he would argue, cannot resist the temptation to use heroin, and once fallen they are quickly launched into the short, nasty, brutish life of a degraded, enslaved addict.

Apart from its empirical inaccuracy, this argument is noteworthy for its anti-democratic stance: other, weaker adults are not fit to make a choice about drugs, so their votes and preferences are to be discounted or prohibited. To sweeten this unpalatable fascism, reflexive mention is made of children. Children must be saved from dangerous temptations, so we must execute the tempters. But state intervention is actually not very important in most children's lives as they already toil under the close protection and dictatorial control of their parents. Since children are so closely regulated by these extra-legal forces, the case for state intervention is weakest for children and strongest for adults. (I will return to child protection in Chapter Three.)

Continuing with adult preferences, I suspect that very few people would prefer any given physical harm over the opportunity to participate in any given vice offence. Even minor harms, like theft of $10, would not be chosen over being offered an illicit drug. This choice is sensible. Vice offences are usually consensual, and thus being offered the chance to indulge causes no harm since one can readily decline. But drug-related costs are, to some extent, imposed on innocent third parties who have not consented. I may decline to purchase heroin while my neighbour makes the opposite choice. Consider then a forced choice between having your neighbour take an illicit drug and having your bicycle stolen. In the case of caffeine, alcohol or tobacco most of us are indifferent to our neighbour's habits or even welcome their drug use because we enjoy our own use of these drugs more when in company. Illicit drugs are different, even if pharmacologically equivalent, because they are illicit. Users of illicit drugs (outside medical circles) now diverge from the norm by being younger, more rebellious, more often male, less often white and middle class than average. Some people will interpret the forced choice just presented as a choice between a bicycle theft and living beside the sort of person who "does heroin." But I want the

69

choice to convey a situation in which one's neighbours remain the same except for their occasional or frequent recourse to some illicit drug. If forced to actually investigate the real costs such drug use would impose (by observing the drug-using neighbour's reactions), most people would not prefer to suffer the theft of their bicycle. Indeed, there are probably many nuisances more annoying then drug-using neighbours. Consider neighbours who burn garbage outside, who let their property deteriorate, who race motorcycles on the street at night, who are aggressively rude or who keep dogs that bark constantly. The results of a carefully conducted forced-choice survey should demonstrate that our neighbours' drug use is hardly on a par with nuisances, let alone serious crimes.

b. Fairness and Universality

State intervention must be proportional to the harm defended against and it must also be fair. Take, for example, the justice of parking meters and parking violations. These state-sponsored measures are justified as necessary devices to ration scarce parking space. But it is also necessary for motor vehicle drivers to be treated alike. Exempting the sons and daughters of high state officials, as was recently the effective practice in Boston, is unfair. Choosing to punish A but not B for the same offence is unjust. Individual cases should not be isolated and rationalized on the grounds that since A committed the infraction A is fairly penalized, regardless of what is done to offenders B,C or D. Davis properly argues that if equality of treatment is one ingredient of justice then we cannot know whether punishing A is just without looking at all other cases.[70] There may be good reasons for exempting police, military and fire department vehicles in active service from parking rules, but if private individuals or groups receive special treatment through selective enforcement then all other parties should be offered legal protection. In the case above, A should be able to escape a parking violation upon proof that B was enabled to illegally avoid paying such fines. This protection would force the government to either penalize B or exempt A. Either way, both would be treated the same. Fairness requires equal treatment of like offences and offenders.

The evidence presented in Chapter One suggests that the use of any psychoactive drug is a "like offence," and therefore fairness requires that drug users face regulations formulated according to identical rules. If it is determined, for example, that a fitting and proportional response to drug-based externalities is the imposition of an excise tax, then every drug user should pay a tax whose rate is based on a uniform formulation. Under such a rule, drug smokers might pay a higher tax on their products than drug eaters if it was demonstrated that smoking was a more socially damaging mode of ingestion. What would not be fair, however, is to tax tobacco products but not caffeine if it could be shown that both drugs generate some level of social cost. Similarly, if investigation, analysis and democratic choice judged mandatory medical prescription to be the best, most fitting response to drug use, it would be unfair to put diazepam in and leave heroin and alcohol out. Rules for impaired diving, for crimes committed under the influence of drugs, for a minimum age for drug use, for advertising, and so on, must be administered according to non-biased guidelines if fairness is to be achieved. An unfair rule would prohibit the advertising of marijuana whereas a fair rule would prohibit the commercial promotion of any drug whose use creates a certain scale of social harm. Fairness means the equal opportunity of every drug user to be regulated according to non-partisan principles.

Fairness plays a central role in contract theories of justice. Experience shows that the fairest contracts are those negotiated between equally resourceful parties. The best recipe for deriving fair laws is therefore the placement of legal contractors into the same position. John Rawls achieves that equality in a hypothetical way by placing his "original contractors" behind a "veil of ignorance" where they know nothing of their own personal attributes or social status.[71] Legislators making drug laws from this position would not know if they were cocaine smugglers, tobacco addicts, brewers, college students, marijuana plantation owners, physicians, police or inner city unemployed youth. These lawmakers would be appraised of the historical and scientific information about drugs, but they would not know their own class preferences or class interests. Under such constraints, legislators would not re-invent current drug laws because those laws reflect the unjust exploitation of social power and majoritarian interests. Skolnick instructs an American legislator, as a lesson in fairness, to "ask himself how he would respond to penal sanctions forbidding the smoking of cigarets, the

71

drinking of coffee,...or any other commonly practiced activity which, if 'excessively' indulged in, might lead to social and personal harm."[72]

The essence of fairness is to balance one's rights against one's obligations. Your rights are obligations someone else owes you. Your obligations are someone else's rights. The lender's right to be repaid is the flip side of the debtor's obligation to repay. The right to hear the truth counterpoises the obligation not to lie. A citizen's right to vote is the government's obligation to permit that vote. The perpetual difficulty in effecting justice is that we naturally tend to demand excessive rights while denying our full obligations. This imbalance is painfully evident in the case of drug users. Alcohol users demand, as a right of self-defence, that potential users of cannabis, cocaine or morphine not engage in using these drugs. Yet at the same time, alcohol users ignore the reciprocal claim from marijuana users. In other words, alcohol users demand an obligation from others that they themselves refuse to honour. Fairness requires that we demand only those restraints on other's drug use that we also inflict on our own drug use. To protect ourselves from some drug use while imposing drug-related costs ourselves on other people is the rankest kind of injustice. Henry Anslinger, former head of the Narcotics Bureau, spearheaded this injustice in the U.S. and is aptly described by King as "one of the most tyrannical oppressors of his fellow citizens ever to be sustained in public office by this republic." A close parallel to J. Edgar Hoover, Anslinger was, if anything, more fanatical and anti-democratic.[73]

The inquiry into what sort of drug control systems we should adopt can be conducted in a fair way only if voters are forced to choose a system that will affect all drug use, including their own. Only this choice accords with the standards of universality espoused by Kant and modern moralists like Feinberg.[74]

What drug control system would be preferred if the same standards applied to everyone? Chapters Four through Eight consider the full range of drug control options now in place. The basic options evaluated are criminal law prohibition, medical prescription, rationing, taxation and private law. According to the criteria outlined, how do these control systems compare? From a cost-benefit perspective, prohibition and prescription tend to be high cost/low benefit systems. Indeed, it is questionable whether the general public receives any benefit from these methods. The other three options — rationing, tax and tort controls — all tend to be low cost/ high benefit systems. Analysis of which system best delivers a level of restraint proportional to common drug-related dangers leads to similar conclusions. Even at its mildest, criminal law may be too harsh an instrument for the regulation of ordinary drug use and sales.

Which system, or mix of systems, would voters choose if the choice had to affect their own drug use? Again, few would choose prohibition or prescription. This much is clear. The choice between the other three options is less certain. One form of rationing, for example, could be very popular. Tort law, on the other hand, promises numerous advantages, but because private law controls are more difficult to understand, voters may prefer a system based primarily on tax controls or rationing.

To emphasize the fairness requirement, I consider each of the five alternatives in isolation as a single, uniform control system applied to every drug user. Many drug policy analysts prefer to assign different drug users to different systems. While I oppose such discrimination as being scientifically unwarranted, readers need not accept my methodology to benefit from the following analysis. Chapter Five, for example, considers the wisdom of assigning psychoactive drugs to mandatory medical controls. Chapter Six can be read in isolation as an evaluation of how far tobacco and alcohol negligence suits against producers can and should go. Similarly, Chapter Four, on criminal law controls, illustrates that there is significant scope for changing drug laws even while retaining prohibition.

Advocating a single, universal regulatory model for all users, producers and sellers of psychoactive drugs does not mean that within any one system drugs are treated identically; that all must have the same rate of tax, for example. But is it not inconsistent to treat drugs differently within a control system, while advocating that all drugs be treated alike by being assigned to the same control system? The answer lies in the scale of variation. Putting drug users into different legal categories allows for great differences in treatment — compare the legal status of coffee and cocaine users. The most important legal decision is whether to assign a drug to tax controls, criminal prohibition, rationing, tort law or medical prescription. Differences within any one system are relatively minor.

Tax rates, for instance, can vary widely and high tax rates can duplicate some of the side-effects of criminal prohibition, but taxes at any rate have far more in common with each other than they do with criminal law controls. Ultimately, the issue is an empirical one, because it rests upon the evidence that use of different drugs creates, minor not major differences, in effect. Arguably, the scale of differences can justify minor variations, like different ration quotas, but cannot justify major discrimination, like prohibiting one drug and rationing another.

We should also consider what kind of democratic framework and constitutional structure would permit the adoption of fair drug regulation. In the Rawlsian ideal, laws reflect voluntary agreements between comparable and unbiased contractors. People, in practice, are neither equal nor unbiased, but I believe our individual differences are less of a barrier than institutional imperfections. Most democratic systems are merely "representative." In this lowest form of democracy voters have such little influence that they are "rationally ignorant" about government activities. Two solutions are possible. Either voter input must be drastically increased and/or stringent constitutional limits must be enacted to limit the laws governments can pass.

Before going on to consider the political question and to examine in detail each of the five alternate drug control models, I want first to briefly survey reform proposals and justice-based arguments of leading drug law reformers.

Notes

1   R. Nozick, *Anarchy, State and Utopia* (New York: Basic Books, 1974) 23-26.

2   See D. Maloff *et al.*, "Informal Social Controls and Their Influence on Substance Use" (1979) 9 *Journal of Drug Issues* 161.

3   E. Garfield, "Alcohol: Are the Benefits Worth the Risks?" (1981) 15 *Current Contents* 5-13.

4   J. Fort, *Alcohol: Our Biggest Drug Problem And Our Biggest Drug Industry* (New York: McGraw-Hill, 1973).

5   H. Gray & I. Walter, "The Economic Contribution of the Tobacco Industry" in R. Tollison (ed), *Smoking in Society* (Lexington Books, 1986) 25, 3-5; P. Taylor, *Smoke Ring - The Politics of Tobacco* (1985), 152.

6   T. Akiyama & R. Duncan, "Coffee and Cocoa Trends" (1983) 20 *Finance & Development* 20-33.

7   C. Huang, J. Siegfried & F. Zardoshty, "The Demand for Coffee in the United States, 1963-77" (1980) 20 *Quarterly Review of Economics and Business* 36-50.

8   A. Middleton, *Tobacco Coast* (Virginia, 1953).

9   "Profits Without Smoke" *The Economist* September 19, 1987, 37; *Globe & Mail*, May 20, 1987, B1.

10   E. Single, "The Costs and Benefits of Alcohol in Ontario: A Critical Review of the Evidence" in *Economics and Alcohol: Consumption and Controls* M. Grant, M. Plant & A. Williams (eds), (London: Croom Helm, 1983) 97-106.

11   P. Bucholz, "Legal Aspects of The Control of Tobacco" (1980) 4 *Legal Medical Quarterly* 14, 17.

12 See D.G. Garan, *The Key to the Sciences of Man* (1975) or *Relativity for Psychology* (1969) (New York: Philosophical Library).

13 B. Alexander, *Peaceful Measures: Canada's Alternatives to the War on Drugs* (Toronto: University of Toronto Press, 1990) Chapter Six.

14 See, for example, T. Duster, *The Legislation of Morality* (New York: Free Press, 1970) 237-8.

15 R. W. Johnson, *Disease and Medicine* (London: Botsford, 1967) 5, 11.

16 R. Calder, *Medicine and Man* (London: George Allen & Unwin, 1958) Part 9.

17 Philip Smith, *Arrows of Mercy* (New York, 1969) 3-10; see also Epstein, "Life Without Pain" *The Atlantic Monthly*, June, 1982, 39-58.

18 See I. Illich, *Limits to Medicine* (London: Marion Bogars, 1976).

19 See R. Mendelsohn, *Malepractice* (Chicago, 1980); G. Lorea, *The Hidden Malpractice* (New York: William & Morrow, 1977); C. Dreifas (ed.), *Seizing Our Bodies: The Politics of Women's Health* (New York: Vintage Books, 1978); D. Evenson, "Midwives: Survival of an Ancient Profession" (1982) 7 *Women's Rights Law Reporter* 313, 315; B. Levy, *et al.*, "Reducing Neonatal Morality Rate with Nurse-Midwives" (1971) 109 *American Journal of Obstetrics & Gynecology*.

20 K. Makela, *et al.*, *Alcohol, Society and the State* (Vol. 1, 1981) 110.

21 M. Kinsley, "Glass Houses and Getting Stoned" *Time* June 6, 1988, 76.

22 J. Feinberg, *The Moral Limits of the Criminal Law* (Vol. 1, 1984) 189. In contrast, see D. Beauchamp, "Exploring New Ethics for Public Health: Developing a Fair Alcohol Policy" (1976) 1 *Journal of Health, Politics, Policy and Law* 338-359, 347.

23   R. L. Dupont, Jr., *Getting Tough on Gateway Drugs: A Guide for the Family* (Washington: American Psych. Press, 1985); J. Knowles (ed.) *Doing Better and Feeling Worse* (New York: W. W. Norton, 1977); "The Growing Militancy of the Nation's Non-Smokers" *The New York Times* Jan. 15, 1984, 6E.

24   J. S. Lublin, "Cost of Equality" *The Wall Street Journal* (14 January, 1980).

25   J. H. Knowles, "The Responsibility of the Individual" in J. H. Knowles, (ed.), *Doing Better and Feeling Worse: Health in the United States* (New York: Norton, 1977) 57, 59.

26   See S. Berger and G. Wiseman, "Kick it! Report on Anti-Smoking Legislation, 1976" Non-Medical Use of Drugs Directorate.

27   R. J. Bonnie, "Discouraging Unhealthy Personal Choices: Reflections on New Directions in Substance Abuse Policy" (1978) 8 *Journal of Drug Issues*, 199, 201.

28   L. Nelkin, "No Butts About It: Smokers Must Pay for Their Pleasure" (1987) 12 *Columbia Journal of Environmental Law* 317-341.

29   B. Ward, "Non-smokers take fight for clean air to the workplace" *The Ottawa Citizen* (26 January, 1985) B1.

30   W. Scanlon, *Alcoholism and Drug Abuse in the Workplace* (New York: Praeger, 1986) 1, 2.

31   R. McDonnell & A. Maynard, "The Costs of Alcohol Misuse" (1985) 80 *British Journal of Addiction* 27.

32   R. Leu & T. Schaub, "Does Smoking Increase Medical Care Expenditure?" (1983) 17 *Soc. Sci. Med.* 1907-14.

33   For a different result see Weis, "Can You Afford to Hire Smokers? (May, 1982) *Personnel Administrators* 71; Kristein, "The Economics of Health Promotion at the Worksite" (1982) 9 *Health Education Quarterly* 27.

34   G. Oster, G. Colditz & N. Kelly, *The Economic Costs of Smok-*

ing and Benefits of Quitting (Lexington: Lexington Books, 1984).

35 Makela, *et al.*, *supra* note 20, 41.

36 See W. Thompkins & H. Anslinger, *The Policeman's View of Marijuana* (1953); J. Margolis & R. Clorfene, *A Child's Garden of Grass* (Los Angeles: Cliff House Books, 1975).

37 L. Schrifrin, "Societal Costs of Alcohol Abuse in the United States: An Updating", and E. Osterberg, "Calculating the Costs of Alcohol: The Scandinavian Experience" in *Economics and Alcohol, supra* note 6, 62, 82. For a critical appraisal of alleged drug-related employee costs, see J. Morgan, "Impaired Statistics and the Unimpaired Worker" (1989) 1(2) *The Drug Policy Letter* 4-5.

38 L. Solomon, *Energy Shock* (Toronto, Pollution Probe, 1980).

39 S. Feinhander, "The Social Role of Smoking" in R. Tollison (ed.), *Smoking and Society - Toward a More Balanced Assessment* (Lexington Books, 1986) 171-174.

40 N. Wald, S. Kiryluk, S. Darby, R. Doll, M. Pike, R. Peto, *United Kingdom Smoking Statistics* (Oxford University Press, 1988).

41 See J. Brody, "The Growing Militancy of the Nation's Nonsmokers" *The New York Times* (15 January, 1984) 6E; V. Ross, "Manners Going Up in Smoke" *Maclean's* (21 January, 1980) 40-41. On how tobacco became an integral part of 20th century culture, see *Drug Scenes: A Report on Drugs and Drug Dependence by the Royal College of Psychiatrists* (London: Gaskell, 1987) 82-88.

42 R. Lacayo, "All Fired Up Over Smoking - New Laws and Attitudes Spark a War" *Time* April 18, 1988, 42-53; "A Smoke-free Zone for Europe?" *The Economist* March 29, 1986, 40.

43 See W. J. Rorabaugh, *The Alcoholic Republic* (New York: Oxford, 1979); M. Lender & J. Martin, *Drinking in America: A History* (New York: Free Press, 1982).

[44] Royal College of Psychiatrists, *Alcohol: Our Favorite Drug* (London: Tavistock, 1986) 12.

[45] P. Berger, "A Sociological View of the Antismoking Phenomenon" in *Smoking and Society* (1986) 235.

[46] T. Szasz, "A Plea for the Cessation of the Longest War of the Twentieth Century - The War on Drugs" (1988) 16 *The Humanistic Psychologist* 314-322.

[47] See J. Cloyd, *Drugs and Information Control* (Westport: Greenwood Press, 1982) 56-57; R. J. Bonnie and C.H. Whitebread, "The Forbidden Fruit and the Tree of Knowledge: An Inquiry into the Legal History of American Marijuana Prohibition" (1970) 56 *Virginia Law Review* 971.

[48] Scanlon, *supra* note 30. See also "Battling the Enemy Within: Companies fight to drive illegal drugs out of the workplace" *Time* 17 March, 1986; "Taking Drugs on the Job" *Newsweek* 22 August, 1983, 52-59; "Mission just possible" *The Economist* 30 September, 1989, 72.

[49] W. Shugart & R. Tollison, "Smokers versus Nonsmokers" in *Smoking and Society* (1986) 220-221.

[50] The "Partnership" placed a full-page advertisement in *The New York Times*, May 7, 1988 depicting a young job applicant. The caption read "In her job interview she'll tell you all about her MBA. If you want to know about her THC, coke and crack, you'll have to dig a little deeper." Digging "deeper" means testing her blood, saliva or urine or spying.

[51] E. Imwinkelried, "False Positives" *The Sciences* September/October 1987, 22-28.

[52] A. Hoffman, *Steal This Urine Test - Fighting Drug Hysteria in America* (NY: Penguin Books, 1987).

[53] "Drugs on Wall Street" *The Economist* May 9, 1987, 76.

[54] J. Kagel, R. Battalio & C. Miles, "Marijuana and Work Performance: Results from an Experiment" (1980) 15 *Journal of Human Resources* 373.

55   "Snort and be tested" *The Economist* March 15, 1986, 20.

56   H. Abrams, "Who's Minding the Missiles? Too Often, People with Drug, Drinking, or Psychiatric Problems" (1986) *The Sciences* July/August 22-28.

57   K. Zeese, "Drug Hysteria Causing Use of Useless Urine Tests"(1987) 11 *Nova Law Journal* 815; J. Felman & C. Petrini, "Drug Testing and Public Employment: Toward a Rational Application of the Fourth Amendment" (1988) 51 *Law & Contemporary Problems* 254-296.

58   P. Bookspan, "Jar Wars: Employee Drug Testing. The Constitution and the American Drug Problem" (1988) 26 *American Criminal Law Review* 359-400.

59   See J. Marmor, "Psychosocial Roots of Violence" in R. Sadoff (ed.), *Violence and Responsibility - The Individual, the Family and Society* 11 (1978), where he writes that the "role of drugs in violence is a significant one... Alcohol is probably the most important drug in this regard, acting by depressing frontal lobe function and thus blocking out the acquired social controls that ordinarily restrain the acting out of violence."

60   See H. Silving, *Essays on Mental Incapacity and Criminal Conduct* (Chicago: C.C. Thomas, 1967) 228-34; J. Goldstein, *Aggression and Crimes of Violence* (New York: Oxford Press, 1975) 79; A. Zeichner & R. Pilhl, "Effects of Alcohol and Instigator Intent on Human Aggression" (1980) *J. Stud. Alcohol* 265.

61   See S. Morse, "Undiminished Confusion in Diminished Capacity" (1984) 75 *Journal of Criminal Law & Criminology* 29.

62   See H. Hutchison, *et al.*, "A Study of the Effects of Alcohol on Mental Functions" (1964) 9 *Canadian Psychological Association Journal* 33-42.

63   See J. Kaplan, *The Hardest Drug: Heroin and Public Policy* (Chicago: University of Chicago Press, 1983) 24 ff.

64   See D. Strug *et al.*, "The Role of Alcohol in the Crimes of Active Heroin Users" (1984) 30 *Crime and Delinquency* 551.

[65] See J. Zenter, "Heroin: Devil Drug or Useful Medicine?" (1979) 9 *Journal of Drug Issues* 333.

[66] On Israeli legal treatment of Palestinians, for example, see J. Stout, "Management Without Objectives" *Reason* October 1988, 42-45.

[67] See N. Boyd, "The Origins of Canadian Narcotics Legislation: The Process of Criminalization in Historical Context" (1984) 8 *Dalhousie Law Journal* 102.

[68] See L. Wallack, "Mass Media and Drinking, Smoking and Drug-taking" (1980) 9 *Contemporary Drug Problems* 49, 57-58.

[69] This analysis follows M. Davis, "Setting Penalties: What Does Rape Deserve?" (1984) 3 *Law & Philosophy* 61, 83.

[70] K.C. Davis, *Discretionary Justice: A Preliminary Inquiry* (Baton Rouge: Louisiana State University Press, 1969) 170.

[71] J. Rawls, *A Theory of Justice* (Cambridge: Belknap Press, 1971).

[72] J. Skolnick, "Coercion to Virtue: The Enforcement of Morals" (1968) 41 *Southern California Law Review* 588, 624.

[73] R. King, *The Drug Hang-Up: America's Fifty-Year Folly* (New York: W.W. Norton, 1972), 69.

[74] J. Feinberg, "Harmless Immoralities" in *Rights, Justice, and the Bounds of Liberty* (Princeton University Press, 1980) 88-92.

III A Comparative Survey of Drug Reform Proposals

North Americans face both a drug problem and a "drug problem" problem. Naturally, a number of analysts have responded to the drug-regulation challenge by advocating various reforms.

Some propose legalizing all psychoactive drugs. This group includes Milton Friedman, C.P.Freund, Erich Goode, Ron Paul, Marie-Andree Bertrand, and Thomas Szasz. Others would legalize all "recreational drugs": this group includes Norvil Morris, David Boaz, Neil Boyd, Ethan Nadelmann, M. Smith, E. van den Hagg and Norman Zinberg. Zinberg and Grinspoon would "phase in" legalization, starting with marijuana, rather than opting for a wholesale re-classification. Others would legalize only marijuana (David Richards, M. Rosenthal) or would legalize everything but heroin (John Kaplan, Rufus King, Frank Logan, W.F. Buckley, Jr.) or everything but cocaine (Arnold Trebach,1984). Trebach more recently favors legalizing all drugs. Mikuriya, del Gatto and others, favor converting illicit drugs, especially heroin, to prescription-only status but Smith, Szasz and van den Hagg strenuously oppose that move. Most agree that legal drug use should be denied to youngsters under a certain age, that treatment for drug abusers be expanded, and that focus should shift from police action to education. Some point out, however, that drug education as presently practiced is frequently counterproductive. A few analysts want all drug advertising prohibited. Caballero proposes drug rationing but others oppose such a scheme. A few want medical clinics to provide drugs to certified "addicts," usually of the heroin-using variety. Only Richards considers tort law for control of drug-related behaviour, but he rejects it as insufficient.[1]

Three central points emerge from a survey of drug-reform proposals. First, many of these proposals are preliminary and underdeveloped. Almost none of the advocates of age limits for legal drug use offer any discussion of the advantages and disadvantages of age limit laws, although there are serious questions as to whether such limits are enforceable, constitutional or even necessary. Second, most proposals gravitate toward an alcohol-regulation model for currently prohibited drugs. Serious consideration is not given to rationing or tort law, and only a few proposals consider extending medical controls to morphine, LSD, cocaine and the like. Finally, the disagreement evident among the various reformers cannot be resolved without a good understanding of the reasons behind their proposals. Do those favouring the legalization of only marijuana discriminate against other drug users because there are less of them, because they have less social status than marijuana users, because their drugs are more dangerous or because, at this time, marijuana reform is the most politically feasible strategy? In order to facilitate a consensus about drug-law reform, this chapter tries to sort out and assess the reasons behind the more fully-developed reform proposals now on the table.

1. Costs - Benefits and Rights

Drug law reforms are conceived within two analytical frameworks. The first is cost-benefit. Cost-benefit analysis seeks a regulatory system that will achieve maximum benefit at minimum cost. The challenge in such an analysis is to make an accurate and comprehensive assessment of all relevant costs and benefits. To date, all cost-benefit analyses of drug regulations are to some degree inaccurate or incomplete. As noted in Chapter Two, medical and recreational drug costs are repeatedly underestimated while drug benefits are exaggerated. With illicit drugs, costs tend to be overestimated while benefits are denied. Nonetheless, a rough consensus exists in the drug-law reform field that criminal control of drugs generates costs in excess of benefits.

The second reform framework is based on human rights. In its pure form, the rights-based approach does not construct an economic or social calculus. Instead, it begins by affirming the existence of certain legal rights affecting privacy, due process, democratic choice, equality, fairness and freedom from unwarranted punishment. Armed with these legal and ethical premises, analysts construct a drug control system that will not conflict with the elucidated rights. In its pure form, a rights-based analysis requires logical consistency rather than empirical accuracy. In practice, however, legal rights are not isolated, abstract entities. Guaranteeing equal protection before the law for all people will not, in itself, overcome a social context wherein certain races or genders are widely regarded as inferior.

Conceivably, cost-benefit analysis may produce reform proposals quite at odds with programs based on human rights. Publicly executing a small number of drug users would be an excessive punishment, but perhaps it would cheaply and effectively deter millions of people from taking psychoactive drugs. This pure deterrence reasoning is in fact practiced by some drug enforcement officials. Drug agents may, in moments of candour, admit that strip searches, police entrapment and other intrusive techniques compromise traditional privacy rights. Yet they justify such trampling, or at least tiptoeing, on rights as the price paid for effective drug control. Rights advocates can respond to such self-proclaimed pragmatism in two ways. The weak response is to argue that certain rights must be honored regardless of social cost. This approach appears to contrast pragmatism with civil liberty, by assuming that privacy, for example, is worth more than reduced drug consumption. Understandably, this elevation of apples over oranges is not likely to resolve disputes about drug control. However, a second and stronger argument is that abusive enforcement measures are ineffective and that ethical controls are the most effective controls. Note that government cannot even eliminate illicit drug use in prisons where civil rights are minimal. Cost-benefit and rights-based analysis are inter-related and complementary. High benefit/low cost regulations will best protect human rights. Or approached from the other side, regulations designed to respect democratic choice and ethical rights will deliver high benefits at low costs.

If my proposition is correct, if cost-benefit and rights-based analysis are mutually supportive, why do all drug reformers not rush to the same conclusions? With purely cost-benefit approaches the basic reason for divergent conclusions is factual inaccuracy. A cost-benefit analysis is only as good as its data. To some extent, empirical inaccuracy also bedevils rights-based arguments, since the logic of legal equality is frequently abandoned in the face of presumptions that women, blacks, children, communists, witches or heroin users are inferior. The other central failures in these arguments, which the following sections illustrate, are a lack of respect for fairness and an unwillingness to recognize the basic equivalency of psychoactive drug use. Some decriminalizers advocate a new legal policy for cannabis or cocaine or LSD, but are not willing to generalize their system to include all psychoactive drugs. Some offer very

85

detailed, technical reforms that tinker with the present system without dealing with issues of human rights. Representative of this group is Michael Rosenthal, a past consultant on drug reform to the U.S. federal government, who proposes a jerry-built system of "partial prohibition" for all "controlled substances" except marijuana, which he would legalize.[2]

2. Taking Human Rights Semi-Seriously

One group of reform advocates recognizes that current drug laws abuse human rights, but their own proposals fail to take rights seriously enough. The most frequent obstacle is a failure to treat all drug users equally before the law. Typical of this genre is a comment made by Mark Danner in introducing a symposium entitled "In the Age of Cocaine — What is America's Drug Problem?"[3] Danner suggested to the conference participants that "perhaps the best way to start is to divide the monolith we call the drug problem into its constituent parts. What drugs in particular are widely used today? Are some drugs becoming more popular and others less so?" These questions are not inappropriate but neither are they sufficient. Opponents of slavery in the 1800s did not merely ask: What category of blacks are most widely-used as slaves today? Is slavery becoming more popular in Alabama and less so in Virginia? Danner is closer to the central issue when he asks: "Is legalization of some or all drugs a realistic option?" But even here his emphasis is pragmatism, not democratic choice or ethics.

David Richards, in law review articles and in his book *Sex, Drugs and the Law: An Essay on Human Rights and Overcriminalization,*[4] promotes a rights-based approach to drug law reform. Richards does not reject a cost-benefit approach. He admits current drug laws are wasteful and ineffective, paying out low benefits at high cost. Yet he criticizes other reformers for relying too heavily on cost-benefit arguments. Their mistake, he claims, is a strategic one. In the reform cause, Richards considers it more important to argue that criminalizing drug use violates human rights. This makes considerable sense given that legal institutions — the courts, judges, legislators and jurors — are accustomed to thinking in terms of rights. All vice offences should be decriminalized, according to Richards, in order to reaffirm basic and traditional rights. Following Kant and Rawls, Richards contends that traditional rights centre on respect for equal personal autonomy of all persons. This means that ethical laws must reflect principles of mutual respect — treating others as one would like to be treated in comparable circumstances — and of universalization — judging the morality of principles by the results of their universal application.[5] Richards himself, however, does not adhere to the principles he espouses.

A major strength of the rights-based argument is that it casts a seemingly new and radical position in a familiar form. Decriminalizing psychoactive drugs would in many ways return us to the legal status quo of 1875, prior to the wave of alcohol and opiate prohibition that swept the U.S. and Canada. In 1900 many American courts still viewed a person's right to use and produce alcohol as self-evident. The Prohibition of alcohol was considered a drastic, unusual and highly controversial act. Canadian legislators after 1918 took the very rare step of leaving the issue to direct referenda. Americans assumed that such a novel interference with legal rights required a separate amendment to the Constitution. Now, psychoactive drugs are added to the list of prohibited or controlled substances by low-level bureaucratic decisions.

Working within a rights-based framework, Richards addresses the standard issues of proportionality, fairness and equality. On the issue of proportionality, he is correct as far as he goes. The easy task is to reject the criminal prohibition of drugs as disproportionately severe. Richards demonstrates that the reputed criminality of illicit drug users is ridiculously exaggerated, that habituation or drug dependence is miscast as enslavement, and that all illicit use is falsely portrayed as serious abuse.[6] The reason law enforcement agents engage in this deception is plain — they need to magnify the harm caused by illegal drugs to match the scale of the penalties inflicted. If legislators decree that marijuana possession deserves a maximum of seven years imprisonment, by inference, marijuana possession must be very dangerous. For Richards, the solution is obvious: lower the penalties so they match the actual scale of drug-related social harms. Unfortunately, Richards is not clear about what penalties would be appropriate. At one extreme, he judges criminal law punishments to be too severe. At the other extreme, he rejects a purely market sanction/civil law regime as too lenient. One bowl of porridge is too hot, and one is too cold: which one is just right? Rationing, taxation or medical supervision?

Some reformers propose moving marijuana from criminal controls to rationing. Richards rejects rationing on two grounds. First, rationing marijuana but not other drugs would be unfair. Richards argues that if rationing is inappropriate for alcohol and tobacco use, then "it would seem a *fortiori* that it should be rejected in the case of marijuana." Rationing marijuana but not alcohol is "hypocritical" because alcohol is the more dangerous drug. He then suggests, on broader grounds, that rationing drugs is inappropriate because it does not sufficiently respect personal choice. Thus, criminal law is too harsh, private law is too weak and rationing too inflexible. While his analysis of these regulatory methods is undeveloped, his tentative conclusion that marijuana should be treated like alcohol has merit. My problem is with Richards' proposal for heroin, mescaline, LSD and certain other drugs. Richards feels that these drugs should be made available, but only on prescription from state-authorized physicians. No evidence is cited to indicate that heroin or mescaline are more damaging than alcohol, nicotine or cannabis. Nevertheless, Richards assigns these drugs to medical control. If medical prescription of alcohol is inappropriate, what makes it appropriate for heroin? Richards does not adequately explain.

Richards realizes that all psychoactive drugs can be used for artistic, ceremonial, recreational or medical purposes. This understanding places in sharper relief his failure to explain why physicians rather than lawyers, coaches, teachers or clerics should have supervisory control over certain drug use. Prescription is described as a "kind of license" the state grants to physicians in order that they exercise "proven medical competence" to minimize drug-related damage.[7] Both of these claims are unsupported by the evidence, a point to be explored in detail in Chapter Five. Physicians' competence as drug experts is not proven. More importantly, physicians lack the enforcement resources necessary to act as drug police and their fiduciary obligations to their clients should preclude physicians serving as quasi-drug agents. Physicians are supposed to act in confidence and in their client's best interests. Only in extreme cases involving contagious diseases should public obligations force physicians to act as informers or law enforcers. Richards is also off the mark in characterizing prescription as a reasonable constraint. Under a prescription system, individuals have no right to controlled drugs. They may have a right to treatment, but this right is limited by the power of the medical profession to define treatment. Recall that many drugs now classified as illicit were once accepted as official medical treatment. Furthermore, government has established its own power to legally define "treatment." Following passage of the Harrison Act in 1914, federal agents and courts in the U.S. redefined certain prescribing practices as non-medical and thus non-authorized. The statute gave physicians the legal right to prescribe narcotics in the course of "professional practice." However, the U.S. Supreme Court interpreted the statute so as to prohibit drug prescribing "to addicts." In *Jin Fuey Moy* (1920) and *Behrman* (1920), the Supreme Court ruled that the prescribing of narcotics was an unwarranted "gratification of a diseased appetite for these pernicious drugs."[8]

Richards is not alone in proposing special medical controls for certain drugs. Mark Moore at Harvard and other supporters of selectively decriminalizing drugs point to the British system of medically supplied heroin as a viable alternative.[9] Such reform would convert illicit drugs back into semi-medical substances, transform criminal users into "patients" and replace outlaw traffickers with state-approved physicians or pharmacists. Arnold Trebach, who directs the Institute on Drugs, Crime and Justice at American University, argues in *The Heroin Solution* (1982) for special heroin controls.[10] Like Richards, Trebach is a foe of criminal controls of drug use. He condemns American legislators because they have in this century "criminalized heroin, converted addicts into criminals, and proselytized this repressive policy to the world."[11] Trebach's solution, which may be the only one that is now practical, is to replace criminal controls for heroin users with slightly less repressive medical controls.

Trebach knows that 90% of all heroin users are not addicts and that most users take the drug recreationally, not medically. He also calls for drug control programs that are "democratic" a term implying a willingness to respect individual rights and to promote equal treatment before the law. Nonetheless, he advises that each drug or group of drugs be examined separately and a fitting system be devised for each. As for heroin, Trebach judges it to be "a medical problem." He would only permit heroin to be supplied to "addicts" and only through the offices of a supervising physician. Marijuana? It should be sold in stores along with alcohol. Cocaine? He would "seriously consider decriminalizing possession," which means that selling cocaine would remain an offence.[12] While marijuana use is a bad habit, heroin use for Trebach is a "disease"; he speaks of a "global epidemic" for which there is no "complete cure." Despite the absence of a cure, Trebach urges government to "bring addicts into a varied system of medical, caring treatment," and he praises the British medical dispensing of heroin for helping "addicts" to come "in out of the criminal cold into the warmer arms of legitimate medical practice." [13] But are prescription controls "warm" only in relation to the cold Gestapo-like procedures of narcotics agents? Rufus King also compromises an otherwise excellent analysis of drug controls by advocating special "medical" supplies of drugs for "true addicts." Generally, however, King proposes a unified approach to drug regulation wherein under-regulated users of tobacco would face more restrictions and over-regulated users of cannabis would face less government intervention.[14]

Trebach does not adequately explain why heroin should be made a restricted prescription-only drug while cocaine and marijuana are to be treated more like alcohol, nor does he consider whether any drug should be subject to mandatory medical control. This is an oversight at a time when a number of thoughtful commentators have criticized the entire program of medical prescription. Trebach, instead, defers to the presumed expertise of physicians. Under his proposal, physicians could prescribe heroin but only to the "organically ill and the addicted." Since he knows almost all heroin users are not "addicts", Trebach apparently intends to prohibit their access to heroin. Meanwhile physicians are to be given wide therapeutic scope to experiment with every "rational approach" to drug user rehabilitation from methadone maintenance to Zen Buddhism. Physicians, as state agents, will be permitted in this system to operate scientifically dubious programs like methadone maintenance, or co-opt sacerdotal rituals, but priests and faith healers will not acquire the right to compete with medical practitioners. Physicians can preach but preachers cannot treat.

The scientific evidence about whether heroin is more or less dangerous than alcohol or diazepam is not a central issue for many reformers in this field. Beauchamp, as a final example, is concerned with protecting personal autonomy. He stresses the importance of Kant's principle that any moral rule should be capable of applying to everyone. He also remarks, quite properly, that whereas individuals can be restricted for the common good, no person should face a legal burden "except in expectation that everyone in similar circumstances is similarly burdened." Finally, Beauchamp judges that prohibiting alcohol defeats the goal of protecting the common good. He reasons that the results of a total ban on alcohol "simply outweigh any gains to the health and safety of the public. (This is why an individual can with consistency be for the prohibition of hand guns, and even heroin, but still oppose the prohibition of alcohol.)"[15] Beauchamp's second line is a throwaway. He cites no evidence to distinguish opiates from alcohol.

3. Foes of John Stuart Mill

John Stuart Mill, a leading utilitarian and social theorist of the 19th century, was a staunch opponent of alcohol prohibition. Mill generalized his distaste for such paternalistic legislation in an 1859 essay entitled "On Liberty."[16] Mill's familiar argument is that government is generally not justified in compelling people to act or to avoid acting merely for their own good. Putting this doctrine into practice, Mill defended the opium trade and the liberty of the opium smoker. He also attacked mandatory prescriptions for drugs. Mill even objected to punitive taxes on alcohol though he did not object to revenue-motivated alcohol taxes. In Chapter Eight, I counter Mill's view on taxing drugs and argue that punitive taxes are more ethical than pure revenue taxes. Nozick recently reiterated Mill's "harm principle" in contending that state coercion is justified only in the interest of genuine self-defence. We can arrest persons who try to assault us, but we should not have the authority to arrest persons who merely try to assault themselves, by means of tobacco chewing or opium smoking. Mill concluded that prohibiting the use of alcohol or other drugs is not warranted on self-harm grounds. State action is justified only if harm to others is involved, and then only to a degree proportionate to that harm. Smoking in public harms others, but not to a degree justifying criminal charges and imprisonment. Mill held that adults should almost always be permitted to explore "tastes and pursuits" of a private nature, including the use of drugs.

Mill's argument is well-known and well-debated. For a century it has stood as a beacon for libertarians and a target for prohibition-ists. As a target it serves present purposes well since a number of drug reformers have attempted to refute Mill's propositions. The first analyst I will consider is John Kaplan.

Kaplan pioneered in the fight to decriminalize cannabis.[17] But while an opponent of drug prohibition in the case of marijuana, Kaplan does not generalize that policy to include all drugs. It is not that he ignores the scientific evidence about drug equivalence: he admits that heroin and alcohol are more alike than most people realize. Still, he feels that "pharmacological symmetry is by no means the most important factor shaping a rational drug-control law."[18] In other words, drugs should not be treated alike simply because they are alike. And, since Kaplan believes public law restric-tions on drug use are justified not only to prevent social harm but also to mitigate self-harm, his policy deliberations necessarily con-front the spectre of J.S. Mill.

Mill's dictum against paternalism allowed for two exceptions, ei-ther of which, Kaplan claims, can be expanded to defeat any grant of a general right to use drugs. Mill's first exception concerned depen-dent youngsters. Mill accepted that young children must be pro-tected against their own actions. While this is true, both Mill and Kaplan err in thinking that the protection of children necessarily justifies state action. Mill mistakenly believed that society has "absolute power over [children] during all the early portion of their existence."[19] In fact, the state, as the social collective, in 1850 had only marginal power over children. The legal doctrine of *patria potestas*, dominant until the fourteenth century in England, did not allow for any state intervention over children. Later, the *parens patriae* doctrine allowed the state to assume the powers and obliga-tions of the natural parents in very limited circumstances. In Mill's time it was thus the *parents* who controlled children, not the state. Because real paternalism or maternalism is far more powerful and important than state controls, the state traditionally has been a minor factor in children's lives. Since 1850, state intervention concerning children has increased substantially. Statutory limits concerning child labour and compulsory schooling, social welfare agencies and child subsidy payments from government exemplify the change. Still, modern parents hold nearly absolute power to dictate their children's religious, political, ethical, cultural and dietary indoctrination. State prohibitions applying solely to youngsters tend to compete directly with parental control and are usually perceived to be in violation of parental prerogatives.

Mill's exception clearly justifies parental regulation of children. Children should be restricted by their parents in a number of ways. Parents should prohibit bad posture, outlaw rudeness, dictate study schedules and lay down the law about excessive television viewing. Similarly, parents should severely limit their children's access to drugs even before the child's birth. Drug damage appears to increase inversely with the age of the drug taker, so abstinence is especially important for children. Restricted drug use is also important from a socializing perspective. Children should not be taught that chemical solutions are easy, costless and totally acceptable. Parents should not set a drug-dependent example. But the need for restraint does not justify state prohibition. The state is not justified in enacting legal prohibitions against sibling rivalry, bad posture, sexist toys or beer consumption by ten year olds in their own homes. Where laws do prohibit "underage" drug use, they are frequently unenforced and irrelevant. At the federal level in Canada and in 47 U.S. states, tobacco use is prohibited to persons under a specified age, usually 16 years. These statutes were enacted during a period when legislators were busy prohibiting opium, cocaine and alcohol for both children and adults. Between 1870 and 1930, U.S. cigaret consumption increased one hundred fold. Regulators, determined to save young boys from tobacco, had prohibited sales to minors in 26 states by 1890. By 1909, 15 states had outlawed all cigaret sales but not sales of cigars and pipe tobacco.[20] In 1899 the Anti-Cigarette League was founded by Lucy Gaston. As usual, the drug habits of upper class men (pipes and cigars) and upper class women (abstinence) were either tolerated or regarded as ideal.

As for protecting minors, laws against underage tobacco use were rarely if ever enforced. To the contrary, Brecher suggests that these early anti-cigaret laws served to publicize smoking and to make the practice more attractive.[21] Today no detectable difference in tobacco use among adolescents exists between states with minimum age laws and those without.[22] Alcohol age limits are more energetically enforced because alcohol retailers and licensed outlets must check clients' ages to protect their liquor licences. However, outside licensed premises underage liquor offences are extremely common. Since all provinces and all states legislate alcohol age limits, no alternate system exists for comparison purposes in North America, and hence no study has measured the long run effects of imposing or of changing age limits for alcohol use and possession.[23] Alternative models do exist, though, in Britain and other European countries in which no general age limits apply to alcohol use. In addition, North Americans allow drugs like aspirin, tranquilizers and especially caffeine to be consumed by children from an early age. Parents in New York may be aghast at parents in Lisbon giving diluted wine to three-year olds, but it is not at all clear that aspirin and caffeine are significantly safer for children than small amounts of alcohol.

Mill's exception for state control of children's drug use, therefore, makes little sense. Parental control and parental example are the critical ingredients. By usurping parental responsibility for monitoring children's drug use, the state will likely worsen the situation. Parents have the means to enforce compliance with family standards of drug use, whereas the state does not. By taking on the task of banning "under age" use, the state encourages parents to leave drug control to government authorities. Competent private authority is thereby weakened in favour of incompetent public authority.

Note also the contrast with serious crimes. Murder, assault and robbery are prohibited to adults but not to children. In many states, children under a certain age (usually 12-14 years) are not liable for criminal acts. Even adolescents up to 16, 17 or 18 years of age are subject to special provisions that diminish their criminal liability. A child with an illegal weapon is treated more leniently than an adult, whereas a child with a bottle of beer is treated much more harshly. To be consistent, even if we were to prohibit drugs to adults upon pain of criminal prosecution, we should not prosecute children for the same offences. The paradox here is that while children should be, and generally are, subject to far more severe social restraints than adults, this does not mean they should be exposed to many state controls. As Donald Black observes, the amount of law varies inversely with the amount of social or non-legal restraints.[24] Since children live under severe parental restraints, special legal restraints aimed at children are mostly superfluous and often counterproductive. But the ineffectiveness of state control over children's private behaviour ironically invites an escalation of repressive measures. In this sense Kaplan is correct: Mill's exception for children can lead to the utter ruin of his general premise. Modern prohibitionists frequently justify criminal penalties against adults on the grounds of child protection. If children are to be denied any opportunity to acquire a certain drug, then it follows reasonably that adults must be denied access as well. It is widely known that adults provide "underage" users with alcohol, and the same is bound to be true for legal marijuana, heroin and cocaine. It is also known that parents lead their children by example, that users of alcohol and nicotine are more likely to raise children who take these drugs. Child-proofing society against drugs is impossible unless adults are also restricted. Mill also made an exception for people in societies he called "savage" or "barbaric." Since Mill failed to distinguish effectively between his own society and the "savage," this too opens a door through which a whole host of paternalistic laws could pass. Marxists likewise claim that all pre-communist societies are "immature," a view that naturally heralds intrusive and paternalistic governments, at least until maturity and the millennium finally arrive.

Mill's second exception allowed the state to prohibit "voluntary slavery" because Mill reasoned that it is "not freedom to be allowed to alienate [one's] freedom."[25] Kaplan accepts this argument and attempts to apply it to heroin addiction by suggesting that for some heroin users the "metaphor of slavery... is not so farfetched."[26] Actually, the metaphor is far-fetched. In addition, Mill's second exception itself is problematic. What is "voluntary slavery"? Slavery, like employment, is not a simple institution that can be defined or understood outside a cultural and legal context. Slaves in America were racially and culturally very different from slave owners. Slaves in Imperial Rome, on the other hand, were not always racially separate, nor at an educational or cultural disadvantage compared with slave owners. Roman slaves could buy their way to freeman status.

In a strict sense, voluntary slavery cannot exist in a culture that lacks slavery. To sell one's self into slavery in an archaic hunting-gathering society is a meaningless concept. How can one be a slave if there are no slave owners, no slave markets, no rules about treatment of slaves and no work designated the province of slaves? Similar barriers face a would-be slave today in a Western economy based on employment, market relations, commercial values and labour unions. Since slavery exists outside normal employment relations, the closest one can come to slavery today is in non-commercial family relations. Specifically, one thinks of the housewife and mother whose work is not commercially valued, whose daily pay is not affected by any legislation, whose ability to transfer to another housewife position is extremely limited, and whose occupational choice has been largely dictated by the accident of being born a woman.[27]   Housekeeping is still the largest single occupation in North America, and 99% of its practitioners are women. While the slavery aspect of being a housewife is quite apparent to feminists, most people do not recognize it. For them "slavery" means blacks picking cotton in Alabama under the whip of a sadistic overseer. Naturally, slavery did not bother most white southerners in 1820, nor does the inferior position of housewives bother most men today.

Outside the family, the closest thing to voluntary slavery is a pre-paid employment contract for work as a servant, gardener, athlete or chauffeur. Under certain circumstances some people might choose to be paid in advance for forty years of service. However, this would hardly be the classic case of slavery, because one could buy out of the contract at any time. Furthermore, the terms of employment would not necessarily be unpleasant or unrewarding, nor would relations between master and servant be without legal obligations and rights. Thus Mill's objections to "voluntary slavery" are much weaker than first impressions would suggest. Weaker still is Kaplan's portrayal of drug habituation as a kind of slavery.

Slavery constrains choice. In most slave cultures, slaves were closely regulated in their daily activities and could not easily change positions. They usually had no political power, could not qualify for public office and were excluded from most high status professions. In the most severe cases of slavery, as in the American south, slaves could not buy an end to slavery either for themselves or their children. To what extent does drug addiction restrict choice? This question can be answered generally or specifically. Generally, most drug addicts or drug dependents are not seriously restricted. Take for example the millions of alcohol, nicotine and caffeine addicts. Their drug habits require an expenditure of from $200 to $2000 a year per drug, and may occupy from 60 to 180 hours a year per drug. This last cost is not usually significant since people can take drugs while they do other things. Given an ample, legal and convenient supply of their drug, most drug users lead productive lives. Admittedly, they are vulnerable to trade embargoes and strikes by suppliers, but the same applies with a number of commodities on which people are dependent, especially oil, gas and electricity. The obvious solution is to stockpile such commodities.

On average, drug habits are not very constraining. In extreme cases, however, drug habits become a serious drain on money, time and human resources. For a small proportion of users, drug intake consumes most of their time and money. Skid-row alcoholics provide the best example. Yet even here the slavery metaphor is far-fetched. Slavery is always politically constraining, drug addiction need not be. Slaves are controlled by other people and by social institutions. Drug addicts are controlled by their own biochemistry, needs and passions. Slavery of the American sort was almost totally inescapable. Drug addiction, even amongst heavy heroin users and alcoholics, is not permanent. To compare the minor, flu-like pain of heroin withdrawal, which lasts a week or two and never kills anyone, to the lifelong struggle of black slaves is inappropriate. It demeans the memory of those sold into bondage and it exaggerates the plight of the drug user. This exaggeration is motivated by the same impulse responsible for misrepresenting illicit drug use as an instigator of violent behaviour. By magnifying the appeal of illicit drugs, government agents justify their imposition of harsh penalties against users. If drug addiction is a fate worse than death, a walking hell or a living nightmare, then a five year prison term or involuntary commitment to a psychiatric institute is a small price to pay for deliverance.

The strength of this argument rests on its empirical accuracy. If a heroin habit is inherently no more beguiling or debilitating than a nicotine or alcohol habit, then extreme measures to prevent self-harm are inexcusable. Bernard Crick, a political scientist, assumes that in the case of certain "hard drugs", addiction is either irreversible or reversible at such great cost that the only answer is to prohibit the drug and thus prevent people from ever starting the habit.[28] Crick cites no valid evidence to back up his views about addiction, he overlooks the ineffectiveness of prohibition, and he does not explain why it matters so terribly whether some proportion of the population are regular and long-term users of heroin. Britain pioneered the Industrial Revolution and the rise of modern science, conquered a large part of the world and implanted her legal and cultural systems almost everywhere while comprised of people addicted to alcohol, tobacco and caffeine.

Prohibitionist Sidney Cohen, borrowing from Kant, agrees that drug laws now infringe individual freedom, but he explains "what a greater encroachment it is to be locked into a 'speed, smack or downer' habit where the degree of freedom is reduced to the next fix!"[29] Richards properly rejects this drug slavery metaphor as unfounded, adding that "there is something morally perverse in condemning drug use as intrinsic moral slavery when the very prohibition of it seems to be an arbitrary abridgement of personal freedom."[30] So silly are views on illicit drug habituation that in 1958 *The Pharmacological Basis of Therapeutics* (L. Goodman and A. Gilman) advised that "Narcotic addiction, even in terminal cases, should be avoided if possible." What is the worry, that people will go to heaven craving morphine? Contrast these uninformed views with the historical evidence on pre-1914 opiate users. As Lauderdale and Inverarity report:

> Addicts were usually indistinguishable from other community members in terms of occupation, appearance and public behaviour... Since opiates were not viewed as a serious menace to society, little popular support existed for legislation to ban their use... If this climate had continued, opiates might still be considered in much the same way as nicotine is today.[31]

Finally, on the issue of self-harm, Kaplan considers the response of a hypothetical Rawlsian contractor. According to Kaplan, an unbiased contractor establishing drug controls might consent to laws that made "reasonable efforts to prevent his weakness from causing him great damage."[32] But do drug habits usually threaten "great damage"? And what are "reasonable" legislative efforts? Kaplan implies that to protect themselves from heroin and certain other drugs, Rawlsian contractors would willingly impose on themselves a total criminal prohibition. But would they? A criminal record and imprisonment can be more detrimental than the self-harm caused by voluntary drug use. Present, biased voters happily support prohibition of exotic drugs they know nothing about and never expect to use, but Rawlsian contractors are not in such a position: they know about pharmacology but they do not know their own personal preferences or biases. The odds are about 1 in 4 that they will be users of prohibited substances. Risk-averse contractors may accept some manner of legal restraint to save them from their own appetites, but their choice will not include criminal law controls.

Just as the child exception expands to destroy Mill's injunction against paternalistic laws, so too can the "voluntary slavery" exception be twisted into rationalizing almost any level of state coercion. Prohibitionist rhetoric is full of inaccurate slave analogies. Illicit drug users are alleged to be sick victims of irresistible impulses. Major support for the slavery model comes from determinists who since the early 1800s have portrayed more and more human choices as being psychologically or socially compelled. Adolescents are drawn into addiction by peers, by ruthless "pushers," or by social pressures. Drug addicts are not personally responsible, they are pawns, victims of parental or capitalistic or racist or sexist oppression. They do not desire or pursue their wretched state; rather they are exploited by giant pharmaceutical firms, by evil foreign powers, or by gangsters. Taking their drugs away by force is like compelling someone caught in a cross-fire to duck. Mill did not do enough to counter this view because he himself did not understand the paradoxical basis of human psychology. For Mill, a life of impulse and moral licence was not "truly free"; only the self-restrained were "completely free." Actually, self-restraint is the most restrictive form of control. The self-restrained are the least free. They feel free, however, because they accept without notice restraints acquired through conditioning.

As mentioned earlier, an advantage of a rights-based approach to drug controls is that it combines radical and traditional messages. Kaplan acknowledges the critics who charge that present heroin laws exceed traditional levels of legal intervention by a large margin but his answer is to identify an "endless" list of other non-traditional legal initiatives, from building codes to minimum wage laws.[33] His response can be faulted on two grounds.

First, critics do not suggest that narcotics laws are the only instance of excessive and inappropriate law making. Kaplan's linking of narcotics controls with minimum wage laws provides no ethical support if the latter is as counter-productive as the former. The major impact of minimum wage laws is to force young, entry-level employees into unemployment. Minimum wage laws do most damage to groups who are supposed to benefit.[34] Similarly, heroin laws are a greater threat to drug users than heroin.

The second problem with Kaplan's argument is that he fails to establish or discuss criteria for determining the acceptability of paternalistic laws. This lacunae allows him to equate narcotics laws with consumer protection laws on labelling, weights and measures and building codes. Yet the differences between these two types of state coercion are monumental. Narcotics laws entail criminal prosecution of individuals and imposition of extreme penalties. In contrast, pure food laws entail setting standards for business operations and provide for minor, non-criminal penalties. Packing undersized lobsters may, in fact, be as socially harmful as using heroin, but that is not how our present laws treat these matters.

Kaplan does not seriously consider the legal tradition that for centuries permitted personal drug use as a matter of assumed right. Instead, like many analysts, he writes about drugs like heroin as if they were major innovations and presented truly new problems. Actually, what is mostly new is the legislative criminalization of drug use and the creation of mandatory medical prescription. In the end, Kaplan rejects Mill's argument, observing that "no modern state... has ever followed Mill's principle with respect to all activities."[35] But Mill did not discuss "all activities." His rule against forcing people to act or forebear merely for their own good applied, by definition, only to self-harming behaviour. Since drug use imposes some level of harm on others, it does not fall within Mill's pure self-harm category. Here is where Mill can be faulted. He assumed that drug use did not require public law controls because the harm it caused to others was too remote or indirect. Without the aid of developed social science techniques and modern research information, Mill underestimated the harm to others caused by drug consumption. But compared to the prohibitionists of his era who outrageously exaggerated certain drug-related dangers, Mill's assessment of the scale of harms is closer to the truth. Faced with a choice between total prohibition and market controls, Mill's libertarian program would be superior. Most people readily exercise restraint in moderating their intake of tranquilizers, amphetamines, alcohol and caffeine. As Bakalar and Grinspoon correctly conclude, the "picture of drug abuse as a potentially uncontrollable epidemic is vastly overdrawn."[36]

Drug use does generate social costs but fortunately we are not limited in regulatory choices to the black and white, total control/no control dichotomy of Mill and the prohibitionists. Tax disincentives are a form of state coercion, but they can be extremely mild and unintrusive compared to criminal law penalties. However, to give Mill credit, his simple "no state coercion" position regarding drug controls may have reflected his understanding of political possibilities. He perhaps realized that once a tax control system was legislated, prohibitionists in bureaucracies and the courts would eventually transform the tax into a prohibition. Indeed, this is what happened with the U.S. Harrison Act of 1914 and the Marijuana Tax Act of 1937. The Harrison Act imposed an excise tax at the modest rate of one penny per ounce on opium and on coca leaves, but the Act was administered so as to affect a police powers prohibition of use.

4. Taking Human Rights Seriously

Drug reform analysts who take rights seriously begin with a commitment to fairness and legal equality. Starting with an affirmation of traditional legal protections is important because it puts the onus on regulators to justify state intervention. State agents naturally employ a reverse onus rule, whereby the state need only accuse and conviction follows. If marijuana cannot be shown to be entirely harmless, users will continue to be criminally prosecuted. In contrast, rights advocates argue that cannabis use should be unregulated unless the government can factually demonstrate that its use harms others and that equivalent harmful activities are similarly regulated. Equal treatment before the law requires that like persons and like activities be subject to equivalent legal controls.

Erich Goode, in *Drugs in American Society* (1984), recognizes that current drug laws abuse civil liberties. For Goode, one of the major costs of prohibition is the sacrifice of "privacy, civil liberties, freedom from surveillance, the rights of suspects...and freedom from cruel and unusual punishment."[37] While each drug represents some special problems of regulation, Goode stresses the need to regulate the use and sale of all psychoactive substances. The central policy question Goode poses is not drug specific; rather he argues that given a "population of heavy drug users... how can we minimize

101

harm to everyone involved?"[38] He argues that the fuss over a relatively minor group of heroin users is misplaced, that drug laws are prejudiced against young, non-white, poorer and non-medical users, and that illicit drugs are not scientifically distinct from licit drugs. Moreover, drug use is comparable to other risky or impairing activities like mountain climbing, motorcycling and playing football. Goode does not propose a regulatory program for either drugs or these "social psychoactives," but his work points toward some form of uniform control built on a recognition of a right to use drugs. He suggests that a basic right to alter one's consciousness may be no less fundamental than the freedom to read or to experiment with sex, food, music or sports. To be legally accurate, though, I should emphasize that in the U.S. and Canada, citizens have no right to eat what they choose, wear whatever clothing they choose, or listen to whatever music they wish. Like drug users in 1850, music consumers today are not seriously regulated, but there is no constitutional guarantee that their favorite composers will not be banned tomorrow. Such things do happen - in Turkey, Kurdish music is outlawed. As Oteri and Siverglate demonstrate, our own legislators could prohibit German Baroque music merely by asserting that Beethoven and his ilk are overly exciting, habit forming stepping stones to "hard" music like heavy metal rock, that German music threatens interest in local composers and encourages passive, socially unproductive behaviour.[39] As for clothes, compulsory motorcyclist helmets may be only the beginning. Legislators could also force bicyclists, joggers and pedestrians to wear safety clothing. After all, requiring pedestrians to wear safety helmets topped by revolving blue lights after dark would save far more lives than helmets for motorcycle riders. Specific limits to legal intervention in these areas do not exist.

David Bellis, in *Heroin and Politicians - The Failure of Public Policy to Control Addiction in America* (1981) is, like Goode, ready to look at the evidence. Bellis notes that "there is little or no valid evidence that sterile, unadulterated, properly administered heroin is any more dangerous than tobacco or alcohol." A scientific regard for the data leads Bellis to conclude that "we have identified the drug abuser in our society and he seems to be nearly everybody."[40] Bellis does not advocate a particular drug control structure, but he does reject "repression and rehabilitation", that is criminal law and medical control, and he stresses that "drug abuse" is a general issue touching all psychoactives and almost all people.

James Bakalar and Lester Grinspoon, in *Drug Control in a Free Society* (1984), also tend to treat drug use as a general phenomenon and compare it broadly with sports, music and television. They cite the Iranian police campaign after 1979 against alcohol, heroin and Western pop music.[41] The Iranian authorities prohibited pop music because they claim it is addictive, licentious, socially harmful and associated with increased violence. Islamic fundamentalists, like the Puritans, view music and some forms of personal adornment in the same way that North American politicians view marijuana and cocaine. The Iranian "war against rock music" may strike us as silly, but their lawmakers acted with as much scientific evidence and concern for civil liberties as ours do in warring against drugs. The authors also compare television viewing and seat belts. Television's critics claim it is a habit forming, socially disruptive practice that is especially harmful to children's ethical and intellectual development. They may be right. In some countries, television is restricted by law, as Bakalar and Grinspoon mention, but North Americans often let television baby-sit their children. Similarly, seat belts reduce traffic accident costs and insurance premiums and are mandatory in some jurisdictions, but not in the U.S. Finally, the authors note that the typical diatribe against recreational drugs can, with the substitution of a few words, be applied to sports such as mountain climbing, hang gliding and football. All are dangerous, habit forming exercises in escapism, but the similarities with drug use tend to be ignored. Even Bakalar and Grinspoon, after pointing out the parallels, explain that "obviously we do not want to find ourselves comparing the effects of marijuana on high school students with the effects of football."[42] Why not? Football may be more damaging. If an accurate accounting were performed, one might find that football kills more people, wastes greater resources and weakens society more than does the current level of marijuana consumption. Football promotes sexist, anti-intellectual values and is plainly corrupting college sports programs throughout the U.S. Researchers find that in secondary schools, the greatest status is achieved through sports, which easily eclipse academics.[43] Marc Fasteau notes in North American culture a "skewing of values which tend to make sports a compulsion for many boys, the mandated centre of their lives."[44] Professional football viewing is indulged by millions, wasting substantial sums of money on a process that is at best socially unproductive. Even less can be said for boxing, which kills 25 to 30 boxers a year. Soccer violence has resulted in over 200 deaths in a single match: moats, barbed wire and armed police are now necessary to protect players, referees and fans.[45] Many will reject this drug/sports comparison out of hand, but when critically analyzed, most defenses of sports are hollow rationalizations. Take the case of helicopter skiing. Every year skiers die in accidents and avalanches. These deaths generate high rescue costs and indirect social damage. What benefits counter-balance these costs? Fitness? The skiers could stay at home and jog much more safely. Communing with nature? They could forget the noisy and polluting helicopter and study biology or geology in nearby woods and hills. Careful exercise is clearly beneficial to health but sports are a different matter. Indeed, the popularity of sports seems to be directly proportional to the amount of obesity and degenerative disease in society.[46] In societies where physical fitness is the norm, organized sport is generally absent.

Richard Schroeder and Steven Wisotsky also take the fairness issue seriously. In *The Politics of Drugs (1980)*, Schroeder correctly observes that marijuana's possible harmfulness cannot justify prohibition in light of alcohol and tobacco controls. Alcohol is equally or more harmful, yet it is not outlawed. The same is true of tobacco; yet smokers "do not run the risk of being sent to jail."[47] Schroeder does not spell out the logical conclusions of his comments, but the implications are clear — if marijuana users are imprisoned, to be fair, alcohol and tobacco users should also be imprisoned. This willingness to make even-handed judgments contrasts sharply with official opinions like those expressed by the U.S. Shafer Commission and the Canadian Le Dain Commission. Both of these state-appointed review bodies rejected the non-criminal regulation of cannabis because they feared it would institutionalize a transient phenomenon. This argument makes some sense only if one assumes marijuana use is a unique problem, and even then prospects for eradicating use of this one specific drug are not good. When psychoactive drugs are viewed as a general class, the argument is unrealistic. After thousands of years, drug consumption can hardly be described as "transient." Furthermore, even without drugs, humans can alter their mood in drug-like ways through hypnosis, self-suggestion, fantasy, overstimulation of endorphins, acupuncture, electrical stimulation and mob-scene revival meetings. Why prohibit indulgence A when indulgences B through Z are not even socially constrained?

While Wisotsky's article "Exposing the War on Cocaine: The Futility and Destructiveness of Prohibition" deals specifically with cocaine, much of his evidence and reasoning applies equally well to all the illicit substances. Wisotsky's work is technically and legally sophisticated, but he properly recognizes that the most intelligent reform proposal in the world cannot overcome the "war-on-drugs mentality." This mentality is vulgarly deterministic and "profoundly totalitarian." It views people as objects, not responsible actors. One passage from Wisotsky is particularly apt:

> Seven decades of government propaganda about the evils of drugs have deprived the public of the power of critical thought respecting drugs, or cowed it into silence. Fear of arrest and prosecution silences consumers of illegal drugs. People who do not use drugs but who object to the status quo on grounds of principle or expedience are silenced by the powerful stigma attached to the advocacy of freedom of choice to use cocaine or other drugs. Notably, no counterpart of the National Organization for the Reform of Marijuana Laws (NORML) exists for cocaine, heroin or even prescription drugs.[48]

Wisotsky's attack on totalitarian drug laws is not drug-specific. Instead, he stresses that the "war on drugs" is actually "a war on the American people" and that the government "operates within a context of irresponsibility."[49] Charlotte Twining's exploration of totalitarian legislation in the U.S. is even broader. It portrays the drug laws as merely one example among many of a fascist tendency for governments to acquire excessive, unregulated power.[50] In the end, Wisotsky's proposal for cocaine control looks very much like present alcohol regulations.

Randy Barnett suggests that an analysis stressing the injustice of drug laws is preferable because, if done properly, it will render most cost-benefit calculations superfluous.[51] Detailed strategies for regulating drug behaviours are endless: one cannot possibly test them all. But a rights-based approach to drug control eliminates in advance all the methods that abuse human rights. The more stringent the rights, the fewer control methods will survive to be tested. Barnett also favours rights as the best device for constraining legislators. The problem with basing policy decisions on a consequential analysis is the pervasive ignorance policy makers have about the consequences of their laws. If facts about costs and benefits are to matter, the necessary incentives need to be built into the legislative process. Such incentives are largely absent, which is why legislators can prohibit drugs merely by declaring them to be hazardous.

Thomas Szasz is probably the leading advocate of liberating drug users from both police and medical supervision.[52] Szasz realizes that drug use is self-harming, sometimes severely so. Nonetheless, he argues that citizens should have the right to ingest any drug, just as they have the right to freedom of speech and religious observance. Naturally, this right to take drugs would not be an absolute or unfettered right. Freedom of speech is not unlimited either, self-expression can harm others, sometimes to a degree beyond any counterbalancing benefits. The state therefore imposes restrictions on speech that amounts to libel or slander, sedition, false advertising, copyright infringement, obscenity, or hate literature. Freedom of speech also fails to excuse a public nuisance created by amplified broadcasts. Clearly, difficult distinctions must be made between freedom of speech and limits warranted in a democratic system. Obscenity restrictions, for example, might only be justified for public broadcasts and public signs, but not private reading material like magazines. Or perhaps public law obscenity prosecutions should be replaced by private suits and the award of monetary damages. Neither the elucidation nor the precise treatment of fundamental rights is firmly settled. Still, enough has been agreed about civil liberties to fill out the bare bones of Szasz's recommendation that voluntary drug use be treated as a basic legal right constrained only by reasonable laws in aid of public defence. Szasz explains that like most rights "the right of self-medication should apply only to adults, and it should not be an unqualified right..."[53] Since drug use is not significantly more or less damaging than harmful pursuits not prohibited or assigned to medical control, Szasz reasons that justice should preclude dissimilar legal treatment for drug users.

New rights, such as the right to use any drug, are normally

rejected as "odd, frightening or laughable," according to Christopher Stone, who cites as examples the development of legal rights for children, women and minorities. Stone explains that the American Founding Fathers "could speak of the inalienable rights of all men, and yet maintain a society that was, by modern standards, without the most basic rights for Blacks, Indians, children and women. There was no hypocrisy, emotionally no one *felt* that these other things were men."[54] Today most judges similarly feel that certain drugs users deserve special oppressive treatment.

Critics may object to drug users' rights on the grounds that drug use is discretionary, unlike racial and sexual characteristics. This objection is misplaced because the most apt comparisons to drug use are not race, sex or age, but religion and politics. If drug use is largely discretionary, as I have argued, why should it matter if we permit some drug use and prohibit others? Consider the same question about religion. Religions, like drugs, are largely interchangeable to uncommitted observers. Why then should the state guarantee freedom of religious choice if one creed or cult can substitute for any other? The answer involves fixation and cultural conditioning. Babies are indifferent as to whether they grow up to be Christians or Buddhists. But once they have been conditioned to accept certain beliefs and behaviours as proper, their habits cannot easily be changed. What begins as cultural accident becomes through fixation, pre-ordained righteousness. Since different people undergo different aculturation, their versions of the True Way clash. In multicultural empires or large federal states, the necessary civil-war preventative is religious and political freedom. The same analysis applies to drug cultures. While people traditionally follow their parents' examples in religion, politics and drug use, adherence is not inevitable. Over the very long term, all political, religious and drug fidelities can be altered but, in the short term some people will fight to the death to protect their habits, even if their behaviour is objectively equivalent to that imposed by their enemy. With drugs, this reluctance to change will be most pronounced where use of a specific drug is associated with important social rituals, with perceived superiority, or with facets of one's personality. In Western culture, alcohol use is integrated in a thousand such ways. But the same is also true subculturally for outlaw drugs like heroin and marijuana. In contrast, obscure medical psychoactives that have not acquired brand loyalty and life-style associations could be readily replaced despite physiological habituation.

A second key point is that freedom of drug choice should not depend on proof of harmlessness. Voting rights are protected despite the possibility of voters making harmful choices. Church independence is protected despite church members entertaining fantastic beliefs. Religion may be an intoxicating "opiate of the masses" as Marx suggested, but Szasz would not on that account prohibit church membership. Conversely, freedom of religion should also preclude government from subsidizing, encouraging, honoring or exempting from legal or taxable liability specific churches. Unfortunately, freedom of religion in the West has traditionally meant the freedom to choose between official, state-supported Christian congregations. Likewise, freedom of drug choice has meant the freedom to use whatever brand of beer, cigaret or coffee one desires. I do not mean to be entirely disparaging. These are genuine freedoms when compared to regimes that compel allegiance to one church or that permit production of only one brand of beer.

Szasz's position expands upon that of Richards or Kaplan because he takes seriously the requirement of legal equality. He also criticizes drug criminalizers for failing to recognize or admit that medical and licit drugs as well as many other pastimes are as dangerous as prohibited substances. The lack of fairness in current drug regulations is the primary clue needed to expose the actual objectives of the prohibition. If prevention of social and self-harm were the real purpose, then why are damaging drugs like alcohol and nicotine not banned? Nor can concern for the well-being of illicit drug users be the real reason for narcotics laws, since these people would be healthier under non-criminal controls. Drug prohibitions fail to protect children and encourage rather than discourage organized crime. What then is the purpose of prohibiting marijuana, cocaine, LSD and heroin?

Szasz suggests that certain drugs are outlawed as symbols of wickedness. As symbols, these drugs are burdened with fictional characteristics by authorities who create the "drug problem" under the guise of solving it. Since framing certain drug users as scapegoats, outlaws, revolutionaries or social dissidents has nothing to do with fairness, pharmacology or human rights, these elements are all irrelevant to current drug laws. As Eldridge noted in 1967, almost all drug control analysts begin with a preconceived, usually implicit assumption that illicit drug use is "an intrinsically depredating evil." This view, Eldridge suggests, is the product of "misconceptions...kept viable by a succession of inaccurate information, sometimes innocent and sometimes artful, which has in time created a whole body of dope mythology effectively blocking public support for a dispassionate inquiry."[55] The antidote to the misconceptions and deceptions is to recognize and publicize the fact that psychoactive drugs are a unified class of substances. Drug laws are unethical on two counts: first because they unfairly distinguish between drugs, and second because they unfairly distinguish between drugs and other socially harmful behaviours. The remaining issue, which Szasz does not develop and which this book addresses in detail, is what legal restraints on the right to use drugs would be reasonable and just.

A just system of regulating drug use is determined according to such criteria as proportionality, equality, democratic choice and fairness. Taking legal equality and fairness seriously leads one to conclude that psychoactive drug use should be subject to a broadly uniform system of regulation. If we then turn to a cost-benefit analysis within the constraints of justice, we will find general agreement between the two analytical frameworks. Criminal prohibition is a rights-abusive, democratically unjustified system, and it also delivers low benefits at high cost. Prohibition is probably not a wise choice for drug control of one drug or for all drugs. However, if legislators are forced to treat drug users fairly, the social drawbacks of prohibition, tolerable if restricted to a few of the less popular psychoactives, become intolerable. A potential for political transformation is achieved by adding the rights-based analysis. Cost-benefit analysts tend to view government as an impartial instrument dedicated to furthering social good. They need only point out the social gains to be derived from an enlightened policy and legislators will enact it. In contrast, rights-based analysts are self-consciously political; they assume that the major challenge is to regulate the regulators. According to this view, an enlightened policy about drugs is likely to evolve only if incentives, procedures and controls are altered in the political market. This means assigning new rights, convening constitutional conferences, altering methods of voter input and changing legislative procedures.

In the following five chapters, each of the basic drug regulation methods is considered. Each method is evaluated as it would function if it were the only regulatory regime controlling the use, sale, production, importation and promotion of psychoactive drugs. Examining these alternative methods in isolation will force our cost-benefit analysis to operate within a specific ethical framework. Technically, the five systems can stand separately, but special mention should be made of the private law/market control system. It is easy to envision a system of drug controls left entirely to private law regulation, but it is also possible to integrate this system with public law mechanisms. The same integration is not so readily conceivable with the other mechanisms. All drug use cannot simultaneously be prohibited through the criminal law and rationed. Similarly, a full medical prescription system of drug delivery precludes the retailing of taxed drugs to the general public. However, private law actions can be readily integrated with all the other systems. For example, both drug traffickers and physicians could be sued in tort law for causing drug-related injury through negligence.

Notes

1. See, generally, the symposium on marijuana decriminalization in *Contemporary Drug Problems* Fall 1981; "America
After Prohibition", *Reason,* October 1988 22-30; N. Morris &
C. Hawkins, *The Honest Politician's Guide to Crime Control* (U.
of Chicago Press, 1970); T. Mikuriya, "A Comprehensive
Proposal to Legalize Drugs" *California Physician* December,
1989, 19; M. Bertrand, "Beyond Decriminalization and Legalization" forthcoming, (1990); the symposium on "American
Drug Policy and The Legalization Debate" (1989) 32 (3) *American Behavioral Scientist.* For other references see notes to
this chapter as well as chapters 1 and 2.

2. M. Rosenthal, "Partial Prohibition of Non-Medical Drug Use:
A Proposal", (1979) *Journal of Drug Issues* 437.

3. "In the Age of Cocaine - What is America's Drug Problem?"
Harper's Magazine December 1985 39-51.

4. David Richards, *Sex, Drugs, Death, and the Law: An Essay on
Human Rights and Overcriminalization* (New Jersey: Rowman
and Littlefield, 1982); D. Richards, "Drug Use and Rights of
the Person: A Moral Argument for Decriminalization of Certain Forms of Drug Use", (1981) 33 *Rutgers Law Review* 607.

5. Richards, *ibid.,* (1982), 7-10.

6. Richards, *supra* note 4 (1981), 681.

7. *ibid.,* 680.

8. See S. Wisotsky, "Exposing the War on Cocaine: The Futility
and Destructiveness of Prohibition", (1983) *Wisconsin Law
Review* 1305, 1419.

9. See M. H. Moore, "Regulating Heroin: Kaplan and Trebach on
the Dilemmas of Public Policy", (1984) *American Bar Foundation Research Journal* 723, 724-728.

10   A. Trebach, *The Heroin Solution* (New Haven: Yale University Press, 1982).

11   *ibid.*, 289.

12   *Harper's, supra* note 3, 45.

13   Trebach, *supra* note 10, 292.

14   R. King. *The Drug Hang-Up: America's Fifty-Year Folly* (New York: W.W. Norton & Co., 1971) 346-350.

15   Dan Beauchamp, "The Individual, State and Alcohol", in M. Grant & B. Ritson, (eds) *Alcohol - The Prevention Debate* (London: Croom Helm, 1983) 166, 170.

16   J.S. Mill, "On Liberty" in R. Wollheim (ed), *Three Essays* (London: Oxford University Press, 1975).

17   J. Kaplan, *Marijuana: The New Prohibition* (New York: World Publishing, 1970).

18   J. Kaplan, *The Hardest Drug: Heroin and Public Policy* (Chicago: The University of Chicago Press, 1983) 111.

19   Mill, *supra* note 16, 15, 101. Schonsheck's recent application of Mill's "harm principle" also favours age limits on drug use, J. Schonsheck, "On Various Hypocrisies of the 'Drugs' In Sports Scandal" (1989) 20(4) *The Philosophical Forum* 247, 279.

20   See, R. Troyer and G. Markle, *Cigarettes: The Battle Over Smoking* (New Jersey: Rutgers University Press, 1983) 34-37, 101.

21   E. Brecher, *Licit and Illicit Drugs* (Consumer's Union, 1972) 232.

22   H. Diehl, *Tobacco and Your Health: The Smoking Controversy* (New York: McGraw, 1969).

23   K. Makela, *et al.*, *Alcohol, Society and State* (Addiction Research Foundation, Toronto. Vol, 1 1981) 65.

[24] D. Black, *The Behavior of Law* (New York: Academic Press, 1976).

[25] Mill, *supra* note 16, 126.

[26] Kaplan, *supra* note 18, 105.

[27] See B. Bergmann, *The Economic Emergence of Women* (New York: Basic Books, 1986) 199-202.

[28] B. Crick, *Crime, Rape and Gin - Reflections on contemporary attitudes to violence, pornography and addiction* (London: Elek/Pemberton, 1974) 72-73.

[29] See C. Brown & C. Savage, (eds), *The Drug Abuse Controversy* (Baltimore: Friends Medical Science Research Center, 1971) 34.

[30] Richards, *supra* note 4, 660.

[31] P. Lauderdale & J. Inverarity, "Regulation of Opiates" (1984) 3 *Journal of Drug Issues* 567.

[32] Kaplan, *supra* note 18, 108.

[33] *ibid.*, 102-3.

[34] See, for example, M. Friedman, *Capitalism and Freedom* (Chicago: University of Chicago Press, 1962) 180.

[35] Kaplan, *supra* note 18, 106.

[36] J. Bakalar & L. Grinspoon, *Drug Control in a Free Society* (Cambridge University Press, 1984) 145; see also J. Langer, "Drug Entrepreneurs and Dealing Culture", (1976-77) 24 *Social Problems* 377-387.

[37] E. Goode, *Drugs in American Society* (New York, Alfred A. Knopf, 1984, 2nd Ed.) 270.

[38] *ibid.*, 254-55.

[39] J. S. Oteri & H. A. Silverglate, "The Pursuit of Pleasure:

Constitutional Dimensions of the Marijuana Problem", (1968) 3 *Suffolk Law Review* 55.

[40] D. Bellis, *Heroin and Politicians - The Failure of Public Policy to Control Addiction in America* (Westport: Greenwood Press, 1981) 11, 208.

[41] Bakalar & Grinspoon, *supra* note 36, 19.

[42] *ibid.*, 16. But see I. Pollock, "Football: brutality as sport" *The Globe & Mail* January 24, 1986 A7. The same question can be asked about all-terrain vehicles (ATVs). In 1983 emergency room reports in the U.S. indicated 42 deaths and 27,554 injuries from ATV incidents. This increased to 48 deaths and 66,956 injuries in 1984. The Consumer Products Safety Commission is seriously considering halting further sales of ATVs. See D. Owen, "Deterrence and Desert in Tort: A Comment" (1985) 73 *California Law Review* 665, 672.

[43] See James Coleman, *The Adolescent Society* (New York: Free-Press, 1961) and B. Avedon, *Ah, Men* (New York: A & W Publishers, 1980) 72.

[44] Marc Fasteau, *The Male Machine* (New York: McGraw-Hill 1974) 105.

[45] "Take Me Out to the Brawl Game" *Time* October 29, 1988, 86.

[46] "Getting an F for Flabby" *Time* January 26, 1987, 56.

[47] R. Schroeder, *The Politics of Drugs: An American Dilemma* (Washington, Congressional Quarterly Press, 2nd. ed. 1980) 51.

[48] Wisotsky, *supra* note 8, 1423.

[49] *ibid.*, 1425.

[50] C. Twining, *America's Emerging Fascist Economy* (New York: Arlington House Publishers, 1975).

[51] R. Barnett, "Curing the Drug-law Addiction - the Harmful Side Effects of Legal Prohibition" in R. Hamowy (ed), *Dealing*

with Drugs - Consequences of Government Control (Lexington Books, 1987) 98-100.

52   For a recent statement of Szasz's position, see T. Szasz, *The Therapeutic State* (Buffalo, Prometheus Books, 1984) 263-266.

53   T. Szasz, "The Ethics of Addiction" in C.C. Brown & C. Savage (eds), *The Drug Abuse Controversy* (Baltimore, National Education Consultants, 1971) 39, 47.

54   C. Stone, "Should Trees Have Standing? - Toward Legal Rights for Natural Objects" (1972) 45 *Southern California Law Review* 450, 455.

55   W.B. Eldridge, *Narcotics and the Law - A Critique of the American Experiment in Drug Control* (Chicago: University of Chicago Press, 1967) 11, 12.

IV Uniform Criminal Law Controls

The primary injustice of current drug laws is that some sellers and users of drugs face criminal prosecution whereas others do not. This unfairness can be remedied either by removing all psychoactives from criminal law jurisdiction or by criminalizing all drugs. This chapter evaluates the full criminalizing option whereby the production, sale and perhaps also the use of recreational, OTC and prescription-only (Rx) psychoactives would be criminalized. For most people, this proposal will seem ludicrous and unworthy of serious consideration. Treating all psychoactives the way government now treats cannabis will be dismissed as impractical, self-defeating and unpopular. Current drug laws exist for ritualistic, superstitious and political purposes that cannot be satisfied if the scientific equivalence of psychoactives forms the basis of our legislation.[1] Still, I believe the issue is worth exploring in some detail.

Present criminal controls on cannabis use may simply represent the criminal law system at its worst. Grinspoon and Bakalar argue that criminal law is a "very expensive and clumsy instrument" for handling drug use, and that this "would be true even if the law were used in a subtle and flexible way, but it is not ... it is wielded aggressively and stupidly."[2] These authors may be right, but their claim still needs to be investigated. Perhaps there is some version of prohibition that could effect an agreeable solution to drug regulation. But deciding if prohibition, even at its best, should be accepted depends, ultimately, on voters preferring it to other regulatory systems. After considering how a uniform prohibition might function and then weighing the costs and benefits, few people would willingly choose the criminal prohibition of all psychoactives.

1. Administering Uniform Prohibition

All criminal law controls incorporate certain features that distinguish criminal law from tort law, tax controls, rationing or medical supervision. To begin with, criminal law is prohibitory. Certain standards are set: no murder, no robbery, no motoring in excess of posted speed limits, no littering. Transgressions against these standards are met with penalties. Law breakers are apprehended and plead guilty or are tried and convicted on an individual basis. Even though most offenders and almost all traffic offenders plead guilty, they do have a right to a trial. Each case can, therefore, be considered on its particular merits, with the outcome varying according to an accused's state of mind, past record, character, social status, age, sex, appearance and legal representation. Criminal law also tends to be formal, legalistic and dominated by lawyers and judges. Criminal law doctrine is subtle and complex; criminal law procedure is convoluted, obscure and expensive. Finally, criminal law is usually associated with intentional torts, extremely immoral acts and serious breaches of social obligation. By customary usage a "crime" still denotes a major wrongdoing. Some analysts distinguish true "crimes" from mere "offences," like traffic regulations, on the grounds that moral condemnation only attaches to crimes.[3] Both crimes and offences are variations within a prohibitory, formalistic and personalized system of behaviour regulation.

Within this prohibitory or criminal framework are a number of variables. Three variables of particular interest to drug regulators are the prohibition's coverage, the penalties inflicted for breaching the law, and the law's enforcement. Should we prohibit all trading and consumption, or only commercial sales? Should drug offences be penalized like murder or like jaywalking? Should drug enforcement agents be granted extraordinary powers and huge budgets, or should they be legally constrained and grossly underfunded? Should courts take constitutional rights seriously, or should they compromise at every turn in order to aid the bitter war on drugs? Clearly, the nature of drug prohibition will vary a great deal depending on the answers to these questions.

The first variable is coverage. What drug-related behaviours are to be outlawed? A pure prohibition would forbid the production, sale, possession and use of all psychoactives under any circumstances. Merely being present while others consumed drugs could be prohibited and perhaps, at the extreme, expressing an interest in or desire for drugs could be declared a crime. The Canadian *Criminal Code* now makes it an offence to import any printed matter that "advocates the consumption of illicit drugs." For the first offence, the maximum penalty is a $100,000 fine or six months in prison. Under this law, *High Times*, a U.S. publication featuring cannabis gardening tips, is illegal.[4] Present controls on illicit drugs like cocaine and peyote come close to the extreme model, but even under the current system two legal exceptions are permitted — religious use and medical use. How would these exceptions be interpreted in a universal drug prohibition?

A safe prediction foresees the judicial affirmation of tradition. Alcohol would be permitted in Christian churches and perhaps at Christian marriages, but secular drugs like coffee and marijuana would probably not be permitted a ceremonial, sacred role. Many Rastafarians of the Ethiopian Zion Coptic Church revere ganja (marijuana) as a Biblically-approved sacramental herb. Their rituals have not gained legal exemption to date but legislators could establish a broad "religious" exemption to include any drugs employed by groups in controlled settings for educational or metaphysical purposes. The wider the religious exemption, the more popular the prohibition would be. Drug use could thereby be permitted in contemplative, organized and ceremonial settings. Even if the religious exemption was widened to include bacchanalian and ribald celebrations, much drug use would still be restricted. Solitary, casual or profane use would be illegal, as would commercial sales. All use would be by groups within systems of private, ceremonial controls. Such a system would, in many respects, duplicate drug controls in pre-industrial societies. However, two significant differences must be noted. First, the regulation would be backed by criminal law sanctions, not merely social sanctions. Solitary, anti-communal drug users would face social ostracism and disapproval as well as legal penalties. Second, the system would not be drug- or church-specific. Groups using cannabis, cocaine and Peruvian pipe music to celebrate their metaphysics would co-exist with groups using caffeine, alcohol and Handel. Separation of church and state, to be effective, must extend to all religious, ceremonial trappings including vestments and drug use. If the state forbids certain beliefs or self-directed activities, it transforms the police into armed clergy empowered to enforce the state's official religion.[5]

The other potentially broad exemption often permitted under criminal law controls is medical use. During the federal prohibition of alcohol in the U.S., physicians wrote over 10 million prescriptions a year for the drug.[6] In 1921 the *Willis-Campbell Act* was enacted to limit this medical exemption. Thereafter no beer could be prescribed, and liquor was restricted to one-half pint per person every ten days.

The most restrictive medical exemption would permit psychoactive drug use only in hospital. The next level would permit medical use on a physician's premises. The least restrictive exemption would permit any psychoactive's availability upon prescription. The medical exemption at its broadest could permit wholesale drug distribution for recreational purposes. The *Webb* case in 1920, for example, involved a physician selling opiate prescriptions to all comers at 50 cents per prescription.[7] Such "script doctors" still exist under current medical controls. These medical issues, however, deserve special treatment; the next chapter evaluates a system that prohibits all drugs except when prescribed under medical supervision.

A full prohibition would outlaw both commercial drug distribution and private consumption. The major variation on this theme is the "vice model" in which only suppliers and producers are criminalized. Prostitution exemplifies the vice model because sellers, not buyers, are prosecuted. Under partial prohibition, drug users could partake in private, as is now permitted marijuana smokers in Spain and in eleven states, including Alaska (in the last case because of a 1975 decision by the Supreme Court of Alaska based on the constitutional right to privacy).[8] However, all public use would be prohibited and no legal suppliers would exist. Perhaps home production and gifts would be permitted, but no commercial sales would be allowed. This system is seriously touted as a solution for marijuana. In 1973 the National Commission on Marijuana and Drug Abuse recommended that, unlike other illicit drugs, marijuana should be decriminalized for personal use and distribution without profit, that possession in public of less than an ounce result in forfeiture and of more than an ounce to forfeiture plus a fine of $100. Sale and distribution for profit would continue to be treated as felonies.[9] Most marijuana offences now involve possession, so partial prohibition would effectively decriminalize 90% of marijuana crimes.

Partially prohibiting a legal drug is a much different matter, though, since coffee, unlike cannabis, is produced and marketed commercially by large, well-established businesses. These businesses would be destroyed by partial prohibition. Nonetheless, partial prohibition is the only plausible form that a uniform drug prohibition could take, given that most citizens are drug users. From past experience, we cannot expect that judges, police, army officers and legislators will quit alcohol, coffee, tobacco, aspirin and the like simply because they are illegal. Under full prohibition there would be a drastic shortage of non-drug users to administer the laws. Under partial prohibition the problem is largely solved because the various legal authorities, while continuing to consume drugs, will not usually be drug traffickers. For criminal law to function effectively over the long term there must be some positive behavioral basis of distinguishing law-breakers from law enforcers. With partial prohibition, the difference will be that between suppliers and consumers.

Under either full or partial prohibition, commercial drug sales will be illegal, thus enterprises now in the legal drug business will be forced out. Drug production and distribution, by default, will fall into smaller and more numerous hands. After 1920, most large American brewers, distillers and vintners were replaced by a million persons engaged in smuggling, bootlegging and running small stills.[10] One side effect of replacing large, legitimate sellers with numerous, small illegitimate sellers is the greater availability of drugs to youngsters. This occurs because adolescents find it easy to enter the illicit drug distribution business. Start-up costs are low, their peers serve as customers, and criminal penalties reduce competition from adults who are more at risk of conviction. Where children under 12 or 14 are exempt from criminal liability, they provide an ideal supply of drug delivery boys or girls. Under uniform prohibition, drug delivery routes could become so lucrative for young entrepreneurs that thousands would abandon school for the business world.[11]

As commercial sales are fractured into small bits, distinguishing users from sellers becomes difficult. Surveys of the cannabis market indicate that nearly half of all users at some time also sell the drug. The prevalence of the user/distributor could lead to a *partial* "partial prohibition," where "trafficking" would be defined to exclude small sales. Perhaps all off-premise alcohol sellers possessing less than ten litres of absolute alcohol would be exempted as "private." This would allow bootlegging and door-to-door sales but prohibit warehousing, commercial retailing and on-premise sales. That would mean no bars, no coffee houses, no liquor stores, no wine in restaurants, no gourmet coffee at the supermarket, no OTC psychoactives at the pharmacy, no cigaret vending machines, no smoke shops, no licit tobacco industry and no sports sponsorships by drug producers.

The second important variable determining the impact of criminal law is the scale of penalties assessed against breaches of the prohibition. Should we take the Malaysian example of executing heroin sellers and extend it to all drug hucksters? Is illegal possession of coffee to be punished by life imprisonment; six months plus a $5,000 fine; banishment; probation; or a $2 fine? Should convicted drug offenders also face collateral penalties such as the denial of a driver's licence, a passport, student loans and public housing benefits?[12]

If most adults are to be drug offenders, the best model is traffic offences. A majority of motorists exceed posted speed limits and thus qualify as offenders. Popular revolt against speed limits is muted, however, because the penalties are small fines and the likelihood of being caught is very slight. The same applies to drug law violations, which is why millions of marijuana users are apathetic about law reform. Popular acceptance of a uniform prohibition will vary directly with the scale of penalties imposed. Milder penalties will increase support, while severe penalties will minimize support. Nebraska's reform of marijuana penalties in 1969 may provide an illustrative case of political dynamics.[13] Nebraska's legislature reduced penalties for marijuana possession to a maximum of seven days in jail. Liberals favored a lower penalty because it reduced oppressiveness, while reactionaries supported the change because the old law was not being enforced. The senator who advocated the penalty reduction intended to *increase* the net impact of criminal sanctions. Generally, a law's deterrent impact depends on its severity, its frequency of application, its timing and its perceived fairness. Raising drug offence penalties from a $100 fine to five years in prison will have little effect if the odds of being convicted per offence are one in ten thousand, or if so many people disagree with the penalty that no jury would convict. With illicit drugs, a $10 fine, frequently enforced, could have more impact than current life sentences that are rarely handed down or fully served.

Mention should also be made of judicial discretion and discriminatory penalties. Traffic penalties tend to be mechanical and fixed: a conviction for going through a red light earns a flat $53 fine with no variation. In contrast, traditional crimes promise large maximums and often no minimums. Manslaughter in Canada is subject to penalties ranging from life imprisonment to an unconditional discharge or suspended sentence. Citizens are less likely to accept prohibition if judges are allowed discretion on sentencing. Both in business and in law, people prefer to know in advance what they are getting. Between a fixed $20 fine and a range of penalties from absolute discharge to a $2000 fine, most people will opt for certainty. A prime example of judicial discretion attaches to Canada's *Narcotic Control Act*. Although the Act does not distinguish between opium, morphine, cocaine and cannabis, judges have created a major difference in effect by treating cannabis offenders much more leniently than other drug offenders.[14]

We must also consider penalty variations between different drug violations. Much of the fairness gain in a uniform prohibition would be lost if unwarranted penalties were assessed against certain drugs. Criminal law could prohibit the sale of both alcohol and cocaine without treating the sellers fairly. Alcohol sellers could face a $5 fine while cocaine sellers face execution. The onus must be on the government to demonstrate convincingly that a factual basis compels discrimination. The law should begin with the presumption that all drug users or drug sellers are equal unless and until proven otherwise. The last important variable is enforcement. How many drug agents will be hired? How rigorous will be their enforcement efforts? What powers of arrest, search and seizure, interrogation and entrapment will they be granted? The prohibition of tobacco for minors illustrates the possibilities of pure non-enforcement. Police apparently devote no resources to curbing underage tobacco use and make no arrests; there is no Tobacco Enforcement Agency or Bureau of Nicotine. The result comes close to free availability of tobacco to children. Benign neglect has its attractions, and many voters might support a general "symbolic" prohibition on the understanding that police would not actually enforce the law. That non-enforcement is a realistic possibility is indicated by the lack of marijuana prosecutions in Denmark and The Netherlands, despite no formal change in the law. But can the police be counted on to shirk their obligations? While police can sometimes be compelled to enforce laws, they cannot be compelled not to enforce laws (though they can often be bribed into non-enforcement).

Marijuana provides a good example. Canadian police could arrest 100 or 1,000,000 marijuana offenders, depending on how they assign priorities and resources. The natural result of police discretion is selective enforcement against young men from lower socio-economic backgrounds who fit the rebellious or delinquent stereotype. Twelve men face cannabis charges for every woman, although surveys of cannabis use show only a slight disparity between the sexes in actual cannabis consumption.[15] Economists, legislators, famous entertainers, law professors and engineers could be arrested if the police pursued them. If all drug sales were prohibited, police would enjoy new opportunities to discriminate between coffee and LSD sellers or between illegal brewers and illegal tobacco growers. The solution is either to take drug control out of police hands or to create powerful constitutional protections against selective enforcement. The constitution could compel judges to invalidate any criminal law that was not enforced against at least one out of every ten offenders, or that was enforced primarily against an identifiable subclass of offenders. As it stands now, a one out of ten rule would invalidate all vice offences and all the bizarre or obsolete criminal laws that police rarely enforce.

Assuming that police intend to enforce prohibition brings up the question of police power. Police now possess extraordinary powers to combat the drug "enemy." Such powers include entry without warrant, wiretapping, strip searches, undercover operations, purchasing illicit substances, and plea bargaining with informers. Police also enjoy the illegal but *de facto* power to perjure themselves, to violate accuseds' rights and to threaten and intimidate suspects. These powers are not inherent in the criminal law system. Police could be regulated and forced to play by different rules. For example, drug agents need not be armed. From 1920 to 1930 in the U.S., an estimated 1,550 persons were killed by state and federal agents, and while this "shotgun enforcement" of alcohol prohibition was most pronounced in the South, everywhere suspects were frequently shot from behind or died accidentally from "warning" shots.[16] Strip-searches need not be permitted either. Currently, Canadian police can detain all the patrons of a given tavern, separate the men and the women, and strip-search every person for illicit drugs.[17] Police leaders in Britain complained recently that Britain was the only European country "where the law did not allow intimate body searches to be made of people suspected of carrying Class B drugs."[18] Mayor Koch of New York City proposed that visitors from Mexico, Thailand and Indonesia be strip-searched at the New York international airports.[19] Even worse, police have been permitted to use choke holds and induce vomiting to prevent suspects from swallowing illicit drugs. Such tactics and strategies recall John Helmer's characterization of drug crusaders as "zealots for normalcy."[20]

Drug informers play a vital role in current law enforcement, but informers need not be rewarded with reduced penalties, lesser sentences or immunity from prosecution. Whether or not an accused person informs on former friends and associates is irrelevant to retributive justice in their own case. Accused persons who inform should be treated like any other informer, and rewarded by money payments. Buying non-privileged information with money is a standard and ethical practice, but buying information with special legal outcomes is a mockery of justice. Finally, a major benefit of permitting private possession and use is that it would shield individuals from police investigations and abuses. Children would not be encouraged by state authorities to inform police that their parents were hiding rum in their fallout shelter or holding illegal coffee klatches. Prohibiting only commercial transactions pits the police against a more equal adversary, namely illicit businesses.

At its most severe, criminal control would prohibit all drug-related transactions including private use, threaten law-breakers with severe penalties, and grant police and courts abusive, extraordinary powers. At its mildest, criminal law regulation would prohibit only certain commercial drug transactions, impose minor penalties, severely restrict police and prosecutorial powers, and grant broad religious and medical exemptions. With these variations in mind I turn now to an evaluation of prohibition's potential benefits.

2. The Social Benefits of Uniform Prohibition

In prohibiting certain drug-related behaviours, government hopes to deter socially-detrimental activities. Deterrence will occur either by reforming those punished or by warning away potential law-breakers. Naturally, the value of deterrence varies according to the restraint achieved and the harmfulness avoided. Slightly deterring very harmful acts can be more beneficial than totally deterring scarcely harmful acts. Criminal prohibition also teaches that certain acts are wrong and inflicts a retributive penalty against wrongdoers.

Drug prohibitionists usually begin and end with the benefit to be wrung from general deterrence. Prohibition's appeal is heightened by exaggerating drug-related costs and by overestimating the deterrent impact of criminal law controls. As noted, a favorite ploy links drug use with violence or acquisitive crime. Marijuana was once described by narcotics agents as a cause of uncontrollable lust and homicidal mania. Heroin users are so criminal that by one New York City estimate they stole over ten times the amount taken in all thefts reported to police.[21] In Australia, Ian Elliot surveyed official police reports on the illicit heroin trade's financial costs and concluded that "a moment's reflection is sufficient to show that these estimates must be wildly and absurdly wrong."[22] Arthur Phillips, former chairman of the British Columbia Police Commission, claimed in 1978 that heroin users in that province committed 60% of all property crime and accounted for 50% of the total cost of police, criminal courts and jails. These ridiculous estimates were backed by an unsupported claim that selling heroin was the province's 4th largest industry.[23] A year later, Rafe Mair, B.C.'s Minister of Health, admitted that there were few heroin users in the province and most of those were not addicted. Finding heroin users in short supply for their new Brannan Lake treatment centre, the Ministry quickly decided to admit alcoholics as well.[24]

At various times, coffee, alcohol, tobacco, and nitrous oxide were branded as grave social menaces threatening the very existence of civilization. Grave social menaces do exist. Twentieth-century wars have claimed about 80 million lives so far. Starvation, parasites and infectious diseases are also major threats, as are pollution and environmental degradation. Drug use is *not* a major threat. Drug use mostly injures drug users themselves, and the injuries are mostly chronic, with late onset. Drug use kills people, but primarily by limiting their old age, not by cutting them down as young adults. I estimated in Chapter Two that drug use constitutes enough of a social cost to merit some public intervention. The cost, however, is not huge. Even if prohibition could enforce total abstinence, our major problems would still be with us.

How close can prohibition come to achieving the elimination of all psychoactive consumption? The answer cannot be found in history because no industrial society has every attempted a uniform prohibition. We find precedents only with selective prohibitions. In that context, prohibition may have deterrent effect. The *Volstead Acts'* first five years saw U.S. alcohol consumption rates fall by 66% compared to 1913 rates. By 1927-30, however, alcohol use was down only 33% compared to 1913. Moreover, alcohol use at this time declined even in countries without prohibition.[25] Surveying the performance record of legal prohibitions against drug use, Bakalar and Grinspoon conclude that prohibition works best "in the short term, and especially when the drug problem is concentrated in a small sector of the society."[26]

Why are deterrent effects not long-lived? At the beginning of a fresh prohibition, citizens face the threat of unknown enforcement. What penalties will the courts hand down?. What is the likelihood of arrest and conviction? With experience, people learn that their initial caution was unjustified because the chance of arrest is very small. As Becker concluded in his 1963 report on marijuana users, over time "the user discovers his fears [of criminal sanctions] are excessive and unrealistic."[27] Law breaking therefore increases over time. The criminalization of impaired driving followed this pattern, first in Scandinavia and later in North America.[28] But notice that alcohol use and impaired driving were both widespread before criminal controls were enacted. A different outcome is possible when the prohibited drug is unknown or unfamiliar. In that case, prohibition may lead to increased drug consumption. Police warnings and sensational media coverage advertise the drug's existence and create a perversely attractive mythology. If the police say its bad, it must be good! Using the forbidden drug may become a badge of courage, a sign of fashion or a symbol of rebellion. In 1937, when about 200,000 Americans used cannabis, the federal government enacted new prohibitive laws against use of the drug. Forty years later, 20 million Americans consumed cannabis regularly, many self-consciously aware of defying their government's edicts.[29] After a thorough analysis of cocaine prohibition, Wisotsky concludes that "the war on drugs has been and promises to be a losing proposition" because — given the private, consensual nature of drug offences — the "systematic detection of offenders is not possible within politically realistic budgets and the existing constitutional limits upon law enforcement techniques."[30]

With established drug habits, deterrence also decreases over time because alternative marketing and production methods develop. Prohibition forces large distillers to close shop, but eventually numerous illegal stills are built to take up the slack. Similarly, smuggling networks gradually replace the once-legitimate importers. Investments flow into black market facilities. Clandestine labs are created and production apparatus is miniaturized. New plant strains are devised to grow locally what was once a foreign crop (like coffee, coca, tea, chinchona, marijuana and peyote). Drug potency is jacked up to reduce product size and smuggling risks. Government agents are bribed. Politicians are persuaded or bought. All of this takes time; even underworld empires are not built in a day. The end result is creative adaptation to new legal conditions. Prohibiting popular drugs is a bit like applying pesticides. The first application works wonderfully. Unfortunately, succeeding generations of pests adapt or evolve resistance until eventually the once-effective chemical is useless. Like insects, humans are adaptable. Productive ingenuity under adverse conditions is frequently noted during war. The British and German Armed Forces bombed each other's industrial centres for years during World War II. Yet in 1944 both were producing more war material than in 1939. Similarly, marijuana production increased in the U.S. during the 1970s even as arrests doubled.[31] War often strengthens one's adversaries.

The potential social upheaval from prohibition increases with the economic importance of drug production. In countries like Bolivia and Colombia, two drugs — coffee and cocaine — dominate the national economies. If the commercial production, distribution and exportation of such drugs is forbidden, the natural result is the growth of a counter-government. Now-illicit producers are cut off from government services and are thus forced to create their own police forces, hospitals, airports, roads, pension plans and taxes. Coffee and coca barons become increasingly powerful until the underground economy outperforms the official economy. Such an inherently unstable state will be followed by civil wars or, more likely, swift coups — such as the one in Bolivia in 1980. Industrial states are not as vulnerable because no single drug products dominate their economy. Nonetheless, there are regions in France, Italy,

Ontario, South Carolina and California that are heavily dependent on drug production or distribution. The scale of black market activity also increases dramatically when we consider a uniform prohibition affecting every psychoactive drug: from 5% to 10% of an industrial economy could be forced underground.

Besides working best over a short term, prohibition is said to be most effective when applied against a marginal social group. The advantages of focusing scarce enforcement resources on a small group are obvious. We must also note the limited objectives of specific prohibitions. After 1945, Japanese by the millions developed a taste for amphetamines. The government responded in 1953 with restrictive legislation. Amphetamines faded away and were replaced by narcotics. The government responded in 1963 with a new law aimed at opiates. Subsequently, Japanese barbiturate use increased.[32] Irish authorities cracked down on whisky in the 1890s and thereby sparked a boom in ether use. The Islamic campaign against alcohol spurred the development of coffee drinking, a habit Arabia bequeathed to the world. The current repression of marijuana use in India appears to be causing a switch to alcohol. In some cases people switch rather than fight, particularly with drugs like cocaine and amphetamine that are very close substitutes. But to some extent, all psychoactives have substitution potential within a given population. Thus, to ascribe success to a prohibition that merely shifts people from one drug to other drugs is to employ a peculiar criterion of success. If our objective is to reduce total drug-related costs, then mere drug substitution may be entirely futile. Temperance advocates were blind to this problem when they shunned alcohol in favour of "soft" drinks like Care-Cola, Dope Cola, Wiseola, Coca-Cola and Kola Ade, all of which contained cocaine.[33] In 1890 cocaine was "soft" and alcohol was "hard," whereas in 1988 cocaine is the "steel drug" and "soft" drinks contain caffeine.[34]

The case for general deterrence appears then to be weak. New drugs like coffee, tea, opium, tobacco, gin, LSD and amphetamines have been outlawed in various historic contexts without marked success. Reginald Whitaker describes some of these drug battles:

> In sixteenth century Egypt, sales [of coffee] were
> banned, stocks burned, persons were convicted of

having drunk the evil substance, and warnings de-
nouncing its pernicious properties were circulated
widely... chocolate roused a storm of violent disapproval when it was first introduced into Europe... In
the nineteenth century, a long struggle was waged
against cigarettes, which led the *New York Times* to
solemnly warn its readers in 1884 that 'the deca-
dence of Spain began when the Spaniards adopted
cigarettes and if this pernicious practice obtains
among adult Americans the ruin of the Republic is
close at hand.'[35]

Actually, the decline of Spain is mostly attributable to its government's counter-productive tax laws but that is another story.

Prohibition of specific drugs has brought substantial decreases
in consumption, which may prove to be temporary, or has led to the
substitution of other drugs. At its worst, prohibition publicizes
unknown drugs and engenders curiosity and desire — the "forbidden fruit" effect. New York's famous Rockefeller drug law with its
mandatory minimum prison terms caused no decrease in heroin
activity.[36] The case for specific deterrence is also weak. Persons
punished for cannabis crimes report that punishment did not alter
their attitudes or drug use.[37] Recidivism rates for compulsory treatment are high. This inability of prisons and forced withdrawal to
affect permanent or even temporary personal reform is consistent
with the overall performance of present "correctional" services.
Traffic fines do not appear to reform drivers, nor does rehabilitation
of criminals in general appear to work. There is no reason to think
drug offenders are any more susceptible to imposed rehabilitation
than rapists, arsonists or tax evaders. Rehabilitation, after all, presumes that offenders are somehow personally flawed and in need of
repair. Criminals are portrayed as relatively rare deviants needing
help to conform to orthodox standards. Drug use, however, *is*
orthodox behaviour. The rare deviants are those who avoid all psychoactives.

Prohibitionists also claim that criminal law is educational.
Rudolph Giuliani, a former federal associate attorney-general and
anti-drug campaigner, explains that "The most general purpose of
the law is to teach. Laws against the use and sale of drugs say

firmly that it is *wrong* to use these things."[38] I agree: criminal law does instruct by creating an official scale of values. But is the lesson in the case of prohibited drugs effective or accurate? The wrongness of drug use can be conveyed through a variety of means. Posted warnings, punitive taxes, rationing and private tort actions all educate the public about drug-related social costs. Indeed, all laws are educational. The problem with criminal law is what it teaches. If drug users are threatened by long prison terms, the law teaches that drug use is as wrongful as robbery and murder. This false lesson is confusing. It also misallocates enforcement resources and misplaces public condemnation. A recent survey of 600 young adults at Michigan State University found that almost all respondents picked heroin as the most socially and personally harmful drug.[39] This is what the current criminal law teaches, despite all the contrary evidence from pharmacology. Conversely, the survey found that respondents were remarkably unaware of the social and health costs associated with legally accepted drugs like aspirin and nicotine. Ironically, while 98% selected alcohol as the second most deleterious drug, 75% of them had consumed alcohol in the week prior to the interview.

Selecting the right scale of punishment for drug-related behaviour is critical for educative purposes. If public officials equate illicit drug use with murder or theft when drug users know it is not even equivalent to disorderly behaviour, government credibility suffers. In 1970, H.J. Anslinger, for 33 years the commissioner of the Bureau of Narcotics, was still claiming that marijuana use was "a sign of incipient insanity," that users were "psychologically and socially maladjusted people," that alcohol "has nothing to do with the drug problem" and that under marijuana's influence a man can become "so violent that it takes five policemen to hold him down."[40] In 1937, Anslinger and a small number of supporters propounded this nonsense at a Congressional hearing prior to passage of the Marijuana Tax Act. In a chapter entitled "The Inevitable Failure of Our Drug Laws," Brown, Mazze and Glaser describe Congressional hearings on opiate control after 1945 where again "testimony was dominated by the Bureau [of Narcotics] and by various local enforcement officials whom it recruited. They reemphasized their drug fiend mythology and called for more severe penalties, thus justifying larger budgets for their agencies."[41] Since the Bureau's policy was built on fabricated, falsified and manipulated data it was natural that Anslinger attempted to impose a blackout on drug research. This research clamp down became almost total by the 1950s and continues in more subtle form today, as the response to Norman Zinberg's work on the moderate use of illicit drugs illustrates. Robert Gordon of Johns Hopkins University reviewed Zinberg's 1984 book *Drug, Set and Setting: The Basis for Controlled Intoxicant Use* and advocated its censorship because Zinberg was spreading the "fantasy" (read "heresy") that moderate, periodic use of opiates was possible.[42]

Illicit drug users, for good reasons, learn to distrust politicians and to perhaps view all government pronouncements with similar skepticism. That is, if legislators are foolish and ignorant about drugs, perhaps they are equally unreliable on foreign affairs, tax policy, labour law and national defence. Other difficulties arise if drug activities, like tobacco smoking, are under-punished. In that case the law teaches that legislators are ill-informed, irresponsible, or in the pay of drug producers who have successfully lobbied for special leniency. Finally, the criminal law now teaches that different drug users should be subject to very different penalties. Prohibiting every psychoactive drug would be a major educational breakthrough. However, the same breakthrough could be achieved by any other uniform regulation.

3. The Costs of Criminal Prohibition

The costs of criminal controls will vary according to the penalties, powers and enforcement resources employed. If the laws are not enforced, costs will be low. Lack of enforcement, however, cannot be assumed. Prohibition of alcohol lacked full public support but was nonetheless enforced to some degree. Assuming a modicum of enforcement, two types of costs can be anticipated. Intended costs include direct expenditures on law enforcement agencies, foregone tax revenues and burdens inflicted on drug offenders. Unintended costs include organized crime, police corruption, disrespect for the law, increased violence, impaired health, foreign policy setbacks and a power imbalance between government and the governed. Unintended costs are the major problem, but as Theodore Schneyer pointed out in 1971, these "externalities" of law-making are rarely considered by legislators or attributed to them by voters.[43] Almost everyone is blamed for drug enforcement side effects except the politicians responsible.

a. Intended Costs

Criminal law controls can be expensive. Under the limited drug prohibition now in effect, 650,000 Americans are arrested per year, mostly for cannabis possession. The federal Drug Enforcement Agency (DEA) employs 4,000 persons. Total federal enforcement outlays are about $3 billion per year, including funding for crop eradication and other anti-drug campaigns abroad. Overall, at both state and federal levels, the criminal law suppression of drug users cost $10 billion in 1984.[44] Police expenditures are high because drug offences comprise an important portion of police work. Approximately three-quarters of all search warrants involve drug offences. A survey in Los Angeles County during the 1970s found that a third of all felony charges involved drug offences. In the U.S. during 1986, drug offences accounted for about 23% of the 583,000 persons convicted of felonies in state courts. Enforcement costs are high because the system is individualized and cumbersome. From four to eight hours of police time are required to process a single marijuana arrest in Canada.[45] According to one estimate, prosecuting a Canadian heroin trafficker cost the taxpayers $3 million (1979).[46] In 1976, New York State spent $100 million arresting 29,000 cannabis offenders.[47]

Drug enforcement fuels police expansion. At least thirteen U.S. federal agencies are funded to punish, lecture or treat illicit drug users, and to enforce more than 900 federal laws pertinent to drug use. There are also over 100 federally supported "drug squads" composed of state, county or city police, plus about 700,000 officers in general law enforcement who make drug-related arrests.[48] Naturally, every hour of police time spent on drugs cannot be spent on homicide, domestic violence, theft, rape, assault, industrial sabotage or illegal waste disposal. This is one reason why greater police efforts meet with higher real crime rates. Nor are police agents the only public servants being misdirected by the drug crusade. James Beniger of Princeton, who studied the growth of drug controllers in the 1960s and early 1970s, found that higher salaries, promotions, research funds, larger budgets, media exposure and status led drug specialists to become addicted to drug control. Thereafter, competition among agencies and individuals led to what Beniger calls "trafficking" in drug users and offenders.[49]

Punishment is another key factor in determining enforcement costs. Imprisonment is expensive both for the taxpayer and the offender. Prison costs run from \$10,000 to \$40,000 per prisoner per year. Because a uniform prohibition of drug use would criminalize millions of citizens, imprisonment would not be a financially viable sentence. Even under a partial prohibition, the number of drug offenders would preclude jail sentences. Fines are much more attractive. They are far less of a burden to the offender than prison and raise revenue rather than expending it. Depending on the schedule and the efficiency of enforcement, fines could raise enough revenue to offset all enforcement costs. On similar grounds, the DEA is now lauding the benefits of property confiscation made possible by new forfeiture provisions in the 1984 Comprehensive Crime Control Act. Airplanes, cars, boats, houses and factories employed in making or distributing illicit drugs are legally seized by the DEA. After conviction of the owner, the seized property is sold, with the proceeds going to government. According to Giuliani, who cites no figures, DEA costs "are almost entirely offset by the cash and property seized during drug arrests."[50] Of the DEA's Miami fleet of 200 cars in 1986, 119 were seized from drug offenders. Under full prohibition, a significant portion of private property would be subject to government seizure. Such seizure is apt to be more punishing than fines; imagine motor vehicles being seized for traffic violations.

Another major cost is tax revenue foregone. Under a uniform prohibition, government would lose present excise revenues from taxes on tobacco and alcohol, plus potential revenue from excises on drugs that are now illicit, medical or otherwise untaxed. In addition, income from drug-related commercial activities will go underground, and income tax yields will fall. These revenue losses will easily exceed the few billion dollars of direct enforcement costs. In the United Kingdom, alcohol and tobacco taxes earn \$9 billion annually. An exact estimation of revenue loss is impossible because we must guess at the tax rates and the tax yield from excises on drugs like cocaine, marijuana, diazepam and caffeine. These issues will be explored in Chapter Eight, which deals with the uniform tax control of psychoactive drugs. As a general estimate, however, a full drug prohibition would cost, in direct and potential losses, from 5% to 15% of present tax revenues from all sources.

The other intended cost of prohibition is the damage inflicted on convicted drug offenders. At the extreme, this damage includes imprisonment, social ostracism and criminal record. A criminal record by itself precludes career opportunities, deters prospective employers, and even prevents acceptance into educational institutions.[51] This may be acceptable for serious crimes and career criminals, but it is not acceptable when a majority of the population behaves criminally. In their mildest form, criminal sanctions against illicit drug behaviour would inflict a small fine, with no record kept of the incident. Fines would not escalate with subsequent convictions so there would be no distinction between first time offenders and others. Escalation of penalties would result only from failure to pay a fine. Drug offence procedure in this case would be modelled on the administration of vehicle parking fines. Millions of fines would be levied and paid. The first fine for the illicit possession of tobacco would be the same as the 100th fine for that offence. Input from lawyers and courts would be minimal. Very little social stigma would attach to those convicted and fined. Illicit drug use, like illegal parking, would be regarded perhaps as impolite and self-centred, but not as reprehensible or evil. Incidentally, illegal parking in cities like Rome probably causes more damage and aggravation than illicit drug use.

b. Unintended Costs

I now want to consider the side effects or unintended costs of criminal prohibition. These costs have been analyzed by Kaplan, Hellman, Schneyer, Wisotsky, Szasz, Richards, Nadelmann, and others, so this section will do no more than briefly canvass the literature and review the general consensus that prohibition's costs exceed its benefits. Ostrowski provides the most recent and detailed estimation of prohibition's costs and benefits in the U.S. He estimates costs of about $80 billion for 1988, against few, if any, benefits.[52]

Under either full or partial prohibition, commercial drug interests will become illegitimate. Taverns, tobacco farms, brewers, and pill assembly lines will only be able to function illegally. This will inflate prices and curtail consumption, but it will also force legitimate businesses either to leave the trade or turn to the black market. Black marketers are at a disadvantage because they cannot rely on police protection, operate overtly or take their business disputes to court. Protecting property and enforcing debts becomes their own responsibility. As a result, illicit drug traders must operate as the Western pioneers did before the law arrived. This means private armies, weapons, reliance on a code of honour, family businesses and private vendettas.

Criminalizing drugs increases the murder rate because black marketers kill one another far more frequently than do legitimate business competitors. Over 100 people were killed in Dade County in 1980 for drug-related reasons: enforcing debts, repaying betrayal to the police, protecting an exclusive business territory, obtaining a dealer's money or drug supplies.[53] If tobacco is prohibited, illicit tobacco traders will behave in like fashion. Criminalizing drugs also creates a sizeable economic sector which is both heavily armed and antagonistic to the government. Currently the war on drugs is a limited witch hunt. Under full prohibition, the battle against drugs could escalate into a civil war.

If personal drug use were permitted in a partial prohibition, customers would still turn to black marketers for their supplies. Millions of citizens would thereby come into frequent contact with organized criminals. Organized crime, as a popular service industry, will necessarily confound the ethical distinctions between good and bad, legal and illegal. Criminals were romanticized during Prohibition, while the police were cast as meddlesome, incompetent spoilsports. Large black markets also interfere with public planning. Numerous tax, pension and welfare adjustments are geared to official statistics concerning unemployment rates, farm production, retail sales and gross national product. Black marketers do not report to the government, thus official figures diverge from reality. A uniform prohibition of drug sales combined with income tax evasion, illegal immigration and non-standard employment will result in 25% or more of the economy ceasing to officially exist.

The growth of organized crime is usually exploited as a justification for more government in general and more police in particular. This is doubly unfortunate because increased police corruption coincides with increased police power. In measuring the costs of heroin prohibition, Kaplan cites the "staggering levels of police cor-

136

ruption" : from one third to one half of all narcotics agents engage in blatantly illegal practices.[54] The reasons for police corruption are familiar. Agents often work undercover buying and using illicit substances and fraternizing with illicit traders. Bribes to police are large, because of the high crime tariff, and undercover agents can easily conceal bribe taking. Furthermore, many agents have no moral compunctions about taking drug money since they recognize that the illicit drug trade is not intrinsically worse than the alcohol or tobacco trade. Being placed in a position to risk one's life for the sake of halting a minor nuisance would demoralize most people, especially when those efforts were mostly ineffective. If the best police efforts manage to intercept only one tenth of the illicit drug trade, what practical difference does it make if another few kilograms or tons get through? Police are also capable of recognizing that millions of citizens are demanding and paying for these drugs and are thus undercutting all police efforts. A police force cannot remain honest or effective without strong public support. With cannabis and cocaine prohibition, the public is divided. Millions see the police as the enemy, while others demand more vigorous police action. With alcohol, caffeine, nicotine and aspirin prohibition, this ambivalence would likely fade, with most people giving the police considerably less support than they now enjoy. The end result of total drug prohibition might be the transformation of police into para-military troops patrolling hostile streets in armoured cars, returning at night to fortified bunkers. Conversely, the police might engineer a coup and remove the civilian government in order to revoke prohibition.

When governments lose public support, the classical response is to proclaim martial law, suspend elections, and institute a police state. In the last decade or so, this strategy was pursued in Chile, South Korea, Argentina, Grenada, numerous African states and in the Philippines. Such open and ruthless dictatorial maneuvers are not as readily achieved in the older democracies. American politicians speak of drug "wars," but so far none have attempted to proclaim an official war-time status. However, there is a wide middle ground between total military/police take over and genuine democratic rule. Both the U.S. and Canada are plainly advancing over that middle ground by instituting increasingly draconian measures ostensibly aimed at drug offenders. Many of these measures are so broad they affect everyone. Partly to prevent the "laundering" of drug proceeds, the U.S. federal government passed banking laws requiring reporting of all cash deposits above $10,000. The Bank Secrecy Act of 1970 instructs banks and certain other finance businesses to file Internal Revenue Service Form 4789 whenever they receive more than $10,000 in cash. In 1985, the Bank of Boston paid a $500,000 fine for failing to report $1.2 billion in cash transactions.[55] Government officials claim that $170 billion earned annually from drug dealing, gambling, loan sharking and prostitution is being laundered with the help of banks.[56] Late in 1988, Congress ignored foreign bank protests and passed a measure forcing all off-shore banks with U.S. ties to maintain records of cash transactions of $10,000 or more, and to divulge such records to U.S. drug offence investigators on request. Of course, the whole money-laundering problem arises only because government criminalized these businesses in the first place. Now, with dozens of banks under investigation, organized crime is turning to casinos, stock brokers, race tracks, grocery stores and other businesses with rapid cash turnover. Ultimately, under pressure from a uniform drug prohibition, government might prohibit cash sales over $5, and require all other transactions to be recorded electronically. Rising tax evasion is already pushing Washington and Ottawa toward such neo-feudalistic interventions.

To help police catch illicit drug producers, U.S. courts have interpreted the fourth amendment so as to allow police searches of open fields without warrants. Even supporters of drug criminalization like Saltzburg warn that U.S. courts have "cheated" by "turning their backs on fundamental constitutional principles ... in order to aid the war against illicit drugs." Saltzburg adds that the Supreme Court decision in the marijuana case of *Oliver* is "indefensible in virtually every respect."[57] But Saltzburg's concerns merely scratch the surface. In recent years members of Congress have proposed bills that would, if passed, permit the military to assist in drug law enforcement, create a northern Arctic "gulag" for drug offenders, restrict bail for drug suspects, permit disclosure of IRS data, eliminate the exclusionary rule, punish foreign drug producers, and repeal the prohibition against use of herbicides abroad.[58] Military law is also being transformed by the "war on drugs." In a recent U.S. article, Stephen Kaczynski analyses "the more aggressive posture of the services and the new tools given the enforcement authorities within the last four years." Kaczynski, a drug war supporter, concludes that every case opening up new vistas of law enforcement power has been a drug case, and that "Freed of artificial and substantial impediments, commanders and prosecutors alike now have the weapons and mandate to wage virtual total war [against soldiers using illicit drugs]."[59]

Border operations to catch smugglers inconvenience every traveller. Shoot-outs between police and drug traders endanger bystanders. There is also the problem of limiting the field of operations for special drug enforcement units. E.J. Epstein, in *Agency of Fear: Opiates and Political Power in America*, argues that Nixon created a new drug agency in order to have his own police force that could circumvent the FBI and the CIA.[60] According to Epstein, the White House staff planned to expand and consolidate its power over domestic investigations by exploiting public fears of illicit drugs. Under a general prohibition, federal police agencies would wield tremendous power because most citizens would be criminal drug users or would associate with criminal drug suppliers. Thus most people, including members of opposition parties, critical journalists, and unfriendly academics, would be vulnerable to drug prosecutions. The stage could then be set for blackmail and selective enforcement for partisan objectives quite unrelated to drug use. Illegal drug use could become the equivalent of Stalin's "crimes against the state", which everyone committed. Expanding the scope of criminal controls is a classic device for conducting a reign of terror. A narrow criminal law is popularly regarded as protective because people are more likely to be victimized by crime than prosecuted for it: a uniform drug prohibition would reverse the equation.

Prohibition will reduce total drug consumption, a change that will likely decrease chronic health problems. With less alcohol consumed there will be less liver disease, fewer heart problems, less cancer. On the other hand, prohibition may increase the rate of acute reactions because of poor quality control, adulterated products and mislabelling. Customers will use less drugs but they will also use worse drugs. Familiar drug products, if alcohol in the 1920s and heroin in the 1960s are good precedents, will become increasingly fatal. Smuggling requirements favour highly potent drugs in concentrated form. Legal opiates were eaten, smoked or consumed in liquid form, usually mixed with alcohol. Illegal opiates became concentrated and more potent. Morphine replaced opium, which was then supplanted by heroin (effectively a concentrated form of morphine). Smoking and drinking opiates were replaced by injections. Similarly, prohibition curbed beer and wine use and shifted drinkers to distilled alcohol. These spirits were sold with counterfeit labels and sometimes contained industrial contaminants. Mixed drinks or cocktails became popular because they disguised the taste of inferior liquor. Legal efforts to control ether, used to produce cocaine hydrochloride, has increased cancer risks to cocaine users because South American producers replaced ether with benzene. Prohibition is also likely to shift consumption patterns toward periodic binging, which reduce illicit drug "episodes." Given an equal annual consumption rate, however, binging is more dangerous than moderate daily intake, particularly with drugs like alcohol and diazepam for which the lethal dosage is only about twice the very inebriated dosage.

Prohibition perverts journalism because crime control is presented in exciting, dramatic, and simple-minded terms.[61] Police opinions, police theories and police estimates of the extent of the illicit drug trade are presented uncritically and without a balancing counter-opinion.[62] The result is media dissemination of propaganda. Commentators climb over one another in search of the "nation's number one drug problem": Mike Wallace on *60 Minutes* said it was PCP, TIME used to say it was heroin, then cocaine, then "crack". Later, the *Boston Globe* discovered "bazuko" in Colombia, a form of cocaine even cheaper, more thrilling and "more dangerously addictive" than crack. Naturally, bazuko use is spreading in "epidemic proportions" as a new "scourge against humanity."[63] Robert Bomboy's press survey found that most drug reporting by major newspapers reflects ignorance, fear and misconceptions.[64]

Popular drug coverage focusses and thrives on police controls for a number of reasons. Journalists enjoy a symbiotic relationship with the police at all times, but prohibtion adds naturally appealing elements. Daring drug entrepreneurs take unusual risks and earn extraordinary incomes. Under prohibition, armed police officers track down wily and dangerous criminals, engage in high speed chases, intercept airplanes and speedboats, and conduct surprise raids. People hunt or fish for sport, so it is no surprise they enjoy films, television series and news reports about police hunting traffickers. As in sport, there is no ultimate victory or defeat, rather it is the game that matters. Furthermore, journalists revel in the opportunity to be "war correspondents" in the Hemingway tradition, especially as the "drug war" fronts are down the street, and the "enemy" rarely shoots outsiders or takes hostages.

Under prohibition, illicit drugs are portrayed as incredibly enticing, dangerous and criminogenic substances.[66] This portrayal supplies three enduring fictional characters: the tragic self-destructive drug user, the resourceful trafficker, and the crazed killer. Each of these characters is naturally entertaining, supplying writers with easy, off-the-shelf motives capable of propelling along the flimsiest story line. Thus best selling films and novels are heavily populated by caricatures of junkies, ruthless drug dealers and drug-crazed homicidal maniacs, while almost no one depicts brewers, tobacco farmers, tax collectors or liquor store owners. Television series feature Elliot Ness and Al Capone, not John Kenneth Galbraith in his war-time role as rations and price controls czar.

In contrast to drug war coverage, the important aspects of drug-related behaviour are rather dull and uninteresting. Worse, the experimental evidence is plainly discomfiting and insulting. Pharmacological and sociological studies indicate that government has been foolishly wasting billions of dollars and unnecessarily disrupting thousands of lives; that parents, editorial writers, film stars and teachers have been hypocritical in warning children about "drugs," and that narcotics agents are more dangerous than protective. Presenting these facts requires careful preparation, extended discussion, lengthy study and a willingness to buck widespread prejudices. Presenting police reports, drug seizure tallies and body counts requires very little talent, but sells more advertising space and attracts wider readership. However, if all drug use or all drug sales were prohibited, many of the fabulous myths about illicit drugs would be exposed. Both drama and criminal law require dichotomy, contrast and the juxtaposition of incongruous elements: good battles evil, righteousness challenges sin, police gun down criminals, and drugs are soft or hard, medicinal or dangerous, welcome or reviled. Uniformity, equivalence and unchanging fundamentals may be good science but they are bad theatre. Prohibiting all drugs would, in many ways, spoil the fun.

4. Crime and Public Choice

Authorities on drugs, particularly those of an orthodox stripe, frequently refer to "society's" views on drug-related issues. One reads that "society was concerned about opium in patent medicines" or that "society feared an upsurge in marijuana use" or that "society has decided that hard drugs must be eradicated."[66] Society should not be personified or construed as an intelligence capable of having single views or opinions. "Public opinion" is a better term of reference, since we are all aware that on any topic a variety of opinion exists. Furthermore, public opinion can be tabulated whereas vague references to "society" represent untestable mysticism, laziness or an effort to obscure a lack of public support. It is now well recognized, for instance, that opium, cocaine and marijuana prohibitions were enacted without wide public support or concern.[67] The present abiding interest in illicit drugs was created by government agencies, specific politicians and sensationalist media. The law led, rather than responded, to popular demand. Be that as it may, the task at hand is to consider which method of drug regulation most people would prefer. The key to producing an answer that is not only popular, but fair as well, is to rule out in advance all the unfair choices. Public opinion polls suggest that most people are adamantly opposed to decriminalizing heroin, but this position is unjust and almost entirely weightless, since very few people use heroin or know anyone who does use heroin. The fair question takes a different form. It asks, what restraints will you accept on your own drug use in order to protect yourself from the drug use of others? Worried about cocaine users? Will you then allow your alcohol, coffee and aspirin use to be prohibited in order to deny cocaine to other people?

Rights do not come unburdened by obligations. The right to not be murdered is matched by the obligation not to murder other people. Similarly, the right to be protected from drug-related costs is balanced by the obligation not to inflict drug-related costs on other people. As it stands, caffeine users are quite free to pass costs on to others, but cocaine users are threatened by severe sanctions. Not surprisingly, caffeine users outnumber cocaine users by a very large margin. While most realize that it would be unfair for the majority to vote in a special tax applied only to people named Smith,

142

the same unfairness is not so apparent when a drug like morphine is prohibited. Of course, after the tax or the specific prohibition is enacted there will be fewer Smiths and fewer morphine users, but not all will be deterred. Some tax-oppressed Smiths will refuse to change their name to Psmith or Smythe, perhaps for sentimental reasons, just as some opiate users will refuse to heed the government's discriminatory commands. As noted, people can change their choice of drugs under legal pressure, just as they can change their name, their religion, their diet or their music. But while such changes are possible, they are not costless. More importantly, the majority act unjustly when they support unwarranted legal discrimination.

The fair question then is: Will voters select a uniform prohibition of drugs to protect themselves either from their own weakness or from the threat posed by other people's drug use? The answer is probably no. The costs of uniform prohibition plainly outweigh any possible benefits. Murder merits prohibition: drug use does not. Prohibition offers little social protection because it cannot curb drug use in the long term, because it shifts users to stronger, poor quality drugs consumed on unregulated premises and purchased from underworld suppliers, and because it corrupts everything it touches. As for protection from self-harm, a vigorously enforced prohibition would cause most people more harm than would the free availability of psychoactives. Criminal law is antagonistic to personal autonomy and tends to justify massive public intrusion into private affairs. A uniform prohibition would be fair in theory but unjust in practice because of the large degree of unavoidable discretion left in the hands of police, prosecutors, defence attorneys and judges.

Notes

1   See Peter Manning, *The Narcs' Game: Organizational and In-formational Limits on Drug Law Enforcement* (MIT Press, 1980) 256.

2   L. Grinspoon & J. Bakalar, *Cocaine: A Drug and Its Social Evolution* (New York: Basic Books, 1985) 236.

3   See J. Kleinig, *Punishment and Desert* (1973) 28-29.

4   "No Time for High Times" *Globe & Mail* November 1, 1988, 23.

5   Wayne Morgan, *Drugs in America - A Social History, 1800-1980*, (Syracuse University Press, 1981) 93.

6   S. Cashman, *Prohibition - The Lie of the Land* (New York: Free Press, 1981) 40, 153.

7   R. King, *The Drug Hang-Up* (New York: Norton, 1972) 41. See *Webb* vs. *U.S.* (241 U.S. 394, Sup. Ct.).

8   M. Rosenthal, "Partial Prohibition of Non-Medical Drug Use: A Proposal", (1979) *Journal of Drug Issues* 437, 442; "Streets of Shame" *The Economist* March 26, 1988, 46.

9   *ibid.*

10 Henry Lee, *How Dry We Were - Prohibition Revisited* (New Jersey: Prentice Hall, 1963) 86-88.

11 J. Lamar, "Kids Who Sell Crack" *Time*, May 9, 1988, 18-25.

12 M. Isikoff, "U.S. seeks tougher 'zero tolerance' drug policy" *The Detroit News* June 8, 1988, 3A; "Antidrug or Antipeople" *Time* September 19, 1988, 28.

13 J. Galliher, J. McCartney, R. Baum, "Nebraska's Marijuana Law: A Case of Unexpected Legislative Innovation" in *Crimi-nology: Power, Crime and Criminal Law* (Illinois: D. Forsey

Press, 1977); J. Galliher and J. Cross, "Symbolic Severity in the Land of Easy Virtue: Nevada's High Marijuana Penalty" (1982) 29 *Social Problems* 376; J. Galliher and L. Basilick, "Utah's Liberal Drug Laws: Structural Foundations and Triggering Events (1979) 26 *Social Problems* 284.

14 N. Boyd, J. Lowman & C. Mosher, "Case Law and Drug Convictions: Testing the Rhetoric of Equality Rights" 29 (1987) *Criminal Law Quarterly* 487-511.

15 *ibid.*

16 Lee, *supra* note 10, 168.

17 R. Solomon, "Drug Enforcement Powers and the Canadian Charter of Rights and Freedoms" (1983) 21 *University of Western Ontario Law Review* 219.

18 B. Whitaker, *The Global Connection: The Crisis of Drug Addiction* (London: Jonathan Cape, 1987) 291.

19 Arnold Trebach, "In the Age of Cocaine - What is America's Drug Problem" *Harper's* December, 1985, 45.

20 John Hellmer, *Drugs and Minority Oppression* (New York: Seabury Press, 1975) 152. Manning recommends disbanding all specialized police drug units, including the entire U.S. federal drug enforcement structure, and warns that because police organizations do not closely control their drug agents' actions a minor reform, like decriminalization of use or reduced penalties, will do little to alter police tactics. Manning, *supra* note 1, 258-61.

21 John Kaplan, *The Hardest Drug: Heroin and Public Policy* (University of Chicago Press, 1983) 51.

22 I. Elliot, (1982) "Heroin Mythologies for Law Enforcers" 6 *Criminal Law Journal* 6, 8.

23 A. Phillips, "A total war on heroin addiction - can B.C. win it?" *The Globe & Mail* March 18, 1987, 10.

24 *Maclean's* January 21, 1980, 26.

25 K. Makela, *et al.*, *Alcohol, Society and the State* Volume 1 (Toronto, Addiction Research Foundation, 1981) 7.

26 J. Bakalar and L. Grinspoon, *Drug Control in a Free Society* (1984).

27 H. Becker, *Outsiders: Studies in the Sociology of Deviance* (New York: The Free Press, 1963) 72.

28 See H. L. Ross, *Deterring the Drinking Driver* (Mass: Lexington Books, 1982).

29 E. Goode, *Drugs in American Society* (New York: Alfred Knopf, 1984) 256.

30 S. Wisotsky, "Exposing the War on Cocaine", (1983) Wisconsin Law Rev. 1305, 1381; see also J. Anthony, "The Effect of Federal Drug Law on the Incidence of Drug Abuse" (1979) 4 *Journal of Health Politics, Policy and Law* 87.

31 Goode, *supra* note 29, 256.

32 L. Grinspoon, *Marijuana Reconsidered* (1977) 344.

33 J. L. Phillips & R. D. Wynne, *Cocaine: The Mystique and Reality* (New York: Avon Books, 1980) 53. During this era, Vin Mariani, a bordeaux wine and cocaine mixture was popular with leading figures such as Ulysses S. Grant, a U.S. President, and Pope Leo XIII. While the primary American psychiatric textbook in 1980 explained that moderate use (two or three times a week) of cocaine "creates no serious problems" the *New York Times* in 1986 piously intoned that such an idea "had become an anachronism for the second time in a century." In short, styles in cocaine changed again. The *New York Times* November 17, 1986, B6.

34 P. Erickson, E. Adlaf, G. Murray, & R. Smart, *The Steel Drug: Cocaine in Perspective* (Mass: Lexington Books, 1987). Typically, these researchers found cocaine users who dabbled with the drug or who found it unappealing, users who have been "underrepresented in the media's sensational coverage of 'ruined lives.'"(129)

35   R. Whitaker, *Drugs & The Law: The Canadian Scene* (Toronto: Methuen, 1969) 4-5.

36   Kaplan, *supra* note 21, 94.

37   P. Erickson, *Cannabis Criminals: The Social Effects of Punishment on Drug Users* (Toronto: ARF Books, 1980); N. Boyd, "The Question of Marijuana Control" (1982) 24 *Criminal Law Quarterly* 212-232.

38   *Harper's*, *supra* note 19, 44.

39   A. Vener, L. Krupka, J. Climo, "Drugs (Prescription, Over-the-Counter, Social) and the young adult: Use and Attitudes" (1982) 17 *International Journal of Addictions* 399, 405.

40   "The Drug Revolution", *Playboy* February, 1970, 55, 58, 70.

41   J. Brown, R. Mazze & D. Glaser, *Narcotics, Knowledge and Nonsense: Program Disaster Versus a Scientific Model* (Mass: Ballinger Pub. Co., 1974) 91.

42   See J. Blackwell, "Academic Censorship and the 'War on Drugs': The Case of Responsible Drug Use" (1989, forthcoming).

43   T. Schneyer, "Problems in the Cost-Benefit Analysis of Marijuana Legislation", (1971) 24 *Standford Law Review* 200.

44   Bakalar & Grinspoon, *supra* note 26, 110.

45   P. Bailey & R. Solomon, "Police Processing of Cannabis Cases" (Unpublished Research Study: National Dept. of Health & Welfare, 1979).

46   Phillips, *supra* note 23.

47   J. Blackwell, "Decriminalization of Cannabis in the United States" in *Cannabis - Options for Control* (U.K.: Quartermaine House Ltd., 1979) 93.

48   Manning, *supra* note 1, 11.

[49] James Beniger, *Trafficking in Drug Users: Professional Exchange Networks in the Control of Deviance* (Cambridge University Press, 1983).

[50] *Harper's, supra* note 19, 46.

[51] N. Overend, "Marijuana Possession: A Criminal Act or Compliance Problem", (1984) 42 *University of Toronto Faculty Law Review* 114, 121.

[52] J. Ostrowski, "Thinking About Drug Legalization" Cato Policy Analysis (1988). See, also, M. Kurzman & H. Magell, "Decriminalizing possession of all controlled substances: an alternative whose time has come" (1977) *Contemporary Drug Problems* 245; L. Fink & M. Hyatt, "Drug Use and Criminal Behaviour", 8 *J. Drug Education* (1978); H. Greenstein & P. Dibianco, "Marijuana Laws - A Crime Against Humanity" (1972) 48 *Notre Dame Lawyer* 314.

[53] Wistosky, *supra* note 30, 1401.

[54] Kaplan, *supra* note 21, 97. See also J. Dombrink, "The Touchables: Vice and Police Corruption in the 1980s", (1988) 51 *Law & Contemporary Problems* 201-232.

[55] *Time,* March 25, 1985, 64.

[56] *Time,* November 12, 1984, 83.

[57] S. Saltzburg, "Another Victim of Illegal Narcotics: The Fourth Amendment (As Illustrated by the Open Fields Doctrine)", (1986) 48 *University of Pittsburgh Law Review* 1, 4.

[58] Wisotsky, *supra* note 30, 1302-5.

[59] S. Kaczynski, "America at War: Combatting Drugs in the Military" (1984) 19 *New England Law Review* 287, 333.

[60] E. J. Epstein, *Agency of Fear: Opiates and Political Power in America* (New York: G. P. Putnam, 1972) 250-261.

[61] L. Wallach, "Mass Media and drinking, smoking and drug taking", (1980) *Contemporary Drug Problems* 49.

[62] See Erickson, *supra* note 34, 23-32.

[63] Reprinted in the *Ottawa Citizen*, September 13, 1986, F1.

[64] R. P. Bomboy, *Major Newspaper Coverage of Drug Issues* (Drug Abuse Council, April 1974).

[65] See D. Smith & G. Gay, *"It's So Good, Don't Even Try it Once": Heroin in Perspective* (New Jersey: Prentice-Hall, 1972).

[66] Eldridge, for example, writes that "Society has made a judgment that indulgence in narcotics is wrong." W.B. Eldridge, *Narcotics and the Law* (1967) at 13.

[67] C. Mitchell, review of *Health Protection and Drug Laws* (Canada, National Health and Welfare, 1988) 21 *Ottawa Law Review* (1989) 303-305.

V Uniform Mandatory Medical Prescription

Psychoactives such as Dexedrine, Librium, imipramine, Miltown, Secondal, Dalmane, chloral hydrate, methaqualone, phenobarbital, Tuinal, Amytal, diazepam and many others are available legally only when users obtain permission from a licensed physician. For such drugs a prescription is mandatory by law. Some reformers advocate shifting heroin, cocaine, cannabis and other illicit drugs from police to medical control. Since it is unfair to subject only certain psychoactives to prescription control, in this chapter I consider the potential impact of shifting every psychoactive to Rx status. Physician authorization on an individual basis would then be required before one could purchase, possess or use caffeine, nicotine, alcohol, aspirin or cocaine. If this system works for most sedatives, why should it not work for all sedatives, including alcohol and cannabis? But does it work? Before evaluating a uniform prescription-regime, it will be helpful to understand how the present prescription-only system started and how effective that system is in its limited form.

In 1900, with the exception of cocaine and opiates in some jurisdictions, all existing psychoactives could be obtained without physician approval. Drugs were frequently sold "on prescription," but such prescriptions were not like today's versions. Instead, prescriptions were voluntary and non-restrictive, like recipes. Once issued by a physician, these medicinal recipes could be used repeatedly by the initial customer or others. Pharmacists sometimes copied formulas and sold them as, say, "Dr. Smith's Cough Remedy," hence many physicians dispensed drugs directly.[1] Drugs that were prescribed could also be purchased without prescription. Since 1913, but mostly from about 1938 in the U.S. and 1940 in Canada, availability has been legally curtailed both for recreational and medical psychoactives. Now hundreds of psychoactives are either prohibited or made available only through physicians, who hold a legal monopoly as gatekeepers interposed between pharmaceutical producers and consumers.[2] While the laws creating mandatory prescription purport to protect the public interest, the evidence

151

available indicates that public protection does not justify mandatory prescription control of any drugs.

1. Drug Prescription and Medical Monopoly

a. Professional Hegemony

The laws and regulations establishing any profession's special status are invariably represented by the profession as guaranteeing competent service, facilitating access to such service, and promoting health, safety, fair prices or justice.[3] A substantial critical literature disputes such claims, and argues that the characteristic features of professionalism serve to further professional self-interest at the customers' expense.[4] This literature generalizes about the behaviour of professional groups and their organizing bodies. In all cases, diversity exists. Some physicians, for example, disapprove of their medical association's positions and would willingly abandon medicine's various legal monopolies. Some physicians refuse to prescribe any psychoactive drugs, except in emergencies. It is important to recognize and encourage such mavericks, yet we must realistically focus on general attitudes and average behaviors.

The "learned" professions such as law and medicine grew out of the medieval church, as close associates of the university and the landed aristocracy, and led a wave of professional formation in the mid-1800s. Since that period, professions have succeeded in expanding their power and influence. Several hypotheses attempt to explain this phenomenon. The public choice analyses of political decision making suggests that concentrated, producer groups such as plumbers, electricians or surgeons naturally dominate diffuse consumer groups in influencing legislation and, more importantly, in influencing the administration of laws.[5] Mancur Olson charts a consistent tendency among all producer groups to create monopolistic cartels so that given time, political stability and the absence of legal impediments, the rise of business, labour and professional cartels is inevitable.[6] According to Olson, public concern about incompetent or unethical practitioners provides "ideal cover" for forming a professional cartel. Industrial development is not a pre-condition of professionalism: witness India's occupational caste system, which is the end result of a thousand years of professionalism. Other explanations suggest that buoyant professionalism is a purely capitalist phenomenon, or that professionals seized on licensing laws to create occupational monopolies in order to counter-balance the growing power of large corporations.[7] Neither of these hypotheses satisfactorily explains why the relative dominance of a nation's medical profession appears closely related to national wealth rather than political structure. Economic development and political stability relate directly to the scope of medical powers in China and Cuba as well as in Canada, France and the United States.[8]

Every professional group pursues two goals: lessening competition and expanding their occupational field. Once the profession gains the ability to certify and, later, to license practitioners, control of the qualification procedure leads to market control. Over time the stringency of entry procedures increases: apprenticeship periods lengthen and become less financially rewarding; formal schooling is extended to accommodate a more academic curriculum and entry quotas are set. Critics charge that there is insufficient connection between medical school performance and competence in practice, that the curriculum is not always appropriate, that residency conditions discourage quality service and that a major objective of the process is to foster fraternal solidarity.[9] Concurrently, competitive techniques such as advertising, price cutting and innovation are made unethical or even illegal. The term "ethical drug" comes from the American Medical Association's 1847 code of ethics, which forbids advertising. The effect of this ban was probably to make "ethical drugs" more expensive than the "proprietary" medicines that were advertised. In states now prohibiting the advertising of eye glasses and related services, prices are 25% to 100% higher than in states without such "ethical" restrictions.[10] More to the point, a 1975 study in the U.S. estimated that restricted advertising of prescription drugs resulted in $400 million worth of higher prices.[11] A Canadian study of 13 major professions concluded that the average practitioner's earnings were increased 11.8% by fee schedules, 10.8% by advertising restrictions and 4.3% by barriers to interjurisdictional mobility.[12] Clients lack access to information about the relative competence of practitioners. In 1980 the AMA was sued by the Federal Trade Commission for injuring the public by conspiring to restrict physician advertising.[13]

Considerable evidence substantiates the claim that professional initiatives to restrict entry, fix prices, exclude competitors and repress internal criticism conflict with the medical profession's avowed fiduciary duty to clients. Numerous authorities report that the AMA and local medical organizations consistently work to the detriment of clients.[14] Olson advises that professional and government intervention in the medical care system "mainly helps physicians and other providers."[15] Professional self-regulation and physician-staffed disciplinary boards are exercises in conflict of interest: the profession usually unites against complaining clients.[16]

Medical professional bodies evidence standard monopolistic features. Indeed, the medical profession is often regarded as the leading model of professional hegemony.[17] The medical profession's special success is attributable in part to the rise of scientific medicine in the late 1800s, although the effectiveness of modern medicine has been exaggerated.[18] Evidence indicates that dramatic increases in medical input (hospitals, physicians, nurses, drugs) have not been matched by equivalent increases in health output.[19] John Knowles reports that half of the reduced mortality rate accomplished over the past 300 years was achieved prior to 1900. In the last 100 years, medicine contributed about 10% of the longevity gain. Furthermore, the nature of this gain is usually misunderstood or misrepresented: almost all of it occurs in childhood. Gains at ages 40, 50 or 60, when drug therapy intensifies, are minor.[20] (Of course, minor improvements generally can mean a great deal in single cases: without medical advances in chemotherapy for treatment of leukemia, for example, I would not have lived to age 40.) Finally, while much attention is paid to expensive technology and heroic surgery, Lewis Thomas argues that the most effective medicine is "relatively inexpensive, relatively simple, and relatively easy to deliver."[21] Nonetheless, a scientific core did provide a framework for professional unification. The mechanical germ theory of disease was, in Knowles' words "simple, unitary and compelling," and thus it meshed well with a growing faith in science and technology.[22] This mixture of science, superstition and professional hegemony is well illustrated by antibiotics.

Antibiotics, the fruit of scientific investigations, are dramatically effective, within limits, but are ritualistically and inappropriately prescribed. Though antibiotics entail some risk of adverse reactions, they are often prescribed needlessly for conditions they cannot effect. Internationally, Silverman reports that antibiotics are "among the most widely mispromoted, misprescribed and misused of all prescription drugs."[23] Similarly, mood-altering drugs developed in the 1950s were credited with emptying psychiatric hospitals and curing much mental illness, although total psychiatric beds increased along with the indices of mental illness. Ikegami reports that in Japan, the "greatest increase in psychiatric beds occurred at a time of wide-spread use of psychotropic drugs, regarded in many countries as instrumental in decreasing the in-patient population."[24] Officially, inmates in U.S. mental institutions fell from 550,000 in 1955 to 300,000 in 1975, but as Schrag reports, "vast increases in the resident population of nursing homes and halfway houses more than compensated for the decline."[25] By 1978, there were 1.8 million psychiatric clients treated in hospital and 4.9 million treated outside.

Professional organizations strive to exclude extra-professional competition. Lawyers compete with accountants, tax preparers, bankers, investment counsellors, real estate agents and social workers. Similarly, physicians compete in some aspects of their work with nurses, midwives, pharmacists, paramedics, priests, psychologists, and other counsellors. Physicians to date have managed to dominate the other health care professionals,[26] even in areas such as psychotherapy, counselling, birth and drug advising where physicians are not demonstrably superior providers of service.[27] With birth control, Paxman argues that "the requirement that a physician's prescription precede the issuance of oral contraceptives is still one of the single most effective limitations on roles for non-physicians."[28] One key to physician dominance is third party insurance coverage, which reimburses clients only for physician- provided services. Thus drug advice from a physician is covered by medical insurance, whereas consulting a pharmacologist results in out-of-pocket expenses.

Besides dominating related health care competitors, physicians have broadened the accepted definition of what constitutes a medical problem. Examples of medical colonization include the application of the disease model of inadvertent ailments to alcohol and tobacco use, and also to antisocial behaviour.[29] In an article entitled "Medicine as Patriarchal Religion", J. Raymond identifies a consistent tendency of physicians to appropriate greater chunks of life into the medical domain by means of "theological paradigms."[30] Medical imperialism in crime or drug control is not founded primarily on scientific understanding or effectiveness, but is rather the result of proselytizing, political control, ideological conviction and historical circumstances.[31]

The literature on professional aggrandizement raises suspicions about the supposedly essential nature of mandatory prescription. Since most professional prerogatives and legal privileges prove, on close inspection, to be self-serving, it is likely that mandatory prescription is no exception.

b. Prescribing Professional Advantage

As it happens, physicians did gain significant benefits from the move to mandatory prescription.

First, physicians expanded demand for their services. Prior to 1930, about 32% of medical sales involved prescription; after 1940, figures indicate a major shift, with Rx drugs comprising from 70% to 80% of all medical sales by 1980.[32] Economist Sam Peltzman calculates that prescription regulation doubled the demand for physician services.[33] From 1965 to 1978, U.S. domestic sales of Rx drugs increased 220% and exports grew by 560%.[34] Between 1950 and 1976, prescriptions per person per year in the U.S. increased from 2.4 to 6.9.[35]

Second, writing prescriptions was the kind of business general practitioners (GPs) wanted. Through to the early 1900s, the medical profession was fragmented, competitive, poorly paid and overcrowded. Thereafter, restricted entry, specialization and the growth of hospitals improved conditions for some physicians, but often not for the GP. Larson reports that by the late 1920s the GP was "increasingly marginal."[36] The subsequent economic depression put additional financial pressure on these small entrepreneurs of medicine. Mandatory prescription was a welcome antidote to the GP's plight. The same economic conditions are apparent today in less developed countries where poorly paid physicians "have a strong incentive to maintain a virtual monopoly over not only the prescribing of drugs but also over the dispensing of drugs."[37] To prevent clients from buying the recommended drug illegally, some physicians refuse to even identify the drug.

Prescribing is one of the easier medical tasks. GPs in the 1930s increasingly abandoned major surgery, obstetrics and specific dis-

156

ease groups to specialists; however, prescribing was a task they could readily handle. In 1940 a dozen or so substances accounted for most prescriptions. By 1941 the Food and Drug Administration's list of Rx drugs contained about 30 drug categories (of which only one is still considered effective). The ordinary medical practitioner treats primarily by prescribing drugs, seeing about 90 clients a week for an average of 15 minutes each.[38] Koumjian suggests that prescribing "simplifies practice."[39] The diagnosis that precedes prescription may be very difficult and time consuming, but prescribing is usually easy because the client's problem is routine, because the substance is given as a placebo, or because only symptomatic relief is provided. GPs write prescriptions more often than specialists, and more of these prescriptions involve psychoactive drugs.[40]

In the 1940s, the FDA prosecuted pharmacists in several key cases for selling Rx drugs OTC.[41] The pharmacists were convicted of selling misbranded drugs and of illegally practicing medicine.[42] Under the post-1940 system, pharmacists gained a near-monopoly role as prescription fillers. The financial gain this represented may have rendered the sacrifice of professional autonomy worthwhile. Most pharmacists are now overtrained for the routine role they play.[40]

As a third advantage, physicians are the gatekeepers on whom pharmaceutical manufacturers must focus their promotional resources. Physicians receive the flattering attention of sales representatives who supply gifts and sample products. Pharmaceutical firms sponsor symposia and conventions and fund research projects, many of dubious value.[44] The influence peddling here ranges from the innocuous to the corrupt, but in all cases physicians are the major beneficiaries. After chronicling the pharmaceutical industry's bribing of physicians, Silverman concludes that the benefit flow encourages staunch medical opposition to any significant reform of drug regulations.[45]

A fourth advantage of mandatory prescription for physicians is that it establishes them as the leading drug experts. Liberal, democratic logic prompts the following line of reasoning: physicians are the legally authorized gatekeepers; only the best qualified experts would be given such authority in an enlightened democracy; we live in an enlightened democracy: therefore physicians must be the

157

most qualified drug advisers. This reasoning is assailable on two grounds. First, the legislative process creates laws according to political influence not merit. That is, physicians bought mandatory prescription just as lawyers and other professions gained their legal entitlements, usually with no legislative debate, opposition or even notice. How was mandatory prescription enacted? In the U.S., a chemist employed by the Massengill Company fatally poisoned over 100 children by using diethylene glycol as a solvent in a sulfa preparation. This sulfanilamide incident is widely credited with inspiring the 1938 *Food, Drug and Cosmetic Act*.[46] The Act aimed to protect consumers by requiring pre-marketing proof of safety and more honest disclosure in labelling. No mention was made of Rx drugs. The Act, however, gave special status to all drugs labelled: "Caution: to be used by or on the prescription of a physician." Such drugs were exempted from the Act's labelling requirements. Drug producers found this exemption very useful. As Yingling points out, producers labelled products as prescription drugs "even though they contained ingredients which were readily available in the OTC market products."[47] Almost all new drugs, appearing at the rate of 50 per year in the 1950s and 20 per year in the 1960s, were marketed as prescription products. The exemption was also exploited by FDA administrators who decided that certain drugs were dangerous, and thus misbranded, if the "used on prescription" legend was missing. The FDA declared that "all drugs which may be dangerous to health unless used under appropriate supervision" would be misbranded without a prescription. This decision was formally approved by the *Humphrey-Durham Act* amendments in 1952.[48] At the 1951 Congressional hearings, witnesses claimed, without evidence, that regulating drug quality and safety was the same as restricting the public's right to self-medication. No consumer advocates appeared for the public. Physicians were the expert witnesses. But certain evidence raises doubts about the image of the expert, well-informed, scientific and altruistic prescribing physician. While some physicians are genuine drug experts and leaders in drug research, most are not dispassionate or well trained advisors in pharmacology; they rely unduly on industry sources for information and their incentives do not encourage restrictive prescription. Peter Dews, a professor of psychobiology at Harvard Medical School, concludes that the training physicians receive about drug action is an "overwhelming failure."[49]

Representing all physicians as drug experts creates a second myth about the power of medical supervision to transform "dangerous drugs" into life-saving medicines. This myth enjoys greatest currency in connection with psychoactive drugs. Substances such as the natural and synthetic opiates are either respectable medicines or dreadful scourges depending not on pharmacological properties, but on the legal and social status of the person giving the drug. This ruse is useful to physicians since it permits Rx distribution of popular drugs whose therapeutic value is indistinguishable from recreational and illicit drugs.[50] Since psychoactive drugs, as a class, tend to be euphoric, habit forming, teratogenic and health impairing, the physician's medical role as prescriber of such drugs is precarious. To bolster their position, physicians adopted a new role as drug control police, whereby psychoactive drug use becomes "medical" when it is purportedly limited in dosage, duration and purpose. An added objective of medical supervision is thus to prevent chronic or habitual use, and thereby avoid the social harms caused by "abuse" of psychoactives.

2. Police Power, Prohibition and Physicians

a. Drug Prohibition Prior to Mandatory Prescription

Prior to 1900, the burgeoning temperance movement against alcohol, as well as tobacco and opium, often conflicted with medical interests. Alcohol-and opiate-based medicines were widely prescribed.[51] Opium imports increased five fold between 1860 and 1900, by which time about 1.5 million Americans used the drug, many with medical encouragement.[52] A major obstacle for alcohol abolitionists was the opposition of the medical profession, according to Longmate, as growth of the temperance movement in the 1870s coincided with a "craze" for prescribing alcoholic medicines.[53] Organized medicine was ambivalent about the value of both tobacco and alcohol consumption. In 1922 the AMA held a referendum on alcohol Prohibition. Asked if whiskey was a "necessary therapeutic agent in the practice of medicine," 49% of physicians said no while 51% said yes.[54] The AMA eventually fought Prohibition, partly because the government restricted the capacity of physicians to prescribe alcohol.

Some analysts attribute early drug laws to non-medical

influences. According to Smart, Canada's *Proprietary and Patent Medicine Act* of 1908 was fueled largely by temperance groups offended by the alcohol content of many OTC panaceas.[55] Murray speaks of a "plurality of interests" behind the *Act* but he stresses the major role played by pharmacists and physicians who were losing revenue to patent medicine sellers.[56] Helmer similarly argues that the American *Pure Food and Drug Act* of 1906 reduced competition in the medical drug market and divided that market between physicians, the larger drug producers, and their go-betweens, the pharmacists.[57] The result was higher prices, not necessarily safer drugs. By 1900, eight states had prohibited sale of opiates and cocaine except when prescribed by a physician. Once in place, the federal prohibition of opium, and later of alcohol, led to recurrent enforcement crises which were countered by an escalation of police powers. Cashman cites examples such as Michigan's *Habitual Criminal Act*. This authorized life sentences after four convictions under the state's alcohol control law. Nearly 40% of all American federal prisoners in the 1920s were convicted under the *Volstead Act*, which prohibited the sale or distribution of alcohol.[58] Increased criminal law penalties led, in turn, to exaggerated vilification of drug offenders to justify the excessive penalties. This occurred more with opiate users than alcohol users because of the demographic transformation of the opiate user from a private, middle class, iatrogenic female consumer to a low class, urban male hustler.[59] The *Volstead Act* failed to generate the same effect because alcohol users remained a mainstream majority, despite Prohibition.

In the 1920s, prohibtion of alcohol and "narcotics" adversely affected physicians in various ways. Their prescription rights were abridged, and what was once accepted medical practice became a criminal offence. Under the U.S. *Harrison Act*, after 1919 thousands of physicians were charged with selling narcotics and many served prison terms.[60] This is ironic because the Act appeared at first to grant physicians a monopoly on the sale of opiates. A major Canadian court decision in 1928 paralleled American jurisprudence by confirming that control of morphine use was a police affair, and that medically prescribing morphine could be an offence.[61] After 1925, an amendment to the *Opium and Narcotic Act* made unlawful prescription an indictable offence in Canada, punishable by a minimum of three months imprisonment. Thousands of physicians and pharmacists in the U.S. were licensed to prescribe and sell liquor during Prohibition, but their discretion was restricted by the *Willis-Campbell Act* of 1921. Thus, the precedent was firmly established that legislators could restrict or prohibit use of popular and frequently prescribed medical substances.

Politicians and bureaucrats thus threatened physicians' livelihood and power. Apparently, drug prohibition interests were more powerful than medical interests. Even the normally influential lobbyists for brewers and distillers were unable to halt the 18th Amendment. Prior to 1930, physicians were still consolidating their professional position. Raising barriers to entry, closing medical schools, and creating other monopolistic devices required the cooperation of government because only the legislatures and courts could ultimately grant and protect such anti-competitive measures. Being dependent on the government for their profession's protected position meant that physicians could not hold the high ground in confrontations with law makers. Finally, physicians were seriously divided on the issue of prescribing opiates, alcohol and other dependency-inducing drugs. Many physicians wanted to distance themselves from the opiate- and alcohol-based preparations available on the commercial market. Physicians were also divided about the nature of opiate and alcohol addiction. One school held that addiction was a natural consequence of repeated drug consumption, and that opiate users were normal people often started on their habit by physicians. This school advocated continued prescription and voluntary withdrawal under medical supervision. The opposing schools held that opiate or alcohol addictions were functional diseases triggered by underlying mental disturbances. The American Association for the Cure of Inebriates was founded in 1870 to promote what would become the leading theory in the period from 1880 to 1915. This school advocated mandatory institutional treatment. This medical portrayal of opiate users as disturbed deviants lent support to law enforcement agencies propagating the myth that "addicts" were dangerous, compulsive persons requiring incarceration.[62]

As the political scapegoating of opiate users gathered strength, physicians' incentives became clearer. By diagnosing opiate users as diseased deviants, physicians could garner the support and cooperation of powerful law enforcement bureaucracies. Conversely, by arguing that opiate users were like other people and deserved access to their preferred drug, physicians would reap official condemnation. And, should they actually supply opiates, physicians could lose their license or face criminal charges. Given these incentives, most physicians understandably adopted the official line on narcotics.

b. Drug Prohibition After Mandatory Prescription

The legislative and judicial framework for prohibiting use of psychoactive drugs was entrenched by 1940. Politicians could thereafter add or subtract drugs from the list of prohibited substances as they saw fit. The creation of Rx drugs at the instigation of the medical lobby added a new category of almost-prohibited substances in what, I suggest, was partly an effort to pre-empt further political control of medical practice. Having removed the opiates and cocaine from medical practice, government could, with equal justification, remove barbiturates, amphetamines and all other psychoactives. A logical medical response to this danger was physicians' adoption of a quasi-police role whereby they would supervise the use of "dangerous" drugs and eliminate the possibility of indulgent recreational use. If successful, this quasi-police role would help physicians avoid further criminal prohibition of drugs and prevent new drugs from being added to the list of narcotics. This program naturally led to certain strategies.

First, all new psychoactives were developed and promoted as medicines. Had they been advertised as competitors to alcohol or cocaine, their use would have been prohibited. Second, the euphoric potential, addictive properties and long-term detrimental health effects of the new psychoactives were consistently underplayed.[63] When Timothy Leary started to publicize the euphoric, playful effects of LSD in the early 1960s, the drug's status as medicine was jeopardized, and eventually lost. As medicines, amphetamines were considered "remarkably safe" by physicians but later, as illicit drugs, their use reportedly created high mortality risk. Researchers now conclude that neither of these views are empirically valid.[64] Medical authorities confidently proclaimed that barbiturates, amphetamines and benzodiazepines, in their turn, were safe, non-addictive and of limited interest to potential drug "abusers." Their aim was to distinguish medical psychoactives from recrea-

162

tional drugs and from illicit narcotics. Perhaps the height of this deception occurred when synthetic opiates like methadone were substituted for morphine and heroin.[65] The third strategy was to gradually reassert the therapeutic properties of illicit drugs to enable physicians to reclaim some medical jurisdiction over heroin, cannabis, cocaine and the rest. In 1981, THC, the active ingredient in cannabis, was reclassified by the FDA as a Class C drug having "clinical applications."[66] In Canada, physicians successfully re-established their right to administer heroin in certain circumstances.

The second type of "dangerous" drugs that mandatory prescription was alleged necessary to control were substances that are toxic in small doses or that may adversely affect certain users. This maternalistic rationale creates negative incentives. If the medical monopoly is founded on clients' inability to protect themselves, then physicians can strengthen that justification by promoting client incompetence. Client vulnerability to drug-related harms can be encouraged in a number of ways. Ignorance about drugs can be maximized by prohibiting direct advertising, by avoiding package inserts or rendering them unintelligible, by choosing brand names, generic categories and classifications that are obfuscating, and by simply withholding information in the physician/client interview. Havighurst and King argue that through monopolistic controls, physicians have "found ways to limit the consumer's ability, either directly or through others acting on his behalf, to obtain, evaluate, and act on information."[67]

Client incompetence can also be increased by fostering a medical relationship built on faith and on clients' uncritical acceptance of "doctor's orders."[68] A vicious circle then develops: the client has faith and so feels no need to question the prescriber, this reliance deepens the client's ignorance, which increases the need for faith, further entrenching the client's vulnerability. Ironically, physicians' clients may know less about the drugs they are consuming than illicit consumers of the same substances. Since the illicit users operate independently of medical supervision, they require and hence develop an elaborate folklore of evaluative information. This non-medical pharmacopeia employs broader classifications ("uppers" and "downers") more accessible names ("bennies," "Yellow jackets," "speed") and less biased evaluations. The benzodiazepines, for example, were called "solid booze" years before medical

163

authorities admitted the equivalence between alcohol and diazepam. Similarly, while M.D.s in the 1950s insisted that barbiturates were safe drugs devoid of recreational potential, thousands of drug "abusers" knew otherwise.

3. Public Health and Safety

a. Dangerous Drugs and the Need for Medical Supervision

Potential dangers from drug use include accidental poisoning, adverse reactions, health impairment and habituation. Mandatory prescription is premised in large part on the existence of such dangers. The logical problem with such justification is that Rx psychoactives are no more or less dangerous than OTC or recreational drugs, whether licit or illicit, consumed by millions without benefit of physicians. Consider an example from each category: aspirin, alcohol and cannabis. Aspirin, one of the most potent OTC analgesics, is a leading cause of fatal poisonings, allergic reactions, ulceration, cardiac problems and hearing impairment. Alcohol is a potent central nervous system depressant that temporarily alleviates a variety of symptoms, but is a source of health impairment and premature death. Cannabis is apparently not as dangerous as alcohol or as habit forming, but its use too can be impairing. If aspirin, alcohol or cannabis had been developed after 1940 they would be Rx drugs.

Critics might reply that what we have here is not a logical failing but a political one, namely the incapacity of physicians to have aspirin, alcohol and other dangerous drugs reclassified Rx. This argument is unassailable, but it cannot be applied to recreational drugs because their legal status also depends on their alleged lack of therapeutic efficacy. If it is admitted that alcohol, cocaine, heroin, nicotine and caffeine are as dangerous and as therapeutically useful as the Rx psychoactives, then only two resolutions are possible. Either medical psychoactives should be available for purely social purposes, or current recreational drugs should be elevated to Rx status. The same logic applies to OTC formulations, which are often manufactured by prescription drug producers and may contain identical substances.[69]

Obviously physicians lack the power to reclassify alcohol as purely medical, and they would not want to declassify medical psychoactives because this would discredit current medical practice and reduce demand for medical service. There would also be a risk that declassified psychoactives such as diazepam would be redefined as "narcotics" and thus lost to medicine as heroin was in the 1920s. Since psychoactives do have valid therapeutic uses, such a prohibition would be a measurable loss. A rough stalemate therefore permits only minor changes, with some recreational drugs rehabilitated as medicines, some Rx drugs shifted to OTC or illicit status, while alcohol remains as neither drug nor medicine nor narcotic. To abandon this illogic is no easy matter because the legal status of drugs is now imbedded in the political structure.

b. Effects of Mandatory Prescription

Prescription controls are justified as being necessary to protect uninformed users from accidental harm, including fatal poisoning. Peltzman tested this hypothesis by comparing accidental poisoning rates in the U.S. before and after 1938 and by comparing countries that enforce prescription-only laws with countries that do not. According to Peltzman, "enforcement of prescription only regulation does not significantly improve the health of drug consumers — [and], if anything, poisoning mortality is higher than expected in countries which enforce prescription regulation."[70]

The explicit premise of compulsory medical supervision is that physicians' superior knowledge and expertise is required to reduce the excessive, foolish or inappropriate drug choices people would otherwise make. Unregulated users of OTC and recreational drugs do engage in a considerable amount of fruitless and even harmful drug consumption, including the "semi-religious" ritual of taking daily vitamins.[71] However, it is doubtful that physician control improves on that record. Brackings found that physicians are often in no better position than their clients to prevent or perceive drug-related injuries.[72] Temin concludes that physicians "cannot and do not make informed choices among competing drugs."[73] By scientific standards, physicians routinely overprescribe, even in the face of clear warnings about serious consequences.[74] The prescription of clioquinal (Entero-Vioform) in Japan, which led to perhaps the world's worst drug disaster, illustrates the limitations of physician supervision. Clioquinal was developed in California in the 1930s for amoebic dysentery. It was not useful for ordinary diarrhea or for prevention and, because of significant dangers, warnings were is-

165

sued by the developers not to use the drug for more than two weeks. Yet millions of Japanese were prescribed the drug from 1950 to 1970 and used it daily for extended periods. The damage award of nearly $500 million was paid by the Japanese government and the producer, Ciba-Geigy, not by physicians.[75]

Prescribing choices are strongly affected by fashions and medical customs often unrelated to therapeutic indications.[76] In addition, physicians are apparently as susceptible to commercial promotions as the public. The AMA argues that only physicians have the knowledge, ability and responsibility to decide about prescription drug use. In response, Mintz counters that physicians are uncritical, and ill-informed about drug dangers and "passionate" advocates of psychoactive drugs.[77] Silverman and Lee second this critical appraisal, noting that a lack of knowledge about drugs is the "greatest deficiency of the average American physician."[78] Layne adds that "the average physician's knowledge of medications is rather cursory compared to other health professionals."[79] Prescription control also appears to be an insufficient guard against either habitual use or self-poisoning.[80] Even the mere imposition of an intermediary may increase the potential for harm. A survey by *American Druggist Magazine* recently found that half of the respondent pharmacists had made dispensing errors because of physicians' sloppy handwriting.[81]

When reasons are sought for the poor performance of prescribing physicians, the following are often cited: inadequate medical training, the high volume of new products, drug industry inducements, over-eager and irresponsible clients, uncritical media praise of "miracle" drugs and the pressures of practice.[82] More basic critiques spotlight physicians' over-reliance on chemotherapy, their aggressive proselytizing of chemical solutions, and their use of drugs for inevitable events, such as pain and death, where treatment is often useless.[83] By exaggerating the merit of anti-infectives and by misrepresenting medical psychoactives as different in kind than recreational drugs, physicians probably increase drug consumption. From Britain, Prescott and Highley report that there is no evidence that regular use of psychoactive medicines aids those with social problems; indeed, "these drugs may be positively harmful."[84] A case in point is the controversial prescription to 40,000 Canadian children, mostly boys, of Ritalin.[85] Taken for "hyperactivity," Ritalin is an amphetamine-like drug popular among illicit users. Excessive prescribing may be one reason why a recent comparison study in the U.S. found that those with improved access to physicians and hospitals experienced worse health than those not provided free medical services.[86]

Whether physicians have led or merely responded to increased demand for drugs is not clear. Prescription drug sales have expanded faster than OTC or recreational drug sales, but this may be because most new drugs have been marketed under medical supervision. New prescription psychoactives may simply serve as substitutes for alcohol. Crutchfield and Gove argue that alcohol use can be characterized as "self prescribed medication aimed at inhibiting deterioration of the user's mental health."[87] It is therefore logical to assert that prescribed psychoactives can substitute for alcohol either recreationally or medically. Physician control will deter drug use insofar as it raises prices, impedes access and results in more cautious behaviour. On the other hand, physician control will promote drug use insofar as it results in subsidized costs, pro-drug advertising, unreasonable expectations, and incautious behaviour. While all these factors are operative, the promotional aspect of prescription controls seems to dominate. Layne's list of the effects of mandatory prescription include reinforcement of physicians' medical monopoly, increased cost of treatment, greater client dependency and an easier rationalization of excessive drug use.[88] Rosenberg observes that medical users of amphetamine "overlook the basic euphoria and sense of powerfulness that goes along with amphetamine use, believing instead that they are taking the amphetamine for weight reduction, or because the doctor prescribed it."[89] Examining the incentives to prescribing physicians helps explain why prescription controls do not function as a major restraint force.

c. Incentives for Prescribing Physicians

Physicians' prescribing deficiencies are often criticized as if mere reporting of the problem will result in remedial action. Medical students' lack of adequate pharmacological training has often been attacked in this manner.[90] Inadequate attention is paid to the incentives for prescribing physicians whereby it may not pay for them to be more knowledgeable about drugs.

Physicians rely primarily on the drug industry supplied *Physician's Desk Reference* in the U.S. and Canada, but even specialized researchers have difficulty acquiring information on comparative drug risks, benefits or costs. Since relevant information on Rx drugs is costly or inaccessible, physicians tend to prescribe according to "medical custom."[91] There are instrumental reasons why information about drugs is restricted. First, drug producers volunteer the minimum data required by law. When disclosure was not mandatory, as before 1906, almost nothing was disclosed. While certain states prohibited non-prescription sale of cocaine in 1900, cocaine use increased until 1906 because commercial remedies like Coca-Cola did not have to disclose their ingredients. Today, American and European pharmaceutical firms provide much less data about their products in countries with less stringent or less enforced regulations.[92] Producers minimize release of product information partly because drugs are often riskier than they first appear. Producers want to extol a drug's virtues and underplay its risks for commercial reasons.

Physicians will tend to share the producers' preference for limited information under an Rx system that makes physicians the prime beneficiaries of the industry. In addition, neither producer nor prescriber is anxious to be well-informed about negative consequences because such knowledge restricts business, increases the likelihood of being found negligent, and troubles the conscience. Antibiotics are frequently prescribed as placebos — over 60% were so used in one study — despite serious risks for users.[93] An ignorant physician can engage in such practice with less guilt than can a well-informed prescriber. Cynics suggest that physicians prescribe new drugs early and often before their dangers are exposed and their use limited or condemned.[94] Physicians' desire to ignore the fundamental similarities between Rx and non-Rx psychoactives also motivates them to curtail information about drugs.

Making drug assessment costly and difficult ensures that the public will not acquire such information and will be forced to rely on medical custom. Should a familiar, accessible and cheap source of information exist, clients could gain in independence at the loss of professional dominance. Clients, however, are not presently in a position to generate effective demand for such information because, even if they become better informed than their physician, they must still submit to medical supervision in choosing and acquiring Rx drugs: hence their rewards for learning about drugs are minimized. This does not apply to individuals who use Rx psychoactives for recreational purposes without physician approval, but as "criminals" their potential political opposition to mandatory prescription is weakened.

Acquiring skill or knowledge is costly. Just as drug producers provide only the information they are forced to give, physicians acquire only the skill level they are forced to have. Since they possess a monopoly, physicians are not forced by competitive pressures to provide high quality, cost-effective drug advising. According to one study, pharmacist supervision of prescribing led to a reduction in the use of inappropriate or unnecessary drugs and a lower level of adverse drug reactions. Pharmacists' drug advice is also considerably cheaper. Despite these and other similar results, physicians retain control.[95] One result for medical clients is higher costs — a natural consequence of systematically disabling the purchaser's decision-making capacity. A more important problem is higher health risks. Theoretically, the threat of tort or civil liability should deter careless, incompetent and negligent prescribing, but in practice, tort law generally fails to effect significant deterrence.[96] There are, in addition, a number of reasons why physicians are particularly unburdened by tort liability for prescription-related injury.

The first obstacle involves causation. Drug injuries are more difficult to recognize, diagnose, document or prove than ordinary physical injuries. Damage may be spread over generations, as is the case with DES or any teratogen.[97] Yet even when the causal connection is established, the manufacturer is held liable, not the prescriber, despite the fact that physicians are by law interposed between producer and consumer to take responsibility for preventing such damage.[98] Drug producers are often instructed by law to convey information about drug risks only to the prescriber. Inconsistently, physicians then argue that they cannot be held liable for their failure to fully inform clients of such risks.[99]

Physicians are also criticized for permissively prescribing according to client demands; a typical *Lancet* blame-the-patient editorial speaks of "patients, who may be reluctant to leave surgery or clinic without a prescription."[100] Fredman and Burger take the same line. They admit that physicians are the "drug middlemen for conventional middle-class America," but physicians, they claim, are just "eager to please": the impetus for over-prescribing "comes from the patients," and physicians give in to client demands for drugs because they lack the "time or ability to cure the psychosocial problems of their nonsick patients."[101] Why are medical experts seeing the "non-sick"? Worse, why are physicians knowingly "treating" what they cannot cure?

Some legal analysts, usually counsel to physicians or medical associations, are equally apologetic. Teff, for instance, declares that the invention of benzodiazepines meant physicians in 1974 "no longer felt compelled to prescribe barbiturates..."[102] Since barbiturates are almost entirely discredited as medicines, why were physicians once *compelled* to prescribe them? And why is it that physicians dominate their clients in all areas except drug prescribing? The evidence is actually more ambiguous. In an English study, more patients felt their physicians were too inclined to prescribe, rather than too reluctant. Other reports suggest that prescribing psychoactives worsens the physician-customer relationship and that customers are most satisfied with information, not drugs.[103] Some researchers found that the prescribing of psychoactive drugs was not based on client expectations.[104] Moore claims it "distresses" physicians to prescribe to opiate users who come seeking "not improvement, not a better life, not rehabilitation, but drugs to stick in their veins." Logically, physicians should be distressed by the continued prescription of any psychoactive, but such is not the case.[105]

While demand for tranquilizers and other psychoactives may be declining, it is still financially tempting to meet the demand. Furthermore, mandatory prescription amplifies the physician's incentive to prescribe. If prescriptions are optional and the physician advises against a drug on health or safety grounds, the determined client can purchase the product at a pharmacy. When prescriptions are mandatory, a frustrated client must seek another physician, and thus a reluctant prescriber is more likely to lose clients. In the first case the physician can afford to be more objective because what is being sold is information about drugs, not permission to take them.

Permissive prescribing is most attractive in the case of Rx psychoactives. Being no more dangerous than the alcohol consumed by millions of people throughout their lifetimes, the Rx psychoactives are relatively safe to prescribe. They are effective short-term symptom alleviators, and they are also habit forming, a trait that builds repeat clients. Cooperstock reports that most sedative/hypnotic Rx drugs are prescribed for much longer periods than indicated and that from 25% to 45% of medical users are dependent.[106] Again, the incentives foster relaxed prescribing. Refusing a client's request may send that client to a less reputable physician; perhaps a "super-prescriber" or "script doctor."[107] Or worse, the refused client may turn to illegal sources and so risk criminal penalties and injury from adulterated drugs. A reasonable physician may decide that moderately permissive prescribing is the best solution. One psychiatrist worries that desperate clients denied Valium might "steal tranquilizers, or they might *take to alcohol*, or they might lose their jobs, their families, their dignity. It is the *same dilemma* we faced with alcohol during Prohibition (emphasis added)."[108] What would change this calculation is a government enforced edict against certain drugs, as occurred with amphetamines in the early 1970s. The result was an immediate and drastic decline in amphetamine prescriptions.[109] Government enforcement resources are required to achieve such results because physicians lack the interest or capacity to control illicit sources or effectively police clients.

Arguments against self-medication are usually flawed because important variables are accepted as fixed factors. For example, consumers cannot make intelligent decisions now because information is scarce, sanctions against misinformation are ineffective, physicians promote client vulnerability and ignorance, tort liability is easily avoided, and pharmaceutical producers are improperly regulated. Attempts to remedy these specific problems without reference to an overall objective, like the primacy of self-medication, will probably stir up as much opposition as the more radical goal, but will accomplish less.[110]

4. Public Choice and Mandatory Prescription

Prescription control of all psychoactive drugs is administratively possible. Every drug would be available, but only for medically-approved use, like whisky as a sedative to be taken three times daily, with meals. Nicotine would still be taken, but probably as a pill or gum, not smoked. Opium, heroin, LSD, mescaline and MDMA would be taken therapeutically, as would laudanum, an old alcohol-opium favorite. Besides its Classic Coke, Coca-Cola could market a truly original version containing cocaine, but a prescription would be required. Aspirin, caffeine, nicotine, cannabis — all would be Rx drugs. The political question is: would voters willingly inflict an Rx control system on their own drug use?

A probable lack of public support for full prescription control is foreshadowed by a singular fact — only two types of psychoactives are normally assigned to medical monopoly. These are new drugs, like Valium, that initially lack an existing body of users to protest, and illicit drugs, like heroin, whose users are already severely criminalized. Reclassifying coffee, tobacco, aspirin, antihistamines and alcohol as "controlled substances" would cause great inconvenience. Under uniform prescription, recreational drug retailing would be transformed. Tobacco, coffee, and aspirin would be removed from grocery stores, restaurants, vending machines and even drug store shelves. Liquor stores would be converted into pharmacies. There would be no self-serve and no bulk buying. Persons with alcohol or other drug prescriptions would be limited to small, medicinal rations. Providing large amounts of caffeine or alcohol to wedding guests would become legally impossible: under current laws, prescribed drugs cannot be shared. Offering prescribed drugs to another person is, after all, tantamount to practicing medicine without a licence.

Some good news for consumers is that without punitive taxes, alcohol and tobacco prices would fall sharply. Government would not dare tax therapeutic chemicals like alcohol and nicotine any more than they now tax diazepam. But the bad news is that non-taxed prices would be countered by physicians and pharmacist's fees and by the major inconvenience of waiting to see overbooked medical doctors. Perhaps worse, every prescription seeker would face medical scrutiny. The nature of this medical interview would vary. With script doctors, the money-for-prescription transaction would be brief and relatively painless. But some physicians would insist on being convinced of a client's genuine medical need. In that case, drug users would have to couch their motives in therapeutic terms, a not impossible task given that "medicalese" is a fluid language. Millions would still take alcohol, caffeine and nicotine, but their intake would become therapeutic. Their drugs would relieve headache, help cope with depression, aid social adjustment, explore the subconscious, improve self-actualization, control mood swings, reduce aggression, increase assertiveness, ease pain, lessen anxiety or alleviate stress. Officially, no one would take drugs simply for fun: all use would be medically instrumental. Taverns would be transformed into group therapy centres with psychiatrists, nurses and sex therapists replacing bartenders and waiters. Drug spas would specialize in hallucinogenic "discover yourself" weekends. Uniform prescription would effect some positive changes, but even with liberal prescribing the program would not be very palatable. Presently, physicians prescribe Rx psychoactives mostly to children, young women and housewives. These are the least powerful groups in society, which is why their drug access was easiest to control medically. Users of recreational drugs are not so powerless. Users of alcohol, tobacco and coffee include most voters, most men, and occupational groups such as politicians, lawyers, accountants, business executives, truck drivers, unionized employees, and others who are as powerful as physicians. These groups will not willingly cede control of their traditional drug habits to physicians. For many drug users, the greatest cost of prescription alcohol would be submitting repeatedly as a humble petitioner before a physician for permission to do what is now a matter of personal choice.

Despite its high costs and its assault on personal privacy and autonomy, universal prescription would not provide sufficient protection against either self-harm or drug-related social harm. Physicians are ill-suited social protectors because they lack policing resources and the incentives to practice restrictive prescribing. Government stepped in to ration medical prescription of alcohol in the 1920s because physicians were not self-restrained. The same would occur in a uniform Rx system. As the sole gatekeepers of access to all psychoactives, physicians would stand to reap enormous monopoly profits. All drug producers would join pharmaceutical firms in bribing physicians with gifts, free samples, sponsored symposia in Hawaii, and "research grants" to test new drugs. At the same time, a black market in Rx drugs would flourish, and millions of illicit traders would practice medicine without a licence. Unless they prescribed permissively, physicians would risk losing control of the drug trade to organized crime.

Prescription controls would also fail to properly reduce self-harm. People willingly seek professional expertise for special knowledge or skill when errors would be costly. But most drug-taking poses few risks compared to surgery. Drugs also require little in the way of expert knowledge. Drug users take the same drugs repeatedly over many years and know what to expect. They learn drug lore from their parents and discuss drug effects at great length with their peers. In any case, under monopoly conditions physicians are not reliable or cost-effective sources of expertise, partly because of major conflicts of interest between physician and client. There is much evidence of abusive practice. Physicians over-promote drugs and psychotherapies that are unnecessary and counter-productive. Physicians in the 1970s treated 75% of their clients by drug prescriptions, the most prescribed drugs being tranquilizers, analgesics and sedatives.[111] Wohl estimates that about $21 billion is lost per year to "unnecessary drug-related hospitalizations."[112] Physicians are not disinterested scientists or public servants; they are members of powerful guild organizations designed to promote their pay, power, prestige and security. Loyalty to the guild usually supercedes loyalty to patients or the public. Medical priorities are evidenced in a number of revealing ways: by collusion among physicians not to testify in malpractice suits, by the reluctance of medical associations to remove or restrain all their unfit members, by anti-consumer lobbying, and by chauvinistic aggression against female patients. On the issue of drug information, for example, the AMA fought against a 1963 U.S. federal law requiring the publication of every medical drug's contraindications. In Crichton's words, for the past four decades "the American Medical Association has worked to the detriment of the patient in nearly every way imaginable."[113] There is no reason to expect better performance under a prescription control scheme.

Physicians, as noted, would face strong prescribe-or-perish incentives, primarily from black market pressures. Under prevailing laws, the pressures to prescribe are not effectively stymied by countervailing pressures. In particular, physicians are not made effectively liable for drug-related damage either caused or suffered by their clients. If prescribed Valium use causes harm, the physician who made that use possible is rarely forced to compensate the injured party. Since physicians reap the benefits of prescribing while avoiding most of the costs, they are encouraged to over-prescribe.

To control prescribing, government can set certain ceilings, as happened with alcohol prescribing in 1921, or establish punitive tax disincentives. Other strategies include compulsory no-fault liability prescriber's insurance or annual licence-to-prescribe fees. If these financial disincentives accurately reflected drug-related costs, physicians would refuse to prescribe any psychoactive except on an emergency basis for surgery or in hospital. Emergency-only prescribing would also protect people from self-harm and from damage caused by other Rx drug users. But while this would settle the medical issue, it would not settle the drug issue. Extreme medical restraint in prescribing psychoactives would fuel a pervasive black market. To limit the illegal market, physicians would need to prescribe generously. But they could not prescribe liberally and accept liability for drug-related damage, so physicians would have to prescribe only on condition that drug takers assume full responsibility for all damage. Such a condition, however, negates the rationale of compulsory prescription, namely that physicians will take responsibility.

Physicians should rarely act as police agents. Their medical duty is owed to their clients, not to government. But because physicians lack the resources to enforce a prescription-only system, they would be forced to enlist government assistance; hence physicians could succeed as social protectors in the drug field only if they operated alongside law enforcement agencies. Such a partnership is unstable, however, because government can administer effective drug controls without assistance from medical associations.

In summary, mandatory prescription for all psychoactive drugs is a high cost/low benefit system that does not adequately respect individual autonomy. The high costs follow naturally from organized medicine's monopolistic practices and from the cumbersome, inefficient mode of administration. Psychoactive drugs are taken daily by the majority of adults. To funnel each drug user through periodic medical interviews would be expensive and time consuming. The system's low benefits are due to a number of factors including physician's inability to significantly reduce drug use, control black markets, compensate injured parties, or inform users about risks. Finally, medical control of drug use is an excessive limitation of personal autonomy. Public surveys would clearly indicate that caffeine, aspirin, alcohol and nicotine users generally do not want compulsory medical intervention in their drug affairs. They may want cannabis or cocaine to be Rx drugs, but if prescription-only alcohol is the price they have to pay, the majority of voters would just say no.

Notes

1   Peter Temin, *Taking Your Medicine - Drug Regulation in the United States*, (Harvard University Press, 1980) 22-23.

2   H. Grabowski & J. Vernon, *The Regulation of Pharmaceuticals* (American Enterprise Inst.: Washington, 1982).

3   See Jethro Lieberman, *The Tyranny of the Experts* (New York: Walker & Co., 1970) 12-14; Temin, *supra* note 1, 21.

4   A well-documented critique of medical controls is found in C. Baron, "Licensure of Health Care Professionals: The Consumer's Case for Abolition" (1983) 9 *American Journal of Law & Medicine* 334. Also recommended is R. Hamowy, *Canadian Medicine - A study in restricted entry* (Fraser Institute, 1985). See also Magali Larson, *The Rise of Professionalism* (University of California Press, Berkeley 1977); Philip Elliot, *The Sociology of the Professions* (Macmillan, 1972); I. Illich, *et al.*, *Disabling Professions* (London: Marion Boyars, 1977); S. Shortt, "Physicians, Science and Status: Issues in the Professionalization of Anglo-American Medicine in the Nineteenth Century", (1983) 27 *Medical History* 51.

5   See, for example, Dewees, Mathewson & Trebilcock, "The Rationale for Government Regulation of Quality", in *The Regulation of Quality* D. N. Dewees (ed) (Toronto: Butterworths, 1983) 20-23.

6   Mancur Olson, *The Rise and Decline of Nations* (Yale University Press, 1982) 37, 44, 86.

7   See H. Waitzkin & B. Waterman, *The Exploitation of Illness in a Capitalist Society* (1974); Temin, *supra* note 1, 21.

8   Ivan Illich, *Limits to Medicine* (1976) 70-74. Ugalde cites evidence from China, Cuba, Honduras and elsewhere regarding the "almost total control" physicians exercise over health policy and the promotion of their own economic interests that this control allows. A. Ugalde, "Physicians' Control of the

Health Sector: Professional Values and Economic Interests - Findings from the Honduran Health System", (1980) 14 *Social Science & Medicine* 435. On the relationship between GNP and "health" spending, see J.P. Newhouse, "Medical Care expenditure: a cross national survey", (1976) 12 *Journal of Human Resources* 1.

9 See Andrew Allentuck, *The Crisis in Canadian Health Care*, Chapter 8 (Toronto: Burns & MacEachern, 1978); Michael Crichton, *Five Patients - The Hospital Explained* (New York: Knopf, 1970) 202; Robert Mendelsohn, *Confessions of a Medical Heretic* (New York: Contemporary Books, 1979) 130, 160.

10 L. Benham, "The Effect of Advertising on the Price of Eyeglass", (1972) 15 *Journal of Law & Economics* 340, 345.

11 J. Cady, *Drugs on the Market* (Lexington: Heath, 1975) and *Restricted Advertising and Competition: The Case of Retail Drugs* (Washington: American Enterprise Institute, 1976).

12 See, M. Trebilcock, "Regulating Service Quality in Professional Markets" in *The Regulation of Quality* (1983) D. Dewees (ed) 102. On the benefits of medical competition, see also Paul J. Feldstein, *Health Care Economics* (New York: Wiley, 1979).

13 See R. Kraft, "Attitudinal and Legal Factors in Professional Advertising", (1985-86) 1 *Journal of Law & Health* 61, 64.

14 See, for example, Howard & Martha Lewis, *The Medical Offenders* (New York: Simon & Schuster, 1970) 294-305; Crichton, *supra* note 9, 62; E. Cray, *In Failing Health - The Medical Crisis and the AMA* (New York: Bobbs-Merrill, 1970); J. Knowles, "The Responsibility of the Individual" in *Doing Better and Feeling Worse* J. Knowles, (ed) (New York: W. W. Norton, 1977) 76.

15 Olson, *supra* note 6, 174; also *A New Approach to the Economics of Health Care* M. Olson (ed), (Washington, 1982).

16 H. Cohen, "On Professional Power and Conflict of Interest: State Licensing Boards on Trial" (1980) 5 *Journal of Health*

Politics, Policy and Law 291; Robert McCleery, *et al.*, *One Life - One Physician* (Washington: Public Affairs Press, 1971); Lewis & Lewis, *supra* note 14, 29; D. Beveridge, "Regulation of the Medical Profession in Nova Scotia" (1979) 5 *Dalhousie Law Journal* 518, 529.

[17] An early and influential work on the subject is E. Freidson, *Professional Dominance: The Social Structure of Medical Care* (1970). See also Zola, "Medicine as an Institution of Social Control" (1972) 20 *Sociological Review* 3; L. Doyal, *The Political Economy of Health* (1979); T. McKeown, *The Role of Medicine* (1979); I. Kennedy, *The Unmasking of Medicine* (1981); J. Ladd, "Physicians and Society: Tribulations of Power and Responsibility" in *The Law - Medicine Relation: A Philosophical Exploration* S. Spicker, J. Hallway, H. Engelhardt (eds),(1981) 33,41; Paul Starr, *The Social Transformation of American Medicine* (1982).

[18] See L. LaSagna, *The Doctor's Dilemma* (1962) 154: L. Tushnet, *The Medicine Men* (New York: St. Martin's Press,1971) 12-16, 84-86; Crichton, *supra* note 9, ix.

[19] M. Tonkin, "South Africa - A Nation of Pill Swallowers?" ISMA Paper #35, July 1977, 9.

[20] Knowles, *supra* note 14, 57; T. McKeown, *The Modern Rise of Population* (Toronto: MacMillan, 1976); L. Schuman, "Smoking as a risk factor in longevity" 204 in *Aging: A Challenge to Science and Society* D. Danon, N. Shock & M. Marois (eds) (Oxford University Press, 1981) 204; Fries & Grapo, "Physiologic Aging & The Compression of Morbidity" Conference on Health in the 80s and 90s (Council of Ontario Universities 1982) 87; Wildavsky, "Doing Better and Feeling Worse: The Political Pathology of Health Policy" 105, and Eisenberg, "The Search for Care" in Knowles, *supra* note 14, 235. For a thorough view of the impact of anti-infective medication see M. Silverman and P. Lee, *Pills, Profits and Politics* University of California Press, (1974) 7-12.

[21] Lewis Thomas, *The Lives of a Cell* (New York: Macmillan, 1974) 35.

22 See Kissam, "Government Policy Toward Medical Accreditation and Certification: The Antitrust Laws and Other Procompetitive Strategies" (1983) *Wis. Law Review* 1, 21-27.

23 See Tushnet, *supra* note 18, 196-197; Silverman *et al. supra* note 37, 19-20.

24 N. Ikegami, "Growth of Psychiatric Beds in Japan" (1980) 14A *Social Science & Medicine* 561. See also M. L. Gross, *The Psychological Society* (New York: Random House, 1978) 7.

25 P. Schrag, *Mind Control* (New York: Pantheon Books, 1978) 38.

26 Physicians are the only class of health professional whose licenses are unlimited. In addition, laws often compel clients to accept a physician overseer in addition to the other health professional providing primary service. However, since 1975 physician organizations have faced increased anti-trust actions from competitors such as chiropractors. A. Dolan, "Antitrust Law and Physician Dominance of Other Health Professionals" (1980) 4 *Journal of Health Politics, Policy and Law* 675, 681-683. Also, G. Heitler, "Health Care and Antitrust" (1983) 14 *University Tol. Law Review* 577; C. Weller, "The Primacy of Standard Antitrust Analysis in Health Care" (1983) 14 *University of Tol. Law Review* 609.

27 See, generally, Tushnet, *supra* note 18, 102-104; Rogers, "The Challenge of Primary Care" in Knowles, *supra* note 14, 81,99. On the effectiveness of psychotherapy see the survey of literature in C. Mitchell, "Culpable Mental Disorders and Criminal Liability", (1985) 8 *International Journal of Law & Psychiatry* 273. On birth and the merits of physicians versus midwives and others see G. Lorea, *The Hidden Malpractice* (New York: William & Morrow,1977); R. Mendelsohn, *Malepractice* (Chicago: Contemporary Books, 1980); *Seizing Our Bodies - The Politics of Women's Health* C. Dreifus (ed) (New York: Vintage Books, 1978).

28 J. Paxman, "Roles for Non-Physicians in Fertility Regulation. An International Overview of Legal Obstacles and Solutions", (1980) 70 *AJPH* 31, 32.

29 Fox, "The Medicalization and Demedicalization of American Society", in Knowles, *supra* note 14, 9, 11, 18; Tournier, "The Medicalization of Alcoholism: Discontinuities in Ideologies of Deviance", (1985) 15 *Journal of Drug Issues* 39; Poikolainen, "Alcoholism: A Social Construct", (1982) 12 *Journal of Drug Issues* 361.

30 J. Raymond, "Medicine as Patriarchal Religion" (1982) 7 *Journal of Med. & Phil.* 197. See also Koumjian on the medicalization of minor problems such as anxiety and the growth of dependency on symptomatic "medical" treatments such as tranquilizers and on the sedation of elderly nursing home residents as a service to their caretakers. Koumjian, "The Use of Valium as a Form of Social Control" (1981) 15 *Soc. Sci. Med.* 245.

31 See, for example, H. Lennard, *et al.*, *Mystification and Drug Misuse* (1971); MacNamara, "The Medical Model in Corrections", (1977) 14 *Criminology* 439; Morse, "The Twilight of Welfare Criminology", (1976) 49 *South California Law Review* 1253; Ericson, "Penal Psychiatry in Canada: The Method of Our Madness," (1976) 26 *University of Toronto Law Journal* 17; Reisner & Semmel, "Abolishing the Insanity Defense", (1974) 62 *California Law Review* 753, 776; Martinson, "What Works", (1974) *The Public Interest* 35; Wilson, "What Works? Revisited: New Findings on Criminal Rehabilitation," (1980) *The Public Interest* 3.

32 Figures from Temin, *supra* note 1, 3-4.

33 Sam Peltzman, "The Health Effects of Mandatory Prescriptions", (1987) 30 *Journal of Law and Economics* 207-38.

34 Wertheimer, "An Empirical Overview of the Prescription-Drug Market" in *Society and Medication* J. Morgan and D. Kagan (eds) (Mass.: Lexington Books, 1983) 3, 4.

35 Rabin, "Variations in Physician Prescribing Patterns" in *Society and Medication, ibid.*, 17.

36 Larson, *supra* note 4, 165.

37 See M. Silverman, P. Lee, M. Lydecker, *Prescription for Death - The Drugging of the Third World* (University of California Press, Berkeley, 1982) 90-92.

38 See Koumjian, *supra* note 30, 248; Temin, *supra* note 1, 118; J. Graedon, *The People's Pharmacy* 3 (New York: St. Martin's Press, 1976).

39 Koumjian, *ibid.*, 249.

40 See Cooperstock, "Current Trends in Prescribed Psychotropic Drug Use", (1977) 3 *Research Adv. in Alcohol & Drug Problems* 297, 299.

41 *United States* v. *Sullivan*, 67 F. Supp. 192 (M.D. Ga., 1946); reversed, 161 F.2d 629 (C.C.A. 5, 1947); reversed, 332 U.S. 689 (1948). *United States* v. *Marmola Prescription Tablets* 48 F. Supp. 878 (W.D. Wis., 1943); affirmed, 142 F.2d. 107 (C.C.A. 7, 1944).

42 Layne, "Restricting Access to Non-Psychoactive Medications: Public Health Necessity or Disabling Professional Prerogative", (1984) *Journal of Drug Issues* 595, 599. Not surprisingly, physicians who own an interest in a pharmacy or drug supply firm prescribe at above-average rates. Lewis & Lewis, *supra* note 14, 105.

43 For a critical view of pharmacists' knowledge and skill, see G. Banes & N. Chappell, "Pharmacists' Knowledge of the Area of Alcohol, and Alcohol and Drug Interactions" (1981) 15A *Soc. Sci. Med.* 649. The study, however, did not compare pharmacists with physicians.

44 See Richard C. Stroeder, *The Politics of Drugs* (1980) 105, 156. Reportedly, American physicians receive 2 billion free drug samples a year, many of which are given to clients. See also Illich, *supra* note 4, 72, 76; Temin, *supra* note 1, 118.

45 Silverman *et al.*, *supra* note 37, 120-8; Senator Mike Gravel, "Corporate pushers: the only thing amusing about the ethical drug industry is its name", in D. Smith, D. Wesson (eds) *Uppers and Downers* (1973) 124-127.

[46] J. Tyrone Gibson, *Medication Law and Behaviour* (New York: John Wiley & Sons, 1976) 12-15.

[47] Yingling, "Does Self-Medication have a Role in Our Society", 36 (1981) *Food, Drug, Cos. Law Journal* 604, 614.

[48] See Trade Correspondence note in Kleinfeld & Dunn, *Federal Food, Drug and Cosmetic Act* (1938-1949) 561; Peltzman, *supra* note 33.

[49] J. Dekkanen, "The Impact of Promotion on Physician's Prescribing Patterns" (1976) *Journal of Drug Issues* 6.

[50] G. Jonathan, *Tranquilizers* (London: Tavistock, 1986); R. Caplan, *Tranquillizer Use and Well Being* (University of Michigan, Survey Research, 1984); Cooperstock, *supra* note 40, 303-305.

[51] H. Teff, *Drugs, Society and the Law* (1975) 9.

[52] J. Rublowsky, *The Stoned Age - A History of Drugs in America* 122 (New York: Putnam, 1974).

[53] Allan Chase, *The Biological Imperative* (New York: Holt, Rinehart & Winston, 1971) 207. Opium, morphine, injected morphine and opium were, in turn, judged non-addictive by medical authorities.

[54] N. Longman, *The Water Drinkers*, (1968) 172.

[55] S. Goldberg, "Putting Science in the Constitution: The Prohibition Experience" in *Law, Alcohol, and Order* D.E. Kyvig (ed)(Conn.: Greenwood Press,1985) 27-28.

[56] G. Murray "The Road to Regulation: Patent Medicines in Canada in Historical Perspective" in *Illicit Drugs in Canada* (1988) 72, 86.

[57] See J. Helmer, *Drugs and Minority Oppression* (New York: Seabury Press, 1975) 36.

[58] S. Cashman, *Prohibition - The Lie of the Land* (New York: Free

Press, 1981) 205-207. See also R. Solomon, "Regulating the Regulators: Prohibition Enforcement in the Seventh Circuit" in *Law, Alcohol and Order, supra,* note 53, 81.

59   David Courtwright, *Dark Paradise - Opiate Addiction in America Before 1940* (Harvard University Press, 1982) 113,126,147. In contrast, Helmer argues that even before 1920 the opiates were mostly a lower-class habit. Helmer, *supra* note 57, 7.

60   T. Szasz, *Ceremonial Chemistry* (1974) 150. On parallel developments in Britain see, V. Berridge, "Drugs and Social Policy: The Establishment of Drug Control in Britain 1900-30" (1984) 79 *British Journal Of Addiction* 17.

61   *R* v. *Gordon* (1928), 49 C.C.C. 272 (Calgary Dst. Ct.).

62   Helmer, *supra* note 57, 126, 130, 140-44.

63   See S. Fredman & R. Burger, *Forbidden Cures* (New York: Stein & Day, 1976) 174.

64   Kalant & Kalant, "Death in Amphetamine Users: Causes and Estimates of Mortality" (1976) 3 *Research Ad. in Alcohol & Drug Problems* 317.

65   See for example Moss, "Methadones's Rise and Fall" and Dumont, "The Politics of Drugs", in *Drugs & Politics* Paul Rock (ed), (New Jersey: Transaction Books, 1977); P. Kleinman, I. Lukoff and B. Kail, "The Magic Fix: A Critical Analysis of Methadone Maintenance Treatment" (1977-78) 25 *Social Problems* 208.65.22.

66   N. Angier, "Marijuana: Bad News and Good" *Discover* August 1981, 15. Also J. Zentner, "Heroin: Devil Drug or Useful Medicine" (1979) *Journal of Drug Issues* 335.

67   C. Havighurst & N. King, "Private Credentialing of Health Care Personnel: An Antitrust Perspective" (1983) 9 *American Journal of Law & Medicine* 263, 293.

68   An interesting exploration of the physician - client relation-

ship is found in Jay Katz, "Acknowledging Uncertainty: The Confrontation of Knowledge and Ignorance" in *The Silent World of Doctor and Patient* (New York: Free Press, 1984). But for a more critical and insightful analysis see J. Haber "Patients, Agents and Informed Consent", (1986) 1 *Journal of Law & Health* 43.

[69] Silverman & Lee, *supra* note 20, 217-27. See also, Vener, Krupka & Climo, "Drugs (Prescription, Over-the-Counter, Social) and the Young Adult: Use and Attitudes" (1982) 17 *International Journal of Addiction* 399, 400.

[70] Peltzman, *supra* note 33, 229.

[71] See Graedon, *supra* note 38, 3-7; Silverman & Lee, *supra* note 20, 207-229; John Fried, *The Vitamin Conspiracy* 184 (1975); see also J. Levy & P. Bach-y-Rita, *Vitamins - Their Use and Abuse* (New York: Liveright, 1976).

[72] Brackings, "The Liability of Physicians, Pharmacists, and Hospitals for Adverse Drug Reactions" (1985) 34 *Defense Law Journal* 273, 279, 332.

[73] Temins, *supra* note 1, 119.

[74] See Silverman & Lee, *supra* note 20, 15, 22, 82, 296, 301; Mendelsohn, *supra* note 9, 32; Graedon, *supra* note 38, 3, 37, 47; M. Mintz, *The Therapeutic Nightmare* (1965) 217.

[75] Silverman, *et al.*, *supra* note 37, 75.

[76] Tushnet *supra* note 18, 199-203; Temin, *supra* note 1, 118.

[77] Mintz, *supra* note 74, xiii, 73, 76, 86, 185, 217.

[78] Silverman & Lee, *supra* note 20, 50, 203.

[79] Layne, *supra* note 42, 602.

[80] Illich, *supra* note 4, 70 where the author claims that for newer psychoactive "medicalized addiction" by 1975 had outgrown self-directed addiction.

[81] Feldman, "The Handwriting is On the Wall", (1983) 11 *Legal Aspects of Medicine* 8.

[82] Silverman & Lee, *supra* note 20, 301-303. "Ontario plan accused of paying for ineffective, toxic medication", *Globe & Mail* February 10, 1988, A5.

[83] Mendelsohn, *supra* note 9, 46; Illich, *supra* note 4, 93, 105-112.

[84] L. Prescott & M. Highley, "Drugs prescribed for self poisoners" (1985) 290 *Br. Medical Journal* 1633, 1635.

[85] "Questions about a drug" *Maclean's* June 5, 1988, 10.

[86] Diehr, *et al.*, "Increased Access to Medical Care - the Impact on Health", (1979) 17 *Medical Care* 989.

[87] R. Crutchfield & W. Gove, "Determinants of Drug Use: A Test of the Coping Hypotheses", (1984) 18 *Soc. Sci. Med.* 503.

[88] Layne, *supra* note 42, 605.

[89] Rosenberg, "The Abusers of Stimulants and Depressants" in *Types of Drug Abusers* (1973) Cull and Hardy (eds.), 125. See also J. Kramer & R. Pinco, "Amphetamine use and misuse: a medicolegal view" in D. Smith & D. Wesson (eds) *Uppers and Downers* (New Jersey: Prentice-Hall, 1973) 10-11.

[90] Physicians enter practice "with limited training in the field of psychoactive substance abuse." Smith and Seymour, "Prescribing Psychoactive Drugs. A Question of Perspective", in *Society and Medication, supra* note 34, 187; see also S. Grossman & V. Sheidler, "Skills of Medical Students and House Officers in Prescribing Narcotic Medications" (1985) 60 *J. Med. Ed.* 552; M. Gosney & R. Tallis, "Prescription of Contraindicated and Interacting Drugs in Elderly Patients Admitted to Hospital", *The Lancet*, September 8, 1984, 564.

[91] Temin, *supra* note 1, 9, 89, 119. Since prescribing choices are based, in part, on custom, different countries naturally evidence variations in medical customs about drugs. See, Cooperstock, *supra* note 40, 302.

[92] See "Druggists to the third world" *The Economist* March 12, 1983, 90-91; Silverman, Lee & Lydecker, *Prescriptions for Death, supra* note 37, 97-117; M. Muller, *The Health of Nations: A North-South Investigation* (London: Faber & Faber, 1982).

[93] Silverman & Lee, *supra* note 20, 289. Studies show vast differences between hospitals in their rate of antibiotic use; a fact that probably illustrates variations in "medical customs."

[94] Mendelsohn, *supra* note 9, 32.

[95] McGhan and Stimmel, "The Pharmacist as Prescriber", in *Society and Medication, supra* note 34, 120.

[96] Pierce, "Encouraging Safety: The Limits of Tort Law and Government Regulation", (1980) 33 *Vand Law Review* 1281; Teff, *supra* note 51, 114-115; Trebilcock, "Regulating Service Quality in Professional Markets", and Hirshhorn, "Regulating Quality in Product Markets" in *The Regulation of Quality* (1983) 83, 89 and 53, 61.

[97] Trauberman, "Statutory Reform of 'Toxic Torts': Relieving Legal, Scientific and Economic Burdens on the Chemical Victim", (1983) 7 *Harv. Env. Law Review* 177); Stapleton, "Compensating Victims of Diseases" (1985) 5 *Oxford Journal of Legal Studies* 248-253; Rosenberg, "The Causal Connection in Mass Exposure Cases: A 'Public Law' Vision of the Tort System", (1984) 97 *Harvard Law Review* 849, 900-05; W. Freedman, *Products Liability* (1984) 25-27.

[98] Britain, "Product Honesty is the Best Policy: A Comparison of Doctors and Manufacturers' Duty to Disclose Drug Risks and The Importance of Consumer Expectations in Determining Product Defect", (1984) 79 *N.W. Law Review* 342, 369; Fern & Sichel, "Evolving Tort Liability Theories: Are They Taking the Pharmaceutical Industry into An Era of Absolute Liability?" (1985) 29 *St. Louis University Law Journal* 763; Epstein, "The Legal and Insurance Dynamics of Mass Tort Litigation" (1984) *Journal of Legal Studies* 475. In Epstein's article the liability of the prescriber is not even mentioned. As Layne notes, responsibility for misuse of Rx drugs "does not fall squarely on

either the physician's or the consumer's shoulders." Layne, *supra* note 42, 601.

[99] Britain, *ibid.*, 368, 375. Lavigne, "Pill warnings up to doctors, court told" The *Globe & Mail*, September 4, 1985, 23.

[100] "Feedback on Prescribing" *The Lancet*, February 11, 1984, 320.

[101] Fredman & Burger, *supra* note 63, 186.

[102] Teff, "Products Liability in the Pharmaceutical Industry at Common Law" (1974) 20 *McGill Law Journal* 102, 113.

[103] Wartman, *et al.*, "Do Prescriptions Adversely Affect Doctor-Patient Interactions?" (1981) 71 *AJPH*, 1358. See also Tushnet, *supra* note 18, 202; Allentuck, *supra* note 9.

[104] R. Hadsall, R. Freeman & G. Norwood, "Factors Related to the Prescribing of Selected Psychotropic Drugs by Primary Care Physicians", (1982) 16 *Soc. Sci. Med.* 1747.

[105] See Moore, Review Essay, (1984) *Am. Bar. Found Res. Journal* 723, 728; P. Goring, "Drugs and Madness" in E. Bates and P. Wilson (eds.) *Mental Disorder or Madness?* (University of Queensland Press, 1979) 217-233.

[106] Cooperstock, "Some comments on the Clinical Appropriateness of Prescribing Psychoactive Drugs", in *Society and Medication* (1983) *supra* note 34, 158.

[107] See Lewis & Lewis, *supra* note 14, 149; Smith and Seymour, *supra* note 90, 193. One study found that half of the excessive-quantity prescriptions from one clinic were written by 3.4% of the physicians. See, Silverman & Lee, *supra* note 20, 296-298.

[108] S. Rosenblatt & R. Dodson, *Beyond Valium - The Brave New World of Psychochemistry* (New York: Putnams, 1981) 210.

[109] The legislative restriction of amphetamine prescription in Canada in the early 1970s resulted in a 90% decline in con-

sumption. Cooperstock, *supra* note 40, 302. On the US situation see Rosenblatt & Dodson, *ibid.*, 234.

[110] T. Szasz, "The Ethics of Addiction" (1971) 128 *American Journal of Psychiatry* 541-546.

[111] Graedon, *supra* note 38, 3-4.

[112] S. M. Wohl, *The Medical Industrial Complex* (New York: Crown, 1984) 182.

[113] Crichton, *supra* note 9, 62.

VI Private Law Deterrence and Compensation

Prohibition and mandatory prescription are intrusive, expensive methods of drug control. Private law is much less intrusive and costly and, would probably prove more popular as a uniform drug control system than either medical or police controls. But to date, no one has seriously explored the regulative potential of private law in the drug field. Most people know little about private law, while analysts like Kaplan and Richards quickly dismiss private law as too limited or too weak to deal with difficult drug problems. The neglect of private law is also encouraged by influential legal authorities who lament the "appalling inefficiency and ineffectiveness" of private law as an agency of social engineering.[1] Before writing off tort and contract law, however, a distinction should be drawn between the confused and biased state of private law today and the potential impact of a rejuvenated system.

1. The Nature of Private Law

As in the previous two chapters, my aim here is to examine private law in isolation, as if it were the only source of legal intervention affecting drugs. This means wiping the slate clean of hundreds of public laws dealing with drugs. Specifically, a full private law system would do without criminal prohibitions, rationing, liquor licenses, age restrictions, advertising bans, tax disincentives and public agencies overseeing drug testing, labelling and quality control. Private law would also preclude public subsidies to tobacco farmers or other drug producers.[2] As to what a private law world would contain, consider some possible drug-related law suits: tobacco producers sued by millions of customers for negligent failure to warn of risks; employers and restaurants sued for permitting employees or customers to be harmed by sidestream smoke; taverns sued for damage caused by or suffered by inebriated patrons; insurance firms suing alcohol and diazepam producers for the $30 billion cost of drug-related automobile claims in 1990; municipal governments suing opiate producers for drug-related crime, and parent groups suing distillers for not providing alcohol in childproof containers. This brief list of possible law suits should indicate that for some drug-related activities private law can have a major impact.

Contract law and tort law are the two areas of private law relevant to drug control. Contract law involves private agreements that the state helps enforce. A buyer orders LSD, but receives mescaline and amphetamine from the seller. This looks like a breach of an ordinary sales contract, with the seller liable to compensate the aggrieved buyer for certain losses or injuries. Taking a second example, Giant Tobacco Corp. publicly claims that its cigarets do not cause cancer among users. Ten thousand smokers of its leading brand die from tobacco-induced cancers in 1990. This is a breach of contract, and it is also a tort. Torts are general wrongs not dependent on special agreements. In effect, tort law establishes every citizen's legal obligations as part of a social contract. If legal obligations are breached by the commission of a tort, the wrongdoer or "tortfeasor" is liable to legal action. Both contract law and tort law are fault-based systems. Only those who fail to fulfil their contracts or who commit torts are liable. Criminal law is also a fault-based system, but tort law and criminal law differ in many ways.

To begin with, private law is largely enforced by individuals or corporations, not by state agents. In public law schemes, the regulators are motivated by wages and benefits paid from tax revenues. If government cut off the salaries of narcotic squads, custom agents and vice officers, all police regulation of drug activity would cease. Private law is a different story because individuals enforce the law in pursuit of personal gain derived from the wrongdoer. The most common remedy sought by plaintiffs is a money payment from the defendant. Less frequently, plaintiffs request a court order to compel the defendant to take certain action or to refrain from doing something that bothers the plaintiff. With private law the claimant initiates the litigation, gathers evidence and finances the action. The state and taxpayer provide the courtroom, judge, jury and administrative services. The state, through judges or legislators, also provides the rules being enforced. Judges, more than elected politicians, decide what is a tort or what private agreements will be enforced as contracts. For example, courts will not enforce illegal agreements, so the customer who ordered and did not receive LSD cannot now ask the courts for help.

Private law is more decentralized than public law because it necessarily involves citizens in direct law enforcement roles: the onus
to prosecute, to seek redress against a wrongdoer, is on the citizen.
Private law engages individuals in a communal or public task.[3] This
public task is the application of state coercion. Through private
action, the state may compel tobacco producer A to pay $I million to
plaintiff smoker B. As always the question arises: What justifies
this coercive intervention by the state? For the individual plaintiff,
the motivation is personal redress, either through winning a money
award or seeing the wrongdoer punished, or both. In American litigation, plaintiffs recover something in 89% of cases with more than
half receiving less than $10,000.[4] More publicized are the 45 medi-
cal malpractice suits in 1982 that were awarded at least $1 million.[5]
Many legal scholars see compensation as the primary purpose of
tort law, and thus as the ethical justification for state coercion. But
this compensation-first view naturally leads scholars to condemn
tort law as unjustified because even at its best, tort law is an incomplete, imperfect system for delivering compensation.[6]

Tort compensates only those who are wrongfully injured by another person, who know the wrongdoer's identity and who can col-
lect a court award from the wrongdoer. Most injuries or damages
occur through accident (earthquakes, hurricanes, infectious disease) or through one's own fault, and tort does not compensate
such injury. But even where fault exists, recovery is uncertain. An
English survey discovered that nearly three quarters of all potential
plaintiffs fail to initiate a claim.[7] Victims of air pollution, lead poisoning, cancer and other chronic injuries usually do not know the
cause, or cannot attribute the injury to an identifiable wrongdoer.
The other major obstacle is that some wrongdoers have no assets to
seize, no wages to garnishee, no fixed address to find them at, or
they may declare bankruptcy.

Most North Americans buy some combination of automobile,
house, life, disability and health insurance to protect themselves
from a wide variety of risks and injuries. Through American Ex-
press, for example, travellers can purchase $500,000 of life insur-
ance coverage for $6.50 per airplane trip. Insurance is cheaper than
a law suit, and it pays benefits immediately, not five years later
when the last appeal is decided. If private insurance coverage can
provide people with the compensation protection they need, why

should the state provide a tort law system when it could just buy insurance for the poor? Legal enforcement, even of the private variety, is not cheap. Courts, judges, sheriffs and law reports are direct burdens on the taxpayer. The system also countenances large private expenditures on legal costs. The Agent Orange defendants, a group of Fortune 500 chemical companies, spent $75 million on legal costs, asbestos companies ran their legal bill over $600 million and the various Dalkon Shield cases generated $101 million in legal defence costs."[8] Tort critics wonder whether a system that sometimes puts more money into lawyer's pockets than into compensating victims deserves public support. What this theory overlooks is that, for the state, preventing wrongful injury from happening is far more important than compensating injury after the fact. This is why in criminal law, compensation is optional; the primary purpose of criminal law is to prevent wrongdoing. Tort supporters argue that public safety is also the primary justification for tort law. Although, tort law is fueled by desire for personal gain, compensation merely drives the machinery; the purpose of the system should be the promotion of public safety. Oliver Wendell Holmes rejected compensation as the rationale of a fault system, noting that since insurance was available, a state-sponsored compensation tort system was unjustified.[9] According to Kornhauser, tort law "compensates only when compensation promotes deterrence".[10]

State coercion of any kind should be premised on the existence of genuine social threats. This is why tort law is a fault-based system and why the only persons who pay damages or act under court orders are those persons whose misbehaviour generates social costs. According to this perspective, awards should not be based on the plaintiff's needs, but on the defendant's wrong.[11] Attempting to kill someone without lawful excuse is a tort. If the attempt completely fails — the victim spills the poisoned martini before taking a sip — almost no need for compensation arises. Nevertheless, the would-be killer should pay a very large judgment. (Note that tort law does not inflict criminal-type punishments such as execution, imprisonment, flogging, or community service because these would not motivate private enforcement: imprisonment may protect the public, but it does little for the victim.)

A tort judgment against an attempted killer motivates the plaintiff to prosecute. It also punishes the tortfeasor, warns others of the consequences of wrongdoing, reaffirms the resolve of non-tortious actors, and protects the public. Public prosecution rarely compensates the victim, hence often victims do not inform the police or cooperate with the public prosecutor. In criminal law, victims are not a party to the prosecution. If they play any part, they are forced to testify as witnesses, at which time they are frequently victimized again by the accused's lawyer. Deterring socially harmful behaviour is a public benefit, so it makes sense to support either a tax-based police force or a private law incentive system. Both systems are fault-based, so the mere fact of a person sustaining injury does not permit legal action. If, while riding in the subway, A is attacked by B and in self-defence severely injures B, B, now paralysed, cannot sue for $5 million (or even $5) because A was not at fault. Similarly, businesses hurt by honest competition have no claim in tort. Tort liability is tied to fault, which, as in criminal law, is judged according to the harm caused and the degree of intention. An intentional kick to someone's shin is worse than a negligent kick and is much worse than an accidental kick, even if all three kicks raise the same sized bruise. While each kicker should pay compensation, only the intentional kicker should pay significant punitive damages.

Critics charge that tort law cannot effectively deter bad behaviour. Evidence is cited of people ignoring tort rules and failing to alter their behaviour in light of legal decisions.[12] While this is true now, it does not reflect an inherent tort limitation because current systems are, to varying degrees, crippled by government as a matter of policy. Compare tort law in India with tort law in Canada and the United States.

In India, tort law is almost non-existent. Despite an ample supply of wrongful injury, there are no product liability cases in India, no suits against industrial firms, no actions against polluters. Simple tort actions in India take over 12 years to complete and damage awards are small, the median being $658 (U.S.).[13] In contrast, American tort law leads the world in number of product liability cases, awards are larger, and decisions take less time. The weakness of Indian tort law is consistent with generally flaccid public regulation of product safety, employee safety, civil rights and environmental protection in India. A similar, though less extreme difference exists between American and Canadian tort law.

195

Dozens of DES suits have been decided in the U.S., none in Canada. Over a hundred tobacco suits are pending in the U.S., one is pending in Canada. On a proportional basis, American physicians are sued for malpractice more frequently and more successfully than Canadian physicians. What explains these differences? In the Canadian medical case, physicians managed over the years to rule out jury trials, obtain restrictive statutes of limitations, and restrain medical experts from testifying against another physician. Hamowy reports that by 1910 it was "virtually impossible to prosecute a claim for medical malpractice."[14] Even in 1977, more Canadians won $1 million lotteries than succeeded in malpractice actions.[15]

American tort lawyers can advertise, work on contingency fees, and demand jury trials for malpractice: until recently Canadian lawyers could do none of these things. Indian tort law is similarly restricted by high court fees, unspecialized lawyers, long delays, and lack of organizational capacity in law firms. In India, tort law is designed to be ineffective. Powerful producer groups whose antisocial behaviour could be the target of many legal actions have lobbied for a crippled tort system. Naturally, such a lame system fails to deter: suits are too few and awards too small to seriously concern potential tortfeasors. Just as marijuana users flout drug prohibitions, tortfeasors ignore civil liability when their chance of being prosecuted is minimal. Anti-plaintiff interests are powerful. Physicians complain of a malpractice litigation explosion and seek a legislated end to punitive damages, pointing to a 79% increase in malpractice insurance premiums between 1976 and 1984 but during the same period physicians' income increased 89%.[16] Numerous influential figures in the U.S. warn of excessive litigation, flooded courtrooms and a public inflicted with a "fever to sue." Marc Galanter, who found these portentous pronouncements unsupported by evidence, correctly observes that to "identify litigiousness as a problem suggests that any disarray or ineffectiveness in legal institutions is traceable to the undiscipline of the public."[17] Anti-litigation movements promote stagnation and injustice in the name of social harmony and conservatism.

Critics charge that tort awards are too small to properly penalize defendants. This may be true now, but it is hardly a necessary feature of private law. Defendants will also not be deterred much if they can escape paying. This key problem has not been tackled with any enthusiasm by courts and governments. Critics also point to the role of insurance, claiming that bad drivers, for example, are not fully deterred because their insurance bears most of the burden. Insurance companies, however, eventually react to risk disparities among clients, which is why young male drivers pay high automobile insurance rates and obstetricians pay high medical insurance rates. Insurers may also refuse to cover certain forms of misbehaviour: many auto insurance policies for collision damages are void if the driver is drug-impaired. Insurance firms can and should refuse to insure against intentional torts, or at least should require full repayment from the insured in such cases. If these steps were taken, tort liability would deter insured tortfeasors, at least to the extent possible.

2. Intentional Torts

Intentional torts are wrongs committed wilfully with intent to cause injury. All the standard crimes such as rape, robbery, theft, assault and murder are also torts. Intentional torts include battery, assault, false arrest, invasion of privacy, infliction of nervous shock, conversion (theft) and interference with economic relations.[18] People commit intentional torts when they purposefully attack others, play malicious practical jokes, spread false information, make harassing phone calls, defraud, libel, or poison.

The first issue is whether any drug-related behaviour constitutes an intentional tort. An obvious instance is "spiking" a drink with alcohol, LSD, cocaine, aspirin or some other psychoactive. This tort might be committed to sabotage an athlete's eligibility, as Ben Johnson initially claimed in 1988 at the Seoul Olympics after testing positive for steroids. Drugging a business associate could ruin his opportunity for promotion. In its broadest form, this tort could include plying young persons with sedatives such as alcohol. The first-time imbiber in special circumstances might be incapable of giving full, informed consent. In the extreme, this tort includes death by poisoning. In 1983, Tylenol capsules were poisoned with potassium cyanide. Seven people in the Chicago area died as a result. If caught and sued, the drug saboteur responsible would be required to pay full compensation plus heavy punitive damages.

Compensation would include the seven wrongful deaths and the financial loss incurred by the producer. After the deaths, Tylenol's share of the analgesic market dropped from 35% to 7%. Johnson & Johnson's reportedly spent $300 million recalling all Extra-Strength Tylenol packages and devising a new seal.[19] However, even if the defendant killer could pay such a monumental sum, some other kind of penalty would be required. Tort law would merely force the killer to pay damages. Public penalties do little for the victim, but private awards may not do enough for the public.

A second intentional drug tort is the infliction of smoke on other people. Battery is the application of unconsented force against another. Gas molecules are a material force, thus the blowing of tobacco, opium or marijuana smoke into the lungs and nostrils of someone else could be interpreted as a mild but still palpable battery. While I know of no court that has held blowing smoke to be a battery, the potential exists for such a ruling to be made. If sidestream smoke proves to be as harmful as some researchers claim it is, tobacco battery cases may establish new grounds for smoker liability. Sidestream tobacco smoke, unfiltered and fired at lower temperatures than mainstream smoke, contains more carbon monoxide, ammonia, nicotine, toluene and dimethylnitrosamine. In one study, Japanese wives of smoking husbands died from lung cancer at twice the rate of women with non-smoking husbands.[20] Smokers may protest that even if their smoke impacts upon others, the damage is not inflicted intentionally. Sidestream smoke, they could claim, is merely an unavoidable side-effect.

Two responses to this position are possible. The first denies the pose of innocence. For some smokers, part of the fun of smoking is bothering other people.[21] The traditional connection between cigars and domineering men may derive from the propensity of cigar smoke to subjugate all bystanders. Cases no doubt also arise where A purposefully puffs to spite B. Sharon Fischer, who believes people have the right to smoke, admits that if other restaurant patrons complained about her smoking by coughing she would blow smoke at them.[22] The second response notes the equivalence in tort law between intention and recklessness. Saboteurs planting a bomb on board an airplane with intent to destroy the cargo may not intend to kill the pilots, but they realize or should realize the likelihood of human fatalities. If the explosion causes death, the bombers are liable for intentional homicide. In the same way, smokers may not intend to irritate other people, but they should realize that this result is almost inevitable indoors. If they proceed to smoke with knowledge of almost certain annoyance, their state of mind is very close to intent.

Some smokers seek to negate both intention and recklessness by arguing that their nicotine addiction compels them to smoke. Genuine compulsion or coercion is a good defence for many intentional torts, but addiction does not satisfy the legal requirement of an external force threatening immediate physical harm. And even if addiction does compel tobacco use, it does not compel smoking in public: tobacco users could smoke outside or take nicotine by pill, snuff, gum or injection. Free-basing nicotine (in other words, smoking) is the major source of friction with non-users. Tobacco users miss this point because for them tobacco means smoke. One critic of new anti-smoking regulations draws an interesting parallel when he asks: "Can you imagine (police) coming in here and handcuffing a smoker and then taking him out past the heroin addicts shooting up in the street?"[23] Actually, the tobacco smoker may generate more social costs than the heroin injector (discounting heroin costs attributed to prohibition) and yet the to-bacco addict is much more leniently treated. Heroin users are for-bidden non-medical use at all times regardless of the ingestion method chosen, whereas nicotine users are merely asked to not smoke the drug.

Tort actions, whether in battery or in nuisance, against drug smokers by office associates, family members, fellow restaurant pa-trons or employers, could be a plausible source of restraint. For cases in which the parties share space on a continuing basis, an injunction against further smoking would be more valuable than a single damage award. Recently an Ontario court granted a plaintiff an injunction ordering her husband to cease smoking in their home.[24] Jacqueline Reade, the plaintiff, had already lost part of her left lung to cancer. She is also seeking $1000 in damages from her husband. Following the court order, if her husband continues to puff at home he will be in contempt of court and subject to further penalties.

Generally, damages granted plaintiffs bombarded by carcino-genic smoke should be small, but sufficient to motivate private enforcement. Awards of $50 to $500 should suffice, if the losing party must pay the legal costs of both sides, as is the practice in Canada and England. Welcoming sidestream smoke cases to court would open the much-feared "flood gates" judges battle to keep closed, but the flood would quickly ebb. A few hundred law suits would transform the smoking habits of millions. Smokers would quickly respond by switching their mode of ingestion. Many would join smokers' clubs. By mutual agreement, club members and their guests would consent to smoke battery in the same way that martial arts clubs and contact sport teams consent to physical battery. Thus the probable result of making it easy and rewarding to sue smokers would not be endless "trivial" litigation, but rather a short period of test cases that would transform tobacco-using patterns.

Tort regulation of smoking could out-perform the current plethora of anti-smoking laws, while avoiding the rights abuses of public anti-smoking ordinances.[25] Public smoking laws are detailed and arbitrary. In the U.S., about 800 local ordinances affect tobacco smoking. Most states restrict smoking in public places, and a few also forbid smoking by employees on the job. New York State requires restaurants with over 50 seats to provide 70% of them to non-smokers; smaller restaurants and all taverns are exempt.[26] Most cities restrict smoking in elevators, subways, buses, hospitals, gas stations, food stores and places of public assembly. Some Canadian cities, including Vancouver, have stringent rules, whereas others, like Montreal, have minimal regulations passed decades ago more for fire prevention than concern for non-smokers.[27] In any case, all public law smoking controls are under-enforced. In New York City, 70 health inspectors are responsible for policing the new anti-smoking laws in 15,000 restaurants. Whether these laws empower police, by-law personnel, bus drivers, building inspectors or dog catchers to charge offenders, the end result is that few errant smokers are charged. Those who are caught are usually told to butt out. This preventive approach is unlikely to deter future violations. Public enforcement agents are not given the resources, powers or incentives to effectively pursue smoking violations. For the police, the task has low prestige, low priority and low marks for public relations. Anti-smoking laws are assigned to a class of laws, like those controlling littering, dog waste, honking car horns and spitting in public, that are seldom, if ever, enforced.

Private enforcement allows victims themselves to enforce the law. They often have far more at stake than police, and they need not be concerned with public relations or political pressures. Moreover, victims would often be suing people they knew, so the police problems of apprehension and identification are avoided. On the other hand, police enjoy an advantage over plaintiffs in dealing with strangers. One method of alleviating the "unknown defendant" problem is to allow plaintiffs to sue tavern owners, store proprietors or commercial landlords for permitting smoking torts to occur on their property. Such suits would pressure occupiers into taking steps to ban smoking or to prevent non-consenting non-smokers from entering the premises.

Observant readers not imbued with traditional tort doctrine may wonder at this point why tort law restricts enforcement to persons alleging to be victims of the tort. Why should it matter who sues the wrongdoer? For practical reasons, a successful suit is not likely without the victim's evidence and co-operation. On the other hand, no one can compel tort victims to sue, and in fact many do not seek redress from wrongdoers. One solution to this problem of under-enforcement is to let anyone launch a suit, just as anyone in England and Canada can generally launch a criminal prosecution. An open-door policy would not preclude victims from suing — indeed, they should have right of first refusal — but neither would it depend on victims taking the initiative.

Smoking torts are an example of a low-level, widespread wrong that could be amenable to open-ended enforcement permitting "bounty-hunters" to sue for private gain. There are no inherent reasons why at least some police work cannot be re-privatized. In 1838 in England, when public police forces were still in their infancy, between 500 and 3,000 local prosecution societies existed for the voluntary prosecution of crime.[28] Admittedly, public law enforcers — judges, prosecutors, police and legislators — tend to view personal law enforcement with misgiving, but their opinions are colored by professional self-interest. Government has expanded public power and professional monopoly this century at the expense of community initiative and self-reliance. Police have consistently acted within the general trend by broadening their powers and disparaging "amateur" self-protection. Armed self-defence by shopkeepers often generates more police hostility than armed robbery

201

itself. Private enforcement companies could be more attractive than police because they are likely to face greater scrutiny in court. They are also likely to exercise much less power. Naturally, non-victim plaintiffs could not justifiably claim compensation, but they would properly be entitled to punitive damages and reasonable legal costs. In this way, tort's retributive and law enforcement function could be divorced from its role of compensating victims' losses. This separated system of private enforcement would be the opposite of England's prediction that tort law will be superceded entirely by purely public compensation plans on one hand, and purely public, criminal-law style enforcement on the other.[29]

Another example of an intentional drug tort is the deceitful, reckless or intentional marketing of a drug posing a known threat to users. Consider the case of Oraflex (benoxaprofen), which was manufactured and marketed by Eli Lilly Co. in the U.S. as an Rx drug. Oraflex, like aspirin, is a non-steroidal anti-inflammatory drug capable of alleviating symptoms of arthritis. First marketed on April 19, 1982, the drug was withdrawn by government order four months later following reports of fatalities among users. Subsequently, it was discovered that Lilly failed to report the known incidence of adverse reactions.[30] Freedman reports that plaintiffs are suing the pharmaceutical industry "for its failures to test drugs... and for its over promotion and distortion of scientific data concerning its products."[31] Similar cases occur with non-psychoactive drugs as well. The antibiotic MER/29 was marketed by producers later convicted in criminal court for intentionally falsifying or withholding test data. Over 5,000 people suffered serious injury from consuming MER/29, and about 1,500 sued the producers in tort.[32] It should also be possible to sue tobacco and alcohol producers for misleading consumers, hiding drug risks and remaining wilfully blind to the dangers of their product.

3. Negligence

a. Drug User Liability

A negligent tortfeasor causes harm not through intention but through a failure to exercise the expected level of caution, care or concern for others. Ordinary drug use indulged in by millions of adults generates measurable social harm. The issue to be pursued

202

here is whether individual drug users can be held liable in negligence for such damage. Or, to put it another way, could a tort system make it worth-while for us to sue our neighbour for using alcohol coffee, Valium, or other psychoactives? The short answer is no. The first problem is minute damages. As a rough estimate, an average dose of alcohol causes no more than 50 cents in public harm. Equivalent damage is also attributed to the smoking of six cigarets.[33] And this minor social damage is not usually suffered, outside the user's family, by one specific victim. Instead the loss is spread among many people, potentially millions if the costs are borne by government. This means that A's share of B's alcohol-caused damage is a very small part of 50 cents per drink. It makes sense, therefore, for A to be indifferent to being victimized by B's alcohol use. B's family, however, is in a different position, but families rarely rely on legal solutions to internal problems. To make a suit against B feasible we must at least collectivize damages and permit any one to sue on behalf of everyone. But even this would not prompt a suit if the collective damages resulting from B's normal evening of heavy drugging amounted to $18.75. A single alcohol-using episode is not enough of a threat to warrant a private law suit because in tort law, the smaller the case, the less likely litigation will "pay." When American plaintiffs recover less than $10,000, lawyer's fees consume 40% of the recovery; in cases over $50,000, lawyers' fees amount to only 5% of the judgment.[34] Net monetary gain for plaintiffs is much lower in small suits unless lawyers can be avoided.

This brief example indicates why tort law did not produce criminal-type prohibitions of specific drugs: the ordinary, individual user of alcohol, tobacco, heroin or cocaine is not worth suing. Their drug use does not cause much harm, nor is it antisocial enough to warrant significant punitive damages. If moral entrepreneurs and drug crusaders had been restricted to using private law since 1880, heroin would still be treated like aspirin, Coca-Cola would still contain cocaine and alcohol Prohibition would not have taken place. A major advantage of tort law over criminal law is that in private actions actual harm must be proved in each case. Plaintiffs cannot merely assert that their neighbour's heroin use is a terrible breach of social obligation that is causing great harm to innocent bystanders. All claims must be backed by evidence able to withstand critical

203

attack from the defendant. In tort law prior to 1908, when people used opiates no one attempted to sue them. Today, a defendant in such a suit could marshal impressive expert witnesses to deny that opium or morphine use is a serious threat to others. Ironically, Canadian opiate laws were triggered in part by Chinese opiate producers in Vancouver demanding compensation from the federal government for damage suffered in 1907 riots led by the Anti-Asiatic League.[35] In those days, opiate producers were the peaceful victims of illegal attacks which, in retrospect, were perhaps preferable to the legal attacks launched by government after 1908.

Public and private prosecutions differ markedly in their factual underpinnings. Legislators can pass public laws premised on ridiculous, wholly unsubstantiated claims. Drug experts have no right to be heard in legislatures, nor do future offenders necessarily enjoy an opportunity to defend their interests. Once the laws are enacted, prosecutors are not required to demonstrate the harmfulness of cocaine, heroin or LSD use. Heroin users and sellers are severely punished not because they are shown in court to be especially harmful, but because Congress or Parliament alleges that they are harmful. Private law does not operate in this grossly unethical manner partly because in private law the "prosecutor" is the plaintiff, not the state. Judges do not automatically defer to the plaintiff's assertions as they do to government claims underlying criminal law statutes. Judges are state-sponsored, state-appointed agents paid to enforce statutes without being unduly critical. If legislators label cocaine a "narcotic," judges will usually accept that classification despite a wealth of scientific evidence and learned commentary to the contrary. *People* v. *McCabe* (1971), 275 N.E. 2nd 407, is an exception because in that case the Illinois Supreme Court held that classifying marijuana a "narcotic" was unfounded and arbitrary, hence unconstitutional. If legislators demand that cocaine sellers be sentenced to a minimum five year prison term, judges will comply despite a lack of evidence that selling cocaine is comparable to armed robbery, sexual assault or even theft. If an individual plaintiff had made similar assertions about cocaine in 1908, judges would have dismissed the case for lack of evidence.

Superficially, criminal defendants seem better protected than tort defendants. Criminal charges must be demonstrated by the prosecution to a higher degree of certainty, evidence is more readily excluded, and state-funded defence counsel is guaranteed. Appearances aside, though, criminal defendants are processed through a bureaucratic system they neither understand nor control.[36] In contrast, tort defendants direct their own defence, possess equal or superior resources to the plaintiff, argue before a relatively unbiased adjudicator, and face fairer laws. Criminal defendants, even with the best protections, are generally helpless in the face of abusive statutes such as the narcotics laws. So-called "victimless crimes" are possible only under public law. A "victimless" tort is a contradiction in terms, since harm or intended harm to someone must be demonstrated in every case.

Criminalizers claim that vice offences prevent self-harm, but private law, by its nature, has no mandate to prevent people from harming only themselves. Suicide was once an ecclesiastical offence and a crime, but it was never a tort. Seeking an injunction to prevent yourself, with help from the sheriff, to quit smoking or to stay out of taverns is conceivable, but why would the state agree to such suits? Like Ulysses lashed to the mast by his crew to resist the Sirens' song, individuals can have agents or friends help them avoid drugs without state assistance.

Although drug use is generally not very harmful per drug user, it is an important social threat when one calculates the aggregate impact of consuming billions of cigarets, oceans of alcohol, tons of aspirin and shiploads of coffee. Suing one drug user is not an attractive option, but perhaps sufficient rewards would be available if all drug users were sued as a class. Damage awards against the aggregate class could run to billions of dollars, but there are some insurmountable obstacles. First, how would damages be assessed against members of the drug using defendant class? Simply dividing all alcohol-related costs by the number of drinkers would be unfair, given wide variation in consumption rates. How would the courts identify, contact or evaluate the liability of 95 million American or ten million Canadian alcohol users? How would the judgment be collected? Finally, drug-related user torts are not well-suited to adjudication. Discreet incidents like assaults or motor vehicle crashes can be settled by one decision, but drug torts occur on a continuing basis and are so amorphous that one can scarcely conceive of them as disputes. Regulating chronic, repeated torts requires a full-time bureau, not a court.

In some circumstances, drug use is causally connected with major damage. A prime example is fires started by tobacco smokers. De Francesco *et al* estimate that each year cigaret-related fires kill 1,500 Americans, injure 3,600 others and result in $300 million in property damage.[37] Smokers, often intoxicated at the time, cause fires by falling asleep and dropping lighted cigarets onto chairs, bedding, sofa cushions or clothes. The cigarets now marketed smoulder for up to 30 minutes, which allows ample time for upholstery to catch fire. Most victims of these fires are poisoned by toxic gases. Smokers who fall asleep holding lit cigarets are certainly negligent, and are thus liable to compensate those harmed by a resulting fire. But note that the wrongdoing here — negligently causing a fire — is not drug specific. Fires can be negligently started in dozens of ways. The same is true of negligent driving. Driving with over 0.08%, etc. blood-alcohol is a crime, but it is not automatically a tort. Few alcohol-using drivers who blow over the legal limit actually cause damage, or even drive dangerously. In private law, only those causing damage or those driving in a endangering manner are liable. Tort law thereby avoids the injustice of status offences, which make it illegal to be a drug addict, a drug user or a drug using driver. The same analysis applies to intentional torts like conversion or sexual battery. If heroin or alcohol users steal property or rape victims they should be liable. Their drug use, like their church affiliation or taste in clothes, is irrelevant.

b. Liability in Negligence of Drug Producers

Drug producers, distributors, retailers and prescribers owe a legal duty of care in tort law to take reasonable and prudent precautions to avoid injuring their customers. The law for drugs is no different than the private law for food, confections or bottled water. Brewers avoid selling tainted beer because of legal liability, and because their business success requires customer confidence, brand loyalty and good public relations. Market incentives, and to a lesser extent fear of law suits, help ensure a fairly high level of drug quality. This is a major advantage private law offers over criminal law. Prohibition forces drug producers to operate illicitly, and illicit producers cannot advertise, establish brand names, register trade marks, protect innovations or reap the long-term benefits of customer loyalty. By operating so as to avoid criminal liability, illicit businesses also avoid tort liability. Illicit producers are too small, too undercapitalized or too fly-by-night to be worth suing. Negligence suits work best against large, well-established firms. A purely private law system would allow such firms to market cannabis, opiates, cocaine and the rest with the same attention to quality control now given alcohol and coffee. Alcohol may be an inherently dangerous drug, but it need not be doubly dangerous because of negligent manufacture. Private law controls would therefore raise the quality of drugs now classified as illicit.

The quality of Rx psychoactives is a different matter. Presently, these drugs are regulated by agencies of the Canadian and U.S. federal governments. Indeed, the pharmaceutical industry is probably the most closely regulated business in the United States.[38] Under a purely private law system there would be no Food and Drug Administration to oversee the testing of new psychoactives, a change Milton Friedman advocates.[39] Tort law would privatize all the FDA's functions, since drug producers would still be liable for testing, labelling and warning users about their drugs' effects.

Producers labour under a well-established duty to warn potential customers and users about the notable dangers associated with their products.[40] Producers selling drugs without full, adequate and comprehensible warnings should be held liable for all drug-related damage to users caused by this failure. Ortho Pharmaceutical (Canada) Ltd. recently paid out $600,000 to a partially paralyzed plaintiff who had not been adequately warned about the dangers of birth control pills. In general, though, courts have not been supportive of plaintiffs suing for failure to warn. Aspirin, codeine, tobacco and many other psychoactives were traditionally sold without any warnings. Only since 1985 have American aspirin producers agreed, under government pressure, to warn users about Reye's syndrome. Alcohol and coffee products still lack warnings, while tobacco carries a partial warning only because government required it. In 1988 California required all alcohol retail outlets to warn buyers that the drug can cause birth defects.[41] Rx psychoactives carry more complete warnings because of public law regulations, but these warnings usually do not reach the drug taker and are often incomprehensible anyway. Sugarman claims that Rx drug warnings are an example of tort over-deterrence: excessively cautious producers are providing warnings so detailed that users cannot understand them.[42] A more likely explanation of this obscurity is that producers use thick verbiage in standard form contracts and in drug product warnings precisely to discourage customers from either reading or understanding the content. As Merrill observes, Rx drug information "requires more time and pharmacological sophistication than the average physician possesses."[43]

Plaintiffs tend to lose failure-to-warn cases for various reasons, some of which are remedial, some not. Remedial reasons include judges' pro-business bias, restricted access to court, barriers against class actions, convoluted legal procedures, long delays, and resource imbalances between plaintiffs and corporate conglomerate defendants. Recent suits against tobacco firms illustrate these problems. Since the 1950s, when tobacco cases first arose, the U.S. tobacco industry has not paid out a penny. One tobacco producer was found liable for damages in 1988 (see below) but that case is under appeal. Tobacco smoking is one of the more addicting and health-impairing drug habits, so how have the producers escaped liability? Plaintiffs submit that tobacco firms were negligent in failing to warn that tobacco use was addicting and impairing, were negligent in not studying tobacco's impact on health, were negligent in linking tobacco with sports, glamour and youth, and were deceitful in negating scientific evidence linking tobacco use with cancer, heart disease and other ailments. (Tobacco firms probably repressed the bad news about their drug partly from fear of government prohibition). For their part the tobacco firms unleash what the Wall Street Journal calls their secret weapon — "a lavishly financed and brutally aggressive defence that scares off or exhausts many plaintiffs long before their cases get to trial."[44] Typically, the defendants outspend the plaintiffs. This occurs for two reasons. First, the tobacco companies are enormous. A handful of companies control the American market, with two — Philip Morris and R.J. Reynolds — accounting for 67% of total industry sales. Philip Morris is the world's second largest tobacco firm and the world's second largest producer of beer. Like other tobacco firms, Philip Morris is diversifying into food companies and now runs Miller Brewing, Seven-Up and General Foods. None of the six leading cigaret makers is more than 40% dependent on the domestic tobacco trade; all have eliminated tobacco from their corporate name.[45] With total sales of $23 billion in 1984, Philip Morris is the largest U.S. consumer products manufacturer. R.J. Reynold's sales in the same year came to $19 billion.[46] Clearly, these firms as defendants have far greater resources than any single plaintiff. Additionally, each tobacco case is treated as a fight for corporate existence. This "bet-the-company" litigation strategy focuses immense legal resources on a few cases at a time. And the results are impressive. In Green v. American Tobacco Co., the jury found the plaintiff's lung cancer to be cigaret-related, but ruled for the tobacco company because in 1956 lung cancer was "a completely unforeseeable risk" of which the producer "had no opportunity to gain knowledge."[47] Note that producers of new psychoactives are expected to acquire knowledge of dangers before marketing their drugs, but tobacco producers can remain blissfully ignorant after eighty years of cigaret production and centuries of tobacco sales. The jury's finding in Green that the producer could not know "by the reasonable application of human skill and foresight" that cigaret smokers would risk lung cancer was painfully inaccurate.

An obvious plaintiff response is to form class actions, to pool resources, and to seek well-funded allies capable of going the distance against determined tobacco defendants. Increasingly, the tobacco firms are facing more numerous, better-financed opponents. Some cases now pending are led by consortiums of lawyers with experience and funds from successful asbestos litigation. Other tobacco plaintiff groups are being aided by the Rockefeller Family Fund. Law professor Richard Daynard now edits and publishes the *Tobacco Products Litigation Reporter*, a project that will bolster legal expertise for the plaintiff cause. Daynard predicts eventual success, reasoning that if plaintiffs can win on asbestos, where the evidence is weaker, they can win on tobacco as well.[48] For their part, tobacco defendants claim that cigaret smoking does not cause illness and, even if it did, users knew the dangers and voluntarily assumed the risks. Tobacco companies also argue that government-directed package warnings, in use since 1965, meet their duty to warn. Note that in tobacco tort battles plaintiffs do not sue tobacco farmers. Criminal law does not distinguish between growers and sellers; both are defined as "traffickers" and liable to the same penalties. Yet in private law, farmers are ignored, or viewed as innocent bystanders who just happen to grow a dangerous drug. The difference rests on practical concerns. Tobacco users know who produces their cigarets, but they have no idea which farm, state or even country the tobacco leaf comes from. Tobacco farmers are a less tempting target financially, and no direct connection exists between grower and user. Tobacco plaintiffs cannot sue farmers for breach of contractual warranty. Tobacco farmers, like growers of opiate poppies, coffee beans or cannabis, sell unprocessed raw materials, and do not have a duty to warn final consumers.

Tobacco plaintiffs also face barriers such as causal uncertainty. Did the plaintiff begin smoking before or after package warnings? Which brand was smoked? Did the plaintiff engage in other unhealthy activities like mining, sniffing glue, smoking dope, drinking alcohol, or working in a brake factory? Was the plaintiff's heart disease attributable to heredity, bad diet, lack of exercise, or tobacco use? Stapleton observes that tort recovery for the 100,000 premature deaths in Britain purportedly caused annually by tobacco use is impractical because of "hopelessly unsolvable causation issues."[49] Scientists can claim with considerable certainty that tobacco use increases the likelihood of lung cancer or heart disease by a given factor among the population of users, but this certainty fades when an individual plaintiff comes to court. Technical difficulties of a similar nature, however, did not bar recovery in DES cases.[50] Cigaret producers are clearly negligent. They refused to voluntarily warn users, they lobbied furiously against mandatory warnings, and they employed advertising that was biased, incomplete and inaccurate. In the *Pritchard* case, Liggett & Myers came under scrutiny for claiming in advertisements that smoking "makes you feel better" and that a smoker could "Play Safe-Smoke Chesterfield."[51] The Tobacco Institute, an industry-sponsored organ, has for many years tried to counteract research results. At most, tobacco producers admit that a "controversy" exists over the impact of smoking. In fact, the controversy mainly concerns the degree and range of tobacco impairment.

Tobacco users are victims, but not entirely innocent ones. Stapleton talks of "exposure" to tobacco as if smoking were equivalent to malaria. But smokers are not passively exposed to cigarets; they go to considerable effort to acquire and consume tobacco products. The decision to start smoking may be influenced by advertising, but the evidence on that point is not clear (see Chapter Seven). Stronger influences are the examples set by friends, parents and public figures. Once started, few people can smoke heavily without noticing some detrimental impact on fitness and health or without being aware of possible long term impairment. Health warnings about tobacco smoking are not news. In the 1860s the *English Dictionary of Daily Wants* warned readers about the habit-forming nature of smoking and said that cancer's link to smoking was "notorious." The Government Actuary notified the British government of the causal link between lung cancer and tobacco smoking in 1954.[52] Between 1946 and 1954, forty six articles in *The New York Times* reported on the debate about cigarets as a cause of cancer. Even more widely read were three articles in *Reader's Digest* between 1952 and 1954 entitled "Cancer by the Carton" "Can the Poisons in Cigarettes be Avoided?" and "The Facts Behind the Cigarette Controversy." Individuals are obliged to preserve their own health, and this duty is implicitly recognized in tort doctrine. This is why producers of dangerous products can escape liability by candidly informing customers of the risks involved. Since people have a duty to not take unreasonable risks, the informed user of cigarets is personally negligent.

The outcome of tobacco liability cases will depend primarily on proving damages and apportioning those damages between negligent defendant and negligent plaintiff. Most cases involve claims of wrongful death due to negligent failure to warn, but in some cases the plaintiff is still alive and claiming personal injury losses. Pierce reports that for U.S. courts in 1980 the average personal injury award was $181,401, and the average award for wrongful death of an adult was $240,228.[53]   Other more recent sources estimate average wrongful death awards at $1 million.[54]

In tort law, damages are assessed according to a number of criteria: direct expenses, loss of future income, pain and suffering, and loss of amenities. The largest awards occur when young persons are severely injured but will live for many years, or when a high-income earner with dependants is killed. Killing a lawyer is more expensive than killing a bus driver or a housekeeper. Indeed, since housespouses do not earn commercial income, judges are perplexed as to how to value their loss of life or loss of working capacity.[55] Another problem is that judges evaluate plaintiffs' compensation needs without reference to medicare, welfare, disability coverage, pensions and life insurance. Many North American adults with dependants are well insured. High-income earners are usually most insured and thus require less tort compensation than the lowest-income strata, who by current tort doctrine receive the lowest awards for wrongful death or disability. Legal costs would be decreased and delays avoided if awards were standard for damages such as invasion of privacy, loss of a limb, lung cancer, blindness, loss of life. A perhaps typical tobacco plaintiff was the late John Galbraith, whose 1985 case against R.J. Reynolds in California was lost by Melvin Belli. Galbraith started smoking at the age of 19 and continued to smoke two to three packs a day for the next 50 years.[56] He died at age 69 after spending much of his last few years aided by an oxygen machine. Galbraith was retired and probably without financial dependants so loss of income would have been small. Valuing loss of life is the more difficult issue.

Tobacco kills perhaps 30,000 Canadians a year, but these deaths are not comparable to deaths from, say, warfare or auto crashes. A recent privately-sponsored full-page newspaper ad in support of two proposed Canadian federal statutes, the *Tobacco Products Control Act* and the *Non-Smokers' Health Act*, claimed that at "35,000 deaths each year, tobacco industry products kill more Canadians annually than would be killed by the collision of two fully-loaded jumbo jets every week for a year."[57] The comparison is not apt. Airplane crashes are accidents, while tobacco smoking is chronic, consciously pursued and results in disability or shortened life span for some users, not violent death. Furthermore, smokers do not take $125,000,000 airplanes with them when they die. A more apt comparison is premature deaths from overeating.

Tort law doctrine properly recognizes different values for classes of mortality, making death at 69 less of a loss than death at 49 or 29 years of age. Still, Galbraith's cigarets probably cost him from five to ten years. Tobacco smoking also reduced the enjoyments of his last years, but this loss of amenities must be weighed against the initial satisfactions he gained from tobacco. Putting a monetary figure on these losses is a difficult and complex task. At a rough estimate, smokers in Galbraith's position are probably entitled to damages ranging from $100,000 to $500,000. Punitive damages would be added to the total. Punitive damages would be inappropriate if tobacco firms acted responsibly by promoting safe forms of tobacco use, sponsoring scientific research, pushing for product innovations and taking every opportunity to warn customers about known dangers. But because tobacco firms have generally acted in the opposite manner, punitive damages are justified.

The total damages must be apportioned between plaintiff and defendant. R.J. Reynolds was negligent in not warning Galbraith but, he was negligent in risking his own health. Should the cigaret maker then pay 20%, 50% or 90% of general damages? To make this determination, we need to know how much Galbraith would have smoked had he been effectively and completely warned. Obviously, it is impossible to perform this experiment, but future Galbraiths can be tested in the present by providing them with adequate warnings about cigarets, by requiring full-disclosure advertising, and by offering safer forms of tobacco use. Since 1965 a partial form of this experiment has been conducted: from that date cigaret packages, cigaret advertisements and public health notices in the U.S. have warned users that tobacco smoking is detrimental to their health. Despite these warnings, most smokers continue to smoke and millions have started to smoke since 1965. Many smokers learn to ignore the warnings, and in one British test, health warnings were found to increase tobacco use among women smokers.[58] United Nation figures show tobacco use falling by 1.1% per year in the industrial West in contrast to a 2.9% annual increase in Third world nations.[59] As might be expected, trends vary between countries. Canadians maintain a high per capita cigaret rate despite package health warnings and public health advocacy. Canadian consumption dropped from 74 billion cigarets in 1981 to 55.4 billion in 1986, but there was a 1% increase in 1988 over 1987.[60] What this brief survey suggests is that warnings by cigaret makers will likely deter some tobacco use, but that anti-tobacco reactions will not be immediate or drastic. In short, John Galbraith would probably have started and then continued to use tobacco despite adequate warnings. In judging the degree of individual responsibility for cigaret use I estimate, again quite roughly, that R.J. Reynolds should bear 10%-20% of Galbraith's damages plus, of course, all the punitive damages. This apportionment would cost R.J. Reynolds from $10,000 to $100,000 in general damages, and perhaps another $100,000 in punitive damages.

As it turns out, my $200,000 estimate may be low. In the 1988 Cipollone case, a five-year lawsuit in New Jersey against three tobacco producers, the Liggett Group was found liable for 20% of the smoker's damages. This made Liggett liable for $400,000. (The decision is being appealed.) The basis for liability in Cipollone was that Liggett provided, through advertisements, an express warranty that its products were safe when the company knew of research demonstrating tobacco smoking's dangerousness.[61] No punitive damages were awarded. The jury rejected allegations that Liggett fraudulently hid information about smoking hazards from the public. Philip Morris and Lorilard escaped liability because Cipollone only smoked their products after 1966 when cigaret packages included a health warning. On January 5, 1990 the U.S. Third Circuit Court of Appeals ordered a new trial in the *Cipollone* case. The tables are turning, but even so I consider this jury decision to reflect a lenient, accepting attitude toward tobacco producers. The Non-Smokers Rights Association in Canada recently obtained an expert legal opinion advising that tobacco producers could be liable for *criminal* negligence causing death or bodily harm because of failure to warn customers about the inherent risks of cigarets.[62]

While $400,000 is small compared to the millions tobacco plaintiffs are asking for, there are 55 million smokers in the U.S., plus millions of estates representing deceased tobacco users. Now that one tobacco plaintiff has won, other awards may quickly follow. Class actions by injured R.J. Reynolds cigaret customers would cost the company billions of dollars annually. Such suits might seem to spell disaster for the tobacco industry and the one million Americans who earn tobacco-related incomes, but the worst result would merely be corporate reorganization and continued tobacco sales. Some companies might be pushed into bankruptcy or dissolved to pay court awards. Shareholders and some employees would lose out, but new businesses would be formed to market cigarets which, after all, are one of the world's most profitable consumer products. These new tobacco firms would, however, behave differently from their predecessors. Package warnings would be longer and more dire and would be bolstered by detailed package inserts. All lifestyle advertisements glamorizing tobacco products would be dropped, as would sponsorship of sporting events. It is conceivable that under threat of lawsuits, all tobacco advertisements would be voluntarily withdrawn. The new cigaret makers would also support medical research on the drug and give aid to stop-smoking clinics and "weedless Wednesday" campaigns. Those smokers who continued cigaret use under this benevolent corporatism would not be able to shift liability for their impairment to others. Like mountain climbers, race car drivers and parachutists, well-informed smokers would have to assume the normal risks of their chosen activity.

Smokers, however, would still be able to sue over unreasonable or unwarranted risks caused by producer negligence. Over one hundred patents have now been issued for "fire proof" cigarets. One design uses sodium silicate to produce a cigaret that goes out rapidly if not puffed and produces almost no smoke while "idling."[63] Not only do most tobacco firms fail to adopt such innovations, they add chemical compounds to cigaret paper to keep the cigaret burning longer between puffs. Victims of cigaret fires and second-hand smoke may have a good case against manufacturers on the grounds that known design defects were permitted, making cigarets unreasonably dangerous.

A tort law duty to warn would affect alcohol, caffeine, aspirin, mescaline, Valium — every drug would be judged improperly labelled if full and frank disclosure of dangers, risks and contraindications was not included. Since this disclosure must be targeted at the final user rather than a medical or bureaucratic intermediary, the message would have to be readily understood by ordinary people. Courts may find that a variety of messages are required: posted warnings in stores, package warnings, information inserts. Private law may produce more intelligible warnings than public law because the warnings will be tested in private actions initiated by ordinary citizens. The package inserts now required by law for Rx drugs are not graphic, easily grasped, or comprehensive. A uniform private law system would also have the advantage of requiring warnings for every psychoactive. Since media-space and people's attention are limited resources they should be husbanded carefully. The most economical warnings will begin by noting risks that use of every psychoactive entails. Special dangers and comparative risks can then be added to the general campaign. Negligence law could also eventually curtail packaging that is not child-proof and rule out the marketing of drugs administered through intravenous injection or by smoking.

Critics might at this point argue that while tort law offers theoretical protection against negligence, practical barriers to private enforcement will result in continued injustice. Obstacles to effective private prosecution exist in abundance, but it is important to understand that most of these barriers are political. That is, our legal system incorporates centuries of interest group lobbying by producer coalitions intent on hobbling opposition from customers and victims. Garner writes that the tobacco industry's de facto immunity from suit (in 1980) is a judicially-created phenomenon that dwarfs every other issue in modern product liability law.[64] Technical solutions to tort under-enforcement are easily imagined. Punitive damages, which have now fallen into judicial disfavour, can be revived for intentional and negligent drug torts. More cost-efficient means of aggregating suits could be allowed. Class action suits, where permitted by law, are now one-time affairs. In mass cases (Agent Orange, DES, asbestos, cigarets), a group of lawyers on contingency fees forms an ad hoc consortium.[65] After the suit is completed, which may take from three to ten years, the consortium disbands. Conducting expensive legal campaigns against major corporations on an *ad hoc* basis is cumbersome and inefficient. One alternative would permit the establishment of permanent plaintiff-protection law corporations. Such firms would employ lawyers, accountants, medical and drug experts, business managers, and financial officers, and would be free to advertise, solicit clients, issue securities and borrow to finance litigation. Plaintiffs could either sell their evidence and claim for a lump sum prepayment, or contract a contingency fee for a specified portion of an eventual judgment. In a competitive legal market, plaintiff-protection companies would bid energetically for plaintiff claims, which would escalate. In addition, non-victim suits could be permitted in which private businesses could sue drug producers for improper warnings, false test data, misleading advertising or defective products. These companies would combine elements of *Consumer Reports*, public interest advocacy, and bounty hunting.

These kinds of reform would provide the financial platform needed for amassing legal and technical expertise to battle multinational drug producers. In mass personal-injury tort cases today, defendants are always better financed than plaintiffs. Tobacco firms spend millions preparing for a single trial. Although plaintiffs

216

drastically outnumber defendants, they are not as organized. Producers must organize to do business, thus it is easy for them to add a legal-defense division to the company. No cigaret buyer's clubs, no Tobacco Consumer's Institutes, no tobacco user's lobby exist. The costs of organizing a million Pall Mall or Rothman's cigaret smokers would be overwhelming unless some pre-existing institution or business can aggregate the claims in an inexpensive way. Current tort rules inhibit efficient plaintiff protection. Where tort rules are particularly pro-defendant, as in India, no product liability suits occur. American and Canadian courts are less pro-defendant, but the difference between the present system and what is possible is at least as dramatic as the difference now between tort administration in New York and Calcutta.

c. Other Negligence Issues

Two other categories of negligence should be mentioned. The first concerns negligent advice given customers by commercial drug prescribers. Under uniform private law regulations, physicians, pharmacists, nurses, psychologists and others would be free to sell their services as psychoactive drug experts. Their legal status would be analogous to architects. Private home builders do not require an architect's input to legally construct a home, but many find it useful to hire architectural expertise anyway. Once hired, architects are liable for damage or loss caused by their negligent errors. This does not make architects strictly liable for all mishaps. If an unforeseen earth tremor destroys a house that could have been built more earthquake resistant (at greater cost), the architect is not responsible. The same doctrines would apply to expert drug prescribers.

The second area of potential liability for negligence involves the responsibility of those who serve drugs or permit drug use on their premises. Under present public laws, almost every commercial activity involving alcohol requires a licence or permit. Every province and every state boasts a Liquor Control Board or an Alcoholic Beverage Control Board to monitor the serving of alcohol, although no controls attend the serving of coffee or tobacco. Under a private law regime, these bureaucratic alcohol boards would be disbanded, putting alcohol servers on a par with providers of cocaine or coffee. In addition, it would no longer be a felony to offer patrons marijuana, LSD, peyote or Thorazine. Any person or business could

217

serve and sell any psychoactive, subject to certain contractual limits and tort law restrictions.

The first restriction is the familiar duty to warn. On-premise retailers would need to post warnings informing customers of drug risks. Second, and more important, occupiers would have a duty to protect patrons and guests from foreseeable drug-related harm. Depending on the drugs served, different degrees of supervision and care could be required to avoid legal action. Alcohol servers are now made liable for failing to remove potential hazards from their premises. Plaintiffs have sued taverns after slipping on spilt beer or wet tile floors, falling down steep stairways and tripping over entranceways.[66] Drug-serving occupiers must also cope with hazards posed by their customers. In *Gardner* v. *McConnel*, a hotel owner was held liable after one patron, a notorious brawler, injured another customer who was innocently attempting to avoid a fight.[67] Similarly, in *Lehnert* v. *Nelson*, a cabaret owner had to pay damages for failing to eject an obviously disturbing customer who eventually injured the eye of an innocent patron.[68] Liability also attaches to serving persons at special risk. Traditionally, this has meant inebriates, but it could also include pregnant persons and youngsters. Tort law would not automatically preclude serving beer or cannabis to 14-year-olds, but it would discourage serving unlimited quantities or without their parents' presence or permission.

Occupiers may also be liable for damage caused by or suffered to guests after they have left the premises. In *Schmidt* v. *Sharpe et al.*, Sharpe consumed alcohol past the point of intoxication in the Arlington House Hotel.[69] Driving away drunk from the hotel, Sharpe and his car and passenger plunged over a steep embankment. The passenger, who knew Sharpe was intoxicated, was rendered quadriplegic and, in court, was awarded $1,390,000 against both Sharpe and the hotel. Employees of the hotel were negligent in serving Sharpe when they knew or ought to have known that he was intoxicated. (Note that this award was based on the plaintiff's needs, which were extensive, rather than on the hotel's wrongdoing, which was minor.) Conceivably, the same doctrine could be applied to all drug servers, including private hosts. If vigorously litigated, server liability could bring about major changes in behaviour. All known troublemakers, excessive drug users and visibly-impaired customers would be barred entry to taverns, hotels and other hospitality outlets, or ejected if this could be done safely. Private hosts would be encouraged to avoid serving intoxicants or, alternatively, to not let guests drive away impaired. Extended tort liability for private hosts might also help promote a new social etiquette, already visible on the horizon, in which pushing alcohol on guests would be considered boorish and unsophisticated rather than a sign of generosity and concern.

Smoked drugs raise unique issues of occupier liability because smoke bothers or endangers a wide circle of guests. Tort law would not require licenses for selling and serving smoking tobacco or hashish, but it would establish general conditions under which commercial occupiers could permit smoking. Different approaches are possible. For example, occupiers could be held liable in negligence or subject to injunction if they permitted or promoted smoking without the explicit consent of all customers, or without adequate ventilation to counter the possible effects of sidestream smoke.

4. Strict Liability

Strict liability is not fault-based in the traditional tort sense. Instead, the justification for assessing damages is the cost-effective reduction of social costs. Liability is thus targeted on the party best able to deal with, bear or eliminate the loss or injury. Consider the case of automobile mishaps.

About 95 million Americans drive motor vehicles, and every year about 50,000 are killed and 2,000,000 suffer disabling personal injury. In 1985, Canadian road fatalities totalled 4,360. Estimates of the costs of motor vehicle mishaps for New Jersey were $1.5 billion (1981) and for Ontario $750 million (1980).[70] These costs can be allocated in three basic ways. First, in a no-fault insurance plan all injuries, including the self-inflicted kind, would be compensated with the costs spread over all drivers, or all taxpayers. Second, in a fault-based tort system costs would be borne by the injured parties themselves (and their insurers) unless another driver, a highway department, or manufacturer could be blamed. Third, in a strict liability regime one party would be compelled to pay for all foreseeable damages resulting from motor vehicle use. That party could be either drivers, the government, or the manufacturers. Making the

219

government liable would duplicate the effects of a no-fault insurance scheme underwritten by the taxpayer. In the absence of other laws, such a scheme would encourage more driving, especially by high-risk drivers now deterred by the cost of private insurance. Making all drivers responsible is not feasible in a private law regime because drivers, like drug users, are too numerous. In contrast, public controls could easily allocate all costs to drivers by setting the price of drivers' permits, vehicle licence fees, and gasoline taxes at the requisite levels. Sumptuary disincentives borne by drivers would result in less driving, fewer drivers and safer vehicles. As will be discussed in Chapter Eight, tax control would induce similar effects on drugs and drug use.

The other practical possibility is to make manufacturers strictly liable for all auto-related costs. In 1966, William Prosser apparently thought such a scheme preposterous, asking rhetorically if the maker of "good whisky is to be held responsible for the drinking habits of the American public? And is the manufacturer of an automobile to be held liable for the way people drive it?"[71] Prosser did not bother to analyze these possibilities, but other scholars have.

Howard Latin, for example, bases his case for strict producer liability on two major grounds. First, he argues that auto manufacturers are more sensitive to disincentives than drivers.[72] Latin believes it is cheaper to produce safer cars than it is to drive more prudently. Seat belts, padded dashboards, air bags, disc brakes, halogen headlights, collapsible steering wheels and other product innovations reduce damage without requiring better driving. Latin's second argument is that individuals already drive protectively in their own self-interest, so making them strictly liable will not increase their prudence.[73] Actually, there is evidence that people drive to a certain risk level, so that safer cars with better brakes result in people driving faster and leaving less room between vehicles.[74] There is also evidence that a small hard core of bad drivers causes a disproportionate amount of damage.[75] This group of excessively anti-social drivers, as might be expected, appears to share basic traits with habitual petty criminals. Such persons drive aggressively and abusively, not prudently. Under Latin's scheme, drivers' insurance costs would be minimal, while cars would be safer and considerably more expensive. But there would no longer be an insurance penalty against high-risk drivers, and preliminary evidence suggests that without personal liability some drivers tend to drive less carefully.[76]

Similar incentive issues must be addressed when analyzing strict liability for drug-related costs. Under strict liability, producers could not defend themselves on the grounds of consent or contributory negligence on the plaintiff's part. Plaintiffs would merely need to demonstrate that they used drug X and that certain injuries followed as a consequence. Producers would be liable for all alcohol-related mishaps, cigaret fires, damage from sidestream smoke, losses resulting from drug-using employees and drug-induced crime.

Depending on the scale of damages assessed to producers, strict liability could have the following effects. First, manufacturers would raise prices to offset legal costs, and shift to safer drug products. Price increases to pay tort judgments might duplicate the tax-based prices familiar to alcohol and tobacco buyers. Drug production might also shift to smaller, undercapitalized firms better able to avoid judgment by declaring bankruptcy or fleeing. The use of complex corporate structures to shield owners and executives would also hinder law enforcement. Finally, some production would shift to the black market where, free from liability, fly-by-night operators could easily undercut the high tort-induced prices of ethical producers. This last possibility is not likely for auto production because of the heavily industrial nature of the product. However, many drugs can be manufactured in quantity by a few people working in garages, basements, farms or small factories. A possible result, then, of efficiently enforcing a strict liability regime against drug producers for all drug-related costs would be a major re-organization of the industry toward judgment-proof operations. The key empirical question is whether brewers, for example, can raise prices sufficiently to compensate for all damage related to beer consumption.

Making drug producers strictly liable for only third party costs is much less problematic because this avoids the bulk of damages suffered by users themselves. Under this regime, producers could raise prices enough to cover their liability. Prices for various drugs would then vary according to production costs plus the social costs associated with the drug's use. Present law makers argue that heroin producers are "merchants of death" and "enemies of the

221

state" because their drug is so destructive to both users and the public at large. If this were true, under private law controls no one could afford to set up as a legitimate seller of opiates. A legitimate seller of heroin would face suits from the City of New York, for example, claiming $100 million in damages for police expenses, medical outlays, social workers' salaries, public psychiatrists and slum renewal costs. Fortunately for would-be marketers of heroin, New York City could not prove such damages in court. If marketed like codeine, Darvon or aspirin, heroin would not generate extreme social costs. Municipalities would be better advised to sue alcohol and tobacco producers. Tobacco makers, for example, could under strict liability be forced to pay for cleaning up all cigaret-litter. Similarly, the bill for housing alcoholic derelicts could be sent to the local alcohol producers. Victims of impaired drivers would also sue alcohol producers rather than the drivers.

Even if strict liability for drug producers were viable, it raises concerns about drug user incentives. The basic worry is that by avoiding personal responsibility, drug users would consume more drugs and behave less prudently. Likewise, producer liability for drug-related car crashes might increase the incidence of impaired driving. Under strict liability, victims might receive more compensation, but there would be more of them to compensate.

5. Torts and Public Choice

Arguing for private law regulation of drug activities is challenging because the system is difficult to visualize. Private law is decentralized. Anyone can be a prosecutor, and investigations are conducted privately, so no obvious cadre of blue-uniformed police concentrate public attention. Like the market, private law is driven by desire for personal satisfaction. Most plaintiffs will not risk private resources simply to do the public a favour. Paradoxically, though, competitive self-interest in private suits does result in public benefit, just as it does in the market. The market self-interest of individuals is beneficial indirectly because it cancels out, opposes and counteracts the self-seeking interests of others. The social benefit of private legal actions flows primarily from their deterrent effect: one plaintiff's battle prevents others from being injured. Plaintiffs are volunteer soldiers in the war against torts, but unless they are sufficiently rewarded, not enough will step forward to fight.

Public reaction to private law drug controls would likely be more favourable than for either police or medical controls. Private law is inexpensive, relatively unintrusive and capable of protecting rights while enforcing reasonable obligations. Assisted by the litigating parties, judges could work out drug issues more effectively than legislators. Tort liability would affect drug warnings, packaging and advertising, and would increase general availability: more drugs would be available from more outlets at more convenient times and would be served in safer, more pleasant conditions. Taxes on alcohol and tobacco would be removed, but liability-based price increases could cancel some of that gain. Prices for illicit drugs would fall drastically without "crime tariffs". Retail prices for OTC and Rx psychoactives might increase because these drugs would no longer qualify for health insurance coverage, and because producers would face more hostile courts in product-liability actions. Whether average drug prices would rise or fall would depend on how liability was applied and on the efficiency of private law enforcement. If median prices fell, which is possible, overall consumption would increase. Operating against that trend would be the deterrent effect of wider and more complete health and safety warnings. It is also important to note that increased drug use does not necessarily mean greater social costs. If users took more tobacco but in smokeless products or self-extinguishing cigarets, health and social costs might decline. Similarly, more drinking could be associated with less driving and fewer tavern brawls under purely tort rules of on-premise serving and occupier liability. Private law controls also offer two things almost totally neglected by criminal and medical controls: compensation to injured parties, and personal autonomy both for drug users and for opponents or victims of drug use.

Organizations representing police, politicians and physicians will be strongly opposed to private law controls, as will organized criminals. The livelihood of these professions is partially or wholly tied to the continuation of prohibition or mandatory prescription. Conversely, supporters of private drug controls will include many users of illicit drugs, personal injury lawyers, libertarians, and entrepreneurs now excluded from the drug business by licensing limits, criminal law restrictions or medical monopolies.

Private controls probably offer drug users enough protection from self-harm. Under tort liability drug producers would be compelled to market well-researched, quality drugs bearing ample warnings. The risk of adulterated products and uninformed use could be minimized. Product safety appears to be a major consumer concern, and the same concern is probably central to drug users.

Tort liability would not prohibit any drug, which would mean new pharmaceutical products would appear on the market more quickly and in greater numbers, but liability would limit dangerous forms of new drugs. The largest gap in private law control is in protection from low level, diffuse social harm caused by drug users. On the other hand, taxpayers in a private law system are not burdened with expensive police forces and the incidental social costs arising from prohibition or prescription. Thus between the three schemes examined so far — prohibition, mandatory prescription and tort law — private law controls would probably be the preferred system for uniform drug regulation. Finding closer competition for private law necessitates turning to moderate forms of public law regulation, namely rationing and taxation.

Notes

1   R. Pierce, "Encouraging Safety: The Limits of Tort Law and Government Regulation" (1980) 33 *Vanderbilt Law Review* 1281, 1298.

2   A price support and quota system for U.S. tobacco farmers was instituted during the 1930s. The subsidies and barriers to competition result in higher taxes, non-innovative and inefficient farming and powerful entrenched interests in Kentucky, Virginia and the Carolinas opposed to reform. See H. Sapolsky, "The Political Obstacles to the Control of Cigarette Smoking in the United States" (1980) 5 *Journal of Health Politics, Policy and Law* 277, 281.

3   See the discussion on tort and citizen activism in A. Hutchinson, "Beyond No-Fault", (1985) 73 *California Law Review* 755.

4   D. Trubek, A. Sarat, W. Felstiner, H. Kritzer and J. Grossman, "The Costs of Ordinary Litigation" (1983) 31 *UCLA Law Review* 72, 110.

5   S. Sugarman, "Doing Away with Tort Law" (1985) 73 *California Law Review* 555, 595.

6   See, for example, Sugarman, *ibid.*, 591, who writes that over the past twenty years "it has become increasingly popular to view victim compensation as the central purpose of tort law. This idea has particularly infected the courts..." But, for Sugarman, tort compensation now is so random and unprincipled it is like a "lottery."

7   L. Kornhauser, "Theory and Fact in the Law of Accidents" (1985) 73 *California Law Review* 1024, 1039.

8   Sugarman, *supra* note 5, 596.

9   R. Posner, "A Theory of Negligence" (1972) 1 *Journal of Legal Studies* 29, 31.

10   Kornhauser, *supra* note 7, 1032. See also G. Calabresi, *The*

Cost of Accidents (1970); R. Epstein, "The Legal and Insurance Dynamics of Mass Tort Litigation" (1984) 13 *Journal of Legal Studies* 475.

[11]   See D. Own, "Deterrence and Desert in Tort: A Comment" (1985) 73 *California Law Review* 665, 667-676.

[12]   Sugarman, *supra* note 5.

[13]   M. Galanter, "When Legal Worlds Collide: Reflections on Bhopal, the Good Lawyer, and the American Law School" (1986) 36 *Journal of Legal Education* 292, 296-97.

[14]   R. Hamowy, *Canadian Medicine: A Study in Restricted Entry* (Vancouver: Fraser Institute, 1982) 199-207.

[15]   C. Mitchell and S. McDiarmid, "Medical Malpractice: A Challenge to Alternative Dispute Resolution", (1988) 3 *Canadian Journal of Law and Society* 227.

[16]   "The Malpractice Blues" *Time*, February 24, 1986, 66.

[17]   M. Galanter, "Reading the Landscape of Disputes: What We Know and Don't Know (And Think We Know) About Our Allegedly Contentious and Litigious Society", (1983) 31 *UCLA Law Review* 4, 68.

[18]   See R. Solomon, B. Feldthusen and S. Mills, *Cases and Materials on the Law of Torts* (Toronto: Carswells, 1982) 25-225.

[19]   *Time*, March 3, 1986, 48. In Washington State, two residents died after swallowing poisoned Excedrin capsules and random checks uncovered poisoned capsules of Anacin-3. *Time*, July 7, 1986, 49.

[20]   Ben Whitaker, *The Global Connection: The Crisis of Drug Addiction* (London: Jonathan Cape, 1987); "passive smoking" *The Economist* April 2, 1988, 76.

[21]   R. E. Carney, "The Abuser of Tobacco" in *Types of Drug Abusers and Their Abuses*, J. Gull and R. Hardy (eds), (Springfield: Charles C. Thomas, 1974) 160, 170.

22 R. Lacayo, "All Fired Up Over Smoking" *Time*, April 18, 1988, 42, 46.

23 *Ibid.*, 45.

24 Reported in *The Globe & Mail* May 30, 1987, A3.

25 D. Den Uyl, "Smoking, Human Rights, and Civil Liberties" in R. Tollison (ed) *Smoking and Society* (Mass.: Lexington Books, 1986) 189-216.

26 *Time*, February 23, 1987, 14-15.

27 "Hodge-podge of anti-smoking laws abound" *Ottawa Citizen* Sept. 6, 1986, G14.

28 A. F. Wilcox, *The Decision to Prosecute* (London: Butterworths, 1972) 15; D. Hay, "Controlling the English Prosecutor", (1983) 21 *Osgoode Hall Law Journal* 165.

29 I. Englard, "The System Builders: A Critical Appraisal of Modern American Tort Theory", (1980) 9 *Journal of Legal Studies* 27, 49.

30 W. Freedman, *Products Liability for Corporate Counsels, Controllers and Product Safety Executives* (New York: Van Nostrand, 1984), 35.

31 *ibid.*

32 Pierce, *supra* note 1, 132. Mintz cites the MER/29 scandal as an example of flagrantly unethical behaviour by the producer and incredible laxity by the FDA. See M. Mintz, *The Therapeutic Nightmare* (1965) 238-240; R. Merrill, "Compensation for Prescription Drug Injuries", (1973) 59 *Virginia Law Review* 2, 20-23.

33 Whitaker, *supra* note 20.

34 Trubek, *et al.*, *supra* note 4, 120.

35 N. Boyd, "The Origins of Canadian Narcotics Legislation: The

Process of Criminalization in Historical Context" (1984) 8 *Dalhousie Law Journal* 102; A. Comack, "The Origins of Canadian Drug Legislation: Labelling versus Class Analysis", in *The New Criminologies in Canada* (Toronto: Oxford U. Press, 1985) 65, 66.

[36]   R. Ericson and P. Baranek, *The Ordering of Justice* (Toronto: University of Toronto Press, 1982) Ch. 7.

[37]   S. De Francesco, S. Teret & A. McGuire, "Liability for Cigarette-Related Fire Death and Injury", (1986) 17 *Trial Lawyers Quarterly* 9.

[38]   "Testing medicines to death" *The Economist*, January 30, 1988, 54.

[39]   M. Friedman and R. Friedman, *Free to Choose* (New York: Avon Books, 1981) 196.

[40]   See J. Britain, "Product Honesty is the Best Policy: A Comparison of Doctors' and Manufacturers' Duty to Disclose Drug Risks and the Importance of Consumer Expectations in Determining Product Defects", (1984) 79 *Northwestern University Law Review* 342.

[41]   "Business beware" *The Economist* February 20, 1988, 29.

[42]   Sugarman, *supra* note 5, 583.

[43]   Merrill, *supra* note 32, 25. See also D. Bushwood and L. Simonsmeier, "Drug Information for Patients", (1986) 7 *Journal of Legal Medicine* 279.

[44]   Gray, "Tobacco giants would rather fight" *The Globe & Mail* May 2, 1987, B1.

[45]   Sapolsky, *supra* note 2, 284.

[46]   "Tobacco Takes a New Road" *Time*, November 18, 1985, 98.

[47]   Comment, (1963) 63 *Columbia Law Review* 515, 525; A. Rossi, "The Cigarette-Cancer Problem: Plaintiff's Choice of

Theories Explored", (1961) 34 *South California Law Review* 399; Comment, (1964) 42 *North Carolina Law Review* 468, 471.

[48] "Where there's smoke, there's Fire" *The Globe & Mail* January 21, 1987, B1.

[49] J. Stapleton, "Compensating Victims of Diseases", (1985) 5 *Oxford Journal of Legal Studies* 248.

[50] V. Schwartz and L. Mahshigian, "Failure to Identify the Defendant in Tort Law: Towards a Legislative Solution", (1985) 73 *California Law Review* 941.

[51] Comment, *North Carolina Law Review, supra* note 47, 475.

[52] Whitaker, *supra* note 20.

[53] Pierce, *supra* note 1, 1292.

[54] R. Posner, "Can Lawyers Solve the Problems of the Tort System?", (1985) 73 *California Law Review* 747.

[55] See R. Graycar, "Compensation for Loss of Capacity to Work in the Home" (1985) 10 *Sydney Law Review* 528.

[56] *Time*, November 18, 1985, 98.

[57] *Globe and Mail* January 25, 1988, A3.

[58] M. Hyland and J. Birrell, "Government Health Warnings and The 'Boomerang Effect'" (1979) 44 *Psychological Reports* 643.

[59] "Puffing Up Trade in Third World" *The Globe & Mail*, December 4, 1984, 7.

[60] "Cigaret firms puzzled by rise in smoking rate" *The Globe & Mail*, October 11, 1988, 81.

[61] De Francesco, *et al. supra* note 37.

[62] G. Fraser, "Tobacco firms could be held liable in deaths lawyer says" *The Globe & Mail* January 21, 1988, A5.

63 "Shattering the Smoke Freedom. A landmark cigarette ruling" *Time* June 27, 1988, 54.

64 D. Garner, "Cigarette Dependency and Civil Liability: A Modest Proposal", (1980) 53 *Southern California Law Review* 1423; "Cigarettes and Welfare Reform" (1977) 26 *Emory Law Journal* 269.

65 See P. H. Schuck, *Agent Orange on Trial - Mass Toxic Disasters in Court* (Cambridge: Harvard University Press, 1986).

66 R. Solomon, B. Boake and M. Gleason, "One for the Road: A Tavern Owner's Liability As a Provider of Alcohol" (Forthcoming).

67 *Gardner* v. *McConnel*, [1946] I.D.L.R. 730 (Ont. H.C.).

68 *Lehnert* v. *Nelson* [1947] 4 D.L.R. 473 (B.C.S.C.).

69 *Schmidt* v. *Sharpe et al.* (1983), 27 C.C.L.T. 1 (Ont.S.C.).

70 See "The Liability of Providers of Alcohol: Dram Shop Acts", (1984) 12 *Pepperdine Law Review* 177, 178); M. Friedland, M. Trebilcock and K. Roach, *Regulating Traffic Safety: A Survey of Control Strategies* (1989), forthcoming.

71 W. Prosser, "The Fall of the Citadel (Strict Liability to the Consumer)" (1966) 50 *Minnesota Law Review* 791, 807.

72 H. Latin,"Problem-Solving Behaviour and Theories of Tort Liability" (1985) 73 *California Law Review* 677, 686-89.

73 *ibid.*, 691.

74 S. Peltzman, "The Effects of Automobile Safety Regulation", (1975) 83 *Journal of Political Economy* 677.

75 M. Argericu, D. McCanty, E. Blacker, "Criminality Among Individuals Arraigned for Drinking and Driving in Massachusetts", (1985) 46 *Journal Studies on Alcohol* 525; R. Wilson, B. Jonah, "Identifying Impaired Drivers among the General Driving Population" (1985) 46 *Journal Studies on Alcohol* 531.

76 Posner, *supra* note 54, 749.

VII Drug Rationing

Rationing occurs when government intervenes directly in a market to affect public access to goods or services. Rationing is prominent in the command economies of the U.S.S.R. and China, where even procreation is subject to quotas, but it is also subtly prevalent in the West. We ration taxi cabs, radio stations, air traffic, mail services, rental accommodation, electricity, employment, and many imported products. A number of jurisdictions, including South Carolina, Sweden and Canada, introduced personalized alcohol rationing after 1880 as a less restrictive alternative to prohibition.[1] The doling out of heroin in Britain and of methadone in the U.S. are forms of rationing. Cannabis products are seen by some reformers as proper candidates for rationed distribution. For a single drug, and as an alternative to criminal controls, drug rationing may be viable. The broader issue is whether a uniform rationing of drugs would be acceptable to the general population of alcohol, coffee, aspirin and tobacco users.

1. The Nature of Rationing

a. Rationing Justified

Rationing often restricts consumption of a scarce item when price disincentives cannot affect the necessary restraint or allocation, as when water is rationed in a drought, or food in a famine. Since psychoactive drugs are neither scarce nor essential, except in rare circumstances, the scarcity rationale for rationing does not apply. On the contrary, drug rationing's primary objective would be to create an artificial shortage of drugs. There are four justifications for governments creating drug shortages. First, concerns for public safety excuse the rationing of dangerous products such as poisons, guns and explosives. Like mandatory medical prescription, this type of rationing is individualistic because each would-be buyer must first acquire official approval. Explosives require a bona fide purpose in construction, mining or farming. In Ontario, guns are sold only to persons cleared by local police departments, and in most places buyers of poison must identify themselves and have their purchase recorded.

231

The second justification for contrived scarcity is the prevention of self-harm. Government can lower the rate at which citizens ruin their own health by rationing alcohol. Although rationing's aim here is primarily preventive, there is a method of building a compensation function into a rationing scheme, as I will explain below. Compelling drug users to compensate non-drug users for damage attributable to drug use is the third justification for rationing.

The fourth justification is economic. Social critics complain that Canadian, British and American parents spend more on alcohol and tobacco than on their children's education. About 5% of the average Canadian adult's weekly budget is spent on alcohol alone.[2] By comparison, in the U.S.S.R. the percentage of personal income spent on state-produced alcohol was 13% in 1970. If spending on illicit alcohol and fees paid for overnight "sobering-up" stations are counted, Vladimir Treml estimates that 15% - 20% of the Soviet household budget is spent on alcohol, compared with 3% - 6% in Western industrial nations.[3] Furthermore, Treml calculates that some 4 million urban families in the U.S.S.R. expend at least 40% of their income on alcohol. These figures, however, should be treated with caution because Soviet citizens spend a far smaller proportion of their income on basic necessities than do people in the West. According to the Soviet government, for example, apartment rents consume only 3% of family income. Oddly, many Russians spend on alcohol what Americans spend on housing. Similarly, in China, where apartments are heavily subsidized and tobacco is taxed, smokers ruefully admit that cigarets cost them more than living accommodations.

By decreasing the amount of alcohol available for purchase, drug rationers could limit total alcohol expenditure, freeing-up those financial resources for more socially valuable purposes. The present Soviet regime has cut back sharply on alcohol production for three reasons: to protect health, to bolster productivity and military fitness, and to promote economic development by shifting private expenditure away from alcohol. Governments regularly ration products judged to have low social value to encourage investment in higher value goods and services. In war times, Canadian automobile production was severely rationed so that human and physical capital could build airplanes and tanks instead. In militaristic nations such as North Korea, war-time rationing is permanent, with trucks, cars and even bicycles being reserved for government personnel. If American alcohol supplies were cut in half by government decree, hundreds of thousands of alcohol-related employees would be free to pursue other work in agriculture or industry. Economist Abba Lerner allowed that, despite its faults, war rationing was justified as "a form of state guardianship to prevent foolish spending."[4] Lerner did not explain what constitutes "foolish spending," but that category would probably include the purchase of addicting, health impairing psychoactive drugs. Of course, drugs are not the only objects of unedifying expenditure, nor is foolish spending limited to certain groups in society. On the contrary, "foolish spending" is normal human behaviour, although some people are more normal than others.

Two problems confront economic rationing. The first is prices. If drug supplies are artificially limited, demand will push prices up. Per capita aspirin consumption is now about 225 five-grain tablets per year.[5] If regulators imposed an aspirin allotment of only 100 tablets a year, while simultaneously rationing all other analgesics, aspirin prices would climb. A ration-induced price increase would allow some groups to gain financial advantage; the usual beneficiaries being the government and private drug producers. Following the example set by Venice many centuries ago when it established a state monopoly of tobacco distribution for revenue purposes, modern governments often create state enterprises to produce and/or sell rationed drugs.[6] This strategy nearly duplicates the effects of the standard tax on alcohol and tobacco because government rationers force up the market price and then monopolize retail sales so as to claim the extra profit. If government allowed rationing to increase drug prices, the economic goal of rationing would be partially defeated because the drug expenditure decline will not be maximized. One solution to this problem is price controls: supply is reduced, but government enforces prices at the old pre-ration level.

Socialist economies are synonymous with price controls.[7] Apartment rents have not changed much in the U.S.S.R. since the 1920s, still averaging about $18 a month. Food and clothing prices are also held down below market values. The result is shortages, poor quality, long lineups and illicit markets. Meat at Warsaw's state-monopoly butcher shops is cheap, but customers wait for hours and are rationed to 2.5 kilograms per month.[8] Price controls cost the Polish government over one-third of its budget, while in the U.S.S.R. price fixing reportedly costs $115 billion (U.S.) a year; nevertheless, governments like price controls because of the tremendous power they give to politicians and bureaucrats.

A second problem with the rationing is substitution. If controls fix prices too low, perverse misallocations occur, as in the U.S.S.R. where farmers feed bread to livestock because it is cheaper than mixed fodder, or taxi drivers polish their cabs with new children's clothing because it is cheaper than cleaning cloths. These incentives could not occur with controlled drugs if fixed prices were joined to stringent rationing. Then, even if liquor cost less than fruit juice, people would not shift from orange juice to vodka for breakfast because the quantity of liquor available would be artificially limited to a small fraction of the quantity of fruit juice available. Consumers would then use less alcohol than juice, and spend less on alcohol than on juice. A more important substitution effect is that the money saved on buying cheap but rationed alcohol may not be put to a better use. Alcohol users might no longer waste as much money at taverns and liquor stores, but they could re-direct their savings to new expenditures on other drugs, gambling, pornography and so on.

Rationing for economic purposes leads inevitably into the forests of the planned economy. Price and ration controls on alcohol would shift some consumers to cocaine and cannabis, so all psychoactives must be included in the system. Once all drugs are rationed with fixed prices, some spending will shift to the social psychoactives, so they too must come under government supervision. This sequence of legal cat-and-mouse led the Soviet, Korean, Chinese, Polish and other governments to ration a long list of commodities, services and pastimes. While their logic is unassailable, their methods are not. One recurring difficulty is that the ration scheme is too severe or inflexible to be popularly accepted and, as a consequence, significant black markets develop.[9] Despite a state alcohol rationing system in the Soviet Union that forbids the private sale or production of liquor (beer and wine can be made for home use), the per capita consumption of *samogon* (homemade liquor) has increased 600% since 1955, while consumption of legal alcohol increased only 200%.[10]

b. Rationing's Preventive Potential

The preventive potential of general controls such as drug rationing and taxation is denied by the disease theory of drug abuse. According to this view, problematic drug use is symptomatic of personal mental or physical disorder. Popham, Schmidt and deLint explain:

> The view that normal drinkers and alcoholics comprise two quite separate groups... has rendered meaningless or at least of low priority the contemplation of measures intended to affect the prevalence of alcoholism through the general regulation of alcohol consumption. The drinking of the alcoholic came to be seen as independent of other drinking: a symptom of pathological factors peculiar to him, and these not amenable to change by measures that would affect the normal drinker.[11]

This user/abuser dichotomy is championed by drug producers because it exonerates the majority of drug users and precludes restrictions that might reduce total consumption.[12] Police, physicians and other practitioners of individualized "treatment" support the disease theory, in part because it justifies the expensive measures directed at their patients or prisoners. The disease model also allows establishment drug users to disclaim personal responsibility for drug excesses because it claims there is no connection between the total level of drug consumption and the rate of alcoholism, nicotinism or caffeinism.

The disease-model movement calls for both the expansion of individualized alcohol-treatment programs and the liberalizing of restrictions on use. As a result, alcohol taxes fall, while billions of dollars are spent "treating" impaired drivers and "problem drinkers." In the opinion of one research group, the disease model may be seen as "a kind of cultural alibi for the...relaxation of controls [on alcohol]; ...subsequent increases in consumption and in associated problems become arguments for the further expansion of the treatment system."[13] Similarly, the Walsh study in Ireland concluded that the disease concept of drug abuse leads to permissiveness and the illusory promise of a medical cure that blocks a more effective general response.[14]

The counter-position is that the prevalence of heavy drug consumers is a direct function of average consumption rates. This thesis was advanced by Sully Ledermann, a French demographer who studied the distribution of alcohol intake among various populations. In each case he found the same pattern: most alcohol users were light or intermittent drinkers; a considerably smaller number drank regularly, and a much smaller number drank a lot. Ledermann found no sudden shifts that marked off alcoholics; moreover, as average consumption increased, the number of high-risk alcohol users also increased: the entire distribution curve shifted. Ledermann's findings have been confirmed by other researchers.[15] The single-distribution thesis is also consistent with broader discoveries in sociology, anthropology and psychology. Floyd Allport's interest in conforming behaviour led him to examine how people adhere to rules and norms. Allport claimed that people conform or deviate from traffic rules, social norms or employment requirements in specific ways: a large majority closely conform; a smaller number diverge slightly; a still smaller group breaks the rule regularly; and the smallest group ignores the norm completely. Alcohol fits this pattern. In North America, the alcohol norm is light or intermittent use, and most people closely conform to the norm. Individual choice is a minor factor, as cross-cultural or anthropological comparisons of drug use indicate. But social norms are so omnipresent and unchanging that we scarcely notice them, and as a result people believe their constrained use of alcohol reflects free choice and personal control.[16] The *Dictionary of American Slang* lists 313 different words for "intoxication," but not a single word or term that distinguishes between alcohol and non-alcohol cultures. Paradoxically, we are very sensitive to deviations from the norm, although the norm itself, like air pressure, is unnoticed.

The disease model elevates personal factors and claims that individual treatment is the best way to reduce drug abuse. The available evidence does not support the disease theory of alcoholism but does favor the single-distribution thesis.[17] A policy of higher drug prices or lower ration levels affects overall consumption, resulting in less drug use at all levels.[18]

2. Rationing Drug Production and Importation

a. Assigning Drug Quotas

Drugs can be rationed at the production or retail stages. Perhaps the simplest, most impersonal rationing system affects the quantity of drugs produced or imported for the domestic market. The U.S. employs rationing quotas to limit tobacco production. These quotas have declined from 1.19 billion pounds in 1977 to about 700 million pounds in 1987. A ceiling on drug *exports* can be avoided because those drugs will be consumed within another government's jurisdiction. Lebanese who disapprove of cannabis happily export the drug to Europe, and recent concern about tobacco use has not led to a call for limiting exports of American tobacco, which are now growing at 5% a year.

Production or import quotas differ from prohibition because they permit the incremental escalation of drug controls. Criminal laws are absolutist, a typical pronouncement being something like: "as of January 1, 1918 all persons will cease producing or consuming any opium whatsoever." Rationing can impose restraints ranging from very severe to scarcely noticeable. With Canadian cigaret smokers using an average of 10,500 cigarets in 1989, supplies could be rationed to achieve a modest reduction to 10,300 cigarets in 1990. Continuing at that rate, by the year 2000 average annual use would be 8,300, and by 2010, it would be down to 6,300 cigarets a year, a 40% decline over 20 years. This amounts to the median smoker giving up cigarets at the rate of four per week. A gradual, almost imperceptible imposition of rationing could achieve a sizeable impact over time without inciting the opposition engendered by prohibition. People's adaptive capacity must be respected: rationing should proceed at a pace that allows producers and users to accommodate the changes.

If the basic drug supply is to be restricted, drug quotas can be assigned through three different means: government monopoly (nationalization), public administration, and market regulation. If all drug production and importation is nationalized, quotas become direct political decisions by the relevant branches of government. Nationalization of drug production is the most expensive alternative to initiate because government must first acquire the productive

237

capacity of the entire psychoactive drug industry either through purchase or confiscation. And once the drug industry is nationalized, government is caught in a conflict of interest, torn between its duty to promote public safety and its immediate revenue needs. Drug industry employees would become government employees, possibly under one union, and production-cutting policies might be blocked by their power. A less expensive variant of nationalization is for government to establish a retail monopoly, outlawing the sale of drugs except through official outlets at official prices. This alternative will be discussed below in the section on retail rationing.

The kind of administrative systems introduced during the New Deal period to regulate industries such as broadcasting, trucking, and air lines are much less intrusive than nationalization. Under an administrative-control system, legislators delegate authority to a quasi-independent body or Board that is similar to a court of law but has less political independence. For tobacco production quotas, an administrated system would operate along the following lines. A Tobacco Control Act would authorize a Tobacco Rationing Board to "take whatever steps are necessary" to promote the "public good" by means of the orderly, fair and efficient control of tobacco production. Assuming that a certain ceiling has been set on tobacco output, a Canadian Board would divide total permitted Canadian production into, say, 11,000 allotments of 5,000 kilograms of cured tobacco leaf each. These allotments would then be assigned to tobacco farmers for a specified period of time. Existing producers would probably be assigned an allotment equal to or at least proportional to their pre-ration production. Allotment holders would enjoy a temporary licence to produce and market tobacco for perhaps three to seven years. Thereafter, farmers would re-apply to the Tobacco Rationing Board for renewal of their quota. Like broadcasters, tobacco farmers could own their productive capacity, but they could not sell, trade or transfer their allotment or licence. To reduce output, the Board would simply withdraw allotments as they came up for renewal. Tobacco production could, by this means, be gradually curtailed, while allowing farmers and processors the opportunity to stage an orderly retreat from the drug business.

Administrative systems of regulation are not without fault. Politicians would appoint patronage cronies to a Tobacco Rationing

Board, and Board members would tend to favor tobacco producers from their own jurisdiction, or those with the right political connections: frequent re-applications for quota renewal would permit the Board to monitor quota-holders' willingness to meet performance obligations, and perhaps to maintain political party contributions. Because tobacco quotas would not be held as property, quota-holders would be vulnerable to sudden shifts in the tenor of Board decisions. In addition, regulated industries often "capture" the regulatory agency by developing cozy customer/client relations.[19] Members of the Tobacco Rationing Board would commonly resign to work for Imperial Tobacco Co. Ltd., while tobacco executives could expect to retire to a sinecure on the Board. Clearly, the potential for conflict of interest would arise, as it does in most instances of administrative regulation.[20] The Board could also face an endless round of litigation brought by applicants asking for a judicial review of Board decisions.

The third method of assigning production quotas minimizes government intervention by relying on the market. Under a property rights regime, tobacco quotas would be sold at the outset to the highest bidders or to existing producers and, thereafter, could be sold, traded or transferred. A Board would not be needed to regulate quota renewals. Taxi cabs in Toronto and New York are rationed in this manner. New York has not increased the number of its taxi licenses since 1937 when 13,500 medallions were sold for $10 each. As a result, the 11,787 taxi medallions still in existence cost over $100,000 each on the market, which is cheaper than a rationed seat on the New York Stock Exchange.

Under a property rights system, politicians have less opportunity to make patronage appointments or favorable regulatory decisions. To grow tobacco, a farmer would only need enough money to buy a tobacco quota. Political connections, which are more difficult to come by than money, would not be of much use. To reduce tobacco production, government would simply buy up and retire a certain portion of existing tobacco quotas. This process would automatically compensate farmers for abandoning tobacco; moreover, it would preclude court challenges because it would involve willing sellers. A government buy-back program would also maintain the value of the remaining production quotas.

Generally, then, a regulatory system based on property rights

239

reduces the number of actors with vested interests in the status quo. This is an important feature because a long-term objective of production rationing is the reduction of total drug output. The property rights system is clearly the least restrictive, least interventionist alternative, and it is also more flexible and less expensive to operate than nationalization or direct administration. This holds true for every form of drug production, be it agricultural, biological, chemical or industrial.

b. Setting Drug Quotas

At the beginning of the discussion on production quotas, I set the hypothetical Tobacco Rationing Board to work enforcing a ceiling on tobacco output. The next challenge is to determine how one should go about setting a limit on production levels.

A popular method with politicians is the arbitrary but dramatic announcement from the mayor, governor, commissioner or prime minister that their jurisdiction will be "smoke free by the year 2000." With a tobacco-free zone as their goal, regulators can determine how many cigars, cigarets and pipe-tobacco packets are being consumed in 1990, and then calculate the annual roll-back necessary for reaching zero consumption by the end of the millennia. In the U.S., cigaret production would have to be reduced by about 750 million per year. Leaders can also vow to reduce drug consumption by 50%, as Mikail Gorbachev did with alcohol in the Soviet Union in 1986. Such ad hoc goals may not be attainable or even desirable. Criteria are needed to help regulators decide when the ration has been set too low or, at the other extreme, when the quota is too liberal.

One such set of criteria involves measures of proportionality and relative restraint. Assume that under free market conditions citizens purchase 100 units of a given drug. With rationing controls, only 100-minus quantity X could be purchased, quantity X being determined by the social costs and benefits of the drug. For some drugs, like tobacco cigarets , quantity X would be close to 100, since there are safer forms of the drug. However, enforcing a prohibitive cigaret ration would generate high social costs, so additional criteria are required to guide regulators from the time rationing begins and the eventual attainment of an ideal consumption level.

The functional test of a ration floor is how much black market trafficking is generated. Cutting alcohol production by 90% in one

240

year, for example, would spark massive black market trade. Black markets might generate social costs greater than those directly attributable to use of rationed drugs. Extreme rationing would closely duplicate the effects of a partial prohibition, since most production would be illegal. Widespread illegality contingent on overly-zealous rationers occurs in many African "command economies" in which highly-interventionist governments ration everything from asparagus to Zactirin.

The starting point for production quotas will depend on the conditions under which a specific drug is now marketed. According to recent estimates by the U.S. Department of Justice, Americans annually import about 3,600 kg. of heroin, 40,000 kg. of cocaine, and 9,000,000 kg. of marijuana. By comparison, caffeine imports total about 180,000,000 kg., mostly in the form of tea and coffee.[21] Setting quotas at current levels would have different effects on caffeine and cocaine. With caffeine, the quota would correspond to the free market supply, so little change would occur. Imports would have to be cut by 20% to 30% to make significant inroads in caffeine use. More dramatic effects would follow if legal cocaine imports were set at 40,000 kg. per year. First, prices would fall because much of the crime tariff would be eliminated: cocaine importers would operate overtly within the standard framework of legal business protections. Instead of costing $34,000 (U.S.) a kilo, legally rationed cocaine would be wholesaled from Colombia at a price closer to $3,400. Ideally, cocaine consumption would remain at current levels, but consumers would spend 80% or less of the $40 billion now allegedly devoted to purchasing cocaine. The North American trade deficit with Colombia would be eliminated, legitimate importers and price competition would drive out cocaine crime syndicates, and user resources could be re-directed to non-cocaine purchases. Cocaine consumption would remain at about 2% of caffeine intake, a level said to represent a terrible "epidemic."

The critical rationing issue is whether a total U.S. quota of 40,000 kg. of cocaine is too low. The answer depends on a number of related factors including demand, enforcement resources and the ease of smuggling or illicit production. Normally, if the price of a commodity falls, demand increases. This is true for drugs if everything else is held constant. But demand for specific drugs is strongly affected by fashion and, as clothing designers know, even bedrock prices will not move wide ties if thin ties are in. Military

241

music, men's hats, long dresses and cocaine were the rage eighty years ago, but today most adults would not adopt these fashions even if they were paid to. If the current fashion for cocaine is related to the drug's outlaw status and its use by "rebel" entertainers such as John Belushi, J.J. Cale, Eric Clapton, Richard Pryor and Keith Richards, then cheap, legitimate cocaine would probably be much less popular. On the other hand, other segments of society might decide that rationed cocaine is fashionable.

In any case, if low prices were to drive up demand, enforcement efforts against non-rationed production or import would become critical. The government's capacity to prevent extra-quota production would vary according to the nature of the drug's manufacture. Drugs like alcohol and marijuana, which can be produced cheaply in small quantities in temperate climates, make enforcing severe rations an immense challenge. With imported drugs like cocaine and heroin, enforcement means monitoring import quotas, which should not be confused with current efforts to stop all cocaine at the border. Once significant cocaine supplies are legally available at low prices, the financial incentive to smuggle additional quantities will be drastically reduced. Smuggling would continue only if the drug was rationed but prices were not fixed, or if demand increased. Black market activity would signal regulators to increase import quotas. The reasons for illegal trading could be left to law enforcement agents: regulators would simply respond to market signals.

The key criterion for setting the quota floor is therefore black market activity. This leaves the other side of the balance, which is determining when the quota is too high. Perhaps the simplest method of avoiding excessive quotas is to constantly lower them by, say, 1%-3% annually until signs appear that the floor is approaching.

An advantage of a property rights system of alienable quotas, is that regulators could monitor the price of production quotas. For example, assume that in 1990 a cigaret quota is established and the right to produce 10 million cigarets sells on the open market for $35,000. If demand for cigarets falls over the following five years, the market value of the production quota would decline to perhaps $25,000. The quota's decline in value would signal to the rationers that the quota is too liberal. That is to say, the artificially-induced shortage of cigarets would no longer be as stringent as it was in

1990. The government would then intervene to buy up and retire quotas to put upward pressure on the quota value. This action would maintain restrictions on cigaret supplies and protect producers' investment in their quota. Quota setting and price fixing through "marketing boards" is already standard practice with tobacco. Still, despite tobacco cartel formation under Ontario's Tobacco Marketing Board, the selling price for a kilogram of tobacco fell from $5.70 in 1983 to $1.43 in 1987 because the government did not intervene to buy up surplus quotas. What financially endangered tobacco farmers find irksome is that while the price for tobacco leaf fell, tax increases on cigarets between 1980 and 1987 were 179% for federal taxes and 200% for provincial taxes.[22]

Drug rationing could begin and end at the production/import stage without any further intervention in the retail sector. Under this simplest of rationing systems, the Drug Rationing Department would dictate a production ceiling on drugs like alcohol, and then leave producers free to market their limited supply as they saw fit. Retailers' obligations would consist only of not buying any drugs for commercial re-sale unless the product bore an official ration stamp. Enforcement of the law would entail monitoring producers' output and checking retail outlets for unstamped merchandise. One of the advantages of production-only rationing is that enforcement resources are concentrated on businesses rather than individual users. A dozen cigaret factories and two breweries could supply the entire North American market, making it inexpensive to have government inspectors permanently on site to oversee all outgoing shipments. Large, concentrated production facilities are a feature of beer, wine and liquor production and might also be typical of cannabis and cocaine as they became legitimate products. To increase the distance between police and drug consumers, all home production and private, non-monetary exchanges of drug products could be exempted from rationing so that individual drug users would not come into contact with ration enforcement agents. This would preclude police abuse of individuals, instead pitting government agents against legally sophisticated, well-financed businesses able to defend their interests.

A simple, one-stage production quota would probably be the most cost-effective rationing program. For tobacco and wine, this would mean leaving farmers free to grow grapes and tobacco leaf as they chose while limiting producer's capacity to turn those raw materials into wine, sherry, cigars, cigarets or snuff.

Besides rationing drug production in general, regulators can also ration the form or variety of drugs produced. Government could stipulate that out of every 100 litres of absolute alcohol manufactured, 40 litres must be of beer, 40 of wine and 20 of liquor. Complicated rules of this sort are probably not warranted for alcoholic beverages since they are all quite similar from a social harm/self-harm perspective. Perhaps a better case can be made for restricting the proportion of a total tobacco or cannabis quota that can be devoted to smoked products rather than products designed to be eaten or chewed. The empirical basis of such regulations would be whether a gram of cocaine, for example, has a more deleterious impact when smoked, snorted, swallowed as a pill or imbibed in liquid form. If significant differences were discovered among modes of drug ingestion, as appears to be the case with tobacco, then rationers would shift use toward the less harmful forms of a given drug. An additional reason for shifting drug users from one ingestion mode to another concerns the phenomenon of users becoming psychologically attached to the rituals and practices of their favorite method. Cigaret smokers are not only nicotine habitues, they are also fixated on cigarets and the rituals and accoutrements of smoking. At a recent faculty union meeting I attended, a proposal to ban smoking on campus was discussed. One version of the ban extended to faculty offices because most campus buildings are sealed and air is recirculated. A number of impassioned objectors declared that such a ban would force some faculty to quit their positions. Others declared that they could not work without smoking. When I pointed out that the ban was not anti-tobacco and that addicted academics would be quite free to eat, chew, inject or snort the drug, most of my smoking colleagues regarded me with puzzlement, disbelief or horror. For them, tobacco means cigarets and smoking. If rationing encouraged or compelled users to widen their tobacco-using methods, the result could be less dependence on any one method, which might help users wean themselves from their basic dependency. Conversely, users could adopt snuff or chewing tobacco without weakening their cigaret attachment. This question has yet to be investigated.

c. Rationing Drug Advertisements

According to some researchers, drug advertising should be regulated because it encourages people to consume more drugs and also prompts non-users, especially youngsters, to commence drug use. Drug advertising could be banned, taxed or rationed. In this section I will deal primarily with rationing drug advertisements.

The first question is whether commercial drug promotions deserve public-law restrictions. The evidence on the promotional efficacy of advertising in general, and drug advertising in particular, is not conclusive.[23] A review of the econometric research on alcohol advertising's effects found "a stunning array of conflicting conclusions."[24] Various researchers have discovered, amongst other things, that alcohol advertising modestly increases liquor but not beer consumption, that advertising affects market share but not aggregate sales, that advertising in some media increases some kinds of alcohol consumption, that advertising has little effect on alcohol use or market share, and that increased sales lead to increased advertising, rather than vice versa. The simple thesis that more advertising leads to higher per-capita drug use or more drug users is not supported by the available data. For example, banning tobacco advertisements has not achieved the intended effect.[25] The Swedish ban on tobacco messages on television corresponded with declining consumption, but this effect may be due to high tax rates on tobacco, or to the general downward trend for tobacco use noted throughout the West. Though tobacco advertising is restricted in Japan, per-capita tobacco use increased from 1972 to 1978, by which time about 75% of all Japanese men smoked cigarets. The long-term tobacco advertising bans in Hungary and Yugoslavia corresponded with growth in cigaret use of from 20% to 60%. A similar prohibition in Italy, enacted in 1962, was met by a doubling of tobacco consumption through the 1970s.[26] High cigaret consumption is also observed in communist countries where there is no advertising of tobacco.[27]

Per-capita alcohol use increased in Eastern Europe from 1950 to 1980 at the same rate as in Western Europe, again without any advertising. In 1957, when advertising of Scotch whisky was banned in France, imports stood at 157,000 proof gallons. By 1979, Scotch imports totalled 6,294,000 proof gallons. From these and other results, Waterson concludes that advertising has "little impact on national expenditure, or on large sectors of consumers' expenditure in a variety of different markets."[28] Reaching a similar conclusion, van Iwaarden counsels that banning alcohol commercials "will not have any direct impact on the overall use of alcohol. Even in the long run the effects probably would be hardly substantial."[29] The data are not conclusive, but do suggest that some of the more extremist opinions held in this field should be treated with caution. As Strickland warns: "in the areas of both alcohol and advertising, moral bias rather than scientific rigour often predominates."[30]

Even if advertising promotes drug consumption in some subtle, long-term way, the type of advertising ban that the World Health Organization (WHO) and the U.S. Surgeon General recommend for tobacco is not necessarily warranted. First, the WHO is wrong to seek a ban on tobacco advertising unless the ban also applies to every other psychoactive drug. If tobacco ads are banned from television, as they are in Canada and the U.S., then the same ban should extend to sleeping pills, headache relievers, beer, wine and appetite suppressants. Second, the WHO's call for an ad ban ignores constitutional free speech guarantees. Under the Canadian *Charter of Rights*, freedom of expression can only be subject to "such reasonable limits prescribed by law as can be demonstrably justified in a free and democratic society." The harmfulness of smoking is not in itself a justification; an observable link between commercials and tobacco consumption is also required. Representative Mike Synar, Democrat-Oklahoma, who sponsored a bill in 1986 to ban all tobacco advertising, argues that such a ban is constitutional in the U.S. on the basis of the Puerto Rican case of *Posadas* (1986), which upheld a partial ban on advertising for casino gambling. Douglas Kmiec, a Justice Department attorney, disagrees with Synar on the basis of the *Virginia Pharmacy* (1976) case.[31] It is heartening that both Synar and Kmiec make fairness arguments. Synar suggests that if tobacco were regulated by the FDA like other drugs, it would be banned entirely. Kmiec, on the other hand, suggests that the same considerations behind banning tobacco ads also apply to advertisements for automobiles, confections and soda drinks.

The third argument against the WHO stand is that a sudden end to drug advertising would endanger the financial health of many magazines, newspapers and broadcast stations. For 1980, expenditures on alcohol advertising in U.S. magazines exceeded $250 million, with the highest dependence shown by *The New Yorker, Scientific American* and *Psychology Today*.[32] Alcoholic beverage advertising accounts for about 5% of all print media advertising revenue. Two of the major news weeklies, *Time* and *Newsweek*, rely on alcohol promotions for about 10% of their ad revenue. Tobacco ads account for 15% of newspaper advertising, 10% of magazine advertising and 30% of outdoor advertising in America. After the Public Health Cigaret Smoking Act of 1970 restricted tobacco promotions on television, billboards began to advertise tobacco more often than any other product.[33] According to the same source, a recent survey of alcohol advertising in U.S. magazines refuted the notion that advertisers target supposedly "vulnerable" groups such as women, blacks and minors. Instead, as one might expect, liquor ads are aimed primarily at "men's" magazines and at higher income readers. Medical journals are even more heavily dependent on pharmaceutical ad revenue. Tobacco advertising now generates about $13 million annually for Canadian newspapers and magazines.

In some ways, a prohibition of drug advertising would help rather than hurt producers of already established drugs by hindering entry of new competitors and lowering operating expenses. Brewers spend 6.8% of their total revenues on advertising, while the makers of OTC drugs spend about 10%.[34] Without advertising expenses, profits would rise substantially if sales volume remained constant and, as noted above, there is evidence that sales for some drug products would actually increase with an advertising ban. At present, much advertising consists of one company attempting to gain market share from a competitor advertising an indistinguishable product. Miller and Budweiser would probably be better off fixing market share as it stands and then excluding advertising by new breweries, but anti-trust laws forbid such collusion. Michael Schudson in *Advertising, The Uneasy Persuasion: Its Dubious Impact on American Society* (1985) concludes that advertising is not nearly as powerful as its critics suggest, and that the ban of tobacco ads on television helped the tobacco companies save money, maintain sales and avoid anti-smoking advertisements. Schudson also argues that tobacco habits and styles change because of cultural, sexual and demographic influences, and that once a new trend, like women's adoption of cigarets in the 1920s, is underway, advertisers respond to it and help cement or re-inforce the fashion.[35] Peter Taylor, on the other hand, in *Smoke Ring: The Politics of Tobacco* (1985), argues that much of the $2.7 billion spent on U.S. tobacco ads in 1983 was designed to recruit new converts, not merely promote brands to existing users.[36]

Ironically, advertising designed to promote brand-name fixation may actually reduce drug consumption. Despite minimal quality variation among low-cost, homogeneous products like beer, vodka, tobacco and aspirin, some customers purchase branded aspirin when generic ASA retails for 30% of the branded price. Similarly, 100 tablets of the tranquilizer chlordiazepoxide sell for $6.75 generic and $21.95 as Librium (1984 U.S. prices). The extra money appears to be buying a placebo effect; that is, an illusion of greater potency, efficacy, style or prestige. When people spend twice as much for a national brand, they tend to consume less of the drug, trading pharmacological effect for psychic gain.

The ambiguous effects of alcohol and tobacco advertisements do not justify prohibition, and may not even justify rationing. If advertising rationing is instituted, the level of restraint should not be severe. Rationing offers the strategic advantage of avoiding the legal challenges, political opposition and high transition costs of an outright ban. Regulators could ration the quantity and/or the content of advertising.

The quantity of advertising could be rationed in a number of ways. A maximum ratio of advertising to sales revenues of, say, 2% could be stipulated. Alternatively, sellers of advertising space on radio, billboards, magazines and newspapers could be limited in the quantity of drug advertising they could accept. Administering this second control would be easy: the Drug Advertisement Ration Bureau would simply monitor the dissemination of commercial drug messages which, by their nature, are public and accessible. Enforcing limits on advertising-to-sales ratios would be a more complex, expensive task, with greater potential for evasion. The government could also compel drug advertisements on TV to appear in the middle of ad clusters since research indicates such ads are remembered less than the first and last spots.[37]

Canadian federal Health Minister Jake Epp recently made a number of rationing proposals for tobacco and alcohol advertisers.

Epp wants the amount of television ads for beer reduced by 50% and all "life style" ads eliminated. He also wants 15% of the breweries' advertising time spent on warning about alcohol abuse.[38] Epp and his Department probably do not appreciate that under an effective private-law system, drug sellers would voluntarily disclose information about product risks. Epp's bill C-51, the *Tobacco Products Control Act*, would also stop tobacco firms from associating their brand names with sponsored sports or entertainment events. Tobacco producers are currently major sponsors of ballets, theatres and arts institutions. In support of the bill, a member of the Nonsmokers Rights Association pointed out that "You would not have thalidomide sponsoring a cultural event. Or you wouldn't have the Valium Jazz Festival."[39] Diazepam producers do not sponsor public events now because they are not allowed to market their drugs publicly. However, pharmaceutical firms spend a large portion of their budgets sponsoring events for physicians. Compared to this elitist and covert sponsorship, a Valium Jazz Festival would be a major improvement.

There is a basic assumption in our arts-worshipping culture that sports, opera, ballet, theatre and jazz are pure goods tainted by connection with drugs. The Puritans were at least consistent in restricting sports and theatre along with drugs. A final hypocrisy here is that Canadian governments limit tobacco advertisements, while heavily promoting state lotteries. Some psychiatrists report that gambling is more addicting, at least for some people, than any drug.

Instead of regulating quantity, regulators could control advertising content, as Sweden does by refusing to let tobacco ads depict people.[40] There is no evidence that this strategy affects advertising impact: even without restrictions, alcohol advertisers in U.S. magazines use human models in less than 40% of their ads.[41] Animals and animated characters seem to make excellent pitchmen. For decades, the Pillsbury Doughboy has been one of North America's favorite advertising personalities. Morris the Cat and the animated feline Garfield are also popular.

In the 1950s, Ontario allowed beer advertisers to display the label but not the actual bottle. Now beer bottles can be shown, but actors cannot be depicted in the act of drinking. This rule is nonsensical for two reasons. First, most non-drinkers are dependent children who cope with the real-life trauma of seeing their parents drink beer. Second, when the beer commercial ends and the sponsored program resumes, viewers of standard television dramas witness frequent episodes of alcohol intake. Research into alcohol on prime-time television found that although only 16% of total beverage consumption in the U.S. is alcoholic, alcohol drinking episodes on television occurred about three times as frequently as the combined total for coffee/tea, soda pop and water. In other words, 75% of all prime-time beverages contained alcohol.[42] Another survey found alcohol present in 201 out of 249 network programs, with liquor portrayed 120 times more frequently than milk, although, in fact, people drink more milk than alcohol.[43] This over-emphasis is a result of the ceremonial role of alcohol, the dramatic advantages writers gain from using alcoholic drinks as stage props, and the common employment of taverns or night clubs as settings. Some critics claim that this reliance on alcohol is dangerous, but in fact[44] the population's massive intake of television may in itself be the greater danger. Television never accurately portrays real life because, to be entertaining, it leaves out the 99% of life taken up by mundane, repetitive and routine occurrences. What proportion of their time do prime-time characters spend on screen sleeping, shopping for groceries, waiting in line at the bank, or sitting in traffic jams? Television warps everything, not just alcohol. Service or manual workers constitute about 10% of television characters, although they account for 65% of the total North American employed. Men outnumber women on TV three to one, and TV-men are 25-55 years old, while most TV women are 25-35 years old. In an average week a heavy viewer witnesses 15 deaths, and encounters 30 police officers and 10 physicians, the latter being granted near demi-god status. Clearly, there is a possibility that programming is more damaging than advertising, and that television is semi-hypnotic and drug-like, regardless of content.

Concern for impressionable youth frequently leads critics to charge that advertisers are appealing to youngsters by using their peers in ad campaigns. The industry limits alcohol and tobacco advertising to use of models over 25 years of age. By forbidding the use of young adults, the theory goes, one limits the appeal of the advertisement. Yet "old codgers" are used to sell Jack Daniels and, lately, Bartle's and Jayme's Wine Cooler. The theory also exaggerates the frequency of ads using sexual innuendo or "life style" approaches linking alcohol to wealth and achievement.

3. Retail Rationing of Drugs

a. Off-Premise Sales

Alcohol rationing has accustomed many people to retail rationing of drugs. Alcohol sales are typically limited by rationing the number, location and hours of operation of retail outlets. Individual buyers could also be regulated through ration cards, drug coupons and record keeping.

Historically, the most common rationing strategy has been to limit the number of alcohol retail outlets per unit of population. Some researchers, notably Rabow, Watts and Neuman in California, report that increasing alcohol availability leads to higher per-capita consumption.[45] Alcohol sales in grocery stores, where most alcohol is purchased in California, makes alcohol too convenient and improperly treats the drug as a food item, the researchers claim. However, they do not mention the sale of aspirin or caffeine in grocery stores or the much closer association of coffee with food. Other investigators suggest that limiting alcohol outlets is not an important method of restraint except when outlets open in previously "dry" areas, as happened some decades ago in rural Finland.[46] It seems that rationing alcohol outlets does not have a major impact on consumption levels because of customer's capacity to adapt to adverse shopping conditions. Beer outlets are limited in Ontario, but buyers accommodate the restriction by buying in bulk: a case or two of 24 bottles is probably the standard purchase size. Consumers are even more likely to buy other drugs in quantity because most are less bulky and require less storage equipment than beer. An average cigaret smoker could carry on foot a six-month's supply, and a full year's ration of heroin, cocaine, diazepam or aspirin could easily be stored in a small container at the back of the refrigerator. Indeed, for many drugs, as with food, refrigerators make bulk buying possible. In ancient Egypt, beer controls could be more stringent because beer had to be consumed when fresh. The standard barley beer of 4000 B.C. had a shelf-life of only one or two days.[47] A great advantage of distilled liquor in pre-refrigerator days was its extremely long shelf life.

Rationing alcohol outlets need not be associated with a state monopoly, but usually is. Eighteen states and most provinces empower government agencies to distribute alcohol at the retail and/or wholesale level. An American survey in the mid 1970s found total consumption of distilled spirits to be slightly higher in states without government retail monopolies.[48] Other studies, which included beer and wine consumption, did not find significant differences in per-capita alcohol purchases between private and public outlets.[49] Provincial governments in Ontario and New Brunswick recently considered allowing beer and wine sales in grocery or convenience stores. Supporters want increased customer convenience, while opponents worry about increased alcohol consumption. However, neither side will have much effect on what is essentially a lobbying contest between independent retailers and the entrenched alcohol control bureaucracy. The provincial monopoly will probably prevail: since Prohibition ended in the U.S., not one monopoly state or one private-retail state has switched to the alternative system. It seems that whatever legislative choice was made fifty or sixty years ago has become firmly fixed.

State monopolies probably offer an advantage when stringent rations are instituted because government stores are less likely to forgo required record keeping or to make non-authorized sales than are small, independent retailers. Limiting the number of state outlets (but perhaps increasing their size) also helps isolate or spotlight illicit sales. Advantages of private retailing, on the other hand, include better customer service, avoidance of interest conflicts inherent in government sale of drugs, reduced costs to taxpayers, and financial support for small businesses: drug sales are an important, dependable income source for the small, labour-intensive, family-operated retail stores that are now under pressure from supermarkets. The Japanese government grants small retailers certain marketing advantages partly on the theory that such subsidies are better than welfare. Small neighbourhood stores also help reduce automobile use and maintain pedestrian traffic, which helps prevent crime. Private retailers could bid for licenses to operate state-regulated drug outlets if the government wanted to duplicate state monopoly conditions without state ownership.

Critics of private drug retailing complain that private ownership of liquor stores leads inevitably to the promotion of greater consumption. State outlets can ignore standard business practices and discourage buyers, these critics argue. For example, all Ontario liquor outlets once kept stock hidden and required buyers to fill out order slips from posted information boards. Clerks then filled the order from a storeroom, wrapping the purchase in plain brown paper bags. In these stores, described by one critic as "drab holes resembling a cross between a pharmaceutical museum and a public lavatory," impulse buying was less frequent than in Ontario liquor outlets that offered shelf displays and self-service.[50] But buyers will endure spartan conditions if the price is right and, unexpectedly, Spellman and Jorgenson discovered that in monopoly states from 1967 to 1977, distilled liquor sold for less than in "open states": $6.12 as a mean price per bottle versus $6.44.

Another counter-argument is that private alcohol retailers compete for market share rather than trying to expand the overall demand for the drug. The overwhelming importance of market share is related to two factors. First, it is easier to shift a buyer from an existing source than it is to create a new buyer. The number of cigaret smokers may increase or decrease at a rate of 1% - 2% per year, but by capturing existing smokers a new brand's sales chart can register growth rates of 200% or more per year, as occurred when Marlboro went from obscurity to capture 20.9% of the market. In 1983, a 1% market share for U.S. cigarets was worth $170 million, but only six new brands have captured as much as 0.5% of the market in the last decade. During the period of Marlboro's success, Ligget's leading brand, Chesterfield, fell from a 25% to a 3% market share, and American Brand's Lucky Strike Plain went from 40% to 0.8%. Ligget recently fought back by introducing generic cigarets at $1.50-2.00 less a carton. These are selling well without advertising.

Schroeder argues that a government retail monopoly for cannabis may be needed to "ensure sensible marketing procedures," and that "virtually no one wants to see marijuana hawked in the manner of whisky and cigarets."[51] To the contrary, advertisers and potential marijuana marketers would love to see cannabis products sold like alcohol and tobacco so that profits now going to motorcycle gangs and illicit traders would go to them instead. I must also emphasize that nationalization does not ensure "sensible" marketing procedures, nor is direct government ownership a prerequisite of effective regulation. At present, a major purpose of government owned liquor outlets is to create an appearance of effective regulation when, in fact, citizens consume almost as much liquor under a public system of distribution as under a private system. A second important goal of state alcohol outlets is the provision of patronage positions and the opportunity to favour various locales with an outlet.[52] John Kaplan proposes that cannabis retailing should incorporate the many restrictions placed on liquor stores. That suggestion might appease prohibitionists, but it is not defensible otherwise. As Hellman explains:

> In most states the sale of liquor is hedged about with a hodgepodge of restrictions that is probably unique in regulatory schemes. Some of these restrictions appear to be designed to placate temperance or prohibitionist sentiment. Others protect one segment or another of the liquor industry... With few exceptions, these restrictions do not serve any discernible social purpose; their principal effect is to throw a series of petty and annoying hurdles in the way of those who enjoy drinking without significantly limiting access to children or preventing excessive use by adults.[53]

Zoning is a form of rationing whereby retail drug outlets are restricted to certain types of locations and to certain parts of town. Liquor stores, like other commercial enterprises, are rationed in suburbs to preserve the pristine wholesomeness of single-family sprawl. Yet the suburban liquor cabinet remains as well-stocked as its urban counterpart. Zoning rules in many municipalities also stipulate that liquor stores must be a minimum distance from factories, schools or churches. This policy may be directed at alcoholic clergy overly fond of nipping out for a six-pack of beer or it may be intended to exclude the type of customer traffic generated by alcohol outlets. If separating school children from low-life purchasers of beer or wine is the goal then the current zoning rules regulate excessively. All that is necessary is a rule excluding cut-rate liquor stores from school neighbourhoods. The presence of premium stores would serve as a poor lesson in the evils of alcohol since most patrons would be from successful, upwardly-mobile social groups.

Retail hours of operation can also be rationed, making drug

stores operate on what used to be called "banker's hours": 10 a.m. to 3 p.m. five days a week. Moderate hours could be from 9 a.m. to 5 p.m., closed Sunday and a liberal policy might allow sales from 8 a.m. to 11 p.m. seven days a week. Without rationing, of course, drug stores can remain open all the time, as some food outlets do. Rationing retail hours of operation is likely to have the same impact as rationing the number of retail outlets — most customers will adapt to shorter hours by purchasing more drugs per visit. Or at least local customers will adapt in that fashion; tourists and other visitors will have a more difficult time, especially if they are accustomed to a different ration system. Vacationers and foreign guests present rationers a problem because governments usually want tourists to gamble, drink, eat and spend to the limits of human endurance. The usual solution is special rules for tourist regions or for foreign guests. Ontario, until 1989, prohibited retail operations on Sunday except for certain limited cases including designated "tourist areas." Some countries, like the Bahamas, permit casino gambling but prohibit local citizens from indulging. Given the growing financial importance of tourism, sometimes touted as the world's biggest business, the connection between tourism and drug availability should not be ignored. Under either criminal or medical controls, the tourist trade would be devastated because caffeine beverages, tobacco and alcohol would not be generally available. Countries dependent on tourism could not afford such controls for this reason alone. In contrast, private-law controls would permit creation of tourist meccas catering to all drug tastes and appetites in a reasonably safe, understanding atmosphere.

Rationing permits less flexibility and depends on special rules to exempt foreign visitors. Special regulations, bureaucracies and rations are not usually a recipe for attracting foreign exchange, but creative rule manipulation could avoid many problems. Also uniform rationing would make all drugs available, albeit in controlled amounts, so compared to restrictions in unreformed countries, general availability would have novelty value.

b. Personalized Drug Rations

So far I have considered impersonal rationing, but at the retail stage it is possible to ration drugs in a more intrusive, individualistic manner. The Swedish Bratt system, which limited liquor sales to ration card holders, was in force from 1917 to 1955. Revealingly, alcohol rationing was favored over prohibition in a Swedish referendum in 1922. Under the rationing system, a Swedish government agency reviewed each applicant's needs and habits based on their age, sex, drinking history and marital status before granting a ration card for liquor. Women were almost always allowed less liquor than men, and married women were not granted a ration card.[54] Tobacco rations in post-war Germany also discriminated on the basis of gender: men were allowed two packs of cigarets a month and women only one pack. At present, if married women were denied drugs through state rationing it might serve as a serious deterrent to marriage. Considering that on average $1,300 worth of alcohol is consumed per wedding reception, a decrease in the number of weddings could have a positive impact on alcohol control.[55]

Zinberg and Robertson propose a personal rationing system for certain drugs based on acquiring a drug-use license (like a driver's license). Under their scheme license holders could purchase "reasonable" amounts of specified drugs, but supplies could not be resold.[56] Offenders, ex-convicts, psychiatric cases and others would be denied drug-use licenses. Under the Bratt rationing system, no permit was needed to buy wine (which was not then very popular in Sweden) but wine sales were recorded, and if "unreasonable" amounts were purchased by an individual, further sales were refused. Eventually, the system was simplified to allow each ration card holder to buy 4 litres of liquor per month. (In the 1920s, Americans were permitted about 1 litre of medicinal liquor per month under the *Willis-Campbell Act.*) Since Swedes could sell liquor privately, many eligible buyers purchased their full 4 litre quota and sold any surplus. If the same rule applied to a uniform rationing system, which set a personal ration quota on every drug, people would trade rations or sell drugs to maximize their personal drug-consuming preferences. Some people would trade-off alcohol for cannabis or coffee, while smokers might swap any other drug for more tobacco.

A major advantage of allowing non-users to sell their drug rations privately is that it forces drug users to compensate non-users. The only legal method of consuming above the ration limit for a given drug would be to buy someone else's unused ration allowance. Non-users could then choose between limiting overall drug consumption for the social good by ripping up their drug ration cards, or selling their ration for personal benefit. I expect that if people could legally sell their unwanted heroin or alcohol ration, monetary gain would usually triumph over social conscience. Such a policy would short-circuit the current trumped-up outrage about drug trafficking and, by compensating non-users, the sale of rations would duplicate the effects of a collective class-action suit against all drug users. With tobacco cigarets, the Canadian adult per-capita ration would be about 3,200 cigarets a year (160 packs), but the median consumption by smokers is about 500 packs a year. To maintain their present consumption rate, smokers would need to purchase, on average, the tobacco rations of two non-smokers. Under this plan, tobacco prices would increase above the free market floor because users would need to buy a ration coupon to buy the drug. Without taxes, a pack of cigarets would cost about $1.25 instead of $3.25, but the ration card permitting extra consumption might cost $250 on a yearly basis. Surplus or artificial profits would go, therefore, to non-smokers rather than to tobacco producers or government tax-collectors. With all drugs rationed, it is conceivable that abstainers and light users could earn from $1,000 to $4,000 annually by selling their rations to drug users. The opportunity to earn money by selling one's drug rations would also provide a positive incentive to reduce drug consumption because the less one used, the more one could sell. This incentive structure would reduce overall consumption which would, in turn, reduce the market value of a drug-ration coupon. To maintain incentives for people to reduce drug use, government regulators would need to monitor the money value of the different drug coupons and, when values fell, step in to reduce the supply.

Ideally, businesses would be allowed to trade and buy rations, thus avoiding inefficient barter among individuals. For instance, Citizen A might happily trade her annual LSD ration for an extra week's quota of nicotine, but be stymied by lack of contact with non-smoking LSD consumers. Drug ration clearing-houses would avoid these problems by establishing a purely monetary exchange for those buying or selling drug ration coupons. This market would also redistribute drugs nation-wide according to regional preferences. Heavy use of alcohol and tobacco in Quebec could be balanced, say, by higher demand for cocaine and diazepam in Ontario.

In this way, government regulators could ignore production quotas and base the entire rationing system on individual distribution. The drug industry would know in advance the total domestic consumption limit and adjust production accordingly.

I should also note that, to be practical, ration coupons would have to be issued separately for the major drugs — alcohol, caffeine, tobacco, cannabis, cocaine and diazepam — while an "all other drugs" category would include the dozens of marginal psychoactives now prescribed or prohibited. Drug entitlement coupons, like food stamps, would be targets for counterfeiting, hence their manufacture would need to parallel the production of paper currency. Indeed, drug ration coupons would not only look and feel like money, they could even function like paper notes, but with the added advantage of being backed by a limited commodity. Gold and silver are excellent bases for currency because they are inherently limited, but alcohol, tobacco and other drugs could be used as substitutes to a metal standard if the government could effectively limit total drug production. If drug rationing were successful, people might prefer to hold non-inflatable drug coupons rather than paper currency.

Transferable drug coupons issued by Social Insurance Number could be distributed through post offices, or more personal rations could be based on cards issued in each recipient's name. Personal ration cards allowed the Swedish government to cut off citizens' alcohol ration if they were alcoholic or arrested for alcohol-related offences. The Finnish alcohol-buyer surveillance system, launched in 1946, functioned along similar lines. The State Alcohol Monopoly kept files and made note of alcohol "abusers"; persons who made abnormally large purchases of alcohol over a specific period, persons treated for alcoholism or persons arrested for impaired driving, vagrancy, drunk and disorderly behaviour and the like. Note that while Scandinavian alcohol rationers limited or denied alcoholics access to the drug, the opposite policy is pursued by American rationers of methadone, and by British rationers of heroin, who dispense the drug only to habitual users. Obviously, the large majority of non-alcoholic alcohol users would not tolerate a ration system that provided alcohol solely to confirmed alcoholics. Besides the blatant unfairness of such a scheme, it would have the effect of rewarding alcohol abusers. Some people would strive to be arrested for alcohol offences or to be admitted to clinics for alcoholics so as to qualify for an alcohol ration. If only genuine pack-a-day smokers qualified for a cigaret ration, numerous smokers would escalate their intake, at least temporarily, to qualify. This strategy further assumes that rationers have the resources and capacity to properly define and categorize people as "addicts," "abusers" or "dependents," but as noted earlier these terms are subjective and slippery. Moreover, even if a purely objective standard of drug intake is employed to designate "problem" drug users, how could the rationers ever hope to monitor drug-taking behaviour in public when prison officials have trouble measuring drug use behind bars?

Once "abusers" were noted in Finland, sanctions followed, including warnings, home visits by government agents, and suspension of the alcohol purchase permit for one year. This system is akin to probation and, not surprisingly, most Finns regarded it as an "unnecessary nuisance." Studies finding these sanctions to be useless confirmed popular misgivings about the alcohol buyer surveillance system, and it was abolished in 1970. Undaunted, a group of Swedish physicians lobby for return of alcohol rationing, but this time with only 1.5 litres of liquor per month allowed and no transfer of rations permitted, a model closer to mandatory prescription than to criminal probation.[57] Similarly, a study group at the Institute for the Study of Drug Dependence in Britain concluded that a personal cannabis-rationing scheme is feasible. Their proposed scheme would operate in the following way:

> Persons wanting to consume the drug would be required to obtain a ration card containing coupons entitling them to a weekly supply of cannabis. A central registry would probably be necessary to prevent an applicant obtaining more than one card. Having obtained his ration card, the holder could then go... to an "authorized seller of cannabis" to purchase his weekly quota.[56]

The study group noted that the Finnish passbook system for alcohol rationing was "abandoned some time ago, because it proved cumbersome and unpopular." The Finnish example does not necessarily rule out a ration system for a currently prohibited drug like cannabis, which is consumed in much smaller quantities than alcohol, but it is relevant when considering a uniform rationing system for all drugs. Consider the vast record-keeping apparatus necessary to record, retain and recall an individual's purchases of caffeine, aspirin, alcohol, tobacco, cannabis, diazepam, amphetamine and a hundred other psychoactive substances. To add to the confusion, the person buying the drug might not use all or any of the drug purchased: it could be served to friends or given to family members who, for example, are heavy users of caffeine but who rarely do the shopping. Persons making "abnormally large" buys of alcohol may not be problem drinkers at all, rather they may be inveterate hosts or members of large families involved in numerous weddings and anniversaries. Inviting 200 friends to a traditional drug-besotted wedding reception could easily consume a year's worth of an individual's alcohol ration.

The personal surveillance system of rationing presumes a form of drug-taking similar to self-medication in which individuals pick up their daily or weekly ration of alcohol, heroin or cannabis and then slouch off to their living rooms or favorite alleyways for a bout of solitary symptom alleviation. This view ignores the general prevalence of ceremonial and communal drug taking. In 1908, cocaine was not a "party drug," it was primarily a tonic, panacea or cure-all taken for medicinal reasons, and thus when it was made the first Rx drug in Canada, users did not vigorously rebel. In 1989, cocaine is largely a drug for occasions, celebrations and groups, which is why a probation or personal surveillance system would not work well now for cocaine or for cannabis. Nor would it prove satisfactory with drugs like coffee, tea and alcohol that are firmly embedded in our culture as ceremonial substances.

c. On-Premise Sales

On-premise sales account for about 16% of total alcohol use in Ontario, where 7,131 licensed premises produce a density of 10.9 per 10,000 adults.[59] British habits are quite different: there on-premise sales account for 90% of beer and 30% of wine consumption.

The basic decision to be made with on-premise sales rationing is whether the government should encourage public or private drug using. Is society better off if people take beer or coffee home from a store, or if they consume the same amount of the drug in public? Perhaps drug use in pubs is the better choice because entertainment and convivial company may serve as substitutes for drug taking, and peer pressure may mitigate against extreme abuse. Among college students, for example, men drink slower with women than with just other men.[60] On the other hand, communal drug-using can also prolong the period of drug use, and peer pressure to engage in round buying, drinking games and other kinds of competition can lead to increased use. If home drug-using proved to be safer and less socially disruptive than public consumption, then the Drug Rationing Department could divert more drugs to retail outlets and less to taverns, bars, hotels, and night clubs. By making more drugs available for home use and by prohibiting patrons from carrying drugs into commercial premises, the government could gradually shift consumption away from pubs. But would drug use necessarily move back into homes once it had been pushed out of taverns? Some people would move their drug use to semi-private locations such as automobiles, hotel rooms, clubs and city parks.

As for on-premise use itself, current controls are concerned almost exclusively with alcohol. Few regulations apply to serving caffeine beverages or tobacco products (outside smoking restrictions). This discrimination is, as usual, culturally biased. When coffee and coffee houses first appeared in Arabia in the 1500s, they were controversial, and attempts were made to prohibit either the drug itself or its use in coffee houses. The prohibitionists were alarmed because coffee houses were frequently the setting for activities such as gambling, homosexuality and musical entertainment, all forbidden by law. But even in respectable coffee houses, conservative Muslims saw a threat to the social order. To some extent they were right. As Hattox explains, coffee houses changed the Islamic urban environment by mixing groups from formerly segregated city quarters, and by giving men a place to congregate at night other than the mosque.[61] Coffee houses also domesticated games like backgammon, once regarded as sinful, in the same way that taverns domesticated darts, bowls and other games.

The range of possible on-premise controls is similar to those controls previously discussed for retail sales. Just as drug store hours could be rationed, so too could pub hours be restricted. Most jurisdictions do limit pub hours, but insufficient efforts have been made to gauge the impact of such rationing. Rationing tavern hours seems a more plausible restraint than limiting drug store hours because customers can purchase retail drugs in bulk for later use. On the other hand, if on-premise drug use were discouraged by severely rationed hours, users may simply switch to home use. Investigators have chronicled the effect on alcohol consumption of introducing Sunday alcohol sales, of replacing 6 P.M. closing with 10 P.M. closing, and of allowing hotels to open at 6 A.M. rather than 10 A.M. Ian Smith found that men in the early-opening hotels consumed significantly more alcohol per week (at home and in pubs) than comparable drinkers in late-opening bars.[62] From this he concludes that early opening encourages heavy alcohol intake, but it could also be argued that heavier drinkers, given the choice, frequent the type of hotel in Perth, Australia that opens early, rather than hotels that maintain traditional late opening.

The evidence available on rationing pub hours clearly indicates that patterns of alcohol use can be manipulated. Through the 1950s, Australian pubs were famous for their "Six O'clock Swill," as customers got off work at five and had until six to drink their fill of beer. James Michener describes the scene:

> You've finished a day's work and drop into your favorite pub for a couple of quick ones. At the door a blast of foul air, smoke and shattering noise greets you. Around the bar... is jammed a struggling mass of humanity. The barmaids are slinging schooners as fast as their hands will work. They work in a kind of mechanical daze and speak to no one.... At quarter to six, a bouncer begins to bellow in a mournful chant, "Come on boys! Drink Up! Drink up!" At five to six, he cries pleadingly, "Closing, boys, closing!" Men order frantically and those at the bar line up three or four. The bedlam increases. At six, the doors are slammed shut and a frightful gong begins to ring. Now the bouncer cries, "Please, drink up!" The lucky ones at the bar toss off one pint after another.[63]

Women, who by this time had gained the vote in Australia but who did not, as a rule, frequent pubs or work outside the home, kept voting for early closing because while their husbands arrived home drunk, at least they came home on time. As women entered the commercial labour force, started businesses, gained financial independence and developed a taste for beer, they stopped supporting the six o'clock closing. At the same time, the post-war shortage of bottled beer for retail sales ended in the 1950s, and this permitted more home consumption of beer. Drug-serving establishments can also be limited in number and restricted by zoning, but it is questionable if the complications of pub quotas would be worth the trouble and expense. Minor limits would merely guarantee the business success of licence holders, while severe limits would shift users to retail outlets and private consumption; a result that, if desired, could be accomplished overtly rather than in this roundabout way. Controlling location is a more fruitful line to explore.

Pub location is more important than drug store location because customers leave pubs in a drugged state. One of the unfortunate results of modern zoning laws, suburban sprawl and addiction to automobiles is the replacement of neighbourhood pubs with roadside and shopping mall taverns from which inebriated patrons sally forth in their cars. If any individual were allowed to open a pub in his house or store, a flood of small, conveniently located drug-serving businesses could result in more inebriated pedestrians and fewer inebriated motorists. Such a shift would be socially beneficial because impaired motorists threaten others, whereas impaired pedestrians are mostly just a threat to themselves. Allowing pubs of all sizes would result in a proliferation of small outlets, and a case can be made that small is safer than big. Under tort law and statutes, drug servers are obliged, as occupiers, to protect their clients and to prevent excessive drug use. These goals are less likely to be accomplished in large, impersonal bars with thousands of customers per night than in small pubs with a steady clientele known to the owner-occupier.

In this century, government regulators have also seen fit to ration entertainment in pubs, apparently on the theory that making bars unattractive curtails alcohol consumption. A number of regulations have limited amount of window space, number of video games, and periods of live entertainment. Even comfortable chairs and pleasant decor have been restricted in some jurisdictions, possibly in an effort to discourage women. However, the current trend is toward abandoning petty restrictions on pubs, partly because tourists to many states and provinces in the 1950s were not attracted to windowless beer halls furnished with ale-soaked carpets and groupings of arborite tables and early Sears-Roebuck kitchen chairs, set-off to advantage by fluorescent lights and cheap panelling.

Rationing on-premise use could also proceed by controlling individuals. The following could be regulated: amount of drug consumed, time spent on the premises, frequency of visits to the premises and, finally, incidental behaviour while on the premises. With a personal rationing regime, individuals could be assigned drug coupons good only for on-premise purchases, or individuals could be allowed to trade retail coupons for pub coupons at some fixed rate. If the regulators wanted to discourage on-premise drug use they could offer a discount on pub coupons; for example, a retail ration coupon for 6 bottles of beer would buy only 3 bottles in a tavern. The other regulations are less feasible for rationing because they would require direct monitoring of individual behaviour. Like motorists in a car-infested city who are allowed to drive only on odd or even days depending on their licence plate numbers, citizens could be permitted to attend pubs only every other day, perhaps for half an hour. According to one tavern study in Canada, about half of all patrons stay for 30 minutes or less, with the average time being about 34 minutes. A comparison of 1963 and 1978 found that tavern goers now drink less and leave earlier, despite considerable liberalizing of the rules and conditions of on-premise consumption.[64] This increased restraint is probably due primarily to price changes. In 1963, on-and off-premise beer prices were similar. Now, bottled beer in taverns is 250% the price of retail beer, hence it is much cheaper to drink at home.

Time restrictions would be difficult to enforce unless all commercial premises were cross-linked by computer so the entry record of a customer could be immediately perused. But even if this regime could be enforced, its benefits would be doubtful. Upper income groups have traditionally lamented the pub-going habits of the poor but for people who are young, single or transient, pubs may serve as living rooms and extended families. Limiting pub attendance might just enshrine as the legal norm the habits of the middle-aged and married.

264

What use do we now make of taverns? On a given day, about 6% of the Canadian population will visit a public alcohol venue. About eight out of ten alcohol users visit taverns, as do three out of ten non-drinkers. Among all adults, 14% are "regulars" and attend taverns at least once a week; another 18% attend at least once a month. Heavy users are over-represented in taverns: moderate drinkers are more likely found in lounges and nightclubs. Only 2% of a sample of on-premise drinkers said their main reason for being there was to drink. Over 40% came with friends or came to meet friends, and another 20% came to eat. Many also came for the entertainment. Since tavern regulars tend to be unmarried persons in smaller cities who go to socialize, it is not surprising that marital status is almost as strong a predictor of regular pub attendance as is drinking alcohol. Regular patrons generally report a higher level of alcohol use than average, but some are light drinkers or even abstainers.[65]

Incidental behaviour in taverns can also be restricted, again on the supposition that if one cannot have much fun while taking drugs, one will take less drugs and leave earlier. For years, Canadian tavern patrons in some provinces were not allowed to stand at a bar or walk between tables with a drink. In some jurisdictions patrons had to order food with alcohol, a rule that led to recycled sandwiches. Odd rules are still in force. Two young Ottawa entrepreneurs had to endure years of legal battles with the Liquor Licencing Board of Ontario to get permission to open Canada's first combination laundromat/bar and grill in 1987.[66] The cost to taxpayers of creating and enforcing outmoded rules is probably unjustified.

As a final option, the entry of specific groups can be rationed. Until recently in North America, women entering taverns were subject to rules that either separated the sexes, allowed women to enter only when accompanied by a man, or barred women altogether. Up until 1971, women could not work as bartenders in California.[67] Constitutional guarantees of sexual equality are now understood by the courts to rule out discrimination based on sex. Discrimination based on age is also illegal, but only after the age of majority or adulthood has been reached. As was noted earlier, all provinces and states employ criminal-style prohibitions to bar under-age persons from pub premises. This is done partly to limit youngsters' access to alcohol, but the policy is also meant to save youngsters from the bad influences thought to thrive in taverns. A rationing approach might lead to limited access for young people, adult-accompaniment entry or special minors bars where only those *under* 18 years of age could enter. If taverns have traditionally been bad places for children, it was because the law has intentionally rendered them unpalatable for a large portion of the public, and because social customs segregated bars on the basis of sex and social status.

With uniform rationing, youngsters' access to drugs would be far more standardized than it is now. Today caffeine is freely available, tobacco is available legally only to those 16 years of age and over, many drugs are entirely prohibited, and alcohol can be purchased from stores or in taverns only when buyers are over a certain age. The private-law regulation of drug sales would not fix any specific age as a minimum for buying or consuming drugs. Instead, parents, sellers, producers and advertisers would be held to the tort standard of reasonableness. Such a standard would preclude selling drugs to certain youngsters in certain circumstances, but would not dictate that before a person's 19th birthday they can use or possess no alcohol whatsoever, while after that birthday they can buy and drink as much as they want. Avoiding a minimum purchasing age for drugs would not result in the dire consequences that a superficial analysis might suggest. To begin with, current laws are not a serious deterrent. At least 90% of all American high school students engage in illegal alcohol use, and more than half disobey the law regularly. Under-age tobacco use is less frequent, but only because tobacco is a less popular drug, not because of totally unenforced tobacco laws. A child's drug use is primarily determined by parental training (or lack thereof), peer example, and cultural context. Public law has a minimal impact.

A major concern in recent years has been the connection between youthful drinking and driving. As of 1986, states that do not establish a minimum age of 21 for purchasing alcohol or possessing the drug in public risk having the U.S. federal government cut off 10% of their highway fund allocation. The premise behind this law is that a higher age limit will save an estimated 730 to 2,500 lives per year. Mike Males conducted independent tests and concluded that increases in state drinking ages do not save lives. More lives are lost among older drivers than are saved among younger drivers, hence there is no net gain. Questioning the entire concept of minimum-age laws, Males writes that:

> The record of drinking age ups and downs can only be called perverse. During the late 1960s teenage drunk driving deaths peaked after a decade of steady increases. Thirty state legislatures then proceeded to lower their drinking ages. Then, in the early 1980s, after several years of rapidly falling teenage drunk driving rates had produced the lowest level of young-driver alcohol-related crashes in thirty years, Congress and a number of state legislatures moved to mandate a drinking age of twenty-one. At no time have law makers directed concern at the age group causing the largest drunk driving problem: twenty to twenty-four year olds.[66]

It is interesting that the alcohol/driving issue is almost always tackled from the drug side rather than the automobile side. Rationing automobile use or limiting drivers' access to taverns are feasible policies because the requirement of a driver's licence provides government with a powerful enforcement lever, and because changes in tavern location are easier to bring about than behavioral changes in drug users.

Under rationing controls, parents would be able to share their drugs with their dependants. In addition, it would be possible to phase-in a child's public access to drugs in a number of ways. At various ages, children could be gradually permitted to purchase small quantities of drugs in diluted form. Beer with 1% alcohol content, for example, could be made publicly available to all age groups. Access to junior drug rations could be tied arbitrarily to age or to some performance standard, such as grades in school. Such a system would tend to liberalize drug access first for students least interested in drugs, and might significantly increase the status of scholastic achievers. Accelerated access to adult-strength rations or to adult-only taverns could also be tied to community service, lack of juvenile offences, parental permission, police permission, and so on.

4. Rationing and Public Choice

Based on the historical evidence, a uniform program of drug rationing would be least acceptable to the public if it were modelled on the Finnish system of personal surveillance for alcohol use. Cumbersome, irritating and ineffective, that program would be worse when extended to all psychoactives. An administratively cheaper and far more popular ration scheme would supply everyone with drug ration coupons that could be traded, sold or redeemed. This system would have the flexibility to cope with endless variations in popular demand for drugs, plus it would force drug users wishing to consume above the per capita ration allowance to buy from non-users. By providing people with the opportunity to profit by selling unwanted drug rations, this scheme would deliver the most direct and immediate benefits to the largest number of people. For example, the 65% of adults who are non-tobacco users could sell their rations to the minority of smokers. The same situation would not occur with alcohol or caffeine, since most people use these drugs, but there would still be a profitable division between users above and below the median level of consumption. In evaluating this proposal, many people would overrate their ability to limit their drug intake, thereby exaggerating the quantity of surplus ration coupons they would be able to sell. Average performers tend to rate themselves as "better than average," and most people are generally over-optimistic about their future prospects dependent on personal capacities.[69] As a result, this scheme would be even more popular than it deserves to be.

The other potentially popular form of rationing controls on drugs is the production or import quota, especially when rationing is joined by price ceilings. Such a system would promise a gradual, nearly invisible diminution of overall consumption while at the same time fixing prices so that less private resources are devoted to drug expenditures. Compared to a tax-control regime, this rationing system would avoid a massive shift of money from private to public hands. But enforcing production quotas for drugs that are easily produced would be expensive, with the cost rising directly with the severity of the quota restraint. If the rations were too onerous, the result would reproduce the high costs of a partial prohibition. As to how the quota system would be administered, most people would likely prefer a property rights system of transferrable quotas as opposed to nationalization with its high start-up costs, or administrative tribunals with their opportunities for political special-dealing.

As for drug retailing rations, either through stores or through on-premise outlets, a majority of voters would probably prefer to focus on reducing total drug intake while getting rid of some of the regulations concerning hours of operation, number of outlets, advertising limits, zoning restrictions and the like. A difficulty with public opinion in this area is the lack of personal experience with alternative systems. Small, intimate alcohol-serving establishments are familiar in parts of Europe, but are largely unknown in many Canadian provinces and American states where liquor licence bureaux, zoning laws and fire regulations effectively prohibit deviation from the commercial tavern norm. Asking people to choose between a ration system favoring large taverns only, or one permitting pubs of all sizes will be hindered by this lack of first-hand knowledge.

Rationing would probably be preferred to either prohibition or mandatory medical prescription because it is directed toward a reasonable, acceptable and achievable goal, namely the gradual reduction of total psychoactive drug consumption. Reducing overall drug use is probably the most effective social protection measure. As for preventing self-harm, rationing offers a much more modest level of restraint than criminal or medical controls, a level proportional to the threat posed by the self-administration of drugs. Moreover, the scale of restraint under a retail-rationing scheme would escalate with the amount of drug consumed. That is, heavy drug users would operate under greater pressure than light or moderate users because of their need to buy extra ration coupons. Giving up a specialized diet of alcohol or caffeine or nicotine to become a moderate user of every psychoactive would not reduce restraint, because multi-drug users could not trade drug X coupons for drug Y. Once the government imposed a total ceiling on consumption, every drug user would be forced, one way or another, to compete for a limited quantity of drugs.

The disadvantage of rationing over private law controls is the danger of politically powerful groups imposing unjust decisions on less organized groups. Rationing's advantage is that public law can effectively compel drug users to compensate their victims. This end could not be achieved through production or import quotas but it could be accomplished, as explained earlier, through a property rights system of private drug ration coupons. Rationing can also co-exist with a tort law system governing drug safety, advertising accuracy and producer liability.

Notes

1   R. Room, "The Fiscal and Legislative Debate" in M. Grant and B. Ritson (eds), *Alcohol - The Prevention Debate* (London: Croom Helm, 1983) 161.

2   B. Whitaker, *The Global Connection* (1987) 126.

3   V. G. Treml, *Alcohol in the U.S.S.R: A Statistical Study* (Durham: Duke University Press, 1982). In Tunisia and similar countries tobacco smokers also spend a large portion of their salary on the drug. M. Mironowiez, "Puffing Up Trade in Third World" *Globe & Mail* December 4, 1984, A7.

4   A. P. Lerner, *The Economics of Control* (New York: Macmillan, 1944) 50-52.

5   A. Allentuck, *The Crisis in Canadian Health Care* Ch. 7 (1978).

6   Room, *supra* note 1, 162.

7   See M. I. Goldman, *Soviet Marketing - Distribution in a Controlled Economy* (New York: Free Press of Glencoe, 1963).

8   "The high price of price reform" *Time*, July 13, 1987, 40.

9   See "Socialism: Trials and Errors" *Time*, March 13, 1978, 24, 35.

10   Treml, *supra* note 3, Ch. 5.

11   R. E. Popham, W. Schmidt and J. deLint, "The Effects of Legal Restraint on Drinking" in *The Biology of Alcoholism* B. Kissin & H. Begleiter (eds),(New York: Plenum Publishing, 1976) 579, 581, 610.

12   R. Lidman, "Economic Issues in Alcohol Control" Social Research Group, University of California, Berkeley (1976).

271

[13]   K. Makela, *et al., Alcohol, Society and State* Vol. I (Toronto: Addiction Research Foundation, 1981) 65.

[14]   D. Walsh & B. Walsh, "Alcohol and Drink in Ireland in the Post-War Period" in *Alcohol, Society and State*, Vol. II E. Single, P. Morgan and J. deLint (eds), (Toronto: Addiction Research Foundation, 1981) 103, 120.

[15]   D. E. Beauchamp, *Beyond Alcoholism - Alcohol and Public Health Policy* (Philadelphia: Temple University Press, 1980) 103-111.

[16]   D. G. Garan, *Relativity for Psychology* (New York: Philosophical Library, 1963).

[17]   See K. Poikolainen, "Alcoholism: A Social Construct" (1982) 12 *Journal of Drug Issues* 361; I. Vogt, "Defining Alcohol Problems as a Repressive Mechanism: Its Formative Phase in Imperial Germany and its Strength Today" (1984) 19 *International Journal of Addictions* 551 (1984); R. Caetano, "Public Opinions about Alcoholism and its Treatment" (1987) 48 *Journal of Studies on Alcohol* 153, (1987).

[18]   Popham, *et al., supra* note 11, 617. See also J. Rabow and R.K. Watts, "Alcohol Availability, Alcoholic Beverage Sales and Alcohol-Related Problems" (1982) 43 *Journal of Studies on Alcohol* 767.

[19]   A. Downs, *An Economic Theory of Democracy* (New York: Harper & Row, 1957) 255-56.

[20]   See M. J. Trebilcock, "Winners and Losers in the Modern Regulatory System - Must the Consumer Always Lose?" (1975) 13 *Osgoode Hall Law Journal* 619.

[21]   E. Goode, *Drugs in American Society* (1984) 38.

[22]   *Maclean's* June 22, 1987, 30.

[23]   J. A. Brown, *Techniques of Persuasion - From Propaganda to Brainwashing* (London: Penguin Books, 1963) at 165-185. See also C. Mitchell, "The Impact, Regulation and Efficacy of

Lawyer Advertising" (1982) 20 *Osgoode Hall Law Journal* 119, 120.

24   P. Kohn & R. Smart, "The Impact of Television Advertising on Alcohol Consumption: An Experiment" (1984) 45 *Journal of Studies on Alcohol* 295.

25   J. Bourgeois & J. Barnes, "Does Advertising Increase Alcohol Consumption" (1979) 19 *Journal of Advertising Research* 19; E. Brecher, *Licit and Illicit Drugs* (1972) at 235. See also "The Promotion of Prescription and Proprietary Drugs: Corporate Self-Interest Versus Social Responsibility" Symposium Issue, (1986) 6 *Journal of Drug Issues*.

26   "Crackdown on Smoking" *Maclean's*, June 22, 1987, 25.

27   D. L. Wolcott, F. Fawzy & R. Coombs, "Reinforcing Networks: The Medical, Pharmaceutical, Mass Media and Paraphernalia Establishments" (1984) *Journal of Drug Issues* 223, 227.

28   "The Advertising Debate", *supra* note 1, 107-113.

29   M. J. van Iwaarden, "Advertising, Alcohol Consumption and Policy alternatives" in *Economics and Alcohol* (1983) 223, 236.

30   D. Strickland, "Content and Effects of Alcohol Advertising: Comment on NTIS Pub. No. PB82-123142" (1984) 45 *Journal of Studies on Alcohol* 87. This position is also taken by K. Leffler, "Persuasion or Information? The Economics of Prescription Drug Advertising" (1981) 24 *Journal of Law & Economics* 45.

31   M. Synar & D. Kmiec, "Should Tobacco Advertising Be Banned?" *American Bar Association Journal*, December 1, 1986 at 38-39; Comment, "Restraints on Alcoholic Beverage Advertising: A Constitutional Analysis" (1984) *Notre Dame Law Review* 779.

32   D. Strickland, T. Finn & M. Lambert, "A Content Analysis of Beverage Alcohol Advertising" (1982) 43 *Journal of Studies on Alcohol* 665, 677.

[33] K. Warner, *et al.*, "Promotion of Tobacco Products: Issues and Policy Options" (1986) 11 *Journal of Health, Politics, Policy and Law* 367.

[34] Nelson, "Advertising as Information" (1974) 82 *Journal Political Economy* 729, 739.

[35] M. Schudson, *Advertising, the Uneasy Persuasion: Its Dubious Impact on American Society* (New York: Basic Books, 1985). See also J. Boddewyn, "Tobacco Advertising in a Free Society" in *Smoking and Society* (1986) 309-32.

[36] P. Taylor, *Smoke Ring: The Politics of Tobacco* (London: The Bodley Head, 1985).

[37] "Forgettable Commercials" *Psychology Today* December, 1986, 16.

[38] "Beer, tobacco campaigns back in the hotseat" *The Financial Post* March 8, 1986, S.2.

[39] "Ad ban may be hazardous to artistic health" *The Globe and Mail*, July 25, 1987, C1.

[40] R. Arbogast, "A Proposal to Regulate the Manner of Tobacco Advertising" (1986) 11 *Journal of Health Politics, Policy and Law* 393.

[41] Strickland, *et al.*, *supra* note 32, 679.

[42] L. Wallack, W. Breed & J. Cruz, "Alcohol on Prime-Time Television" (1987) 48 *Journal of Studies on Alcohol* 33-37.

[43] Wolcott, *et al.*, *supra* note 27, 228.

[44] See Wallack, *et al.*, *supra* note 42. In contrast, other researchers conclude that the effect of repeated viewing of alcohol consumption on advertising is unknown. E. Futch, S. Lisman and M. Geller, "An Analysis of Alcohol Portrayal on Prime-Time Television" (1984) 19 *International Journal of Addictions* 403, 409.

45 C. Neuman & J. Rabow, "Drinkers' Use of Physical Availability of Alcohol: Buying Habits and Consumption Level" (1985-86) 20 *International Journal of Addictions* 663; J. Rabow & R. Watts, "Alcohol Availability; Alcoholic Beverage Sales and Alcohol-Related Problems" (1982) 43 *Journal Studies on Alcohol* 767.

46 Popham, *et al.*, *supra* note 11, at 585.

47 N. el-Guebaly and A. el-Guebaly, "Alcohol Abuse in Ancient Egypt: The Recorded Evidence" (1982) 16 *International Journal of Addictions* 1207, 1208.

48 W. Spellman & M. Jorgenson, "Liquor Control and Consumption" (1983) 44 *Journal of Studies on Alcohol* 194.

49 Popham, *et al.*, *supra* note 11, 608, 609.

50 C. Israel, "Bureau of Confusion" *Toronto Magazine* October 1988, 63; R. Smart, "Comparison of Purchasing in Self-Service and Clerk-Service Liquor Stores" (1974) 35 *Journal of Studies on Alcohol* 1397 (1974).

51 R. Schroeder, *The Politics of Drugs* (1980) 56.

52 Israel, *supra* note 50; "Unravelling the tangled web the LCBO has woven" *Globe & Mail* October 8, 1988, C10.

53 A. Hellman, *Laws Against Marijuana* (1975) 200.

54 Popham, *et al.*, *supra* note 11, 607.

55 R. Maynard, "Here Comes the Bride" *Report on Business Magazine*, June 1987, 24-30.

56 N. Zinberg and J. Robertson, *Drugs and the Public* (New York: Simon & Schuster, 1972) 260-62.

57 Whitaker, *supra* note 2, 138.

58 F. Logan (ed), *Cannabis-Options for Control* (United Kingdom: Quartermaine House, 1979) 43.

59 E. Single, "The Costs and Benefits of Alcohol in Ontario: A Critical Review of the Evidence" in *Economics and Alcohol* M. Grant, M. Plant and A. Williams (eds), (London: Croom Helm, 1983) 97.

60 W. Ratcliffe, *et al.*, "Drinking in Taverns: A 15-Year Comparison" (1982) 17 *International Journal of Addictions* 869, 874.

61 R. S. Hattox, *Coffee and Coffeehouses - The Origins of a Social Beverage in the Medieval Near East* (Seattle: University of Washington Press, 1985) 113, 129.

62 D. Smith, "Comparison of Patrons of Hotels with Early Opening and Standard Hours" (1986) 21 *International Journal of Addictions* 155.

63 James A. Michener, *Return to Paradise* (New York: Fawcett, 1951) 312.

64 Ratcliffe, *et al.*, *supra* note 60, 874.

65 R. Cosper, I. Okraku and B. Neumann, "Tavern Going in Canada: A National Survey of Regulars at Public Drinking Establishments" (1987) 48 *Journal of Studies on Alcohol* 252-259.

66 "At last, it's legal to drink and dry" *The Globe & Mail* June 5, 1987, B1.

67 Makela, *et al.*, *supra* note 13, 83.

68 M. Males, "The Minimum Purchase Age for Alcohol and Young-Driver Fatal Crashes: A Long-Term View" (1986) 15 *Journal of Legal Studies* 181, 205.

69 See M. Matlin & D. Stang, *The Pollyanna Principle* (1978); L. Tiger, *Optimism: The Biology of Hope* (1979).

VIII Uniform Tax Controls and Price Disincentives

This chapter investigates the regulative potential of tax and price disincentives. The central issues are how to justify a drug tax and how to determine the rate of tax applied. Other questions addressed include the administration, revenue potential and justice of drug taxes. Should drug tax revenue be earmarked to fund special projects such as drug education or the rehabilitation of drug users? Can tax controls be expected to deliver social protection and reasonable prevention of self-harm? Current taxes on alcohol and tobacco purchases will be analyzed as possible models for extension to all psychoactives. Other price disincentives considered include allocating relevant medical costs to drug users and applying discriminatory insurance premiums to drug users for life, disability and automobile coverage.

1. Tax Control Policy

a. Justifying Sumptuary Taxation

In every country where alcohol and tobacco are legal, governments either subject these drugs to special excise taxes or fix their prices through state-owned monopoly enterprises. Special drug taxes have a long history. Egyptian authorities collected a tax on beer and wine more than 3,000 years ago.[1] In 1330, English law required taverns, the only commercial source of alcohol, to pay annual fees.[2] British excises on ale, beer, cider, spirits, tea and coffee were introduced in 1660 and through the 1800s these taxes provided the bulk of peacetime public revenue, a fact that prompted a 19th century MP to praise the habitual drunkard as 'the sheet anchor of the British Constitution.'[3] The first American tax on alcohol in 1791 took effect as quickly as Alexander Hamilton, first Secretary of the Treasury, could manage it (this excise led to the short-lived Whiskey Rebellion of 1794). A federal excise on tobacco followed in 1794, was repealed and then reintroduced in 1864, and starting with Iowa in 1921, various states added an excise on tobacco cigarets until in 1969 North Carolina became the last to tax cigarets.[4]

Despite the well-accepted practice of taxing alcohol and tobacco, the taxes' objectives are not adequately explained either by tax authorities or by tax theorists. State tax administrators view tobacco and alcohol as simply convenient revenue sources.[5] This argument does not explain why excise systems are overdependent on alcohol, tobacco and motor fuel. Together alcohol and tobacco excises yield 44% of Japan's total excise tax revenue. The same relationship for other countries is Austria (49%), United Kingdom (55%), Venezuela (77%), Ghana (64%) and Sierra Leone (96%). If convenience is the objective, why should modern governments not tax equally convenient items in the commercial stream such as rock records, sports tickets, cosmetics or other drugs?

Government revenue need does not justify special taxes since all revenue needs can be met by single rate, broad-based sales taxes or flat rate income taxes. In the case of pure revenue instruments, justice requires the broadest base possible so that everyone is forced to contribute. Exempting food or low incomes is not strictly necessary since welfare needs are better met by direct subsidies such as public housing and food stamps than by indirect tax expenditures.[6] If both an income tax and sales tax were levied on the broadest bases, tax rates on all expenditures, including drugs, would be approximately 5-10%. To depart from neutrality by taxing alcohol purchases more than purchases of orange juice or opera tickets is discriminatory and, therefore, must be justified. Neutral taxes are an extraction of public service; in contrast, special high rate taxes are a penalty and special low taxes are a subsidy.

The most general justification for discriminatory taxes is that some commercial activities or expenditures have less social value than other commercial choices and are thus more worthy tax targets. Of highest value are basic essentials. These not only benefit the individual buyer, they benefit the collective because personal acquisition of necessities avoids welfare dependency and maintains human capital. Consistent with the high social value of human capital expenditures is the fact that governments tend to tax such expenditures at no more than minimal rates. Beyond necessities lies the more diverse field of socially useful expenditures on capital items such as tools, farms, factories, schools and children. Capital expenditures generate positive externalities so government lacks valid reason for taxing them at special high rates. The equation changes, however, when we consider non-capital expenditures on services or items that are personally gratifying but are of little or no benefit to society. Consider the following examples from the U.S. and Canada (Source designated by currency): $300 million a year (U.S.) spent at tanning salons, $3.5 billion (U.S.) spent on pornography, $1.4 billion (Cnd) and $18 billion (U.S.) "invested" in jewelry, $1 billion (U.S.) directed to men's "grooming aids", much of the $14 billion (U.S.) spent on children's toys, $25 billion (U.S. 1982) allocated to 235 brands of soda pop, and $30 billion (Cnd) or $250 billion (U.S. 1986) expended on vacations. Sales tax expert John Due argues that alcohol and tobacco buyers bear special taxes because these products are "considered to contribute little to economic development".[7] But the same can be said for many other products including the items listed above. Economic development depends on capital expenditures. Non-capital items are the fruits of development, not its cause. It is therefore no surprise that many governments world-wide apply higher tax rates to the purchase of cosmetics, jewelry, furs, playing cards, fireworks, yachts, limousines, golf balls and televisions.[8] No government reverses the standard order of social value by taxing food at higher rates and non-capital items at lower rates.

The U.S. tax system, however, is not consistent since excises penalize alcohol while income tax subsidizes "business" drinking. According to James Mosher, in 1982 U.S. businesses purchased over $10 billion worth of alcohol - 12% of total retail alcohol sales.[9] Internal Revenue Service uncritically accepted alcohol bills as tax-deductible, a policy choice that resulted in a $3-5 billion tax loss. The IRS therefore provides free or discounted alcohol to executives, professionals and some white-collar employees. Judges support the IRS, and the alcohol industry, by ruling that whatever the circumstances, alcohol is "good for business". Mosher does not mention caffeine but tax-deductible expenditures on that drug probably run into the billions as well. Allowing tax deductions for the cost of recreational drug use is bad policy but it is especially galling when the same tax law refuses to allow wage earners to deduct their full work-related expenses on child-care, transport and clothing.

Commenting in 1962 on the popular support allegedly accorded alcohol and tobacco taxes, Crombie explained that the two drugs are "in that category of indulgences, of pleasant vices of which it has been good humouredly said that in the interests of taxation there are not enough of them."[10] Perhaps when Crombie wrote there were not enough taxable indulgences and pleasant vices to go around, but that shortage, if it existed, has been amply and affluently overcome. Unprecedented growth in real income provides increased means to buy drugs and major advances in leisure time provide greater opportunity to consume drugs. Moreover, the financial capacity to explore new forms of consumption tends to coincide with breakdowns in the traditional mores which limit expenditure choices. Women's adoption of alcohol and tobacco since the 1920s and the close association observed between youth and drugs since the 1960s, corresponds in both cases with liberation movements and a relatively large and rapid increase in income for previously poor groups. Men traditionally exceed women in drug use and it is men who customarily control discretionary household spending.

Higher taxes on non-capital items are designed not so much to deter buyers but to place the tax burden where it will do least damage. Some amount of tax must fall somewhere, better it rain down on golf balls and cosmetics than on bread, children's clothes or school books. This tax policy will subsidize saving, investment and capital spending and penalize non-capital spending. Drugs should be included as non-capital items, except where specifically exempted, say for hospital use as anesthetics. Once in the same broad category as pornography, cosmetics and the like, psychoactive drugs should bear the same retail tax rates (which generally fall in the 15-30% range).

In search of a justification for even higher tax rates, I note that within the non-capital category there exists a sub-set of commercial choices which not only lack social benefit but generate social costs. For this category, tax may be used for sumptuary or regulative purposes as an alternative to criminal law controls. As Lon Fuller observed, taxes are "close cousins to the criminal law (when) their principal object is ... not merely to raise revenue, but to shape human conduct in ways thought desirable by the legislator."[11] The regulatory aspects of a tax are usually reflected in higher tax rates and the co-existence of prohibitive regimes. State gambling taxes evidence these elements. Tax rates are high: effective tax rates on state lotteries run about 45%. Furthermore, some states prohibit gambling activities, such as casinos, off-track betting, dog racing and lotteries, that other states tax. The same high tax rate - alternative to criminal prohibition pattern is true of alcohol but not of fur coats, vacations, sports and other milder non-capital items. Alcohol and tobacco excise tax rates range from 40-200% and thus tend to be higher than the so-called luxury tax rates. In addition, sumptuary taxes are usually associated with a high degree of government intervention. Where gambling is taxed, the state also supervises gambling operations through state commissions or direct state monopolies. In contrast, a new 12% Canadian excise tax on confections in 1987 was not accompanied by plans to closely regulate the candy bar industry.

Since sumptuary taxes include a decidedly punitive element based on a judgment of wrongdoing, the limits to punishment applicable in criminal law justice should apply to the tax. Unfortunately, there is a great deal of confusion and disagreement about the proper role of criminal law punishment. The confusion is due to misplaced utilitarian and rehabilitative arguments and to a misinterpretation of retribution.[12] All punishment theories agree that legal penalties exist to deter wrongdoing and to subject wrongdoers to special treatment. Where the competing views diverge is on the limits to punishment. Utilitarians limit punishment according to a social benefit calculus or to a pure deterrence analysis, both of which entail problems I will return to below. Rehabilitationists limit state coercion to the level and kind necessary to reform or cure the wrongdoer but that limitation, in practice, tends to be entirely open-ended. The most limited thesis is retributionist. Under retributive guidelines, government can only punish wrongful behaviour, can only punish the wrongdoer, can only punish to an extent and kind proportional to the wrong and must punish equal wrongs equally.[13]

To link tax with punishment and criminal law penalties is not to equate fines with taxes. Both penalize, but procedurally fines are quite different from regulative taxes. Fines require a plea of guilty or a court judgment whereas a tax penalty is based merely on making a purchase. Tax avoids courts, judges and lawyers. Fines are paid after the trial and after the wrongdoing was committed, but tax is anticipatory, being paid before the harm occurs. Fines must be extracted from unwilling offenders so rates of non-payment are high while taxes are collected from willing drug purchasers and rates of evasion are very low. Fines are personalized and may comprise part of an individual's criminal record. Taxes are impersonal. Fines are part of a prohibitory framework, taxes are not. Even if the tax and the fine for buying a litre of liquor are both $10, the fine follows from a law forbidding such drug use whereas the tax is non-prohibitive. Finally, the tax affects a much higher proportion of the targeted wrongdoers and is far less expensive to administer.

b. Taxation and Retribution

Retribution limits punishment to wrongdoing. Earlier chapters contained evidence suggesting that psychoactive drug use falls on the wrongful side of the ledger because drug users breach an implicit social obligation to maintain their own health and, more importantly, because they impose costs on other people. The requirement of wrongdoing is therefore satisfied.

The second requirement is that only the wrongdoer is to be penalized. A special tax on drug-related income is not warranted because drug producers *per se* do not act wrongfully and because business income tax may not be fully passed on to drug purchasers and users. The incidence of business income taxes remains an economic mystery.

A personal income tax on drug users is also not feasible. Granted, we can calculate the portion of the average household budget spent on alcohol, tobacco and other drugs. On alcohol and tobacco alone, the Japanese spend 3%, the Danes 8% and the British 10% of their budgets. According to a recent American survey, the average household spends $21,788 (1984) of which $299 (1.37%) buys alcohol and $255 (1.03%) buys tobacco. Drug expenditures per household decline rapidly after members pass age 65; at 75 and over total expenditure drops to $11,196 but drug expenditures fall even more to $90 on alcohol, $65 on tobacco.[14] (This effect probably corresponds to the longer life span of non-drug using women.) Whatever the expenditure figures, an income tax system could levy a special surcharge on the last 2, 3 or 5% of all taxpayers' income on the assumption that this portion of income buys drugs. This runs afoul of the second rule since the penalty would fall on users and non-users (the innocent) alike. To properly individualize the tax penalty, each income tax payer would need to include annual receipts for drug expenditures. Only that sum would be taxed at the higher rate. Fine in theory, this form of sumptuary tax would fail in practice because of tax evasion. Drug users would grossly understate their drug expenditures in order to escape the surcharge, just as Italian stockbrokers declare an average annual income of $6,900 (1982) to escape income tax. Taxpayers would also resent being forced to keep detailed records of all their drug purchases. To avoid fraud in self-reporting, government could demand that every commercial drug outlet record each person's drug purchases and forward the information to the revenue department. This step is feasible but it would necessarily put an end to cigaret vending machines, which now sell about 10% of all cigarets, and it would place a major administrative burden on a million small retailers and tavern owners.

Excise taxes passed on to alcohol and tobacco purchasers in retail drug prices serve the same function as the personalized income tax but without the complications and administrative difficulties. Taxes on transactions do not require drug purchasers to keep any records and because the tax is collected at the wholesale or retail source, there are fewer tax avoidance possibilities. Excise taxes achieve an automatic fit between amount of drug purchased and amount of tax penalty paid. People who do not buy drugs pay no tax, whereas heavy buyers pay considerable tax. But is the fit between drug wrongdoing and drug purchasing tight enough? In some cases the tax paying purchaser will serve the drugs to other people. If the wrongdoing entails actual use of the drug, then it would seem the wrong person has been penalized. Actually, non-using purchasers lack grounds for complaint because they have voluntarily assumed a tax penalty meant for someone else. A comparable situation is where A donates $15 to B so B can pay a parking fine. Since A is not legally obliged to pay B's fine, the gift of $15 cannot be characterized as a penalty against A.

A far more important concern is that a fixed tax penalty per consumption unit cannot fit every case. Even if we agree that all users contribute to social costs, it does not follow that each drug user contributes the same harm per unit consumed. Some variation can be accounted for by varying the drug tax rate according to the drug purchased, its mode of ingestion and its potency. Some policy analysts suggest taxing low tar and nicotine cigarets at low rates but it is not clear that such products actually reduce tobacco-related social costs.[15] There also exist personal variations in externality production based on age, sex, size, metabolism and behaviour that are beyond the pale for the tax assessor. A flat tax on beer discriminates against people of above average weight because lighter people generally become more intoxicated on the same quantity of alcohol. Similarly, some tobacco users generate fewer social costs per cigaret than others because they never smoke in company or leave ashtrays unattended. Walsh thinks that the "ideal" drug tax would escalate progressively with amount purchased and discriminate between groups of users. Walsh would have youths pay more tax because he claims they are "most likely to cause damage by their drinking patterns", but he concludes that the ideal tax structure is "completely impracticable".[16] Gusfield also criticized tax controls as overly blunt, falling "like sober rain from heaven upon the problem and problem-free drinkers alike". These comments overstate the lack of discrimination. First, Gusfield employed dubious criteria and scant data to conclude that most alcohol users are "problem-free". Second, as Cook points out, the alcohol tax is already quite discriminatory.[17] The top 10% of U.S. alcohol users consume about 40-50% of all beverage alcohol and thus pay approximately 40-50% of the alcohol taxes. This relatively small group exhibits the highest incidence of alcohol-related problems but they also pay the most tax. Conversely, the lowest 10% of alcohol users pays very little tax. Cook concludes that alcohol taxes exact payment from users in at least rough proportion to the social costs they engender.

Cook's case is strengthened when we carefully consider which drug-related costs should be countered by a retributive tax penalty. Serious, acute wrongs such as drug-related murder, assault, battery and negligence already punished or compensated in tort or criminal law should not be subject to additional tax penalties since that would punish the same wrongdoing twice. In calculating the social cost of alcohol at about $1.50 per drink (U.S. 1979), Leonard Schifrin included $4.47 billion in violent crime costs and $6.77 billion in motor vehicle crash costs.[18] These costs should not be included in calculating the alcohol tax rate. The type of costs all users tend to generate are those of a more chronic, diffuse nature such as health costs, lost production, pollution and lack of capital spending. These costs are better candidates for tax penalties because they relate much more closely to the amount of drug purchased and consumed. Over a 40 year period, a heavy cigaret user will smoke up to 30,000 packs of cigarets, whereas a light user will smoke only 1,000 - 2,000 packs. Similarly alcohol users over 40 years will consume from 250,000 drinks down to a few hundred. We cannot predict that a specific heavy consumer of alcohol or tobacco will commit murder, rob a bank or drive over a pedestrian; however, we can predict that they will bother other people, litter common property, have more accidents, die at an earlier age, set a drug-using example to their children and friends, and waste an inordinate amount of resources on a largely useless indulgence.

By restricting tax penalties to diffuse, global wrongs that vary closely with amount of drug consumed, one achieves the best fit between tax and wrongdoing. The next retributive requirement is to make the penalty fit the wrongdoing. Assuming that an excise tax is a fitting punishment one must then apply the right tax rate.

2. Determining Drug Tax Rates

a. Political Rate Setting

The tax rate applied to any drug purchase is obviously the key factor in determining the social impact of a tax control scheme. One merely needs to imagine the contrasting results of taxing retail alcohol sales at 5%, 50% or 500%. Like criminal penalties, tax penalties can range from almost negligible levels to prohibitive rates capable of driving legitimate sales underground. In this section I consider the different methods, principles or criteria by which rates can be set. Melissa Brown argues that there is no technically right solution to the question of how much tax alcohol, tobacco (or other drugs) should bear.[19] I think it more accurate to say that a variety of "solutions" exist and they yield different results, some of which are superior to others. In a preliminary and sketchy way I divide rate setting methods into three categories: political, economic and legal.

The first and dominant method of rate setting is to permit the legislature to establish any rate schedule it wishes. In 1914 Congress amended the Harrison Act to levy a tax of $300 per pound on opium prepared for smoking. No rule prevented Congress from setting such an extreme tax or from taxing opium at all while not taxing other psychoactives. A 1980 survey represented in Table 1 indicates the variation in alcohol taxes between 18 countries. The noted rates aggregate the different tax rates for beer, wine and liquor weighted to consumption levels.

Table 1

Excise taxes per Litre of Alcohol, 1980: Canada = 100

Sweden	315	Japan	146	U.S.	47
Norway	286	Australia	103	West Germany	40
Ireland	247	Canada	100	Spain	39
Finland	186	Netherlands	63	France	31
Denmark	167	Belgium	49	Switzerland	28
U.K.	153	New Zealand	45	Italy	6

Source: J. O'Hagan (1983)[20]

Measured in Canadian dollars (1977) the excise tax per litre of absolute alcohol in Western Europe for beer ranged from 40 cents in France to $14.40 in Ireland. For wine, tax ranged from 0 cents in Italy to $12.40 in the U.K. For liquor, tax ranged from $2.60-$3.50 in Italy to $31.80-$48.80 in Denmark. Not surprisingly, these tax rates tend to correspond with cultural biases; the newest form of alcohol, distilled liquor, is taxed everywhere at higher rates than traditional beer and wine. In addition, tax rates on wine are very low in wine-producing countries where the political power of the industry has long been entrenched. Explaining these tax rates in detail would be quite difficult if not impossible because the political rate setting process is obscure, covert, complicated and strongly affected by historical circumstances. After surveying the rate setting process with alcohol taxes, Johnson, in something of an understatement, concluded that the guiding rules were "not clear".[21]

Johnson alludes to a clear and simple rule when he discusses the rate of alcohol tax that will maximize government revenue. No one knows now but a few decades of rate setting experimentation would suffice to determine the revenue maximizing rate. Whatever the details, such rates should form a parabolic Laffer Curve. As tax rates increase from zero, consumption rates will fall but revenue will rise and continue to rise until a peak revenue rate of, say 300 - 500% on alcohol, is reached. Thereafter, higher tax rates will produce less revenue because of declining consumption and tax evasion. Eventually, at some very high rate, revenue will return to zero because all sales will be illegal. At that point, alcohol prices will resemble current cocaine and heroin prices. One advantage of a revenue maximizing rate is that it precludes prohibitive rates and the black markets they generate. Under this rule Congress would not have taxed opium in 1914 at $300 per pound. Tax rates in different countries would move closer together under a revenue maximizing rule. Rather than the wine tax in the U.K. being at $12.40 per litre of absolute alcohol and the Italian tax at 0 cents, the U.K. tax would increase to something like $20.00 per litre and the Italian to $10.00.

A revenue maximizing rule also poses some problems. Highest tax rates would fall upon drugs not according to their dangerousness but according to the degree to which people are attached to their use. The maximizing rate for Rx psychoactives would be much lower than for alcohol because alcohol is culturally integrated and serves a number of social, ceremonial purposes. Rates would also be higher for drugs that were difficult to smuggle or produce illicitly, a factor of no particular relevance to justice. Finally, revenue maximizing rates have no necessary connection with a retributive analysis based on just deserts. Criminal law fines should not be based on revenue maximizing considerations and neither should drug tax rates. Government has no justification for extracting maximum revenue from drug users.

A second clear but problematic political rule is to set drug tax rates as high as possible. In 1792 one British legislator argued that duties on alcohol should be set so that the "means of intoxication" will be as "difficult to come by as they possibly can".[22] Swiss economist Robert Leu includes this rule among his "political" rate setting methods.[23] On its face, the rule seems unjust. In criminal law its proponents, if consistent, would argue that penalties for theft, counterfeiting, fraud and robbery should be set as high as possible. Indeed, in 1792 British judges and legislators came close to satisfying this rule as they threatened over a hundred crimes with the death penalty. Only the most severe wrongs deserve penalties set as "high as possible" and neither fraud nor drug use falls in that class. A modified form of the rule could specify that drug use merely deserves the highest tax penalty possible. This is more promising and further modifications are possible. What, for example, does as high as "possible" mean? Possible could be interpreted to mean a rate insufficient to stir up black markets because, after serious tax evasion commenced, higher tax rates would not result in drugs being more difficult to come by. If this modified form of the rule is employed, the highest possible tax rates will reach levels comparable to revenue maximizing rates. Hellman believes that marijuana should be taxed like alcohol and tobacco and that the tax rate should not encourage development of a black market but "once that point is accepted it becomes difficult to find other principles bearing on the appropriate rate of taxation."[24]

State tobacco taxes provide a good illustration of how tax evasion and illicit sales limit the "possible" extent of tax rate increases. When neighbouring states impose different tax rates, tobacco is increasingly purchased in the low tax state. Informal smuggling begins when rates vary by more than 3 cents per pack of cigarets and formal, large scale smuggling occurs when the difference exceeds 7 cents a pack. The largest tax gap in 1960 was 8 cents, in 1965 it was 11 cents and in the 1970s the gap increased to 19 cents. As a consequence of the increasing tax gap, cigaret smuggling increased, high tax states stopped raising their taxes and Congress enacted the *Cigarette Contraband Act* of 1978 to bolster law enforcement efforts against cigaret smugglers. Smuggling decreased in the late 1970s but not because of the new law. Between 1955-72, state tobacco tax increases averaged 10 per year with the non-tobacco states like Connecticut, Florida, Texas and Massachusetts pulling away from the tobacco states. In 1963, the non-tobacco states had 40% higher tax rates and by 1975 their rates were 200% higher. North Carolina's tax was lowest at 2 cents per pack, the highest rate states applied taxes of 23 cents per pack. By 1975 interstate cigaret smuggling was a hot issue with some high rate states losing up to 16% of their tobacco tax revenue. In addition, smuggling hurt legitimate wholesalers, incited political corruption and encouraged injury, murder, hijacking and organized crime. Under this pressure, the average number of state tobacco tax increases fell from 10 to 3 a year after 1972. With high inflation and lower tax increases, the real price of cigarets, which had been rising at 1.6% rate up to 1972, fell at 3% per year through to 1981. As the real value of the tax gap decreased, smuggling declined. Smuggling thus abated before the *Cigarette Contraband Act* of 1978 came into effect.[25] What is particularly interesting here is that the tobacco producing states indirectly forced other states to competitively modify their excise rates. The border effect is also a factor in international trade: the Republic of Ireland is now losing alcohol tax revenue because of duty free purchasing and smuggling from Britain.

A third political rate setting method works backwards from pre-determined goals. In a 1977 *Lancet* article, Atkinson and Townsend set as their objective a 20% decline in total alcohol consumption and then calculated the tax rate necessary to achieve a 56% increase in alcohol prices, an increase they estimated would cause a 20% decline in use.[26] This method is simple and technically feasible but only because it begs the initial question of where one should set the consumption ceiling. Why should the government engineer a 20% decline in alcohol use? Perhaps the situation calls for a 50% decline or even a 90% drop in use? Or perhaps current alcohol taxes are already too high in relation to the social costs of alcohol use. Few commentators bother to explain their rate setting choices. Dan Beauchamp considers that taxation should "surely be one cornerstone of a new policy for alcohol", yet his only concrete tax rate proposal is to restore the federal tobacco excise to its 1951 level, which would mean increasing tax per packet from 16 cents to 40 cents. How does he know Congress picked the right rate in 1951?

Another obvious but usually neglected political method of rate setting is direct democratic choice − let voters choose the drug tax rates they want in an open referendum. The outcome of a direct vote will depend on existing patterns of drug use and on the voting rules applied. If a simple, unrestrained majoritarian rule governs the voting then majority-use drugs will be lightly taxed, if taxed at all, whereas minority-use drugs will be heavily taxed. Such an outcome corresponds roughly with current levels of restraint. In all Western countries, caffeine beverages are consumed by over 90% of the adult population. And caffeine is generally not taxed. Instead, in tea, coffee and cola drinks it is regarded as a food. Wine holds a similar place in many European countries and, as noted, Italy, West Germany, France, Spain and Portugal levy few if any taxes on wine. Majority rule is probably also instrumental in changing alcohol and tobacco tax rates over the last twenty years. Except for France, per capita consumption of alcohol is up overall and alcohol is clearly a majoritarian drug. With the exception of Ireland and perhaps the U.K., alcohol taxes have generally not kept pace with inflation so the real price of alcohol has declined in most countries. Compare this to tobacco, a drug no longer used by the majority of voters. In most provinces and states and in many countries, especially in Scandinavia, tobacco tax increases over the past two decades resulted in higher real prices for cigarets. The U.S. federal cigaret excise, which in real terms declined 30% in value since 1965, is an exception.[27] And strictly minority recreational drugs such as cocaine, LSD and mescaline bear a high crime tariff which roughly substitutes for a prohibitive tax rate. The same does not apply to Rx psychoactives despite the fact that tranquilizers such as Valium are used by a relatively small minority. The difference is that people regard medical drugs as a single class and, as a single class, Rx drugs and OTC medications are as majoritarian as alcohol and coffee. In contrast, illicit drug users even as a group remain a vulnerable minority. Different rate outcomes will follow if the voting rules are changed to require either a full consensus on each drug's tax rate or a single tax rate for all drugs.

b. Economic Rate Setting

Economists begin with efficiency. An efficient allocation of resources occurs when voluntary contractors bear all the costs of their transaction. Crimes are diseconomic because the perpetrator by-passes the consensual market to impose costs on an involuntary victim. Buying motor fuel can be diseconomic if the two voluntary parties - the motorist and the seller of gasoline - impose pollution costs on third party victims. Economists refer to the first diseconomy as market by-passing and to the second as a market failure. In public law, the two standard remedies to inefficient outcomes are direct regulation prohibiting the production of externalities or taxes counterbalancing the externalties. The primary aim of the gasoline tax, for example, may not be to prohibit driving or raise revenue but to impose on drivers the full cost of their behaviour. If imposing the full social cost of driving on drivers through a regulative petrol tax results in a 30, 40, 50 or 60% decline in motoring miles per capita, that is the correct result. The process works not by setting a predetermined ration ceiling of automobile use but by letting each motorist choose their desired level of motoring within a full social cost context. Economists expect that higher operating costs will cause motorists to change their behaviour in a variety of ways and the same applies to drug users.

290

To achieve an ideal allocation of resources, an efficiency based tax rate should equal the external costs generated by individual car owners or drug users. This ideal is not achievable, as noted earlier, because most personal variations cannot be monitored or detected for inclusion in a tax equation. A practical compromise is to calculate drug tax rates according to a range of impersonal factors where the general rate level is based on the expected average external costs stemming from using a given amount of drug X. Robert Leu characterizes this method of rate setting as the "insurance approach" because of its parallels with compulsory automobile insurance. Insurance rates are set in two steps: first auto insurance rates must produce enough total revenue to match expenses and claims; second, the average rate per motorist needed to achieve the needed revenue level is adjusted for each motorist according to whether that motorist falls in a high or low risk group.

Setting drug tax rates at levels sufficient to compensate all relevant drug-related externalities is a much easier method than one requiring a measurement of individual costs but even global drug costs are difficult to assess and quantify. The advantage of an efficiency-based tax rate is that it would incite the research needed to compile accurate cost estimates. If all drug tax rates had to be based on demonstrated externalities and were subject to court challenges, then interested parties would gather data in support of their positions. Revenue departments backed by abstainers and light drug users, would push for higher tax rates and so would fund researchers to exhaustively poke into every conceivable connection between drug use and social costs. Drug industries, backed by heavy drug users, would push for lower tax rates and so would establish research institutes to attack and discredit the high cost estimates; and many estimates are, in fact, quite vulnerable. Day, for example, estimated that 25.9% of all fires are "related" to alcohol but a mere correlation is only the beginning of an investigation. Schifrin, more directly, attributes 6% of all fires to alcohol use.[28] Alcohol producers could readily challenge that figure by arguing that most of those fires were due to cigaret smoking, not drinking. Alcohol drinkers who fall asleep or pass out without a cigaret rarely cause fires so if costs are to be attributed to any drug, it should be tobacco not alcohol. Naturally, tobacco producers would reply that alcohol is instrumental in fire damage by causing unconsciousness and by rendering drinkers incapable of rescuing themselves once a fire has started.

Another instance of questionable cost estimation is the frequent assertion that smokers generate health care costs in excess of tobacco tax revenue. Harris claims that in 1975 cigaret smoking caused $7.5 billion in medical costs but yielded only $6.5 billion (U.S.) in tax.[29] Garner, who compares tobacco to cholera, cites 1985 figures indicating that American smokers pay $21 billion in taxes while imposing $20 billion in treatment costs and $40 billion in lost production.[30] If these estimates are accurate, tobacco tax rates should be substantially increased. But are they accurate?. Peter Taylor suggests that "on a purely financial basis, the economic benefits of tobacco far outweigh the health care costs."[31] More to the point, Canadian researchers recently calculated that tobacco-related expenditures on hospital and physician services amounted to less than one-third of tobacco tax revenue.[32] They concluded that if revenue or better health is sought, taxes should go up; but if the objective is solely to correct a financial externality then tax rates should fall. Health costs, however, are not the only externality generated by tobacco users. Nelkin's thorough survey of U.S. tobacco costs cites government estimates that tobacco users bear only 38% of the social costs their drug use generates thus, in effect, forcing every nonsmoker to bear $600 in tobacco costs. Nelkin, therefore recommends the federal excise on cigarets be raised from 16 cents to $2.50 a pack.[33] A recent RAND Corporation study, on the other hand, concluded that U.S. smokers do pay their cost to society through tobacco taxes.[34] The RAND study, however, calculated that alcohol users are seriously undertaxed in terms of alcohol's social costs. In a discussion of alcohol, Bakalar and Grinspoon confidently assert that "it goes without saying that existing taxes on alcohol are not nearly high enough to pay for the costs of alcohol abuse."[35] But current knowledge does not actually permit such confidence.

Setting drug tax rates equal to the average per unit generation of relevant social costs would necessitate the use of a unit tax rather than an *ad valorem* tax. A unit tax is assessed against a physical quantity such as nicotine level, amount of absolute alcohol or gram of pure morphine. Assuming that drug content is the relevant measure of externality generation, a unit tax is required because it does not vary with incidental ingredients as does an *ad valorem* tax. An alcohol tax example can illustrate the difference. Assume that two brands of whisky each contain an identical amount of alcohol which bears a $6 tax reflecting an average social cost per drink (1.5 ounce) of 38 cents. Brand A is a low cost, poor quality whisky aged in plastic barrels for two years. Brand A sells for $1.00 a litre. Brand B is a high quality whisky aged in oak barrels for fifteen years. It sells for $5.00 a litre. After tax, the cheap brand sells for $7.00, the expensive brand for $11.00. This means that pre-tax, B's price is 20% of A's price whereas post-tax, B's price is 63% of A's price, hence B loses most of its comparative price advantage. This example is exaggerated but the effect of a unit tax is always to favour the high price/high quality product. An *ad valorem* tax, in contrast, favors the low quality product. Using the same figures and the same two bottles of whisky, I must apply a retail tax of 200% to raise the same $12 in tax revenue. But this time the post-tax price of A is $3 (not $5) and the price of B is $15 (not $11). Brand A remains at 20% of B's price. The disadvantage of an *ad valorem* tax rate is that tax varies according to non-drug incidentals which have no relation to drug externalities.

For years Britain taxed cigarets on a unit weight basis. This encouraged manufacturers to market short, lightweight cigarets of high quality. France and Italy took the opposite course and employed an *ad valorem* tax which encouraged the production of the low quality tobacco and flimsy packaging characteristic of those countries.[36] Both at the federal and state levels, U.S. governments apply a unit per package tax on tobacco cigarets. The federal alcohol tax is also levied on a per gallon basis. If government inflates the currency, the relative impact of a per unit tax decreases. Inflation in the U.S. reduced the real value of the federal alcohol excise by 70% between 1951 and 1982. As a result, the inflation-adjusted price of liquor declined 48%, beer 27% and wine by 20%. Per unit taxes should be inflation-indexed. *Ad valorem* taxes have the advantage of automatic inflation adjustment.

Per unit taxes levied strictly according to average per unit social costs preclude two common tax practices. The first is the differential taxation of alcoholic beverages with wine and beer favored over distilled liquor. Some early Swedish studies, based on dubious data and sophisticated statistical analysis, reported that the "intoxication effect" of an ounce of absolute alcohol was less if taken in the form of wine or beer than in liquor but later research found no difference in effect between ordinary use of beer, wine or liquor.[37] If alcohol beverages in Canada were taxed fairly, beer prices would climb about 50% and fortified wine, the staple of the impoverished heavy drinker, would increase 100% in price. Naturally, this tax reform policy is backed by the Association of Canadian Distillers.

The second discriminatory alcohol tax policy that has no place in an efficiency-based tax system is the punitive taxation of foreign products. Hamilton's first whisky tax of 1791 set three rates: a high rate on imported whisky, a medium rate on whisky made domestically from foreign raw materials and a low rate on purely domestic whisky. Building in a tariff against foreign alcohol and tobacco is typical of existing excise systems.[38] Discriminating against foreign products cannot be justified from an externalities perspective. If some other valid excuse for a drug tariff exists, which I doubt, it can only relate to an efficiency-based tax if foreign sourced drugs are somehow more dangerous or damaging per drug unit. Generally, the real aim of tariff and non-tariff barriers against foreign products is to subsidize domestic industry at the consumer's expense. This subsidization is probably common in the alcohol and tobacco industries because of the high degree of monopoly concentration and the political advantage such producer concentration offers.

c. Legal Rate Setting

According to economist Leu, the sumptuary taxation of alcohol is a paternalistic policy favored by anti-alcohol groups who stupidly ignore economic efficiency. These people want to deter alcohol use and/or punish alcohol users so they set taxes as high as possible or at a level designed to achieve a specific, pre-determined reduction in use. This view misrepresents sumptuary taxation as necessarily political when, in fact, legal rate setting based on retributive principles subsumes the entire economic efficiency argument and adds an important ingredient – fairness. Kenneth Warner regards a higher tobacco tax as politically ideal because, given an overall price elasticity of - 0.4, real price increases will cut consumption and boost revenue.[39] Like other public health advocates, however, Warner does not consider whether a given tobacco tax rate is fair or deserved.

Retribution and efficiency lead to similar tax policies. The concept of just desert implicitly follows an equilibrium or "economic" model whereby punishment counterbalances the offender's "debt", that is costs imposed on unwilling victims. Retribution requires that only the wrongdoer (debtor) be legally obliged to pay the debt (fine, punishment, punitive tax) with repayment being equal to the debt incurred. Retributive justice prohibits the debt-collector (government) from demanding excessive repayment at the same time as it forbids the debtor to repay an inadequate amount. Under a retributive system, alcohol users should pay a penalty equal to the social harm caused by their alcohol consumption. This social harm is equal to the economist's externality. In addition, the legal analyst considers due process rights.

The first legal process issue is the onus of proof. Since special high taxes are punitive, there should be a constitutionally prescribed onus on the government to justify the tax rate. The legal presumption should be clearly spelled out that all commodities and services should bear a common tax burden unless the case for discriminatory treatment is well-established on at least a balance of probabilities. In other words, all taxable transactions should be innocent until proven guilty. If such rules were in place, alcohol purchasers would not need to prove that alcohol is overtaxed, they would merely need to raise that defence; the onus of proving that the tax rate is warranted should always rest with the state. The target of sumptuary taxation must always get the benefit of doubt. Unhappily, this principle is now ignored in the regulative tax field because courts do not grant taxpayers the same protective rights granted tort and criminal law defendants.

The second legal rate setting issue is equality before the law. Each tort or criminal defendant must be tried according to the same rules and procedures and, if found liable, their legal obligation must be equivalent to other wrongdoers in comparable circumstances. This retributive rule is plainly violated by present tax laws since some drug users are taxed and some are not. If we assume that the current per unit tax on alcohol is justified then the alcohol rate standard can be employed to judge the treatment of other drugs. Users of caffeine and diazepam are obviously undertaxed since they usually bear no special tax at all. Rx psychoactives are, in addition, exempt from VAT and sales taxes and are deductible as medical expenses from personal income taxes. This deductibility is unfair because alcohol can serve an identical medical role. Drugs like marijuana and LSD are effectively "overtaxed" because partial criminal prohibition results in a crime tariff and high prices. Of course, with a crime tariff the "tax revenue" goes to illicit drug sellers and corrupt politicians rather than to the government, but the tariff is still a "tax" in the sense that its existence results from legislative design. Finally, drugs like heroin and cocaine are grossly "overtaxed" through the same crime tariff process. The only drug taxed in even a remotely fair way compared to alcohol is tobacco. Without entering into the details of a social harm analysis, it is easy to predict that if all drug users were taxed fairly, the price of untaxed drugs, like caffeine, would increase whereas the price of prohibited drugs would decrease substantially.

But is the punitive tax rate applied to alcohol users a just rate in the retributive sense? No one knows. Economists and sociologists have started measuring drug-related externalities but not a single legal case, to my knowledge, has addressed the issue of what is a just tax desert for alcohol use. This neglect is not surprising. Courts upheld the U.S. government's right to prohibit alcohol and to jail illicit alcohol sellers for life, so it is not likely that a contemporary court will declare a tax of $9 or $900 per gallon of beer to be "cruel and unusual punishment". Furthermore, judges and legal scholars are trained to differentiate sharply between tax law and criminal law. Government fiscal demands are allowed to excuse most any form of tax even when that tax's design relates to revenue need only in an indirect and flimsy fashion. Legislators now cannot discriminate on the basis of a person's skin colour but they can discriminate on the basis of a person's income or choice of drugs. Graduated income tax rates, which in Britain and Sweden exceeded 90% and even 100% and which drove people out of their homelands, were never found to be unconstitutional. Numerous legal articles describe and criticize the apparently unwarranted variations in criminal law penalties assessed against comparable offenders but I find no legal scholar similarly addressing regional alcohol tax differentials. Such differentials do exist. According to Johnson's figures, the unit tax per gallon of beer was 600% higher in Newfoundland than in Quebec. The wine tax rate was 300% higher in Newfoundland than Alberta and the liquor tax rate was

80% higher in New Brunswick than British Columbia. Most legal analysts regard such rate variations as unremarkable exercises of government's broad power to tax.

Criminal law penalty "rates" are also set by non-retributive judges to deter the offender from repeating the crime or to make an example of the offender so as to deter others. This method is not founded on the degree of wrongdoing but on a prediction of future behaviour. But as it happens, we cannot predict the future occurrence of relatively rare events such as murder and so we cannot tell if a deterrent penalty is "right". Common, everyday events such as drug taking are far more predictable and it is generally true that as penalties for drug taking increase, drug taking declines. Countless examples illustrate the economic truism that higher prices, other things being equal, lead to reduced sales. After a thorough study of the legal, economic and sociodemographic variables affecting U.S. alcohol consumption, Ornstein and Hanssens report that:

> The main determinants of interstate differences in per capita consumption of distilled spirits are price, income, and interstate travel...Control laws are either unrelated to distilled spirits consumption, as in the cases of minimum legal age and Sunday sales, or are related but with very low elasticities, as in the cases of resale price maintenance and print and billboard price advertising. This suggests, not too surprisingly, that control laws affecting price have the greatest impact on consumption. In the case of beer, the primary influence on demand is the youthfulness of the population.[40]

In Ireland, Walsh similarly found that "higher tobacco prices are more effective than anti-smoking campaigns or curbs on advertising as a means of reducing consumption of tobacco."[41]

From their review of the cigaret data, 1954-1980, Bishop and Yoo conclude that the "health scare" had little effect on a declining demand caused largely by higher taxes.[42] McCornac and Filante calculate that a U.S. alcohol excise tax increase of $1 would cause an 8% decrease in alcohol use.[43] Historically, two periods of relaxed alcohol tax restraint in England, the first from 1700-1743 and the second from 1830-1869, led to a "disastrous increase in heavy drinking"; during the first period, the per capita consumption of untaxed gin increased ten to twenty times. Harris predicts that a 12% rise in retail cigaret prices would lead to a 3% decline in the number of adult smokers and a 15% decline in the number of teenage smokers. Elaborating on this last point, Lewit and Coate found that tobacco tax increases had greatest impact on the smoking behaviour of young men and that impact operated primarily on their decision to start smoking rather than to cut back on the amount of tobacco consumed.[44] Teenage price elasticities of demand for cigarets are large, ranging from - 1.2 to 1.4, and it is likely that if young adults do not take up tobacco before they are 25 they never will. With alcohol, Coate and Grossman found that excise tax is a potent method for reducing alcohol use and motor vehicle fatalities among young adults.[45]

Despite these and many other examples of price sensitivity, frequent reference is made to the "inelastic" demand for addictive drugs and the resulting immunity from price disincentives exhibited by addicts. Bernard admits that for years the typical economic analysis of the heroin market accepted the "unchallenged axiom" that heroin users were permanently hooked and that without the drug they faced painful, hazardous effects, including death.[46] This argument errs in two respects. First, the term "inelastic" is an economic misnomer that really means "less elastic" than the idealized item whose sales decrease by 1% with every 1% increase in price. The only true inelasticity occurs when demand remains unchanged despite any price increase. In highly unusual circumstances the demand for oxygen or water might approach true inelasticity. Furthermore, the price elasticity of a given product can change value over different price ranges so that the same item can be very elastic, moderately elastic or minimally elastic. The second error, as already noted, is that because of biases and flawed experiments, researchers failed to get the facts straight about heroin users. Typically, a dozen heroin users who also happened to be violent criminals or subnormal or mentally ill or alcoholics, would be taken as a representative sampling. Bakalar and Grinspoon report that "there is strong evidence that raising the relative price of a drug ... cuts down its use ... it is not true that [heroin addicts] must have a certain daily dose at all costs."[47]

298

Granting a deterrent effect to increased drug prices, however, does not lead to a method for establishing the right tax rate. Theft can be deterred to some degree by $500 fines, 5 year prison terms, flogging or execution but there is no element in a pure deterrence rationale to help us choose between these alternative punishments. A specific target reduction of, say, no theft, or 50% less theft or 25% less alcohol consumption, injects a note of precision into the equation but problems remain. How is the initial target determined? Retribution provides a factual, non-predictive base for penalty setting whereas deterrence depends upon unreliable predictions and legally uncontrollable factors. If a retributive calculus prescribes a $10 tax per gallon of wine it is largely irrelevant whether the price increase over the pre-tax price level results in a 1, 5, 10 or 15% decrease in wine consumption. The tax is "right" because it forces wine drinkers to pay the social "debt" their drug use creates.

Using a deterrence goal to dictate a tax rate puts the cart before the horse. Drug consumption varies not only with price but with changes in unemployment, per capita income, demographic patterns, health concerns, labour market penetration by women, fashion and a hundred other factors. If each country decided to achieve a 10% alcohol reduction by tax increases, the tax rate used would be different in every country and would not necessarily relate to the harm caused by alcohol drinkers. According to Ornstein, price elasticity for beer in North America ranges from 0.3 to 0.4 and for wine, 0.4 to 1.59. This means a 10% rise in price will cause a 4% drop in beer sales and as much as a 15% decline in wine purchases.[48] Beer users will be overpenalized relative to wine users. Generally if alcohol is tightly embedded in the culture, large price increases are needed to achieve small reductions in use because people shift spending from coffee, gambling, junk food and entertainment to maintain their alcohol use. As a result, the tax climbs above a retributive tax level. The opposite case is a country where alcohol is a "newer" drug, less firmly entrenched, so that under tax pressure drinkers shift more readily to other drugs or to social psychoactives. In the second case a small tax increase achieves a 10% reduction so the rate is below the retributive tax level. In the first case, the alcohol users are overpunished because of their stubborn, fixated relationship with the drug, whereas in the second case, users are underpunished because their life styles happen to be different.

299

The third competitor in the criminal punishment debate is rehabilitation. Rehabilitationists in criminal "corrections" restrict offenders in order to treat and cure them and thus prevent their return to a life of crime. Rehabilitation is a specialized, medical form of specific deterrence. The equivalent position in the drug control field advocates taxation as a self-help measure, a way of forcing users to reduce their drug consumption. Philip Cook estimates that doubling the U.S. federal alcohol tax would reduce cirrhosis mortality by 20% and concludes, generally, that taxing alcohol "is an effective public health policy instrument."[49] But why stop at a 20% reduction in deaths from cirrhosis when a total elimination of drinking would reduce cirrhosis mortality by up to 95%? A maternalistic tax designed to protect the health of tobacco users would escalate logically to a prohibitive level. If less drug use is almost always healthier than more drug use, a rehabilitative tax will follow in the path of the "as high as possible" rate discussed earlier. The limits to such a tax are not found in any legal principle of justice but are rather determined by the vagaries of circumstance and the readiness of drug buyers to illegally evade the tax.

3. Drug Tax Revenue

a. Revenue Potential

The revenue potential of uniform tax controls raises two major issues: how much revenue will be raised and how should it be spent? Most of the revenue will flow from the excise tax on drug sales and it is only this revenue that should perhaps be earmarked for special purposes. Other new revenue will be produced indirectly once former black market transactions become subject to existing income and sales tax.

Simon and Witte calculate a 1980 income for the U.S. illicit drug industry of $22-30 billion.[50] At the average federal income tax rate of 20% on taxable income, this undeclared income resulted in a revenue loss of $3-5.5 billion out of a total illegal sector loss of $4.6-7.4 billion. At current values, the income tax loss from the illicit drug business is about $8 billion. For comparison purposes, Roscoe Egger, IRS Commissioner, estimates $120 billion in income tax was evaded in 1985. The $8 billion figure for drugs, however, is a static estimate of a dynamic situation. To tax drug-related income requires a legitimation of the industry, but once cannabis, cocaine and the rest are legal, prices and profits in the industry will plummet. The only certain prediction is that income tax yields will increase by some amount.

The same imprecision applies to potential gains from federal, state and local sales taxes. Once all psychoactives are made commercially available, former illicit, OTC and Rx drugs will be caught by the sales taxes applied by 45 states, almost all provinces and some cities. Revenue estimates cannot be produced from present sales figures, however, because the price, availability and status of these drugs will be undergoing radical transformation. Police estimate that 4 million Canadians spend $2,500 each on illicit drugs for a total of $10 billion.[51] Comparable police estimates for the U.S. are $125 billion or $3,125 per user per year. These estimates seem rather high. For 1979, *Time* quoted police figures to the effect that two million Americans were spending $2 billion on cocaine a year, or $1,000 per buyer.[52] Even if these figures are accurate now, once prohibition ends, sales totals will decline substantially because illicit drug prices fall under every plausible method of tax rate setting. Prices may fall as much as 80% and higher consumption is not likely to offset the effect of lower prices on total sales revenue. At a reasonable guess, Rx drugs, OTC psychoactives and ex-illicit drugs will rack up sales in the $40-80 billion range, slightly ahead of soft drinks. At an average retail sales tax rate of 5%, new sales tax revenue from drugs will total $2-4 billion in the U.S.

Daniel Suits has calculated the potential gain from legalizing and taxing now-illicit U.S. gambling. His estimate was $5 billion for 1974. Unfortunately, Suits gave no thought to the rate setting process as he merely extrapolated from existing tax rates on gambling in those states where gambling is legal.

The revenue yield of special drug excises depends on the rate setting method employed. A revenue maximizing rate is likely to generate far more revenue than an efficiency or retributive tax rate. The problem with the retributive tax rate is that we lack complete or reliable information about the scale of societal harm resulting from drug use. In lieu of such knowledge, I can follow Suit's method[53] and assume that the average tax rates on alcohol and tobacco imposed by governments in North America and Northern Europe are about right and that a similar scale of rates should apply to other

301

drugs. Canada's drug excise revenue for 1982 was $4 billion while in the same year British alcohol and tobacco taxes raised £6.5 billion. This was 6.5% of all taxes and all taxes were 36% of GNP so the existing drug taxes were 2.2% of British GNP. This total is roughly comparable to the estimates of societal damage from alcohol and tobacco use mentioned in Chapter Two. A Finnish estimate for alcohol damage was 1.5% of Finland's GNP and Leu puts Switzerland's annual economic burden from tobacco use at 0.5% of GNP. To include all drugs besides alcohol and tobacco, I will assume that these drugs together will generate about the same level of societal harm as alcohol and tobacco. Coffee is less harmful than alcohol but people drink more of it: Canadian adults on average take 1,140 cups a year. Marijuana is more harmful than coffee and may equal alcohol but few people use it in large amounts. The uniform taxation of drugs should then roughly double drug excise revenue.

Richard Karel in 1989 estimated the tax revenue potentially available in the U.S. from the legal sale of marijuana, cocaine, heroine and opium. By setting tax rates at a black market avoidance level, and by extrapolating from current consumption rates, Karel produced estimates ranging from $10.5 billion to $25.7 billion. About half of these revenues would be produced by the tax on marijuana.[54]

A revenue gain to government is necessarily a tax burden to various individuals. Given the revenue figures above, the per capita drug tax burden in Canada under a uniform system would be $524, in Britain £215 and in the U.S. about $425. (In 1980, the average adult American cigaret user paid $121 in tobacco tax.) But the drug tax is not a simple poll tax levied per person, rather it is a behavioural tax with the burden distributed on the basis of each person's drug use. Some people, including almost all young children, will pay no drug tax whereas others may pay over $2,500 per year. It is necessary to specify young children because youngsters between 12 and 17 purchase (illegally) about $260 million a year worth of tobacco in Canada and more than half that total represents tax revenue.[55]

b. Spending Drug Tax Revenue

Rationing and tax controls both limit access to drugs but only tax controls transfer billions of dollars from drug users to government coffers. Should government pay drug tax revenue into the general fiscal fund, as is done with money from criminal fines, or should drug revenue be earmarked for special projects as is now the case with New Jersey gambling taxes: casino tax revenues must aid the elderly and disabled and lottery taxes fund prisons, schools and similar institutions.[56] The tax's disincentive impact is accomplished regardless of where the revenue goes but deterrence is only part of the story. A retributive tax is also justified in terms of compensation. The problem is that the millions of victims of the chronic, minute and diffuse harms covered by a drug tax cannot be distilled out of the vast complexity of drug interactions. At best, government could rebate net drug excise revenue to each adult citizen in a lump sum every year end. I expect this would be more popular than a purely preventive health program.

Using drug tax revenues to fund ordinary government spending is compensatory in a broad sense because high tax bracket drug users pay more than others, however, not everyone gains from ordinary government spending or, if they do, they cannot recognize it. The billions spent on farm subsidies offer rather narrow benefits while the broad spending on the military offers few direct personal gains. A possible solution to this tax-benefit disconnectedness is to earmark drug tax revenue for special projects about which a definite consensus exists. Public opinion surveys can pinpoint the most popular projects but, at a guess, I expect the list might include wildlife preservation, environmental protection, the Olympics, World Exhibitions, disaster relief funds, medical research, education and space exploration. By establishing one or perhaps a few specific drug-funded objectives, victims could be indirectly but visibly compensated. People would reason that, yes, drug users cause societal harm and we pick up part of the tab but, at the same time, the taxes drug users pay result in this marvelous achievement or positive consequence which we share in as citizens.

Some earmarking of drug taxes already occurs. The provincial government of Prince Edward Island added a 22 cent tax per case of beer in 1971 and promised to use the proceeds to defer provincial expenditures on treatment for alcoholics. A New Brunswick study recommended a special 5% retail liquor tax to fund alcoholic rehabilitation.[57] Brecher and *Consumers Union* urge that drug tax proceeds be "devoted primarily to drug research, drug education and other measures specifically designed to minimize the damage done by alcohol, nicotine, marijuana, heroin and other drugs."[58] These preventive and rehabilitory proposals, which are common in the literature, raise two separate issues: how do they relate to compensation goals and are the proposed projects worthy of public funding?

On the first issue, it would appear that there is at least some connection with compensation. If one societal cost of heavy alcohol use is the expense of special alcoholic treatment facilities, then that cost is properly cancelled out by tax funds raised primarily from heavy alcohol users. In effect, alcohol tax becomes the prepayment of a user-fee for the treatment facilities that alcoholics turn to after decades of heavy drinking. The connection with compensation is more tenuous with projects such as drug education or drug research. These programs, if effective, benefit drug users or prevent future harm rather than compensate for harm already caused. A comparable practice would have motor vehicle tortfeasors pay damages into driver education programs rather than to specific victims. Since the connection between compensation and drug research is rather indirect, such programs should compete with other popular objectives quite unrelated to drugs. A dollar spent on pollution abatement might be far more valuable than a dollar spent on drug education.

The second and more difficult issue is whether the preventive or rehabilitative programs frequently proposed are worthwhile. The medics, nurses, social workers and psychiatrists who create and deliver these programs are firm believers but their self-interest and past failures should raise considerable doubts. In the first fifty years of psychiatry, none of the constant claims of therapeutic efficacy were supported by scientifically valid evidence.[59] The same appears true of rehabilitation programs for drug abusers. Drug treatment is fashionable; witness the Betty Ford Center at Palm Springs' Eisenhower Medical Center and its clients, including Elizabeth Taylor, Johnny Cash and, naturally, Betty Ford herself. Athletes exposed as illicit drug users quickly convert themselves into medical victims by enrolling in posh treatment facilities. More women than ever sign up as candidates for drug rehabilitation even in the previously male preserve of Alcoholics Anonymous. New clients are attracted by stirring testimonials of drug abuse salvation in the same way that diet plans parade before and after miracles of 60 pound weight loss. But Irving Babow after reviewing the evidence on treatment effectiveness, reported that very little verified, reliable evidence existed about drug abuse treatment efforts.[60] Nonetheless, competitors in the drug treatment business routinely argue that their method is "the only effective way", that only ex-addicts, only physicians, only psychiatrists or whatever are qualified to treat drug users. Goldstein, Surber and Wilner at the University of California reviewed all the studies evaluating drug treatment intervention which appeared in any of fifty major journals from 1969-1979.[61] Most of these studies failed to follow up treated individuals, most failed to use control groups for comparison and most failed to define "success" clearly or meaningfully. The Goldstein group concluded that their findings "can only be considered disappointing", that the evaluative studies "suffer from massive design problems" and that very few projects presented their findings "in a manner that can be properly understood, no less replicated". These findings are consistent with the dismal record common to the treatment of neurosis, criminal behaviour, obesity and related activities. Obesity treatment offers many parallels to drug treatment.

To begin with obesity is common: 34 million Americans are classified as obese and the condition is now popularly characterized as a "disease" and a "pervasive health hazard." Causal theories of obesity abound, mostly of a genetic or metabolic nature, but social factors such as education level seem to be better predictors of fatness. Naturally, if social context is the prime determinant, then the medical-style treatment of obese individuals will not work. In fact, no one diet seems any better than others and treatment is no more effective than non-treatment.[62]

If individuals want to buy weight-loss guides or if diet cultists are determined to place Dr. X's diet book in every motel or hotel room, they are free to do so at their own expense. The same is true for self-funded attempts at drug control. Government funding is an entirely different matter. Drug or weight treatment centers should receive funding only if they satisfy stringent measures of effectiveness and only if their effect is of social benefit. By any significant measures of effectiveness, drug treatment programs do not deserve public support except as experiments. Drug treatment is often useless or even worse than no treatment.[63] N. Retterstol calls for more public funding of drug therapy for youths but he offers no evidence of the efficacy of current efforts. Jerome Schwartz, a long-time opponent of tobacco use, favours public sponsored "withdrawal centers" for nicotine dependents but cannot demonstrate that these centers would repay the investment of public revenue.

If voluntary drug treatment programs do not deserve funding, the same conclusion must apply with greater force to compulsory treatment. Under existing laws, drug users may be subject to compulsory treatment after being involuntarily committed to a psychiatric institution or as a condition for avoiding criminal prosecution or for gaining parole.[64] The punishment of dangerous drivers is sometimes waived if they "seek treatment" for alcohol abuse. To a significant extent, therapeutic institutions have evolved into a social control role that compliments and sometimes competes with the criminal law system. Judges feed cases into the treatment complex and psychiatrists operate institutes that serve as quasi-jails. This symbiotic relationship in all its forms, including the transformation of drug users into involuntary patients, should be resisted. Simmons and Gold offer a concise review of involuntary treatment. They find little evidence exists to support the incarceration and treatment of drug users whereas it is clear that forcibly treated persons suffer civil disabilities in losing jobs and in being denied employment or life and health insurance. They also find a confusion of therapeutic theories guiding treatment with the "addict" alternately being considered a victim of too little affluence and too much affluence, or of peer neglect and peer pressure.[65]

So-called "drug education" campaigns, now mandatory in some school districts, are likewise a questionable use of tax revenue. Drug education material is frequently inaccurate, biased and based on untested assumptions. Educators through the early 1970s assumed pupils were ignorant about drug risks, that any amount of illicit drug use was abuse and that total abstinence was the only reasonable goal. Attempts to scare pupils with the "facts" about drugs failed to reduce drug use.[66] Further problems arose as good teachers began to develop scientifically credible material on drugs because such material, as Chapter One indicates, works to the discredit of the drug laws. Because some parents insist that their children learn the official lies about the drug menace, well-informed teachers are caught in another superstition-science conflict except that the drug conflict has far greater legal repercussions for all involved than the evolution-creation debate. Whatever form drug education takes, David Hanson is correct in asserting that the burden of proof lies heavily on those who advocate spending public monies on drug education or making drug programs compulsory.[67]

4. Criticisms of Tax Controls

a. Government Conflicts of Interest

Taxing currently illicit drugs would be criticized as a tacit approval by government of heroin, cocaine and the rest. Objectively, a sumptuary tax is punitive and is applied only against behaviour of which government disapproves. A new punitive tax on caffeine beverages or aspirin would not be regarded as a badge of approval. A punitive tax on heroin signals relative approval only because a tax penalty is so much milder than a criminal penalty. Perhaps the real complaint is that a tax on heroin is a tacit admission that seven decades of persecuting heroin users through the criminal law accomplished a terrible injustice.

Accepting that a punitive drug tax is a mild but still legal form of vice control leads to a second familiar complaint, that by taxing drug users, government is living off the avails of vice, misery, addiction and drug trafficking. This criticism is best countered by earmarking the drug tax revenue and spending it openly and plainly on specific goals or projects. Earmarking makes it apparent that government is not keeping the revenue but is, instead, collecting it to reduce externalities and passing it on to affect some popular public purpose. If this is wrong at least everyone shares the guilt.

A related but more substantial concern is that a revenue raising control policy will compromise a government's ability to act in the general public interest. Even with earmarking, government will still keep a portion of the tax revenue to cover administrative costs. Furthermore, governments profit from their control of the fund transfer system since this control necessitates growth and excuses an expansion of power. The very rapid expansion of the old Health, Education and Welfare department of the U.S. federal government is a case in point. Unless the law dictates otherwise, there is an almost endless array of educational issues that can be manipulated to excuse government intervention: bussing, nutrition, safety, teacher qualification, standard setting, textbook censorship, school prayer, corporal punishment and so forth. Health issues are equally expandable.

Tax controls may also lead to tax reliance and a pro-drug bias in government. The evidence suggests that governments look more kindly on taxed drugs than forbidden drugs. European governments tried to prohibit or restrain tobacco use centuries ago but as Heaton explains:

> All such repressions failed to achieve their purpose, and governments became less hostile when they discovered that smoking addicts were willing to pay high taxes. Richelieu detested tobacco but welcomed the revenue yielded. Venice in 1659 set up a tobacco monopoly. England changed her tune when Virginia ... found that it could grow the plant and thus provide a staple export [and] a source of revenue...[68]

Centuries later tobacco is still an important source of revenue: $4.1 billion in Canada and $21 billion in the U.S. on total sales of $49.1 billion in North America (1986). Politicians' dependence on drug tax revenues is positive insofar as it discourages legislators from scapegoating drug users and prohibiting drugs. But the dependence is unhealthy if the tax rates are set politically and if the revenue is not earmarked for special purposes.

Political control means tax rates will be adjusted to win elections and to lever contributions or political support out of drug producers. Politicians may not gain any personal benefit from the tax revenue itself but that is unimportant - what they want is votes, financial contributions for elections and retirement security. In their successful search for these benefits, members of the Liberal Party of Canada forged such close ties with tobacco producers that the Liberal Party has been called the Tobacco Party.[69] When Louis St. Laurent retired as Prime Minister he became chairman of the board of Rothmans of Pall Mall Canada Ltd. His son, Renault, later served on the same board along with former federal cabinet minis-

308

ters - Robert Winters in the 1960s and Alastair Gillespie in the 1980s. Governor-General Jeanne Sauvé's husband, another Liberal ex-cabinet minister, was a member of the Benson and Hedges (Canada) Ltd. board. Liberal campaign managers, ex-press officers, sons and daughters of party bosses and political bagmen work for tobacco companies. Such coziness has to be prohibited under a drug tax control scheme since retributive or efficiency objectives force the government into an antagonistic relationship with drug users, and by extension, drug producers. Conflicts also arise when drugs like alcohol are retailed through state owned outlets. Government employees benefit directly from drug sales, politically appointed managers make operational decisions and politicians may manipulate prices to favour the incumbent party. I have no direct evidence on this last point, but I expect that tax-price increases tend to occur shortly after an election whereas before an election real prices are allowed to drift down through inflation.

b. Regressiveness

Critics who denounce sumptuary drug taxes as "regressive" assume that every tax should be judged according to a taxpayer's income. O'Hagan considers the Irish alcohol excise inequitable because average wage earners who consume four pints of beer per day pay 7.6% of their income in alcohol tax whereas non-drinkers pay nothing. Furthermore, the four pint a day drinkers who earn only half the average wage pay 15% of total income in alcohol tax. Kay and King likewise report that an alcohol tax is regarded by some commentators as "arbitrary" because it involves "heavy taxation of a commodity that may loom large in one household's spending, but not figure at all in others."[70] This line of reasoning implies that whether or not alcohol looms large in household spending is an accidental matter.

These arguments are inappropriate because behaviour, not income, is the proper basis for judging the fairness of retributive or non-capital expenditure taxes. It is rather obvious that tort awards and criminal penalties should correspond to the wrongdoing committed rather than to the wrongdoer's income level. Most people would be revolted by a criminal law judge who sentenced thieves or murderers on the basis of their net worth or income. In parallel with criminal law, a retributive tax turns on behavioural choice rather than status. Citizens are informed that a certain act (killing, littering, buying alcohol) is wrong and that a certain penalty will be imposed on them if they wilfully engage in that act. In this context a tax penalty is just if the amount paid corresponds to the average social harm caused. In Ireland's case, the alcohol tax rate is probably excessive and is therefore unjust for every alcohol user - the high income earner as well as the poor.

If the tax paid varies according to behaviour and social harm then it is not at all "arbitrary" that some households pay more tax than others. Some households serve more years in prison than others and this is not entirely a matter of happenchance. Admittedly, low income criminals tend to be more severely punished than upper income criminals, but that disparity is a corruption of the judicial and legislative process, not a necessary feature of legal punishment. If the drug tax functions properly, people will put themselves in high or low tax brackets by their drug taking decisions. Persons using no drug will pay no tax but that is perfectly fair since they generate no drug-related social costs. Persons using a variety of drugs to an extreme degree will, proportionally, pay a large amount of drug tax but, again, that is fair since their behaviour is also causing the most damage. Incidentally, it is not obvious that current drug taxes are regressive. The tobacco tax seems regressive, particularly in countries like Britain where heavy smoking is a lower income habit, but the relationship between income and tobacco use is not simple. Some low income smokers are teenagers or young adults who are only temporarily poor. The prevalence of smoking increases with income among women and the poorest Americans have lower smoking rates than middle income groups. The British alcohol tax is slightly progressive because expenditure on alcohol increases more rapidly than income and because higher income earners buy relatively more liquor and wine.

Two other income-related objectives can be noted. The first alleges that tax penalties will not deter the rich. This argument misunderstands the psychological dynamics of income allocation. No one possesses unlimited resources or earns income effortlessly. If coffee is taxed then every coffee buyer can meet the higher price only if they earn more or spend less on some alternate source of satisfaction. In either case, some sacrifice has to be made or less coffee purchased. Suggesting that higher income persons are price insensitive also overlooks the likelihood that their financial status results in part from their being extra sensitive to market signals. A California survey found that higher income buyers were more likely to purchase alcohol in bulk and to actively pursue discount prices. The second allegation complains that the tax will not deter the poor, particularly low income "addicts" who supposedly cut back on food and clothing to afford drugs or who purchase untaxed alcohol substitutes like wood alcohol, nail polish or after-shave lotion. In an article entitled "The Inequity of Taxing Iniquity", McLure and Thirsk argue that sumptuary taxes should not be employed to control "excessive drinking" because demand for alcohol is not very elastic, and thus, for low income users, tax on alcohol will really be a tax on food and clothing. [71] This portrait of the drug user as a compulsive victim is sometimes fleshed out with a causal theory blaming drug use on unemployment or poverty. The effect of the tax penalty is then naturally presumed to be a worsening of the original causal condition. O'Hagan argues this position but without any evidence. In fact, drug use often follows affluence, heavy drug users are not passive victims of permanent afflictions and some alcohol users - the young, the elderly, and marginal imbibers - may be very price sensitive. The tax rate should be set to counteract social costs; whether it deters each and every user by some degree is irrelevant. Furthermore, welfare needs connected with drug use can be dealt with quite separately from the tax system. If some drug users ruin their health or endanger their families through violence or neglect, such major problems can be tackled directly, though imperfectly, through welfare, children's aid departments, adoption, foster homes, food stamps and, where necessary, as a last resort, the criminal law. Minor problems linked to drug-tax burdens will be less responsive or accessible to the heavy hand of government regulators.

5. Additional Price Disincentives

A sumptuary tax on drug users is justified as a means of forcing people to bear the full costs of their drug use. The same policy determinants also justify forcing drug users to pay discriminatory insurance rates. At this time, most forms of insurance do not scale rates according to subscribers' drug habits. This is especially true for group employee plans. Where non-drug users, usually non-to-bacco users, are given favourable rates, the difference is small compared to the actual effect of tobacco on health and longevity.[72] As a result, heavy drug users are subsidized by other people's contribution to the home, health, life, disability and auto insurance pools. The obvious solution is for government to prohibit cross-subsidization in the insurance business but there may be technical barriers preventing such a policy. The central difficulty is to verify and monitor an insured person's drug taking. Simply discriminating between smokers and non-smokers would be unfair because it would put light or periodic users in the same category as two-pack-a-day users. Ideally, insurance rates would vary according to the quantity of drugs used but there is probably no practical method for verifying the insured's declaration. Enforcement would depend on the threat of voiding life insurance coverage altogether if, say, after a client's death the insurer could prove that the deceased used undeclared drugs or undisclosed amounts of declared drugs.

A more controversial disincentive to drug use is to require individuals to pay all medical expenses in the case of self-inflicted ailments. This would shift costs back to drug users, reaffirm each citizen's obligation to preserve his own health and counter the current ethos which teaches that no matter how foolish and self-destructive one's behaviour, government will pick up the repair tab. Arguably, a rule requiring self-payment for self-inflicted injury is fair because the person who enjoys the initial benefits of drug use should also shoulder the negative consequences. The same, of course, is true for sports injuries and other "life-style" diseases. Drugs are not the only source of self-inflicted disease.

The simplest method of allocating medical costs to self-generated illnesses is the traditional user-pay system where all expenses are non-insured. A user-pay method, which dominates in most market transactions, will prevent the gross over-utilization of hospital and physician services typical of the past thirty years. Billing the client directly also reduces the physician's ability to provide incompetent or useless service. Private and public medical insurance are largely premised on the assumption that all medical fees are necessary and that all medical intervention is helpful. Neither proposition is correct. Marcia Kramer discusses billing drug users directly for self-inflicted illness in a context of rising health care costs but if we were really serious about cost cutting we would turn to the core problems: physicians' monopoly, avoidance of external critique and third-party payment.[73] Controlled studies, the consequences of physician strikes and cross-cultural comparisons suggest that much of the billions spent on medical services is wasted.[74] This waste will continue as long as physicians, the main benefactors of insurance, have the power to determine what is proper and necessary medical intervention.

Making drug users pay for self-inflicted injuries in the standard medical insurance system requires distinguishing between accidental and self-inflicted diseases. Kramer is right that putting all ailments consistent with drug use in the non-insured category would penalize some people because not every tobacco user's emphysema is caused by smoking, thus uncertainties should be resolved in favour of the claimant. Kramer is also worried about ability-to-pay; she frets that it is "inhumane to withhold medical care from those sick persons who cannot pay". Actually, in some cases providing treatment is inhumane. With chronic conditions like lung cancer and cirrhosis of the liver and with elderly clients, treatment often manages only to prolong life a few days or weeks at a considerable cost to the person treated who dies away from their home and family. The professionalization of death is a victory neither for health nor the afflicted. In any case, a user-pay system need not involve the denial of necessary treatment. Clients, or their estates, can be billed after the therapeutic intervention with government covering the uncollectible bills. Kramer is correct in stressing that drug taxes are a more powerful disincentive than medical expenses because tax is immediate whereas fear of medical costs, like fear of drug-related disease itself, is far in the future and so is thoroughly discounted. The primary reason for a user-pay approach to medical costs, however, is not to encourage healthier life styles but to avoid burdening innocent parties with avoidable expenses generated by other people.

Three other minor or at least less controversial pricing issues worth mentioning are advertising taxes, returnable bottles and "happy hour" price discounting. As suggested in Chapter Seven, the commercial promotion of drugs probably does not deserve to be banned but it is sufficiently anti-social to warrant some level of tax penalty. As between rationing and taxing drug advertisements, tax offers the advantages of revenue and flexibility.

The second issue concerns re-cycling. Litter is a small but irritating offshoot of drug use that can be partially counteracted by prohibiting or taxing non-returnable bottles and non-biodegradable packaging. A mandatory deposit on beer and pop bottles is a proven instrument for reducing litter and bottle waste.[75] A similar law should be extended to all bottled alcohol and price savings passed on to drinkers of draught beer from re-usable kegs. Cigaret ash and butts should also be eliminated by price differentials strongly favoring so-called "smokeless cigarets" which do produce some smoke but which do not produce ash.

The third pricing issue involves discount pricing of drugs such as that practiced by taverns during "happy hours". A number of states and provinces are considering or have recently banned discount alcohol sales for on-premise outlets. Happy hours were first allowed in Ontario in 1982 and were outlawed again exactly two years later. Opponents of discount pricing complained that happy hours increased traffic mishaps, diverted homeward bound commuters into bars and generally increased alcohol intake. Smart and Adlaf studied alcohol use in selected taverns both before and after the happy hour ban and found no significant effect on aggregate alcohol sales or on individual consumption.[76]

This finding is consistent with earlier evidence that only a small fraction of tavern patrons go expressly to drink. In Canada at least, cost-conscious imbibers take their alcohol at home and happy hour discounting apparently cannot go far enough to remedy the home-tavern price disparity. A different outcome is probable where retail and on-premise drug prices are comparable.

Tavern proprietors have a fairness argument on their side since price discounting is a standard commercial response to slow periods or low demand customers. Price discounts to people over 65, to off-season tourists and to movie goers on Tuesdays are now familiar practices. If tax is justified as a retributive counteraction to drug-related externalities then price discounting is irrelevant so long as the on-premise seller has paid a legal, tax-inclusive price to the drug wholesaler. The only other legal relevance of price discounting concerns incidental issues of false advertising, bait-and-switch tactics or anti-competitive monopolies. Apart from the usual concerns about fair competition, price discounting of on-premise drug sales should be allowed. Providing free drug samples, as the tobacco producers are now doing at sponsored events, is another matter particularly for habituating products such as cigarets. From 1970 to 1983 tobacco producers' spending on cigarets giveaways rose from $12 million to $126 million. The most effective response to drug sample distribution is most likely an outright ban.[77]

6. Tax-Price Controls and Public Choice

For a number of reasons tax-price controls have the potential to win wide public acceptance. There is first the public's familiarity with alcohol and tobacco taxes. At least with marijuana, the "alcohol model" of taxed sales is the most oft-cited reform proposal made by experts and non-experts alike. A second popular feature of tax controls is the somewhat deceptively simple linkage that can be made between tax rates and the level of harm associated with different types and forms of drug products. As long as the tax rate is set according to economic or legal principles, drug users can accept that the tax burden they bear has a reasonable basis. The third source of popularity is the revenue raised by tax controls. This revenue, especially if it's spending is earmarked according to popular choice, will please abstainers and light drug users who comprise the majority of voters.

There are also potential problems and sources of discontent. If unrestricted, government could tax inappropriately by favouring some drug products over others. Tax controls could also become another revenue grab by government in which case a conflict would develop between the duty to limit drug costs and the desire for more revenue. Heavy users, who would pay most of the tax, and the medical/welfare/legal agencies dealing with a client base dominated by heavy drug users, would fight tax controls in favour of personalized restraints. Perhaps some of this opposition could be deflected by involving these agencies in the tax collection and by earmarking some drug revenue for their support.

Notes

1   John F. Due, *Indirect Taxation in Developing Economies* (Johns Hopkins Press, 1970) 60.

2   R. Room, "The Fiscal and Legislative Debate" in *Alcohol - The Prevention Debate* (London: Croom Helm, 1983), M. Grant & B. Ritson (eds), 161.

3   F. Field, M. Meacher and C. Pond, *To Him Who Hath - A Study of Poverty and Taxation* (Penguin, 1976) 90.

4   K. Warner, "Cigarette Excise Taxation and Interstate Smuggling: An Assessment of Recent Activity" (1980) 35 *National Tax Journal* 483.

5   P. Cook & G. Tanchea, "The effect of liquor taxes on heavy drinking" (1982) 13 *Bell Journal of Economics* 379.

6   C. Mitchell, "Taxation, Retribution and Justice" (1988) 8 *University of Toronto Law Journal* 151-183.

7   Due, *supra* note 1, 60, 75.

8   S. Cnossen, *Excise Systems - A Global Study of the Selective Taxation of Goods and Services* (Johns Hopkins University Press, 1977) 53.

9   J. Mosher, "Tax-Deductible Alcohol: An Issue of the Public Health Policy and Prevention Strategy" (1983) 7 *Journal of Health Politics, Policy and Law* 855.

10 J. Crombie, *Her Majesty's Customs and Excise* (1962) cited in J. O'Hagan, "The Rationale for Special Taxes on Alcohol: A Critique" (1983) 370 *British Tax Review*.

11 Lon Fuller, *The Morality of Law* (1969) 60.

12 See, Clarke, "Justifications for Punishment" (1982) 6 *Contemporary Crises* 25; J. Murphy, "Three Mistakes about Retributivism" (1971) 31 *Analysis* 166 (1971); Davis, "How to

Make the Punishment Fit the Crime" (1983) 93 *Ethics* 726.

[13] J. Murphy, *Retribution, Justice and Therapy* (Boston: D. Rei-
      del, 1979); A. Brudner, "Retributivism and the Death Pen-
      alty" (1980) 30 *University of Toronto Law Journal* 337 (1980);
      Nomos Vol. 27, Criminal Justice J. Pennock, J. Chapman
      (eds), (New York University Press, 1985).

[14] B. Harrison, "Spending patterns of older persons" (1986) 109
      Monthly Labour Review 15.

[15] There is some evidence that to compensate for reduced nico-
      tine content, users of low tar/low nicotine products smoke
      more cigarettes, puff more frequently and inhale more
      deeply. N. Benowitz, *et. al.*, "Smokers of low-yield cigarettes
      do not consume less nicotine" (1983) 309 *New England Jour-
      nal of Medicine* 139 (1983); J. Harris, "Taxing Tar and Nico-
      tine" (1980) 70 *American Economic Review* 300.

[16] B. Walsh, "The Economics of Alcohol Taxation" in *Economics
      and Alcohol* (London: Croom Helm, 1983) M. Grant, M. Plant,
      A. Williams (eds) 180.

[17] P. Cook, "Alcohol Taxes as a Public Health Measure" in *Eco-
      nomics and Alcohol* 190-5.

[18] L. Schifrin, "Societal Costs of Alcohol Abuse in the United
      States: An Updating" *Economics and Alcohol* 62, 79.

[19] M. Brown, *Tax Choices* (Washington: The Roosevelt Center
      for American Policy Studies, 1983) 68.

[20] P. Davies, "The Relationship Between Taxation, Price and Al-
      cohol Consumption in the Countries of Europe" *Economics
      and Alcohol* 1431.

[21] J. A. Johnson, "Canadian Policies in Regard to the Taxation
      of Alcoholic Beverages" (1973) 21 *Canadian Tax Journal* 552,
      556.

[22] R. Popham, *et al.*, "The Effects of Legal Restraint on Drink-
      ing" in B. Kissin and H. Begleiter, *The Biology of Alcoholism*
      (New York: Plenum, 1976) 595.

[23] R. Leu, "What Can Economists Contribute?" *Economics and Alcohol* 13, 27.

[24] A. Hellman, *Laws Against Marijuana* (1975) 199.

[25] Warner, *supra* note 4; K. Wertz, "Cigarette Taxation by the American States" (1971) 24 *National Tax Journal* B. Baltagi & D. Levin, "Estimating Dynamic Demand for Cigarettes Using Panel Data: The Effects of Bootlegging, Taxation and Advertising Reconsidered" (1986) 68 *Review Economics & Statistics* 148.

[26] Cited in M. Calnan, "The Politics of Health: The Case of Smoking Control" (1985) 13 *Journal of Social Policy* 279.

[27] D. Garner, *supra* note 30, 424.

[28] Schifrin, *supra* note 18, 75: Day.

[29] J. Harris, "Increasing the Federal Excise Tax on Cigarettes" (1982) 1 *Journal of Health Economics* 117-120.

[30] D. Garner, "Tobacco Sampling, Public Policy and the Law" (1982) 11 *Journal of Health Politics, Policy and Law* 423, 424.

[31] P. Taylor, *Smoke Ring* (1986) 152.

[32] G. Stoddart, R. Labelle, M. Barer and R. Evans, "Tobacco Taxes and Health Care Costs - Do Canadian Smokers Pay Their Way?" (1986) 5 *Journal of Health Economics* 63.

[33] L. Nelkin, "No Butts About It: Smokers Must Pay For Their Pleasure" (1987) 12 *Columbia Journal of Environmental Law* 317, 331.

[34] W. G. Manning, *et al.* "The Taxes of Sin: Do Smokers and Drinkers Pay Their Way?" (1989) 261 *J. American Medical Association* 1604-1609.

[35] J. Bakalar and L. Grinspoon, *Drug Control in a Free Society* (1984) 107.

[36]   J. Kay and M. King, *The British Tax System* (Oxford University Press, 1983) 129.

[37]   Johnson, *supra* note 21, 561; Popham, *supra* note 22, 602.

[38]   K. Acheson, "The Pricing practices of the Liquor Control Board of Ontario: reconsidered" (1983) 16 *Canadian Journal of Economics* 161.

[39]   K. Warner, "Publicity, Price, and Puffing" (1984) 3 *Journal of Health Economics* 179.

[40]   S. Ornstein and D. Hanssens, "Alcohol Control Laws and the consumption of Distilled Spirits and Beer" (1985) 12 *Journal of Consumer Research* 200, 210.

[41]   B. Walsh, "Health Education and the Demand for Tobacco in Ireland, 1953-76" (1980) 11 *Economic & Social Review* 150.

[42]   J. Bishop and J. Yoo, " 'Health Scare' , Excise Taxes and Advertising Ban in the Cigarette Demand and Supply", (1985) 52 *Southern Economic Journal* 402, 410; E. Fujii, "The demand for cigarettes: further empirical evidence and its implication for public policy" (1980) 12 *Applied Economics* 479. But see T. Young, "The demand for cigarettes: alternative specifications of Fujii's model" (1983) 15 *Applied Economics* 203.

[43]   D. McCornac and R. Filante, "The Demand for Distilled Spirits: An Empirical Investigation" (1984) 45 *Journal of Studies on Alcohol* 176.

[44]   E. Lewit and D. Coate, "The Potential for Using Excise Taxes to Reduce Smoking" (1982) 1 *Journal of Health Economics* 121; E. Lewit, D. Coate & M. Grossman, "The Effects of Government Regulation on Teenage Smoking" (1981) 24 *Journal of Law and Economics* 545.

[45]   D. Coate and M. Grossman, "Effects of Alcoholic Beverage Prices and Legal Drinking Ages on Youth Alcohol Use" (1988) 31 *Journal of Law & Economics* 145-171.

319

46 G. Bernard, "An Economic Analysis of the Illicit Drug Market" (1983) 18 *International Journal of Addictions* 681.

47 *Supra* note 35, 103.

48 *Supra* note 40, 203.

49 Cook, *supra* note 17, 194.

50 C. Simon & A. Witte, *Beating the System: The Underground Economy* (Boston: Auburn House, 1982) 149, 180, 291.

51 *Maclean's* September 29, 1986, 36, 38.

52 "Striking at the Source" *Time* July 28, 1986, 10.

53 D. Suits, "Gambling Taxes: Regressivity and Revenue Potential" (1976) 30 *National Tax Journal* 19.

54 R. Karel, "Tax Revenues Possibly Available from Legal sale of Marijuana, Cocaine, Heroin and Opium" (1989) Paper delivered at the 3rd Drug Policy Foundation Conference, Washington, D.C. November 3.

55 *Globe & Mail* September 12, 1987, A1.

56 "Gambling grows into $18.1 billion crop for the Garden State of New Jersey" *Globe & Mail* January 26, 1988, B11.

57 R. Bird, *Charging for Public Services* (Canadian Tax Foundation, 1976) 215.

58 E. Brecher, *et al., Licit and Illicit Drugs* (1972) 538.

59 C. Mitchell, "Culpable Mental Disorder and Criminal Liability" (1986) 8 *International Journal of Law & Psychiatry* 273.

60 I. Babou, "The Treatment Monopoly in Alcoholism and Drug Dependence: A Sociological Critique" (1975) *Journal of Drug Issues* 120.

61 M. Goldstein, M. Surber & D. Wilner, "Outcome Evaluations

in Substance Abuse: A Comparison of Alcoholism, Drug Abuse and Other Mental Health Interventions" (1984) 19 *International Journal of Addictions* 479.

62   G. Kolata, "Obesity - A Growing Problem" (1982) 198 *Science* 905; "Fat of the land" *Time* February 25, 1985, 62.

63   C. Mitchell, "A Comparative Analysis of Cannabis Regulation" (1983) *Queen's Law Journal* 110, 137.

64   C. Webster, "Compulsory Treatment of Narcotic Addiction" (1986) 8 *International Journal of Law and Psychiatry* 133-159.

65   L. Simmons and M. Gold, *Discrimination and the Addict* (1973) 17.

66   P. Goldberg & E. Meyers, "The Influence of Public Understanding and Attitudes on Drug Education and Prevention" in The Drug Abuse Council, *The Facts About 'Drug Abuse'* (New York: Free Press, 1980).

67   D. Hanson, "Drug Education. Does it Work?" in F. Scarpitti and S. Datesman (eds), *Drugs and the Youth Culture* (Beverly Hills: Sage Publishers, 1980) 274. See also H. Parker, K. Bakx, R. Newcombe, *Living with Heroin* (Philadelphia: Open University Press, 1988) 114-116.

68   H. Heaton, *Economic History of Europe* (New York: Harper & Row, 1948) 247.

69   D. Stoffman, "Where There's Smoke" *Globe & Mail Report on Business Magazine* September 1987, 20-28.

70   Kay and King, *supra* note 36.

71   C. McLure and W. Thirsk, "The Inequity of Taxing Iniquity: A Plea for Reduced Sumptuary Taxes in Developing Countries" (1978) 26 *Economic Development and Cultural Change* 487.

72   L. Benham, "Comments on Lewit, Coate and Grossman" (1981) 24 *Journal of Law and Economics* 751-573.

73 M. Kramer, "Self-inflicted Disease: Who Should Pay for Care?" (1979) 4 *Journal of Health Politics, Policy and Law* 138.

74 C. Mitchell, "Strike by Ontario doctors may not be all that harmful" *Ottawa Citizen* May 27, 1986, A9.

75 A. Wagenaar, "Aggregate Beer and Wine Consumption" (1986) 43 *Journal of Studies on Alcohol.*

76 R. Smart and E. Adlaf, "Banning Happy Hours: The Impact on Drinking and Impaired-Driving Charges in Ontario, Canada" (1986) 47 *Journal of Studies on Alcohol* 256.

77 Garner, *supra* note 30, 424.

IX Drug Reform Prospects and Strategies

This concluding chapter considers the future of drug regulation from three perspectives: what should happen, what could happen and what will probably happen. Domestic and international conditions are briefly surveyed to determine whether law-reform prospects in the 1990s differ from those in previous decades. Finally, an assessment is offered of the six law-reform strategies: legislation, litigation, direct voting, civil disobedience, constitutional amendment and political restructuring.

1. A Drug Reform Agenda

Effective reform requires a clear goal and a realistic appraisal of the steps necessary to achieve that goal. The primary goal advanced in this book is to base our drug control system on the three pillars of legal equality, science and democratic choice. Moving in one step from the entrenched discriminatory laws that now prevail to drug laws that take human rights seriously is probably impossible. Except in times of grave crisis, laws are notoriously resistant to change, and voters, even if they had a direct say, now lack the experience and knowledge to make an informed choice. One solution to this problem is to seek a number of intermediate steps that would move at an adaptable pace toward the ideal of fair treatment for all drug users. The following suggestions roughly outline a series of graduated reform steps.

The critical first step is to execute an orderly withdrawal from the drug wars. Domestically this means maintaining the shell of prohibition while instituting a policy of non-enforcement, as in the Netherlands. This policy would shift police resources away from narcotics, make prosecutors avoid possession charges, and abolish minimum sentences to give judges more discretion. The financial costs of criminal controls would be publicized, and cost-reduction goals would be set. Internationally, governments would stop sending drug agents abroad, cut off crop-eradication funds, cease attempts to extradite foreigners on drug charges, and end military involvement in drug law enforcement. Repudiating international drug-control agreements would be too drastic, but these agreements could be redrafted to decrease police powers, explicitly honour national sovereignty, and speak of "effective," "democratic" control methods, rather than specifying methods such as crop eradication.

The second step, which could be taken concurrently, would be to permit the therapeutic use of the major illicit drugs. Physicians could prescribe marijuana, cocaine, heroin and mescaline supplied by pharmaceutical firms. Studies of the comparative performance of these drugs compared to existing medicines could be made publicly available. To increase competition, a broad new category of Rx drugs could be prescribed by nurses and pharmacists as well as physicians.

The third step would facilitate drug-related tort litigation by gradually removing current impediments to plaintiff action. This would mean passing legislation that would hold all drug producers to a higher standard of disclosure and permit businesses to aggregate plaintiff claims and form permanent "plaintiff protection societies."[1] Federal control of new drugs would be replaced by market competition and private litigation.[2]

A fourth step would consolidate the regulation of tobacco, alcohol and caffeine. Existing Alcohol Control Boards would be folded into new recreational drug agencies which would begin to standardize the rules for all recreational substances. Caffeine products would be taxed on the same basis as alcohol and tobacco, with tax rates set according to the legal and economic principles set out in Chapter Eight. This step would be facilitated by reducing federal drug regulation and passing primary authority to local jurisdictions. This change would help pave the way for some state or provincial governments to add marijuana to the recreational drug category, and then legalize commercial production of the drug outside medical controls. Eventually other drugs could be added to the recreational list although still kept on as official medicines in other forms. Cannabis could be sold as marijuana cigarets commercially while also prescribed in tablet form as a THC derivative. The same distinction could be established between smoked opium and medical laudanum. In this way, drugs could be medically deregulated gradually without foreclosing medical choice or antagonizing medical societies.

After twenty to thirty years of non-enforcement, nominal prohibition could probably be abolished. This might lead to pardons for previous drug offenders, and offers to those imprisoned of financial compensation modelled on the packages recently granted to Japanese-Americans and Japanese-Canadians to make amends for unjust World War II incarceration. By 2025, citizens would be accustomed to more peaceful, civilized drug control regimes and would have enough experience with the alternatives to make an informed choice about uniform controls.

This is what should happen: what *could* happen is another matter. If the implausible and the merely possible are considered, the range for speculation is vast. For amusement as much as for instruction, consider the following cases:

1. Variable Discrimination: continue to muddle along without significant change. Most likely case.
2. International War: the drug crusade replaces the fading holy war for and against communism as the U.S. and the Soviet governments turn their guns on new Vietnams and Afghanistans in Latin America, the Middle East and Africa. Most frightening possibility.
3. Civil War: prohibitionists overextend themselves by banning the sale of tobacco. This leads to armed resistance by a loose consortium of tobacco farmers, marijuana growers and drug smugglers. This reprise of the Whisky Rebellion is unlikely.
4. Drug Barons Govern: illicit drug producers in Peru, Columbia or wherever stage a coup and are sustained in office by force of arms and popular support. This government repudiates the international drug agreements as imperialistic and legitimizes all drug exports. A reprise of British India in the mid 1800s, with its opium plantations and exports to China.
5. Commercial Revolution: giant multinational corporations effectively seize national governments and, since these businesses seek profit not war, they force the radical deregulation of all drugs. Thereafter these enormous coffee-alcohol-tobacco cartels take over the formerly illicit trade in cocaine, heroin, hashish and marijuana. The Mafia prove no match for Coca-Cola or Kraft/General Foods, and peace reigns, albeit at monopoly profit levels. Reprise of earlier trading empires such as the British East India Company and the Hudson Bay Company that functioned as governors.

6. Dark Ages: religious radicals overthrow the secular government and erect a theocratic state that, as in Iran, ruthlessly suppresses all forms of dissident behaviour. (Iran hung 70 drug smugglers on a single day in February, 1989.) Millions flee, thousands are killed or tortured, almost all deviant drug-taking ceases. Reprise of the Ayattolah Khomeini.
7. Sick Society: rehabilitation triumphs, all drug users are declared sick but blameless, hence without advertising, promotion or glamour, clinics dispense free generic drugs to all comers. Black markets crumble and the entertainment industry is decimated. Drug users complain that free drugs from medical clinics are about as much fun as holding hands with your parents.

While some of these scenarios possess a touch of the fantastic, all follow historical precedents and extrapolate contemporary trends.

2. The Social Context of Reform

Domestically, significant demographic transformations are altering the drug war context. To begin with, "baby boomers" are aging; the youth counterculture is entering middle age. This maturation process is replacing the Anslinger/Nixon/Reagan generation of cold war/drug war enthusiasts with a generation personally familiar with illegal substances. During the 1970s, something like half of Canadian law students used marijuana, whereas probably almost none did in the 1950s.[3] After 1990, these young lawyers will be moving into political office, donning judicial robes and assuming corporate power. At the same time, greying baby boomers will create a surfeit of mature adults and a paucity of adolescents. As a result, the adolescent cohort in the 1990s will be too small to threaten adults socially. Adults will become more accepting of youthful rebellion, and children will more readily adopt dominant adult values and fashions. One of these adult values will be the pro-sobriety, pro-health outlook typical of maturity. Combining the new open-mindedness with a desire for sobriety will mean more restrictive attitudes towards drugs in general but more lenient views about deviant drug use by the young. This ethic will stand in marked contrast to the passing generation being close-minded about some drugs while making liberal, even unhealthy, use of certain favoured drugs.

Anti-narcotic policy was originally linked to public health, crime control and American accomplishments, and thus possessed a progressive quality. Now, after decades of failure, official hypocrisy and disagreement between scientists and politicians, the drug crusade can be seen as outdated and ill-conceived. Critical, cynical journalists, who often mocked Prohibition, were an important pressure group during the 1920s, but until recently the media has enthusiastically supported the narcotics crusade. This could change, however. For example, R. Cowan, writing in *The National Review*, (April 29, 1983) charged our "drug warriors" with being "an enormous, corrupt international bureaucracy that has been lying for years." Further journalistic comment along similar lines can be anticipated because there are now prominent individuals and organizations, like the Drug Policy Foundation, to offer authoritative opinions that counter government policy. Now that there is a real battle of opinion, it is possible for the reform side to eventually triumph. Numbers and resources still favour the government, but reform opinion carries more scientific credibility. If other opinion leaders such as medical and legal societies join the reform side, the government will probably change course, just as it did in the U.S. with alcohol in 1932. As the debate escalates over the next decade, some newspapers may follow *The Economist's* lead and crusade against the anti-drug crusade. Legalizing illicit drugs could then go from being unthinkable to being self-evident.

Reform pressures on the international front are largely wrapped up with U.S. foreign policy because Americans purchase about 60% of all illicit drugs, their government underwrites more than 90% of police action against the illicit drug trade, and U.S. officials dominate international drug-control agencies.[4] The first source of reform pressure is U.S. incapacity to maintain its current level of domination. Like Britain 100 years ago, U.S. economic power is in relative decline.[5] From 40% of world output in 1955, the U.S. share fell to 25% in 1980.[6] Fewer than one out of 10 American producers faced foreign competition in the early 1960s, but now at least 70% must contend with off-shore competitors.[7] Leadership in world banking and technology is moving east to Japan.[8] Between 1970 and 1987, the proportion of developing countries pegging their currency to the U.S. dollar fell from 60% to 25%.[9] With this relative decline in economic clout comes a corresponding inability to dictate drug policy to countries less dependent on U.S. investment or trade. Recent editorials in France and Australia criticizing the U.S. model of narcotic prohibition exemplify this growing independence.[10]

For the U.S., the war against drugs is part of a larger pattern of economic mismanagement and overextended foreign intervention that Paul Kennedy says is typical of all great military powers in decline.[11] In the face of Japan's industrial challenge, U.S. authorities divert themselves with their fixation on "dirty money." Public education is in crisis and the major innovation offered is a military-style assault on illicit-drug using students. Abroad, drug prohibition provides elements hostile to the U.S. government an ideal trade.[12] At the same time, U.S. allies are blamed, investigated, indicted and even imprisoned on drug charges.[13] As a result, relations with Mexico, Panama, the Bahamas, Jamaica, the Turks and Caicos, and elsewhere are strained. It would be comforting to think that these high costs will convince some future U.S. administration to abandon the drug war, but a substantial thaw in the Cold War could free up resources that could be redirected from fighting communism to fighting "narco-terrorism."

To date, foreign drug producers have been limited by anti-drug laws enforced by their own governments in Pakistan, Colombia, Peru and Jamaica. Declining U.S. hegemony coupled with the rise of new trading blocks in Europe, Asia and South America may pave the way for some countries to permit domestic narcotic production for export, as British India did with opium. The first country legislating legal production of cocaine, cannabis, LSD and so on will derive significant commercial advantages through their monopoly in quality drug products. The producers of the first brand name drugs available to be illegally smuggled into the U.S. or Europe will reap long-term benefits sustainable even after the importing countries legalize domestic drug production in self-defence. Brands like Canadian Club whisky established permanent customer loyalty under similar conditions during Prohibition. It is impossible to say which country will lead the pack in legalizing drug exports. Possible candidates include rogue countries like Paraguay and major producers like Colombia, Lebanon and Thailand. However, the greatest impact on U.S. policy would be the defection of an independent democracy like New Zealand, Australia, Spain, Italy or the Netherlands. Canada or Mexico could best supply the major U.S. market, but both are too vulnerable to steer an independent course on drugs.

328

Speculation aside, it is necessary to recognize that drug reform is part of a larger, complex picture involving population profiles, industrial competition, corporate concentration, the Asian renaissance, foreign alliances, and other factors all interacting in ways that may or may not be conducive to legal change. Perhaps drug reformers can only prepare a reform package and then await an opportunity. Still, there are some active strategies reformers can pursue, and I turn now to consider the various reform methods available.

3. Drug Reform Methods

a. Legislative Reform

Apparently the simplest, most beguiling avenue to reform is for legislators to exercise their lawmaking power by repealing current laws and enacting superior replacements. Nothing could be simpler, or more difficult. The reform record of federal legislators in Canada and the U.S. is discouraging. Despite recommendations from Canadian government commissions to decriminalize marijuana, despite repeated promises to do so from then Prime Minister Pierre Trudeau, and despite the sizeable portion of Canadian voters who have used marijuana, almost no reform occurred.[14] Why?

According to standard political theory, representative governments are effectively controlled so long as legislators must periodically submit their record to the voters in free elections. If laws are unpopular, a critical electorate will defeat the offending government and vote in a reform-minded regime. By this reasoning, a lack of drug law reform indicates that voters are sufficiently satisfied with the present system. If most voters wanted marijuana sold in liquor stores, lawmakers would be happy to oblige. This portrayal of political decision-making, however, is superficial and inaccurate because in general elections voters have almost no opportunity to decide single issues. Instead, they vote for candidates representing a party platform that a government, once elected, is not legally obliged to honour. Voters frequently choose between the least unpalatable party, and they select legislators, not legislation. None of the mainstream parties offer voters drug control alternatives. Conservative parties are staunchly anti-narcotic and their "leftist" opponents support the anti-drug line with equal fervour (except for marijuana).[15] Voters often are subject to laws most of them oppose. No major party opposes income tax or talks seriously of lowering total tax burdens significantly, yet Harris And Roper polls found that 87% of U.S. respondents felt income tax was unfair, 73% resented the ways government spent tax revenue, and 66% thought tax rates were exorbitant. A resounding 5% of British voters judged their income tax rates "about right." Tax cutbacks of significance occur only through direct voting, like California's Proposition 13, which by-pass elected legislators. Most voters support capital punishment for murder, yet most legislatures reject it. Most voters oppose inflation, business subsidies, tariffs, higher salaries for legislators, and deficit financing, yet these policies are almost universal. How can elected representatives deny or oppose majority interests?

Part of the answer is that voters lack control of their elected representatives. In the legislative market, as Tullock, Downs, Buchanan and others explain, legal outcomes depend on who exercises the most effective demand.[17] Exchange occurs because politicians need party endorsement, campaign funds and votes, and in turn their supporters want special services and favourable laws. If party discipline is strong and elections expensive, then voter control will be weak because the legislators' primary allegiance is owed to party and financial backers. Paraguay's Colorado Party is an extreme example: there control was so complete that prior to the 1989 coup, the Colorado-dominated Congress had last disagreed with the party leader in 1959.[18] Citizens vote in Paraguay, but their influence is negligible.

To control legislators, voters must possess information about the issues and about the political process. Without this information, voters cannot have specific policy preferences for politicians to heed.[19] If voters cannot afford to be knowledgeable, their political ignorance is rational and so is their disinterest in voting. Drug legislation illustrates the problem because most voters know little about illicit drugs or drug laws. Surveys indicate that few people are aware of the basic facts about illicit-drug pharmacology.[20] This ignorance is to be expected because the illicit-drug culture is portrayed in the media as "uniformly ugly" and police tend to assume that the worst drug cases are not only typical but also the inescapable result of illicit-drug use.[21] Voters are also in the dark about why narcotics laws were enacted, what they cost to enforce, and what impact they have on society. The history and results of Rx legislation is also *terra incognito*. Even experts find it difficult to fathom the inner workings of pharmaceutical and narcotic regulation. Dozens of U.S. federal and state agencies administer drug laws according to complex, even impenetrable rules that bureaucrats themselves do not always understand.

Unlike most voters, special interest groups and professional regulators focus their attention on specific issues and acquire the information necessary to have informed opinions. People in a trade or occupation have an intense interest in the laws affecting their field, and thus devote time and resources to understanding and modifying those laws.[22] As a result, interest groups lobby effectively, whereas most voters, taxpayers and consumers are diffuse, unorganized and politically ineffectual. To legislators, voters' voices are a discordant chorus, mere background noise, whereas the special interest lobbies chant clear, repetitious mantras. Voters outnumber lobbyists, but they are hobbled by the high cost of organizing and by the "free rider" problem. Potential supporters of NORML recognize that out of millions of marijuana users their absence will go unnoticed but their contribution will benefit many non-contributors. Hence the ineffectiveness of NORML.[23] After studying the problems of broad public interest groups, George Stigler concluded that a broad, voluntary consumer political lobby is not viable.[24]

Drug legislation illustrates the dominance of special interest groups. When mandatory prescription laws were introduced, no party ran on the issue, no public debate occurred, and most voters probably did not even notice the change because initially only a few obscure drugs were affected. Other drug laws have similar histories. Cigaret prohibition was led by cigar producers. The anti-cocaine movement enlisted physicians, who feared that the patent medicine boom would cut into their business.[25] The passing of opiate laws was similarly unrelated to public health or public pressure.[26] Voter support mostly developed after these laws were passed because government agencies made anti-narcotic fervour a measure of patriotism, white supremacy and loyalty. Most voters knew little about the drugs and were not themselves persecuted, so agreeing with the official line cost them almost nothing. On the other hand, the cost of active opposition could be high, a fact voters learned through newspaper diatribes on the horrible fate of addicts

331

and on the prosecution of maverick physicians.[27] Fighting illicit drugs is politically safe because "there are no wealthy or influential lobbies, as there are for tobacco, alcohol, pharmaceuticals, firearms, automobiles and other dangerous products."[28] Joel Fort argues that drugs make an ideal smoke screen for "politicians, editors and publishers, and administrative bureaucrats, who seek, sometimes desperately, for subjects or issues which can easily be oversimplified or distorted, talked about widely, and not antagonize powerful financial blocks. Drugs are ideal for this."[29] Lawmakers find it easier to ignore millions of marijuana smokers than to ignore one organization with the clout of the Tobacco Institute, which contributes campaign funds to hundreds of Congressmen, is staffed by former Presidential aids and politicians, hires the best Washington counsel and dispenses gifts to supporters.[30] Both Presidents Carter and Reagan had close ties to the tobacco industry. In Britain, tobacco producers cultivate an equally cozy relationship with guardians of the public interest.[31] Other legitimate drug producers also form powerful lobby groups, either through industry associations or through giant conglomerates such as Coca-Cola, Seagrams, Allied, and General Foods/Kraft. General Foods and Proctor and Gamble control about 60% of the U.S. coffee market.[32] If marijuana were made legal, pot growers would organize to lobby for price supports, marketing boards, tariffs and other favorable legislation. Once an organized marijuana lobby existed, the re-prohibition of the drug would be unlikely. The great challenge is to get to there from here. Because production is illegal, marijuana producers cannot form a lobby, and without a lobby, marijuana production will not be legalized.

Most existing lobby groups oppose marijuana law reform. Hamowy feels that law reform is unlikely partly because law enforcement officials and medical treatment agencies have an interest in continuing the war against drugs.[33] Illicit drug traders have few reasons to lobby for repeal of prohibition because criminal controls boost prices and exclude low-profit, legitimate competitors. Drug traffickers therefore focus their "lobbying" efforts on police officers, local officials and custom agents to acquire protection and gain competitive advantage over new entrants to the business. Once a trafficker's investment in corruption begins to return dividends, that dealer has an increased stake in the prohibitive status quo.

Even part-time marijuana sellers support prohibition if the alternative, such as a government retail monopoly, would destroy their business.[34]

Besides voters' lack of control over their elected legislators, a second source of anti-majoritarian law is a lack of constitutional protection of minority rights. Unwanted laws occur because each potential political conflict is dealt with as a separate issue, and because in a complex, diverse culture, majorities on single issues are often mere coalitions. Drug regulation is an example of this. If all drugs were included in a single legal classification, then almost everyone would be a drug user and would vote on drug issues accordingly. But when drugs are segregated into discreet units, then most drug-using groups are minorities, except for alcohol and caffeine users. A majority of voters, acting piecemeal, could over time support the legal repression of amphetamine, marijuana, diazepam, cocaine, tobacco, heroin, and so on, even though most people take at least one of these drugs. James Buchanan observes that when the social interdependencies among political decisions are ignored, all voters may eventually be worse off than if no voting and no politicization of social conflicts had occurred.[35] Drug laws are a good example of this: as a society, we would be better off today if no special drug laws had been enacted beginning in 1870. Buchanan concludes that the dangers of excessive politicization cannot be avoided by voting in new parties or new politicians. Instead, he suggests that genuine reform will come about only when constitutional rules limit ordinary majorities from entering too freely into sumptuary regulation.

What can be concluded from this discussion, besides the obvious prediction that under existing rules, significant legislative reform is unlikely? A few positive points can be made. According to an economic analysis of lawmaking, voters are stymied by high information costs. One way to reduce drug information costs is to draw parallels between familiar and unfamiliar drugs. By emphasizing the basic equivalency of drugs, scientists could encourage citizens to apply their extensive knowledge of alcohol, caffeine and nicotine to exotic or illicit drugs. Encouraging people to regard drugs as a unified class could also help counteract the current practice of selective repression. If alcohol users understood that their behaviour could legitimately be assigned to the same legal cubby-hole now assigned to marijuana users, they would perhaps be less excited about oppressing others. Voters are unlikely to understand complicated schemes that would to ration heroin, decriminalize "personal" marijuana use, and move certain drugs from one classification to another. But many voters would understand the simple proposition that legal equality should apply to all drug users. I expect most voters now would vehemently disagree with this proposition, but their minds could change after exposure to the scientific evidence. Over time, legal equality for drug users could become an ethical focus in a way that more pragmatic reforms could not. Schemes such as decriminalizing marijuana possession hold limited interest for voters because they only affect minorities. Equality rights affect everyone.

Public opinion polls that indicate support for even more oppressive, discriminatory laws should not be seen as permanent obstacles.[36] These polls are based on voters' current knowledge about illicit drugs, which is minimal. Public opinion on drugs is emotionally deep and informationally shallow, a combination also typical of foreign affairs, where rapid reversals of opinion are the norm.[37] Public opinion about the Soviets or the Chinese, for example, can be rapidly altered because few voters know much about these peoples. Without knowledge or personal experience, voters tend to rely on directives from official opinion sources in government and the media who, through selective reporting, can quickly transform enemies into allies. If it suited the U.S. government to repudiate the drug laws, it would begin by vilifying past drug control czars, like Anslinger, for lying to and misleading the public. Some gang-of-four drug hardliners could be unmasked as corrupt manipulators, and thrown to the courts and tabloids like fallen TV evangelists. The government would then elevate pro-reform physicians, lawyers and scientists to public offices and commissions and have them recommend abolishing prohibition. Media coverage would detail the medical benefits of heroin and cannabis, hundreds of healthy opiate users would suddenly be discovered by reporters, the end of the black market would be applauded, and within a few years even cocaine users would be transformed both in fact and in public opinion.

b. Litigation

Court decisions cannot achieve the sweeping changes open to

legislatures, but litigation is probably the more accessible route to reform. Courts can change drug laws by extending common-law defences, by interpreting statutory language and by finding laws unconstitutional. The defence of necessity, for instance, has been argued with some success by American marijuana users who claimed that their illness and a lack of efficacious treatment necessitated their consumption of the illegal substance. In *U.S.* v. *Randall* (1976), the *Marijuana Rescheduling Petition* (1988) and *State of Florida* v. *Musikka*, judges accepted marijuana use as necessary for glaucoma sufferers.[38] In 1981, a marijuana-using defendant with multiple sclerosis also succeeded with the necessity defence in Washington State.[39] Judges could broaden the medical necessity defence to include more drugs and more conditions, because some medical authorities would testify that almost all self-administered drug use is "therapeutic."

Judges' capacity to creatively interpret statutes is limited by doctrinal rules and appeal court review, but the latitude judges and juries can take when it suits them is illustrated by the interpretation of statutes that permit abortions only when the mother's "health" is threatened. Constitutional interpretations have the greatest impact because they can invalidate laws or administrative practices. Courts can determine that a specific narcotics provision violates privacy or equality rights, amounts to cruel and unusual punishment, or abridges freedom of religion or expression. Courts cannot replace the invalid law, but they can indicate what sort of legal language would be acceptable.

Petitioning the courts for change is in many ways easier and more productive than looking to the legislatures. Politics is an expensive game compared to the cost of launching a court challenge. Financing criminal litigation can be aided by public clinics, legal aid and *pro bono* lawyers. Civil rights activists and Vietnam protestors often used their limited resources to finance test cases. Unlike legislatures, courts conduct most of their business in public and provide a theatrical forum. Individual cases, like Bob Randall's fight to save his eyesight, have an appeal and urgency lacking in legislative abstractions. Judges and juries must confront the reality of ordinary people summoned often accidentally or arbitrarily to answer drug charges. Courts must also hear the facts of marijuana's medical usefulness or learn about the American natives' ritual use of peyote, while legislators, as brokers, rarely bother to consider the evidence. Courts can therefore serve as a public forum for critical appraisal of the laws created by Congress or Parliament.[40]

The courts also exhibit more diversity than legislatures. Considerable innovation is permitted at the lowest trial levels, where courts are numerous and the decisions have little weight as precedents. Judges generally enjoy tenured job security and so are independent of the forces guiding legislators. As a result, judicial decisions are more diverse, and often more public minded, than legislative enactments, despite judges being, on the whole, more elitist and hidebound than politicians.

Judicial independence is limited, however, because judges are usually appointed by the governing party on the basis of demonstrated political loyalty. Judicial power itself is restricted by the executive's control of the police and army, and by doctrines of legislative supremacy. In consequence, the judicial record on important drug cases is one of restraint and passivity. Both national and state constitutions in the U.S. announce in their preambles that laws must be "reasonable" and "wholesome" and must serve the common good.[41] Since narcotics laws are neither reasonable nor in the common good, how have they withstood most every major constitutional challenge? State alcohol prohibitions were the first drug laws to test the courts' response to the conflict between civil rights and the states' police power. In the *Licence Cases* (1874), Chief Justice Taney of the U.S. Supreme Court wrote for the majority that the states could regulate, restrain or prohibit traffic in alcohol if the legislature "deems" the trade injurious.[42] The Supreme Court rejected lower court decisions holding that prohibiting alcohol deprived citizens of their property without due process and infringed on their rights. Instead, the Supreme Court praised the virtues of judicial restraint and said the courts should question neither the facts behind the law nor the means employed to regulate alcohol.

Courts do not always simply ignore background facts; sometimes they invent them. In 1911 a lower California court accepted that there is "no such thing as moderation in the use of opium" because desire for the drug is "insatiable" and "invariably disastrous."[40] California's Supreme Court in this case re-affirmed the merits of judicial restraint by ruling that the facts about opium were irrelevant; it was enough that legislators believed opium to be a major threat. In early alcohol and opium cases, the courts ignored the traditional requirement that harm be direct and demonstrated, deciding instead that police powers extended to whatever lawmakers happened to think was harmful.[44]

In narcotic litigation over the last century, state power has generally triumphed over constitutional civil rights. The judicial techniques for achieving this result are apparent. Facts can be ignored and replaced by legislative fantasy: in a 1968 marijuana case, a California judge stated that if "reasonable men may entertain the belief that use of these drugs, once begun, almost inevitably lead to excess, such belief affords a sufficient justification for applying restrictions to these drugs."[45] In effect, legislators are deemed to be "reasonable" by definition, a rule that if generally applied would foreclose all constitutional review in civil rights matters. Judges can also base decisions on their own beliefs or on a selective reading of the evidence. In the Louisiana marijuana case of *Bonoa* (1931), the judges referred to two sources, both based on police reports, anecdotes and fantasy.[46] Judges can also act through inaction: two hundred years of commentary has failed to put teeth in the rule forbidding cruel and unusual punishment. A Michigan court in *Sinclair* (1972) did invalidate a poet's nine year sentence for possessing two marijuana cigarets, but few other criminal courts have enforced the rule.[47] Finally, judges can interpret even clear rules to produce surprising results. The American constitutional right to equality before the law did not stop courts from legitimizing slavery, from denying women the opportunity to vote, hold office or practice a profession, or from approving discriminatory taxes and tariffs that penalized Southern states to the North's benefit prior to the South's succession in 1860.

What then are the prospects for court-based reform? Judges prefer to nibble around the edges of a problem; they avoid upsetting entire statutory schemes. American challenges to the marijuana laws on broad constitutional grounds tend to fail, while limited arguments based on medical necessity or privacy have met with some success. Eventually, it may be possible through the courts to secure the right to use any drug in a private home or to receive almost any drug from a physician. Without rejecting prohibition, courts could effectively decriminalize private possession and medicalize most currently illicit drugs. Such developments are possible because they merely extend recent pioneering decisions, because protecting privacy is consistent with traditional values (a citizen's home is her castle), because prescription drugs are sufficiently removed from the "street drugs" used by lower-class youths who engage the most police attention, and because illicit drugs do have therapeutic properties.

c. Direct Voting

An alternative to representative government is direct citizen participation through recalls, initiatives and referenda. Initiatives are the most unconventional because they allow voters to enact laws independently of politicians. An environmental group might back an initiative requiring all alcoholic beverages to be marketed in returnable containers. If a majority of voters approved this proposition, it would become law even if no elected legislator approved of the measure. The referendum involves citizens voting on specific issues put before them either as a constitutional requirement, as with the Swiss tax laws, or at the legislature's direction, as with the Quebec referendum on sovereignty association in 1980. A recall permits voters to impeach elected judges, governors or legislators.

Direct voting has been championed by reformers from the late 1800s onwards as an instrument to battle the "bosses and special interests."[48] Critics have argued that these measures would result in inferior legislatures, poorly-drafted laws, a lack of informed debate, and abusive advertising campaigns. The U.S. record does not support these views. Voter turnout is higher for initiatives than for elections, and most citizens are neither apathetic, cynical or ignorant of the issues. California's legislature is ranked highly by the Citizen's Conference on State Legislatures and voter initiatives are employed frequently in California. A New York State Senate Subcommittee found initiatives as well-drafted as ordinary bills. Initiatives have not been used to oppress vulnerable minorities, nor have citizens cluttered the ballot with trivial issues. From 1918 to 1982, only 29 initiatives were placed on the ballot in Massachusetts. Most were aimed at entrenched political self-interest on such issues as campaign financing, the power of the Executive Council, and legislators' salaries.[49]

338

As economic theory predicts, producer groups almost always react to rather than launch initiatives. Producer groups do not need initiatives; they already enjoy lobbying access to lawmakers. Ironically, it is voters who need to circumvent the democratic system of general elections. Once an initiative is started, however, the lopsided funding typical of most lobbying occurs. In Colorado in 1976, the proponents of four consumer-oriented initiatives received $169,000 in contributions while their business opponents received $1,292,000. In a California anti-smoking initiative in 1978, the tobacco industry spent $6.4 million fighting a proposed law that would outlaw smoking in all public places. The industry claimed that the law would cut cigaret sales by 10% to 15% and establish a dangerous precedent. The anti-smoking groups behind the initiative began with a few dozen people who for years struggled to pay their postage costs. The tobacco industry's spending on Proposition 5 set a new record for California and exceeded the total amount spent by both gubernatorial candidates. Supporters of the *Clean Indoor Air Act* argued that public health was threatened by public smoking, while their opponents argued that smokers' freedom of choice and civil liberties would be infringed upon by the law. Of course, not a penny of tobacco money has ever gone toward fighting for the civil liberties of marijuana smokers. One solution to this problem is to limit the size of individual contributions (R.J. Reynolds alone contributed $2,351,786) and to subsidize public interest advocacy. The tobacco industry raised 99.7% of the money used to defeat Proposition 5, outspending their opponents at least ten to one.[50]

An added advantage of direct voting is that it provides a political avenue for citizens who want to make laws but who do not want to submit to party orders or devote their life to politics. Voter initiatives broaden access to the political process for both campaign organizers and voters.

Where they are available, voter initiatives could affect drug law reform within certain limits. By their nature, initiatives must be immediately popular and consumer-oriented. For drug reform, this means focusing on marijuana, the most popular illicit drug, and on personal use rather than commercial production. Most American or Canadian voters would probably now approve making marijuana available to persons suffering from glaucoma or multiple sclerosis, but there is probably insufficient voter interest to mount a campaign on such a narrow issue. In the next decade, there is little chance that cocaine, heroin or other minority drugs will be the subject of voter initiatives. Even with marijuana, success is uncertain because many people accept the "stepping-stone" theory that links cannabis with drugs saddled with worse reputations. There is also the challenge of generating enthusiasm for defeating a largely unenforced law. Marijuana consumption apparently did not increase after personal use was decriminalized in Oregon and Alaska:[51] this likely indicates that users were not deterred by the law to begin with. If the law is almost irrelevant, then drug users may be unwilling to volunteer sufficient resources to get anti-prohibition measures before the public.

An initiative asking for equal rights for all drug users would be widely opposed because the majority, who are licit drug users, do not want to be associated with the illicit minorities. Like ordinary legislation, initiatives tend to segregate conflicts into discreet, bite-size units. Voters may be balloted on prohibiting tobacco advertisements, but they will not be asked to vote on the fundamentals of free speech. Initiatives on cigaret smoking do not attempt to deal with other comparable nuisances. As a result, initiatives tend to produce patchwork solutions to problems.

d. Civil Disobedience

When governments create inappropriate, overly inclusive laws, deliberate law-breaking can sometimes create substantial reform pressure. Admittedly, the ethics of deliberate law-breaking are debatable. On one side, Lord Moulton held that the measure of civilized status of a people was the degree to which they obeyed unenforceable laws. Wilcox, on the other side, replied that people who obey a law simply because it exists "deserve to be called servile rather than civilized."[52] The ethics of civil disobedience depend on if the law in question, whether practically enforceable or not, deserves moral support. However, the facts of legal life are that laws prohibiting such things as abortion, free speech, religious choice or drug use are vulnerable to civil disobedience because they criminalize far too many people to permit full enforcement (outside a totalitarian police state). As General Ulysses Grant observed: "I know of no method to secure the repeal of bad or obnoxious laws so effective as their stringent execution."[53] A mass surrender of bank robbers would not overwhelm police and prosecutors but if merely one illicit drug user in ten confessed to possession, the courts and jails could not cope. The legal system would be swamped, especially if every accused pleaded not guilty, demanded a jury trial (a constitutional right) and argued every possible defence. The state's enforcement apparatus cannot afford to jail every drug user; indeed, it cannot even afford to arrest every drug offender. Fortunately for the criminal law system, we now live under so many sporadically enforced, widely disregarded laws that most citizens no longer feel it is ethically necessary to openly breach laws with which they disagree. Secrecy is safer. As the Russians say, the nail that sticks out gets hammered.

Civil disobedience need not overwhelm by pressure of numbers to be effective because deliberate law-breaking serves several purposes. It generates political pressure by publicizing disputed laws, it focuses attention on police methods, and it contrasts the ethical standards of the law-breakers with the law enforcers. Members of the Congress of Racial Equality and other American civil rights activists marched and sat peacefully in segregated lunch rooms from Selma to Montgomery and were opposed by the likes of "Bull" Connors with his dogs, water hoses and truncheons. Since crime and confrontation attract media attention, the battles against America's apartheid laws were well publicized throughout the early 1960s. Thousands were jailed, but more joined the battle, including celebrities and many college students.

Mass disobedience by illicit drug users is not likely under current conditions because most users are politically unorganized, do not feel unduly harassed by the law, and are apathetic about reform. Illicit drug users are not a visibly segregated group, like blacks or women, hence they lack an enduring focus for unification. Fashions, like the trappings of the youth counterculture, serve as visible identification but are impermanent. Unless a political drug crisis is generated by the government on a broad scale, illicit drug users will not be marching in the streets or staging mass marijuana "smoke-ins." Perhaps a more probable development is drug-related civil disobedience by a small number of influential people. One hundred MDs smoking marijuana on the steps of a legislature could have considerable public relations impact. Their arrest and subsequent trial would be an international sensation and a great embarrassment to the government that stood behind the prosecution. Protest is risky, though, and while physicians are influential, they

341

are also vulnerable. Possible loss of their medical license probably would deter most medical rebels from even publicly stating a radical position.

e. Constitutional Amendment

If it could be accomplished, adding a right to use drugs to the constitution would be the most effective and far-reaching legal reform: constitutional law is supreme. It overrides ordinary law and limits the scope of legislative action. If an explicit right to use drugs existed, legislators would not have to regulate drug use in any specific way or even regulate drug use at all. However, if lawmakers acted, such a right would probably suffice to defeat the severe prohibition now applied to cocaine use and distribution. A right to use, possess, produce and sell any drug subject only to reasonable and demonstrably necessary limitations would be modelled after established rights of speech, assembly, religion, expression, privacy and mobility. These constitutional rights are not omnipotent; they cannot, for example, prevent private discrimination. A recent American poll found that 85% of respondents would not vote for a Presidential candidate who was an atheist. The chances of a Moslem, Hindu or Buddhist candidate would probably be about the same, and perhaps someday a tobacco smoker's political prospects will be equally dim. Legal rights cannot eliminate personal prejudices, but they can prevent official, state-sanctioned discrimination such as might occur if a public school board refused to hire an atheist or a smoker. Formally ruling out this kind of prejudice has a limited effect on a culture's fundamental orientation. Both the Canadian and American constitutions recognize freedom of religion and a separation of church and state, yet only Christian holy days are statutory holidays, only Christian prayers open Parliament or Congress, only the Christian Bible is used to swear officials into office. In the same way, amending the constitution by adding a right to use drugs would not do much to alter our culture's focus on alcohol, caffeine and tobacco.

Constitutional reform deserves a separate analysis from ordinary legislation both because of the greater importance of the Constitution and because a different political market applies. The generality, supremacy and entrenchment of constitutional rules creates a political calculus more favorable to the wider public interest.

To begin with, constitutional rules are comparatively simple, hence more readily understood by voters. Canada's *Charter of Rights and Freedoms* runs to seven pages with about twenty key sections, whereas ordinary statutes on immigration, income tax, security regulations and the like can run over a thousand pages. Voters are uninformed about most laws because learning about the law and then agitating for change would cost more than could be gained. The same is not true for constitutional rules. Amendments forbidding all tariffs or all income tax exemptions would affect most voters enough to make it pay for them to be informed about the proposed rule. At the same time, by unifying all related issues a constitutional amendment would impede usually dominant special interests because their dominance depends on a single-issue, isolated, beggar-thy-neighbour process. Farmers want tariffs on foreign grains but not on tractors, while farm implement makers want free trade in wheat and rice but tariffs on harvesters. Because tariffs hurt the general interest, and because tariff supporters conflict with one another, producer groups would find it difficult to oppose an anti-tariff amendment. Ironically, consumer groups would have an easier time barring all tariffs than defeating a single tariff.

Constitutional reform promises voters sufficient reward to warrant a higher level of interest and commitment only if the constitution is adequately entrenched. If politicians can easily avoid or change the rules, the constitution will be subject to the usual political market forces. Canada's *Charter* exemplifies the qualities of a weak constitution because many of its provisions can be avoided by legislators declaring that a given statute is valid "notwithstanding" the *Charter*. Quebec's government employed this provision in 1988 to nullify the force of a Supreme Court of Canada decision finding that Quebec's law forbidding commercial English-language signs was unconstitutional. The Quebec government's justification – protecting the French majority's culture – could also be used for drug regulations if Canada's *Charter* guaranteed freedom of drug choice. That is, even if the Supreme Court had the constitutional authority to invalidate prohibition against marijuana users, provincial or federal governments could re-enact prohibitions anyway by arguing, with some plausibility, that oppressing marijuana users was necessary to maintain the integrity of the dominant alcohol/tobacco/caffeine culture. The basic counter-

343

argument to this position is that the force of law should not be available to majorities to allow them to freeze into immobility certain arbitrary or historical features of the status quo. Such laws are fundamentally anti-competitive.

Since radical constitutional amendments regarding drug use or other personal freedoms are unlikely in the near future,[54] reform efforts should probably focus on encouraging judges to interpret present rights so as to create greater legal protections for drug users, producers and sellers.

f. Political Reform

This reform strategy ignores the drug issue and works instead toward primary changes in the entire lawmaking process. This method is really a variation on constitutional reform, except that here attention is paid to the structural aspects of constitutional rules that determine how legislators and judges are chosen, how power is shared between branches of government, and how matters are assigned to federal, state/provincial and municipal governments. By altering basic political structures and incentives, reforms in areas such as drug regulation would occur as by-products.

Take as one example the system of legislative representation. Most countries employ a geographical basis for apportioning legislative seats because this land-based system has its historical roots in an agrarian society in which most people lived and died within a 50-mile radius of their birthplace, and also because it favours establishment interests. If a racial, sexual, religious or drug-using minority comprises 20% of the voting population, it is quite possible that this group will not be able to elect a single sympathetic voice to Congress or Parliament because in each riding or constituency they are greatly outnumbered. For this reason, minorities would be wise to congregate geographically. The other solution is a non-geographical system in which all legislative seats go to the nation-wide candidates ranking, say, from 1st to 300th in votes. This selection system, common in university student elections and some union elections, would permit candidates to appeal to a wider range of commonalities. This would result in feminists, college students, ethnic groups and occupations sending representatives to the legislature. Groups like auto workers, senior citizens, housekeepers, university students, Christian fundamentalists and homosexuals

344

may have more in common with their peers than with the people who happen to live in the same constituency. Under this system, illicit drug-users could have a significant impact because nationally, they are a big group, but are probably outnumbered in most voting districts. Of course, illicit drug-users are a diverse group and probably would not use their drug-taking behaviour as their primary identifier; but if they did, they might be able to elect enough legislators to ensure immediate reforms.

This system of representation would also weaken the power of political parties, permitting representatives to be more sensitive to voters. Critics may charge that such a system would hobble the legislature and impede the creation of laws. If this is true, and there is considerable doubt on that score, whether enfeebled legislatures are a fault or a virtue depends on an assessment of their typical legal output. With drug laws, society would be better off today, if almost every drug-related statute had never been enacted. The same may be true of most laws that regulate industries and occupations. Recall that the primary function of constitutional law is to impede legislatures.

Other possible political reforms can be briefly noted. These include limits to campaign spending, legal actions against breach of campaign promises, subsidies to public interest advocacy groups, voting to elect judges and police chiefs, voter recalls, enhanced division of powers, and stricter approval standards along the Swiss model for certain laws. Legislators in Switzerland cannot vote themselves higher salaries or impose new taxes without first securing voter approval through a referendum.[55] Not surprisingly, Swiss tax rates are relatively low and their politicians are relatively powerless. Decentralizing vice and drug control is another broad reform worth considering. Leaving more regulatory choices to local option will facilitate experimentation and avoid the police-state excesses that are now such a worrisome part of the war against drugs.

For the drug reformer, there are certain advantages to working indirectly through the improvement of democratic control over law-making. A prime advantage is that democratic reform is not issue-specific. It isn't necessary to argue that legislative restraint is needed to stop the unjust oppression of heroin users, sex-trade workers, loan sharks, or other unpopular figures: one can instead broaden the argument to appeal to a variety of disadvantaged

345

groups including taxpayers, housekeepers, women, students, pedestrians, environmentalists and so on, all of whom could benefit from political reform. By itself, the drug issue may be too small or too controversial to provide a sufficiently attractive vehicle for law reform. Another potential advantage is efficiency. Tackling reform in an ad hoc, issue-specific way is like patching cracks in a house that has dry rot in its load-bearing timbers. Solving one problem without affecting structural change may just ensure the appearance of another, similar problem. It may be cheaper in the long run to invest in basic reform, although in the short term that choice is clearly more expensive and more frustrating.

CONCLUSION

When will the drug wars end? Unlike military campaigns, internal wars of persecution are notoriously long-lived. Past wars against witches, Jews, Moslems, Christian martyrs and other scapegoats often lasted for centuries,[56] and the drug war may be no exception. Indeed, the drug crusade is already old. The drug battle lines were drawn up years before the 1917 Communist revolution in Russia, and when the first people to walk on Mars return to Earth sometime in the 21st century, they will probably be greeted by newspaper headlines announcing the familiar, depressing catalogue of drug busts, corruption scandals and violent deaths of inner-city minority youths killed in drug turf battles. For now, compromise seems impossible because governments keep demanding the unconditional surrender of all drug offenders. But possessing no organization, army or headquarters, drug offenders cannot surrender en masse. Strictly speaking, they cannot be warred against; they can only be persecuted.

As modern people we like to flatter ourselves that the problems we face are entirely new. None have passed this way before, so why look for historical parallels? Canada's Supreme Court held in *Hauser* (1979) that "narcotics" were a genuinely new matter, like aviation or telecommunications.[57] The alleged novelty of our problems explains our failure to solve them, and it also rationalizes a reliance on technological fixes, like herbicides, wire-tapping and helicopter surveillance when, at heart, the drug crisis is a replay of the ancient battle between faith and science, between the haves and the have-nots, between the judges and the judged.

That modern drug myths repeat the time-worn divisions of blessed and cursed is apparent from the way the healing properties of medical psychoactives and the destructive properties of illicit narcotics are equally exaggerated in opposite directions. Once it was "God's Own Medicine", now heroin is reviled as a godless curse. Without good evidence, most people accept these exaggerations and lies because they are enshrined in law and re-inforced daily in the mass media. But ours is still a relatively sceptical age, and the weight of pulpit, court and public opinion has failed to prevent

347

certain psychologists, economists, anthropologists, lawyers, physicians, sociologists and other researchers from investigating drug issues and questioning official claims. Such investigation continues to grow and broaden, and a rough consensus has begun to emerge on a number of important points, as I have outlined in this book. At some juncture, the research results will be powerful enough to undermine the drug myths. The vitality and freedom of science must therefore be maintained and, wherever possible, law reforms should concentrate on creating decision-making systems that allow a full and fair consideration of the evidence. We do not yet know enough to provide complete or totally adequate answers about drug regulation, but we do know how to find those answers.

SUMMARY

The Evidence

1. No pharmacological or chemical properties distinguish licit and illicit drugs.
2. Every psychoactive drug may deliver benefits through temporary symptom alleviation, recreation and mood alteration. Benefits are greatest when use is constrained. The immediate gains in satisfaction derived from drug use are probably counteracted by opposite dissatisfactions.
3. Every psychoactive is potentially dangerous because these drugs cause birth defects, health problems and impairments of various sorts. Choice of drug is only one factor in determining the extent of damage. More important factors are dosage and duration of use, purity, mode of administration, setting, age of user and pregnancy.
4. Drug users bear most of the costs of drug use themselves, though some drug costs are passed on to others. These costs have not been fully or accurately measured yet, but the preliminary data strongly suggest that an average drug user generates modest, low-level costs comparable to those costs generated by common nuisances and pollution sources.
5. Drug choices and attitudes about drug use are primarily determined not by the chemical properties of drugs, but by fashions, customs, taboos and laws.
6. Drug laws were not designed to protect society or help drug users, rather drug legislation was enacted to advantage specific occupations, producers, races, age groups, nations and cultures.

The Legal Principles

1. Legal restraint is only justified when it opposes a genuine social threat that is not adequately limited by non-legal controls.
2. Those wishing to impose legal restrictions should be compelled to prove the necessity for their proposed law. Enforcing this rule

may well be the most important single step in minimizing social costs while maximizing personal freedoms.

3. Legal measures should be proportional to the harm defended against and they should be applied fairly both as between wrongdoers and wrongdoings.

4. To protect citizens from abusive government actions, firmly entrenched, specific constitutional limits guaranteeing one's basic choice of food, drug, music, apparel, and so on should be enacted to prevent lawmakers (whether legislators, judges or voters) from creating unjust laws.

The Regulatory Choices

1. **Prohibition**: sets unrealistic goals and even with mild sanctions, imposes disproportionate penalties on both drug use and distribution. In practice, prohibitions are always hypocritical in their coverage and in their administration, and thus prohibition would not be willingly applied to all drugs. The very high social costs and low benefits of current drug prohibitions can be improved upon by adopting the traffic-enforcement model of small, standardized fines and minimal input from lawyers and courts. This system will work best with drugs if production, sale and use in private are all legal and only public use or impairment in public are prohibited.

2. **Medical Prescription:** is clearly superior to severe criminal prohibition but not adequate otherwise. Support for medical controls is based on the false assumptions that physicians, as monopolisitic drug police, can prevent drug-related injuries and stop people from over-using psychoactives. Current medical controls could be significantly improved by granting nurses, pharmacists, psychologists and others the right to prescribe and by permitting them to prescribe any narcotic or restricted drug.

3. **Private law:** this least restrictive legal alternative is a feasible drug control system in theory, but only if tort law is radically revitalized. If the incentives were adequate, and if legal firms and businesses could profitably aggregate plaintiff claims, tort actions would efficiently regulate drug quality and the honest disclosure of product dangers and defects. Seriously injured persons would be compensated for drug-related injuries.

4. **Rationing:** is much better suited than the alternatives listed above for efficiently limiting the total consumption of all drugs. In practice, rationing suffers from a number of defects but these are mostly avoidable. The best system for drug rationing would involve the issuance of drug coupons to all citizens, which they could use, trade or sell freely. This would allow total consumption to be scaled back gradually and it would force drug users to compensate non-users.
5. **Taxation:** is the most familiar alternative to prohibition because of long experience with taxing alcohol and tobacco products. Like rationing, tax controls are well-suited to mass application. Tax controls are not fail-safe, however, and like any penalty taxes should be carefully limited. Drugs should be tax-free until proven guilty, and should bear tax rates proportional to the social harm caused by their use. Ideally, drug tax revenues should be rebated to the public or earmarked for special projects.

Notes

1   See C. Mitchell and S. McDiarmid, "Medical Malpractice: A Challenge to Alternative Dispute Resolution" (1988) 3 *Canadian Journal of Law & Society* 227.

2   M. Friedman and R. Friedman, *Free to Choose: A Personal Statement* (New York: Avon Books, 1981) 196.

3   "The politics of pot" *Maclean's* July 4, 1983. In a 1977 *Weekend Magazine* poll, 35% of Canadian respondents favoured legalizing marijuana use. The pro-reform profile was young, male, higher-income, from Ontario and the West.

4   A. McNicoll, *Drug Trafficking: A North-South Perspective* (Ottawa: North-South Institute, 1983).

5   "Diminished Giants" *The Economist* May 2, 1987, 73.

6   A. Mack, "The Political Economy of Global Decline: America in the 1980s" (1986) 40 *Australian Outlook* 11.

7   R. Reich, *The Next American Frontier* (New York: Basic Books, 1983).

8   D. Morris, "United States Starts Looking Like a Third World Country", Toronto *Globe & Mail* March 10, 1988, A7; L. Thurow and L. Tyson, "The Economic Black Hole" (1987) 67 *Foreign Policy* 3.

9   "Looking Beyond America's Means" *The Economist* Sept. 19, 1987, 76.

10   A. Fontaine, "Beyond Wilson and Rambo" (1987) 65 *Foreign Policy* 33; Editorial (1986) 10 *Criminal Law Journal* 117.

11   P. Kennedy, *The Rise and Fall of The Great Powers: Economic Change and Military Conflict, 1500-2000* (New York: Random House, 1987); D. Calleo, *Beyond American Hegemony: The Future of the Western Alliance* (New York: Twentieth Century Fund, 1987).

12 S. Wisotsky, *Breaking the Impasse in the War on Drugs* (1986); D. Kline, "How to Lose the Coke War" *The Atlantic* May, 1987, 22-27; R. Lee, "The Latin American Drug Connection" (1985) 61 *Foreign Policy* 142.

13 "Wanted Noriega", *Time* Feb. 15, 1988 at 14; "Tears of Rage", *Time* March 14, 1988 at 16; W. Marsden, "laundering 'narcodollars' in the Bahamas" *Toronto Star* Jan. 26, 1986 at G 1.

14 P. Giffen and S. Lambert, "What Happened on the Way to Law Reform?" (1988) *Illicit Drugs in Canada* (1988) 345; "The Politics of Pot" *Maclean's* July 4, 1983. On the U.S. law reform situation, see E. Josephson, "Marijuana Decriminalization: The Processes and Prospects for Change" (1981) *Contemporary Drug Problems* 291-320.

15 N. Dorn and N. South, "Reconciling policy and practice" in *Tackling Drug Misuse: A Summary of the Government's Strategy* (British Home Office, 1986) 198.

16 C. Mitchell, "Willingness-to-pay: Taxation and Tax Compliance" (1985) 15 *Memphis State University Law Review* 127; A. Etzioni, "Tax Breaks and Breaking Points" *Psychology Today* April 1978, 16.

17 J. Buchanan, "From Private Preferences to Public Philosophy: The Development of Public Choice" in *The Economics of Politics* J. Buchanan ed., (UK: The Institute of Economic Affairs, 1978); J. Buchanan, *The Limits of Liberty: Between Anarchy and Leviathan* (U. of Chicago Press, 1975); J. Buchanan, "The Limits of Taxation" in *Taxation: An International Perspective* (Vancouver: The Fraser Institute, 1984) 42; D.T. Dickson, "Bureaucracy and morality: An organizational perspective on a moral crusade", (1968) 16 *Social Problems* 143; M. Olson, *The Logic of Collective Action* (Harvard University Press, 1971).

18 T. Rosenberg, "Smuggler's Paradise" *The New Republic* June 8, 198, 14-16.

19 A. Downs, *An Economic Theory of Democracy* (New York: Harper & Row, 1957) 255-56.

20   P. Goldberg & E. Meyers, "The Influence of Public Under-standing And Attitudes on Drug Education and Prevention" in The Drug Abuse Council, *The Facts About Drug Abuse* (New York: Free Press, 1980) 137.

21   *Ibid*, 143-44.

22   M. Friedman, *Capitalism and Freedom* (University of Chicago Press, 1962) 143.

23   P. Anderson, *High in America: The True Story Behind NORML and The Politics of Marijuana* (New York: Viking, 1981).

24   G. Stigler and M. Cohen, *Can Regulatory Agencies Protect Consumers?* (Washington: American Enterprise Institute, 1971) 49.

25   Cited in P. Erickson, *et al.*, *The Steel Drug - Cocaine in Perspective* (1987) 11.

26   J. Kramer, "From Demon to Ally - How Mythology Has, And May Yet, Alter National Drug Policy" (1976) *Journal of Drug Issues* 390.

27   A. Saper, "The Making of Policy Through Myth, Fantasy and Historical Accident: The Making of America's Narcotics Laws" (1974) 69 *Br. Journal of Addictions* 183.

28   H. Levine and E. Reinarman, "Abusing Drug Abuse - What's Behind 'Jug Wars'" *The Nation* March 28, 1987, 389.

29   Quoted in N. Zinberg & J. Robertson, *Drugs and the Public* (New York: Simon & Schuster, 1972) 237.

30   H. Sapolsky, "The Political Obstacles to the Control of Cigarette Smoking in the United States" (1980) 5 *Journal of Health, Politics, Policy and Law* 277.

31   P. Taylor, *Smoke Ring - The Politics of Tobacco* (1984) 224-26.

32   C. Huang, J. Siegfried and F. Zardoshty, "The Demand for Coffee in the United States, 1963-77" (1980) 20 *Quarterly Review of Economics and Business* 36.

33 R. Hamowy, "Introduction: Illicit Drugs and Government Control" in R. Hamowy (ed.), *Dealing with Drugs: Consequences of Government Control* (1987).

34 P. Erickson, *Cannabis Criminals: The Social Effects of Punishment on Drug Users* (Toronto: ARF Books, 1980).

35 J. Buchanan, "Politics and Meddlesome Preferences" in R. Tollison (ed.), *Smoking and Society - Toward a More Balanced Assessment* (Lexington Books, 1986) 335.

36 "Thinking the Unthinkable" *Time* May 30, 1988.

37 R. Stupak, *American Foreign Policy - Assumptions, Processes and Projections* (New York: Harper & Row, 1976).

38 *U.S.* v. *Randall*, Super. Ct. D.C.Crim. No. 65923-75 (1976); Docket No. 86-22, US Dept. of Justice, DEA; *State* v. *Musikka* No. 88-4395 CF, 17 Judicial Circuit, Florida.

39 *State* v. *Diana*, 604 P. 2d 1312 (1979), Ct. Ap. Wash. Div.

40 Lawyers and environmentalists from the mid 1950s in the U.S. began to take legal action against DDT spraying. These court challenges publicized pesticide hazards, uncovered poor government administration and led to the formation of the Environmental Defense Fund. G. Woodwell, "Broken Eggshells", *SCIENCE* Nov. 1984 115.

41 J. Oteri and H. Silverglate, "The Pursuit of Pleasure: Constitutional Dimensions of the Marihuana Problem" (1968) 3 *Suffolk U. Law Review* 55, 58.

42 R. Bonnie and C. Whitehead, "The Forbidden Fruit and The Tree of Knowledge: An Inquiry into The Legal History of American Marijuana Prohibition" (1970) 56 *Virginia Law Review* 991-993.

43 *Ibid.*, 1003.

44 J. Helmer, *Drugs and Minority Oppression* (1975) 40.

45 Oteri and Silverglate, *supra* note 41, 60.

46   Bonnie and Whitehead, *supra* note 42, 1022.

47   See G. Newman, *Just and Painful* (New York: Macmillan, 1983).

48   J. Zimmerman, *Participatory Democracy - Populism Revived* (New York: Praeger, 1986).

49   *Ibid.*

50   Taylor, *supra* note 31, 202-08.

51   See A. Trebach, *The Great Drug War* (1987).

52   A. F. Wilcox, *The Decision to Prosecute* (London: Butterworths, 1972) 63.

53   Quoted in Wilcox, *ibid.*, 47.

54   H. Greenstein and P. Dibianco, "Marijuana Laws - A Crime Against Humanity" (1972) 48 *Notre Dame Lawyer* 314.

55   C. Adams, *Flight, Fight and Fraud - The Story of Taxation* (Curacao: Euro-Dutch Pub., 1982) 140.

56   T. Szasz, "A Plea for the Cessation of the Longest War of the Twentieth Century - The War on Drugs" (1988) 16 *The Humanistic Psychologist* 314-322.

57   *R. v. Hauser* et al. [1979] 1 S.C.R. 984; 98 D.L.R. (3d) 193; 6 C.C.C. (2d) 481; P. Hogg, *Constitutional Law of Canada* (Toronto: Carswell, 1985) 690-92.

INDEX

357